Guiding Light

American Society of Missiology
Monograph Series

Series Editor, James R. Krabill

The ASM Monograph Series provides a forum for publishing quality dissertations and studies in the field of missiology. Collaborating with Pickwick Publications—a division of Wipf and Stock Publishers of Eugene, Oregon—the American Society of Missiology selects high-quality dissertations and other monographic studies that offer research materials in mission studies for scholars, mission and church leaders, and the academic community at large. The ASM seeks scholarly work for publication in the series that throws light on issues confronting Christian world mission in its cultural, social, historical, biblical, and theological dimensions.

Missiology is an academic field that brings together scholars whose professional training ranges from doctoral-level preparation in areas such as Scripture, history and sociology of religions, anthropology, theology, international relations, interreligious interchange, mission history, inculturation, and church law. The American Society of Missiology, which sponsors this series, is an ecumenical body drawing members from Independent and Ecumenical Protestant, Catholic, Orthodox, and other traditions. Members of the ASM are united by their commitment to reflect on and do scholarly work relating to both mission history and the present-day mission of the church. The ASM Monograph Series aims to publish works of exceptional merit on specialized topics, with particular attention given to work by younger scholars, the dissemination and publication of which is difficult under the economic pressures of standard publishing models.

Persons seeking information about the ASM or the guidelines for having their dissertations considered for publication in the ASM Monograph Series should consult the Society's website—www.asmweb.org.

Members of the ASM Monograph Committe who approved this book are:
Roger Schroeder, SVD, Catholic Theological Union
Michael A. Rynkiewich, Retired from Asbury Theological Seminary

Recently Published in the ASM Monograph Series

Meyers, Megan. *Grazing and Growing: Developing Disciples through Contextualized Worship Arts in Mozambique*

Kim, Enoch Jinsik. *Receptor-Oriented Communication for Hui Muslims in China: With Special Reference to Church Planting*

Lines, Kevin. *Who Do the Ngimurok Say That They Are?: A Phenomenological Study of Turkana Traditional Religious Specialists in Turkana, Kenya.*

Guiding Light

Contributions of Alan R. Tippett Toward the Development and Dissemination of Twentieth-Century Missiology

KEVIN GEORGE HOVEY

Foreword by R. Daniel Shaw

American Society of Missiology Monograph
Series vol. 38

PICKWICK *Publications* · Eugene, Oregon

GUIDING LIGHT
Contributions of Alan R. Tippett Toward the Development and Dissemination of
Twentieth-Century Missiology

American Society of Missiology Monograph Series 38

Pickwick Publications
An Imprint of Wipf and Stock Publishers
199 W. 8th Ave., Suite 3
Eugene, OR 97401

www.wipfandstock.com

PAPERBACK ISBN: 978-1-5326-5419-0
HARDCOVER ISBN: 978-1-5326-5420-6
EBOOK ISBN: 978-1-5326-5421-3

Cataloguing-in-Publication data:

Names: Hovey, Kevin George, author. | Shaw, R. Daniel, foreword.

Title: Guiding light : contributions of Alan R. Tippett toward the development and dissemination of twentieth-century missiology / Author Name.

Description: Eugene, OR: Pickwick Publications, 2019 | Series: American Society of Missiology Monograph Series 38 | Includes bibliographical references and index.

Identifiers: ISBN 978-1-5326-5419-0 (paperback) | ISBN 978-1-5326-5420-6 (hardcover) | ISBN 978-1-5326-5421-3 (ebook)

Subjects: LCSH: Tippett, Alan R. (Alan Richard), 1911–1988. | Missions—Theory.

Classification: BV2063 H6 2019 (print) | BV2063 (ebook)

Manufactured in the U.S.A.   APRIL 10, 2019

Dedication

IN MY LIFE IN missions, I have been blessed by the presence and encouragement of many fellow travelers from many different parts of the world. The collegiate depth is measured in the depth of the conversations, not to mention the depth of the crema on the coffee. These people have been many and frequent, which is why I thank God for all of them.

Then there have been the "fathers" in my life. More than fellow travelers, these people have functioned like a GPS or interactive map, helping me to have perspective on my journey. This list is more focused: my own father—John Hovey; my mission leader for many years—Cyril Westbrook; my Master's degree mentor—Charles Kraft, are examples. Through the writing of this volume, Alan Tippett has joined that list as he has become an ongoing source of information and inspiration. Again, thanks to God for these important people.

For me, there is one person who has traveled the journey with me—but on analysis, actually for me. Glenys, in so many aspects of the forty-nine years of our fantastic life together, you truly have earned the "PHT Award" (Putting Hubby Through Award) which leaves me indebted to you and to God.

Contents

Figures

Permissions

Publishers Permissions have been obtained for the following material:

From *Solomon Islands Christianity*, by Alan Tippett. Figure title "Piety Curve of a Weak Congregation," Alan Tippett, p. 309. Used with permission by William Carey Library, Pasadena, CA.

From *Fullness of Time: Ethnohistory Selections from the Writings of Alan R. Tippett*, by Doug Priest (ed). Figure title "The triangle of personal relationships," Alan Tippett, p. 136. Used with permission by William Carey Library, Pasadena, CA.

From "Conversion as a Dynamic Process in Christian Mission," by Alan Tippett, *Missiology: An International Review* 5.2 (1977) 19. Figure title, "Conversion as a Dynamic Process," Alan Tippett, p. 219. Used with permission by Sage Publications, License Number 4345150804868.

From "Negotiating Identity: Extending and Applying Alan Tippett's Model of Conversion," by Richard Hibbert, *Missiology* 43.1 (2015) 14. Figure title "Socioreligious Identity," Richard Hibbert, p. 63. Used with permission by Sage Publications, License Number 4345150804868.

Foreword

There is much in the philosophy of animism which is in alignment with Scripture, and this should be processed for Christ. Animist religion, on the other hand, is sadly misdirected towards deities who cannot save, and many of its offensive elements are perversions of ideas which could be good if redirected. The animist certainly needs Christ, for Christ alone can meet his needs.[1]

THIS QUOTE FROM ALAN Tippett was written, but sadly not published, over forty-five years ago. Despite the intervening years, the insight and wisdom reflected in Tippett's research and writing does not diminish. His teaching visits to Fuller in the early 1980s gave us opportunity to explore mutual interests in anthropology, particularly as it pertained to mission activity in the Pacific. Through his role as a Professor of Anthropology at Fuller Theological Seminary and his missionary experience, he was chosen to be the first editor of the journal *Missiology* and led in developing our multidisciplinary study.

Among those influenced by Tippett's work was a young missionary sweating and swatting "mossies" (Australian for "mosquitoes") in the Sepik River region of Papua New Guinea. He had discovered Tippett's work on people movements and the impact of power encounters on Sepik River villagers trying to make sense of a colonial-induced message. Witnessing the very things he was reading about encouraged Kevin Hovey to do some creative experimenting among the Sepik River people groups and to seek further education from the authors he had read. This resulted in Kevin and his

---

1. Tippett, *Theological Encounters*, 143.

wife Glenys coming to Fuller where he met and studied under Alan Tippett, Chuck Kraft, and others in the late 1970s. They developed a friendship and their lives intersected, both in America and Australia, until Tippett's death in 1988. Hovey has masterfully captured Tippett's message and uses pithy Tippett quotes that remain relevant to this day! Therefore, having known them both, it is an honor for me to write this foreword and encourage readers to value studying mission from both theological and anthropological perspectives, a study Tippett dubbed "missiology."

As the title indicates, despite Hovey's intimate knowledge of Tippett, his family, and his work, this book is not a biography. Rather it is a well-researched presentation of Tippett's career and contribution to the "development and dissemination of 20th century great commission focused missiology."[2] To accomplish this gargantuan task, Hovey read voluminously, far beyond the Tippett corpus. By doing so, he is able to demonstrate not only Tippett's impact on others, but how others impacted Tippett, who also read voluminously. Hovey connects Tippett's wide reading with his wide experience across the missiological discipline and to the reality of contexts around the world. Furthermore, Hovey applies Tippett's theory and methodological approaches to his own work in the Sepik, as well as to mission in general. I know of no one who has digested Tippett's work and is able to articulate the themes and life stages in order to present Tippett's strategic contributions better than Kevin Hovey. Others knew Tippett well and have applied his ideas to effective cross-cultural ministry—Chuck and Meg Kraft, Darrell Whiteman, Colin Dundon, and Doug Priest,[3] to name a few. But none have identified Tippett's life themes and combined them with the concept of ethnohistory to structure a lifetime of creativity. I congratulate him on this effort from which many will benefit far into the future.

To communicate the value of Tippett's message and demonstrate the significance of his work, Hovey shows how life experience and biblical study enabled Tippett to develop a theology of mission which he combined with a passion for research methods borne of anthropology. Hovey then combines this into a strategy for effective missiology. In other words, he uses Tippett's ethnohistorical method to organize this book. He then identifies five life themes that emerge from Tippett's contributions, and juxtaposes them with

2. Hovey, *Guiding Light*, 12.

3. Doug Priest's editing of Tippett's unpublished manuscripts bring to light Tippett's theological, cultural, and missiological depth and breadth in a series of volumes published by William Carey Library (2012–2015).

the already identified life eras. This masterful interweaving of life path with themes that dominated decisions, interests, research, and teaching, enables him to present Tippett's perspective on theology along with anthropological contributions to research methods and strategic mission practice. From all this emerges guidelines for mission boards and field missionaries—valuable insights, approaches, and practical suggestions reflective of Hovey's own manual for cross-cultural Christian workers entitled *Before All Else Fails Read the Instructions*.[4] Tippett considered this very good advice which he wished he had been given before sailing to Fiji in 1941.[5]

Given my recent interest in "redirecting" (to use Tippett's term in the opening quote) misguided ritual for appropriate worship, I see the theoretical value of this book in Hovey's extended discussion of Tippett's development of Power Encounter (PE) and its relationship to cultural fit. Kraft was helpful with his three encounters: truth, power, and allegiance, which he viewed as a natural "progression" from Tippett's foundational understanding of PE.[6] Hovey's three phases of PE, along with recognizing PE as a progression from paganism to a new church in chapters 8 and 9, is a helpful theoretical contribution with practical missiological consequence. He demonstrates how the three phases of PE he develops from Tippett's writings combine cosmic and earthly themes: God is supreme, God is powerful, and Jesus is Lord. He argues with Kraft's "three encounters" model, showing that cosmic encounters with God demonstrate spiritual power to people who are led to recognize the truth of God's presence and shift their allegiance to Jesus. This paradigm shift moves people from "wrong faith" in spirits from below to "right faith" (as defined by cultural fit) precipitated by the power of the Holy Spirit. I agree with Hovey that Tippett saw PE as representative of more than simply demonstrating the power of one superhuman being over another. PE, then, is "the ocular demonstration of allegiance change that is so necessary for effective Christian growth among people of animistic backgrounds"[7]

I further argue that these concepts apply in any context where human beings express their spirituality. As people process spiritual power in the context of living life, they engage with the spiritual forces around them (from below) or God's presence (from above) for the purpose of living an

4. Hovey, *Before All Else Fails.*

5. Kraft, *SWM/SIS at Forty,* 31–32.

6. Kraft, "Three Encounters in Christian Witness."

7. Hovey, *Guiding Light,* 239.

abundant life as Jesus promised in John 10:10. Satan is a master at twisting truth that results in people using spiritual power for their own benefit, rather than using their rituals and ceremonies to worship the one true God.[8] Satan's lie sets people in search of God (what I call "religion"), rather than honoring God who desires to have a close relationship with people, which in turn results in godly human relationships. Animism, then, must not be seen as a step in an evolutionary sequence from savage to civilized as E. B. Tylor postulated.[9] Rather, spirituality pervades all religious experience and closely resembles what Tippett labeled "animism" as reflected in his research-based writings from such disparate places as Ethiopia, Mexico, First Nations America, Papua New Guinea, the Solomon Islands, and, of course, Fiji. Contemporary human spirituality, animistic or otherwise, must be understood in the context of globalization and lifestyle as lived by people around the world. It is a testimony to Tippett's insights that we can now appreciate animism, not as a step back to an early evolutionary epoch of spiritual development, but rather as a reflection on how human beings, created in God's image, express their nonmaterial experience.

The *imago Dei* is built into every human being ensuring that spiritual awareness reflects our origins as Psalm 8 implies. We are not created a "little lower" than the angels, but rather to represent God's presence on earth—vice royals created to inhabit and inherit the earth in all its fullness. Sadly, Satan ensured this state did not last long, twisting truth and turning God's intent into human depravity. Satan shifted the focus from God to human concern in a context of need. That, however, did not change our status with God who sought out humans, whatever their condition, and desired to be with them and be the focus of their worship. This shifted their allegiance back to God through recognition of Jesus as Lord and Savior. Acknowledging Christ's lordship through the power of the Holy Spirit is crucial to unveiling human spirituality which, by definition, is animistic in the anthropological sense. It entails valuing God's presence among the people and through the power of the Holy Spirit changing the human condition to become what God intended, on earth as it is in heaven. This insight clearly reflects Tippett's connection of theological interests to socioreligious contexts for the purpose of ensuring effective mission. Hovey does us all a service by presenting this message through Tippett's life and

---

8. Shaw and Burrows, *Traditional Ritual as Christian Worship*, 11.

9. Tylor, *Anthropology*, 24–26.

experience, thus moving it out of the twentieth century and contextualizing it for our twenty-first-century benefit.

So why does a now-aging professor of mission, writing about a fellow Australian missionary's life themes and influence, matter in our twenty-first-century world? Because it connects current mission practice to a bygone era in which Alan Tippett was a foremost thinker. We are all products of our day and build on what has gone before—today's missiology emerges from yesterday's mission arguments, failures, and successes. Tippett documented it all through his research, writing, and lectures. Hovey helpfully chronicles it all by applying ethnohistory to Tippett's life themes and vast experience as a missionary, anthropologist, and researcher for the cause of mission. We dare not forget these crucial insights from these hard-learned lessons by others.

Furthermore, we must apply these lessons to the spiritual realities we confront globally as we live in a complex world. God connects today as he did throughout the biblical record and has continued to do throughout the previous twenty centuries. God makes himself known today, no less forcefully, in ways people understand within their context. Only then can Christ be seen as meaningful and relevant to life's circumstances. Researching every context for the purpose of presenting a biblical basis for theologizing enables relevant approaches that bring people from darkness to light. The focus is on God's word in our human environment; today as it has always been. That is the point of all this.

I commend my good friends and colleagues the Krafts and Darrell Whiteman, as well as others who have influenced our brother Kevin and sister Glenys, who began their ministry living in a houseboat on the Sepik River. And I encourage you, the reader, to read these pages with your missional context (the place where you live and work and have your being) in mind. As Hovey did in Papua New Guinea, apply what you learn in ways that fit the context and thereby be a witness of God's presence in that place. In short, allow these pages to influence your thinking for the purpose of missiological engagement that reflects Christ's presence—be incarnational!

R. Daniel Shaw
Senior Professor of Anthropology & Translation
Fuller Graduate School of Intercultural Studies
Pasadena, CA 91182
April 27, 2018

Preface

THE IMPETUS FOR THIS study could be summarized as being the result of two brief encounters in two meetings that occurred virtually thirty years apart. The first, in 1974, in the town of Wewak, Papua New Guinea, is focused on the last ten minutes of a multi-day seminar on theological education by extension, conducted by Patricia Harrison. In those few minutes, Patricia introduced the participants to the Global Church Growth Book Club, pointing out the significance of the books that William Carey Library was publishing that could be ordered from their catalog and shipped to us in our remote locations. I followed her advice, and soon thereafter found myself reading books and articles by Alan Tippett, along with many other helpful authors. Applying this material revolutionized the effectiveness of the ministry my wife and I were involved in while living on a houseboat on the Sepik River of Papua New Guinea. So, midway through our thirty-one years in Papua New Guinea, as a result of that 1974 meeting, I became aware of the Fuller Theological Seminary School of World Mission, from which both my wife and I subsequently graduated with a Master of Arts in Missiology, and from which my thesis was published as *Before All Else Fails, Read the Instructions.*[1]

Having completed that Master's degree, I set a subliminal goal of a PhD. I say "subliminal" because my ministry and leadership roles had to take precedence. So even when I received positive feedback from institutions through whom I could have done such a program, time was simply not available. Then, through a change of roles in 2004, my wife and I founded Global Training Ministries Inc. as a missionary training organization, and the Board granted a twenty percent workload allowance to work on a PhD. This then lead to the second meeting referred to above.

1. Hovey, *Before All Else Fails.*

Having been accepted into a doctoral program, I had to present my research proposals to the Research Committee. I had several in mind, but knew what my priority was. So I suggested a topic about mission in Papua New Guinea that was both close to my heart and that needed research. I'm not sure of the reason, but the Chairman of the Research Committee immediately responded with, "No, you cannot do that for your PhD. So, what is your next topic?" To this day, I have no idea why he said that, but trapped in the meeting for my next topic, I said, "In that case, how about a dissertation on the missiology of the Australian missiologist, Alan Tippett." The chairman, who was not conversant with missiology or Alan Tippett seemed happy with that area of study, so my dissertation, and eventually this book, began.

As I initiated the research, my first concern was that others may have already covered my topic, or, almost as seriously, that nothing had been written about Tippett. In that case, his life story would have to dominate any study to provide a context, and a detailed history was not my goal. I was still thinking about that when I first contacted St. Mark's Library in Canberra regarding access to Tippett's material that Alan Tippett had left to them. I was told that a dissertation about Tippett had already been written by Rev. Dr. Colin Dundon.[2] I discovered a copy of it in Sydney that day, read it that weekend, and was relieved to see that, first of all, it was very well written, but also to see that it was a historical PhD. That then meant that I could fulfill my plan of focusing on Tippett's missiology because his life story had already been written in that study.

This volume then is primarily the dissertation that came from that Research Committee meeting, and which was subsequently accepted for publication as part of the American Society of Missiology's Monograph Series. In its dissertation format, it took eleven years to research and write. In one way, this was due to my other roles during that time, which limited my time for research and writing. However, looking back I can see that there is a conceptual maturity in the study due to working over Tippett's extensive material over such a long time. An example of this is the distillation of Tippett's life themes that I have used in part to structure the study. Tippett did not describe himself this way, however with those years pondering his material, this distillation provided a tool to tame the expanse of his writing and make it manageable in one volume. I had a similar experience while working over his extensive material on power encounter, from which I was

2. Dundon, "Raicakacaka."

able to distill the three phases of power encounter that Tippett wrote about and then make that into a practically applicable whole.

Embedding an analysis of Tippett's insights into a history of the increase and subsequent decline of his influence could easily be seen as being unfair to Tippett as a person, playing fast and loose with the story of his life for the purpose of my dissertation, and now this book. In fact, the reason for including his story is to demonstrate the significance of his insights as they developed, both in league with other people like McGavran, and also with growing networks of people who came to see the significance of these approaches and contributed their insights. Again, the chapter about his declining influence shows the enduring significance of his insights, even though a range of factors impeded Tippett from being at the forefront of those concepts after his retirement. In a most insightful way, McGavran's statement about Tippett after his death captures Tippett's God-given role, and through the legacy of his written material, his enduring significance: "God the Father Almighty laid his hand upon Alan Tippett and made him one of the apostles of effective evangelism throughout the entire world."[3]

As a dissertation, this study had to stop somewhere. So Tippett's influence within the twentieth century became a workable boundary. Yet while writing the dissertation, and now in preparing the manuscript for this published volume, the applicability of many of his concepts to the twenty-first century is evident.

At that point however, a missionary or mission executive not familiar with Tippett's work could easily miss the relevance of his work with respect to their roles and ministries. This is due to Tippett's "unabashed particularism" as I described it in this study. For example, *Peoples of Southwest Ethiopia*[4] hardly seems like it would have any relevance to mission activity in East Asia. Yet many of Tippett's key insights, couched in these specific field studies, have global relevance.

So through the process of reading, researching, and writing this study, I have come to see this completed volume as a heuristic device. As such, it provides current readers access to many of Tippett's significant insights within one volume, thus making them immediately available and applicable. Additionally, it directs readers to Tippett's more detailed published works from which they can source additional detail to enhance their roles

3. McGavran, "Missiologist Alan R. Tippett," 267.
4. Tippett, *Peoples of Southwest Ethiopia*.

as well. For this reason, I am thankful to the American Society of Missiology's Monograph Series and Pickwick Publications for making this study available to others.

Kevin G. Hovey
Parramatta, Australia
31 March, 2018

Acknowledgments

The original dissertation from which this volume comes would not have been possible without the support of many individuals and organizations, and these acknowledgments provide an opportunity to express my gratitude.

Global Training Ministries and Alphacrucis College—my employers during the writing of the original dissertation—have made provision for study time, while my colleagues have been interactive encouragers. I am also thankful to the Sydney College of Divinity and Alphacrucis College, the institutions under which this research and writing has been done. Their structures provided many opportunities to present aspects of my research material over the years of my study.

My supervisory team has been remarkable. Rev. Assoc. Prof. Denise A. Austin, Dr. Darrell L. Whiteman, and Dr. Gerard Goldman have all contributed in significant ways, beyond the call of duty, and with timeliness that has been remarkable.

Alphacrucis College hosted the "Alan Tippett Symposium on Mission and Cross Cultural Mission" in 2013. This was also sponsored by the Australian Association of Mission Studies and Missions Interlink. A total of sixty participants from four Australian states and territories and two overseas nations attended the symposium, including thirteen members of the Tippett family. The librarian from St. Mark's Library was also present, representing their institution, where Tippett's library and archives are housed. This was fitting, considering the degree of assistance St. Mark's staff have given me in this project and their commitment in storing and facilitating research in his collection. Tippett's Mission Board also sent a representative. The participants represented seven other colleges, a number of institutions, or came as individuals. Many presented missiological papers, mostly related directly to Tippett and his material. The December 2014 edition of the *Australian Journal of Mission Studies*[1] primarily comprised articles from that symposium.

A special part of my research has been the privilege of meeting up with, and being encouraged by, Alan and Edna Tippett's daughters, Lynette, Joan, and Robyn, thanks initially to Facebook. The joy of being able to present the first three copies of Tippett's newly published autobiography to them at the opening of the 2013 Symposium is still fresh in my mind.

Alphacrucis College also provided financial assistance for me to attend the Fuller School of World Mission/School of Intercultural Studies fiftieth anniversary and missiological conference in 2015. I was able to present material regarding my Tippett research at a lunchtime roundtable event at that time. That conference was a great follow-up to my Master's degree studies at Fuller SWM thirty-two years prior. Those original studies laid a significant missiological foundation for me, much of which was linked to Tippett's and McGavran's insights and passion, but expanded through the faculty at that time, with Professor Charles Kraft being the mentor for my Master's thesis, published with the subtitle of *A Manual for Cross Cultural Christians*.[2]

My friends, colleagues and fellow missionary trainers, Norman and Roslyn Bradshaw have assisted with effective and expeditious proof reading.

Regardless of how much assistance is indicated from the people referred to above, errors of research, judgement or expression are my own.

1. *Australian Journal of Mission Studies*. Papers presented at the Alan Tippett Symposium on Mission and Cross Cultural Ministry, Alphacrucis College, Parramatta, NSW, 2014.
2. Hovey, *Before All Else Fails*.

Introduction

IN THIS STUDY I will examine the voluminous and conceptually broad writings of Rev. Dr. Alan R. Tippett in order to identify the contribution he made to Great-Commission-focused missiology and mission practice in the twentieth century. Tippett's seventy-seven-year life spanned the majority of the twentieth century, but this volume primarily focuses on the time frame between 1954 and 1988. This was a crucial period for missions globally, with the late 1960s being a watershed, as Tippett observed, "The new ideas and basic missiological theory that was created at the [Fuller] SWM during the second half of the 1960s."[1] Yet little research has focused on Tippett's outstanding life and work. That applies to his field service as a missionary in Fiji (1941–1961), but more especially to his later and more influential role as a missiologist. During this relatively short but extremely significant period of time, Tippett made many vital contributions. I will argue that his input in this way was vital in the development and dissemination of twentieth-century, Great-Commission-focused missiology and strategic missionary practice. Key areas were: the clear theological basis for his missiology; research methodologies that provided accurate data for missiological and strategic reflection suited to a wide range of ministry contexts; his cultural insights which were especially geared for effective mission in non-Western environments; his understanding of societies that were propitious for innovation; societies that had the potential for people movements; the opportunities, challenges, and appropriate ministry approaches in animistic contexts; and approaches that lead to indigenous, culturally appropriate Christianity at the local congregational level and at the level of national church movements. In this study, it will be demonstrated that in each of

1. Tippett et al., *No Continuing City*, 318.

these areas, he served his generation well, and, in doing so, laid a mission and missiological foundation for generations to come.

To facilitate understanding Tippett and his contribution more fully, the first section provides the reader with the historical background to the life of this Australian missiologist, the second examines his theological and research foundations, while the third section elucidates his insights and contributions to strategic, Great-Commission-focused missiology and mission in his era.

While looking at Tippett's life story, it will be observed that Tippett's influence declined quickly after his retirement. This decline in his influence is examined in chapter four, in order to determine if this decline was caused by weak points in Tippett's concepts, or whether it was caused by factors other than his concepts. While a number of factors of a personal and situational nature were noted, the nature of his writing was identified as one element. The point is, many of his best insights were couched in local case studies (Fiji, Solomon Islands, Papua New Guinea, Ethiopia, and the like) which meant that he left no one volume that summarized his key insights in a unified way. Furthermore, he was very particular to ensure a document was ready for publication before he would release it for publication. As a result, quite an amount of his crucial material has only been published posthumously in the last seven years. Added to that is the fact that his insights were so broad and so detailed, they were difficult to access across the books and articles that were published in his lifetime. This study then elucidates five life themes through which key aspects of his life and insights are able to be examined, thus making his key concepts available in one volume, situated within his life story and the mission and missiological world in which he lived.

1

Alan Tippett

Context and Construct

When the Spirit opens a people-movement door and a mission [orga-nization] refuses to see it as of God, could it be that this is an aspect of the negative dimension of "quenching the Spirit"—in that a door opens and closes? We have rethinking to do on all these points.[1]

INTRODUCTION

REV. DR. ALAN RICHARD Tippett (1911–1988), Australian missionary statesman and missiologist, was pursuing further studies in the United States of America after twenty years of missionary service in Fiji when he wrote this confronting statement. It was one of six appraisals that he wrote for his mission-sending agency, regarding their post-World War II mission work in Oceania. The series was entitled, "Australia's Missionary Outreach in Our Time."[2] In that document he acknowledges the influence of his mentors, Donald McGavran at the Institute of Church Growth and Homer Barnett at the University of Oregon, but, as he outlines his theory of practical mission, he points out that he was,

> following a much wider orbit than either of them—the psy-
> chological moment in people-movements, the consumation of

1. Tippett, "Australia's Missionary Outreach," 12.
2. Tippett, "Australia's Missionary Outreach."

1

people-movements, the analysis of the "civilize in order to evange-
lize" fallacy, the multi-individual character of people-movements,
cross-cultural conversion experiences, the relationship of the
people-movement consumated with the concept of indigenous
selfhood, the relation of ethnic renaissance to mission, the qual-
ity/quantity debate and the significance of written records and
statistics.[3]

As shall be discovered in this study, many of Tippett's key concepts are
embryonically encapsulated in these two statements, even though they pre-
date the majority of his writing. He was an Australian pioneer in the field of
mission theory focused on effective missionary practice aimed at the fulfillment of the Great Commission. The term "Great Commission" referred to
here is based around Jesus's post-resurrection statements to his disciples, as
recorded at the end of each of the Gospels (Matt 28:18–20; Mark 16:15–18;
Luke 24:46–49; John 20:21) and in the first chapter of Acts (Acts 1:8). This
is an intentionally narrow focus which will be demonstrated to be representative of Tippett, who then applies this narrow definition in a broad
way. Writing after Tippett's death, Charles Kraft, his colleague at Fuller
Theological Seminary School of World Mission (SWM), described him
as an "anthropologist, ethnohistorian, and missiologist par excellence"[4]
and subsequently referred to his missiological writing as "timeless."[5] Some
scholars have explored key missionaries who served in the Oceanic region,[6]
however, little research has focused on the outstanding life and work of
Tippett. That applies to his field service as a missionary in Fiji (1941–1961),
but more especially to his later and more influential role as a missiologist
who "belong[s] . . . to the world church,"[7] to use his term.

In this study I will examine the voluminous and conceptually broad
writings of Alan Tippett, in order to identify the contribution he made to
Great-Commission-focused missiology and mission practice in his era. I
will argue that his contribution was vital in the development and dissemination of twentieth-century, Great-Commission-focused missiology. Key

3. Tippett, "Australia's Missionary Outreach," 1.

4. Kraft and Priest, "Who Was This Man?," 269.

5. Kraft, *Culture, Communication, and Christianity*, 199.

6. Williams et al., *Fiji and the Fijians*; Weir, "Two Modes of Missionary Discourse";
Samson, "Historical Pilgrimage"; Williams and Cook Islands Library and Museum Soci-
ety, *Narrative of Missionary Enterprises*; Rowe, *Life of John Hunt*; Nettleton, *John Hunt*;
Birtwhistle, *In His Armour*; Tippett, *Road to Bau*; Thornley, *Inheritance of Hope*.

7. Tippett et al., *No Continuing City*, 269.

areas were: the clear theological basis for his missiology; research methodologies that provided accurate data for missiological and strategic reflection suited to a wide range of ministry contexts; his cultural insights, which were especially geared for effective mission in non-Western environments; his understanding of societies that were propitious for innovation; societies that had the potential for people movements; and the opportunities, challenges, and appropriate ministry approaches in animistic contexts and approaches that lead to indigenous or culturally appropriate Christianity. As will be demonstrated in this volume, in each of these areas, he served his generation well and, in doing so, laid a foundation for generations to come.

After establishing the timeline and guidelines for understanding Tippett's writing, this chapter outlines the relevant literature in the field in order to identify a gap in the research. Then working definitions are established and the methodology used in developing the study will be elucidated. The chapter will then overview the structure of the study, showing how the components fit together to achieve its goals.

Time Frame

Tippett's seventy-seven-year life spanned the majority of the twentieth century but this study primarily focuses on the thirty-four-year time frame between 1954 and 1988. This was a crucial period for mission globally with the late 1960s being a watershed, as Tippett observed,

> The new ideas and basic missiological theory that was created at the SWM during the second half of the 1960s was born in confrontation with . . . the jargon of the day . . . *Missionary go home!, the day of mission is dead, dialogue, demythologising, Christian presence, the secular city, the world's agenda, resistant fields.*[8]

During this relatively short but extremely significant period of time, Tippett made many vital contributions. In order to understand this more fully, I will provide a detailed historical background to the rise of this Australian missiologist, with the second and third sections elucidating his insights and contributions to missiology, and mission in his era.

ENGAGING WITH TIPPETT'S WRITINGS

When it comes to an analysis of Tippett's writings, there are a number of things that were specific to his written material that are somewhat different

---

8. Tippett et al., *No Continuing City*, 318.

from other authors who may have been writing on related topics. These are noted here in order to lay a foundation for an understanding of his material.

Prolific, Prolonged, and Purposeful

The first factor is that Tippett didn't write a single comprehensive volume that summarized his insights. This is in contrast with Charles Kraft's volumes on communication, ethnotheology, anthropology, worldview and contextualization, Paul Hiebert's volumes on anthropology and worldview and Gailyn Van Rheenen's volume on animism . This has made it difficult for other scholars to easily interact with his concepts and for practitioners to find the relevant parts of his insightful material that would inform their situations.

In contrast to not having produced a comprehensive single volume, his pen certainly was prolific. In Tippett's "Bibliography 1934–1988"[9] in which he compiles a list of his own writings, 600 items are listed. Even allowing for some duplicates, because some items are listed on the date when they are written but then repeated within the list when he bound them in his unpublished volumes or else when they were subsequently published, the refined number is still very high.

It is also important to recognize that Tippett wrote a very limited number of books and articles that he himself wanted to write. As he describes his own feelings about the two he did want to write;

> . . . I produced my *Aspects of Pacific Ethnohistory*,[10] which has a great deal of basic theory and historiography, and at the very opposite extreme *The Deep Sea Canoe*,[11] aimed at providing a theology of mission in action for Pacific Island audiences . . . These two works gave me a great deal of satisfaction in that each broke new ground, and both were projects I wished to undertake for their own sakes.[12]

This confirms that most of his writing was driven by what others wanted him to write or by his concerns in relation to the mission purposes of others. For instance in his autobiography, *No Continuing City*, he refers to, "The three items of prolonged research in those days, which I value most

9. Tippett, "Bibliography 1934–1988."
10. Tippett, *Aspects of Pacific Ethnohistory*.
11. Tippett, *Deep-Sea Canoe*.
12. Tippett et al., *No Continuing City*, 432.

highly to this day, because they came out of the missionary experience itself (not from my subsequent missiological period)."[13] Here he was referring to "Road to Bau: Biography of John Hunt,"[14] "The Integrating Gospel,"[15] and "His Mission and Ours."[16] As Tippett sees these manuscripts as representing him before he met McGavran, one could assume that these three volumes were all books that Tippett wanted to write. Similarly, *The Christian (Fiji 1835–67),*[17] while not included in the trilogy referred to above, was published before the trilogy and otherwise fits Tippett's criterion.[18]

On closer analysis, it becomes evident that it was other peoples' agendas that precipitated those volumes. *The Christian* was in response to problems occurring on the field caused by the easy availability of a book by Henderson on Thomas Williams' ministry in Fiji[19] that Tippett felt had some "blunders"[20] in it. Additionally he thought that some ridiculous information was being circulated because historians were seriously underestimating Fijian Christianity prior to Chief Cakobau's conversion in 1854, and overestimating it after Cakobau's conversion. "The upshot of all this was my writing of '*The Christian (Fiji 1835–67),*' which . . . reviewed well; a British historian saying the Fijian Church History would now have to be rewritten."[21] Additionally, when reading further in his autobiography,[22] it becomes evident that one book of the trilogy, "His Mission and Ours,"[23] was written in response to a book that "suggested that Jesus' sense of world mission was indirect, and that it lay, not in his statements about it but in his conception of God, and his readiness to take sides with the underprivileged."[24] As will be subsequently observed, this challenged Tippett's core beliefs so he wrote "His Mission and Ours" to refute the argument of

13. Tippett et al., *No Continuing City*, 259.

14. Tippett, "Road to Bau." Subsequently published in a combined volume, Tippett, *Road to Bau and Autobiography of Joeli Bulu.*

15. Tippett, "Integrating Gospel." Subsequently published in a combined volume, Tippett, *Integrating Gospel and The Christian.*

16. Tippett, "His Mission and Ours."

17. Tippett, *Christian (Fiji 1835–67).*

18. Tippett, "Parallaxis in Missiology," 120.

19. Henderson, Fiji and the Fijians, 1835–1856.

20. Tippett et al., *No Continuing City*, 228.

21. Tippett et al., *No Continuing City*, 229.

22. Tippett et al., *No Continuing City*, 260.

23. Tippett, "His Mission and Ours."

24. Tippett, "His Mission and Ours," viii.

that book. Tippett does not name that book, but its identity will be suggested when exploring this more in relation to Tippett's theological basis for mission.

Interrelationship of Concepts

Before subdividing Tippett's concepts for the purpose of analysis, it is essential to note that many of his key concepts are interrelated. To illustrate the point, Tippett emphasized the tools of anthropology and ethnohistory as ways of understanding the culture of the people. He also focused on indigenous forms of worship and structure for the churches and church movements that missionaries are planting. These could easily be thought to indicate that Tippett felt that culture was sacrosanct. It is not until that emphasis is placed alongside his notion that the Christian message itself is a message of "power encounter"—a message that tells of the direct and open conflict between God and all God stands for and Satan and all that Satan stands for,[25] that it becomes clear why he felt it was important for missionaries to understand culture. His goal was that cross-cultural missionaries could effectively participate in God's priority program for this planet and that the churches so produced would be, as much as possible, an undistorted expression of the body of Christ for their own community and beyond. His statements at the beginning of *Verdict Theology in Missionary Theory*[26] and the article "The Gods Must Die" in his privately published "The Liminal Years"[27] demonstrates this well, as seen in the following quote,

> The meeting of Christianity and paganism in Fiji was not a matter of mere dialogue. It was encounter . . . Christianity met paganism and emerged triumphant . . . the young Church was so very Christocentric and yet managed to retain much of the cultural order and orientation . . . in Fiji the Church was Christian and yet also cultural. This characteristic stood by the Church well for the first two or three generations of its Christian history.[28]

25. Tippett, "Liminal Years," 11, 16, 18; Tippett, *Verdict Theology in Missionary Theory*, 89–91.

26. Tippett, *Verdict Theology in Missionary Theory*, 76.

27. Tippett, "Liminal Years," 11, 16, 18.

28. Tippett, "Liminal Years," 11.

Similarly, in *Oral Tradition and Ethnohistory: the Transmission of Information and Social Values in Early Christian Fiji, 1835–1905*[29] he points out that an indigenous church is not an end in itself. The goal is to produce a church that is sufficiently strong in and of itself through the process of indigenization, that it can then fulfill its mission to the world as churches are commissioned to do.[30] In the same work, he argues that being that undistorted expression of the body of Christ does not insure the new church against persecution. He describes how, in the early development of the church in Fiji, because the Christian message and the expression of it in the Methodist Church fitted into Fijian culture so well, that "fit" opened the door for significant impact and influence. The result was that the non-Christian leaders tried to reduce its influence by strongly, sometimes violently opposing it, resulting in serious persecution.[31]

Style Factors

Tippett's writing style must be considered within the context of the time of its composition. For example, he uses the male gender virtually exclusively, as this was the accepted terminology of his day. This illustrates the point that Tippett himself was brought up in one era, even though his material has relevance for later eras.

Referring to those time periods highlights Tippett's use of the King James Version of the Bible, which again seems "behind the times." Although he would have had some other options[32] the audiences he wrote for would have been most familiar with the King James Version. By using that version, any discomfort they felt from his writing came from the information presented rather than from the translation of the Bible he used. Additionally, because he was adept at using the Greek New Testament, when he wanted to argue fine points he tended to use that rather than comparing alternative English translations.

By contrast, where Tippett's expression is sometimes dated, there are other areas where his concepts were well ahead of the times. While there

29. Tippett, *Oral Tradition and Ethnohistory*, 5.

30. Tippett, *Oral Tradition and Ethnohistory*, 5.

31. Tippett, "Dynamics of Church-Planting," 105–8; Tippett, *Oral Tradition and Ethnohistory*, 11.

32. The options would have been: The Revised Version (1885), American Standard Version (1901), New American Standard Bible (1963/1971), New English Bible (1961/1970), and The Living Bible (1965).

is little reference to Charismatic portions of the church worldwide, there are occasional, generally positive references to the Pentecostals.[33] Further, when it comes to his statements about the role and ministry of the Holy Spirit, including the importance of the power of the Holy Spirit in life and ministry, he was considerably ahead of his contemporaries, that is, unless they were involved in the rapidly emerging Charismatic or Pentecostal segments of the church. Even then, his level of articulation of these insights were only matched by Pentecostals and Charismatics much later in their history. This is a reminder that the era in which Tippett wrote should be taken into consideration when viewed through a twenty-first-century lens. Nevertheless, in this study I will demonstrate a number of times that his scholarly contributions were often ahead of his contemporaries.

INTERFACE WITH LITERATURE

As there is an alarming lack of secondary sources that engage with Tippett and his work, this study provides a valuable addition to several broad fields of missiological research. First, it builds on a strong foundation of research already conducted into the history of Pacific mission, anthropology in the service of mission, and Great-Commission-focused missiology. It adds to missiological theory and practical missiology. Finally, it helps fill the gap in the literature concerning Alan Tippett's life and his unique contribution in relation to each of these fields.

Historical Context

History of Pacific Mission

Much work has been done on the history of mission in the Pacific region. The life, ministry and eventual martyrdom of John Williams (1796–1839), often referred to as the apostle of the Pacific, has been the worthy focus of a significant amount of writing.[34] Similarly, a number of works have told the remarkable story of John Hunt (1812–1848).[35] George Brown, famous for leading the first Fijian missionaries to Papua New Guinea in 1875, had his

---

33. Tippett, "Report on the San Juan," 5, 36, 87; Tippett, "No Continuing City," 390.

34. Williams et al., *Fiji and the Fijians*; Williams and Moyle, *Samoan Journals of John Williams*; Weir, "Fiji and the Fijians"; Williams and Cook Islands Library and Museum Society, *Narrative of Missionary Enterprises*; Samson, "Historical Pilgrimage."

35. Rowe, *Life of John Hunt*; Nettleton, *John Hunt*; Birtwhistle, *In His Armour*; Tippett, *Road to Bau*; Thornley, *Inheritance of Hope*.

autobiography published[36] plus his life story.[37] John Paton's (1824–1907) story of his ministry in Vanuatu and Australia is also recorded,[38] while Ruth Tucker's *Jerusalem to Irian Jaya*[39] tells the story of these and others. At an encyclopedic level, Kenneth Scott Latourette's seven volume series includes Pacific-related material.[40] John Garrett's *To Live among the Stars: Christian Origins in Oceania*[41] makes a major contribution in a broader yet detailed look at Christianity in the Pacific. Tippett also contributes to the individual stories of missionaries and key national evangelists in the Pacific,[42] but adds resources and theories behind such historical research in the Pacific with his "The Distribution and Use of Documents in Oceania,"[43] and *Aspects of Pacific Ethnohistory.*[44]

ANTHROPOLOGY IN THE SERVICE OF MISSION

It is vital to understand Tippett's contribution to the development of anthropology in the service of mission, or, "missiological anthropology," to use the term from the subtitle of Luzbetak's book *The Church and Cultures: New Perspectives in Missiological Anthropology.*[45] As well as many of his own contributions, Tippett's book that has been posthumously published as *The Ways of the People*[46] is compiled from the writings of missionaries, then organized into a coherent anthropology text book. In a similar vein, John Hitchen[47] examines the contribution of Pacific missionaries to the science of anthropology. Other scholars came from a background in Bible Translation and linguistics, such as Eugene Nida, who published widely in articles and in books,[48] with his most influential volume being *Customs*

36. Brown, *George Brown.*

37. Reeson, *Pacific Missionary George Brown.*

38. Paton and Paton, *John G. Paton*; Langridge and Paton, *John G. Paton.*

39. Tucker, *From Jerusalem to Irian Jaya.*

40. Latourette, *History of the Expansion.*

41. Garrett, *Live among the Stars.*

42. Tippett, *Deep-Sea Canoe.*

43. Tippett, "Distribution and Use of Documents."

44. Tippett, *Aspects of Pacific Ethnohistory.*

45. Luzbetak, *Church and Cultures: New Perspectives.*

46. Tippett, *Ways of the People.*

47. Hitchen, "Relations Between Missiology and Anthropology," 470.

48. Nida, *Customs and Cultures*; Nida, "Initiation Rites and Cultural Themes"; Nida and Taber, *Theory and Practice of Translation.*

and Cultures; Anthropology for Christian Missions.[49] From that network, the journal *Practical Anthropology* was published from 1953 until 1973, when it merged with *Missiology: An International Review* which started in 1974 with Tippett as its first editor. The two compendium volumes, *Readings in Missionary Anthropology*[50] and *Readings in Missionary Anthropology Vol II*[51] compiled by William Smalley ensured that those resources were available for a longer period of time.

For the sake of the analysis that is taking place in this section, another identifiable group of scholars could be categorized as Christian anthropologists. The footnoted list is only representative, with only a sample list of their publications, acknowledging that they have produced a lot of very valuable material.[52] The significance of their material comes from the depth of their understanding of anthropology and anthropological issues, with those insights already harnessed for the service of mission around the world. This includes their reflection of the strengths and weaknesses of anthropology as a servant of mission.

There are also a number of secular anthropologists whose insights have been fertile in providing models that have been used by missiological anthropologists. Some examples would be Homer Barnett,[53] whose book on innovation was rated by Tippett as the most impacting book on his life after the Bible. Everett Rogers[54] pursued this concept of innovation further. A number of others referred to by Tippett[55] were also helpful on key concepts, such as Bronislaw Malinowski[56] in the development of functional substitutes, F. B. Jevons providing the ability to utilize documents

49. Nida, *Customs and Cultures*.

50. Smalley, *Readings in Missionary Anthropology*.

51. Smalley, *Readings in Missionary Anthropology II*.

52. Tippett, *Solomon Islands Christianity*; Tippett, *Introduction to Missiology*; Luzbetak, *Church and Cultures: An Applied Anthropology*; Kraft, "Dynamic Equivalence Churches"; Kraft, *Christianity in Culture*; Hiebert, *Cultural Anthropology*; Hiebert, "Flaw of the Excluded Middle"; Hiebert, "Critical Contextualization"; Taber, *World Is Too Much*; Taber, *Understand the World*; Shaw, *Transculturation*; Shaw, Kandila; Shaw, "Beyond Contextualization"; Rynkiewich, "Person in Mission"; Rynkiewich, *Soul, Self, and Society*; Whiteman, *Melanesians and Missionaries*; Whiteman, "Melanesian Religions"; Whiteman, "Contextualization"; Whiteman, "Anthropology and Mission"; Whiteman, "Contextualization, Model of."

53. Barnett, *Innovation*.

54. Rogers, *Diffusion of Innovations*.

55. Tippett et al., *No Continuing City*, 429.

56. Malinowski and Kaberry, *Dynamics of Culture Change*.

that had not been professionally prepared as research resources,[57] Anthony Wallace[58] evaluation systems for traditional societies going through culture change in the context of colonialism and Arnold van Gennep[59] contributing his understanding of rites of passage to many aspects of culture change, including Christian conversion and discipleship.

This study will add to this collection of historical narratives by elucidating Tippett's own history. At the same time, it will bring to the fore so much that he wrote about the history of Christianity in the Pacific.

Development of great-commission-focused missiology

The genealogy of literature on "missiology" (as defined below) focused on the Great Commission can be traced starting with William Taylor's 1879 *Pauline Methods of Missionary Work*,[60] followed in 1886 by John Nevius.[61] In his 1912 volume, Roland Allen built upon this foundation through his emphasis of reliance on national workers starting with *Missionary Methods: St. Paul's or Ours?*[62] The publications that follow the theme can be traced in an ongoing lineage: Sidney Clark,[63] Waskom Pickett,[64] John Seamands' legacy of Pickett,[65] and Arthur McPhee's biography of Pickett,[66] followed by Donald McGavran,[67] WCC's "The Growth of the Church,"[68] and McIntosh's

57. Tippett et al., *No Continuing City*, 428.

58. Wallace, *Culture and Personality*.

59. Van Gennep, *Rites of Passage*.

60. Taylor, *Pauline Methods of Missionary Work*.

61. Nevius, *Methods of Mission Work*.

62. In his 1912 edition, he predicted that it would take fifty years for his ideas to catch on. He was correct in that assessment, for it was published again in 1962 which resulted in seven printings by 1972. See Allen, *Spontaneous Expansion of the Church*; Allen, *Ministry of the Spirit*; Allen, *Missionary Methods*.

63. Clark, *Indigenous Church*.

64. Pickett, *Christian Mass Movements in India*; Pickett, *Church Growth and Group Conversion*.

65. Seamands, "Legacy of J Waskom Pickett."

66. McPhee, *Road to Delhi*.

67. McGavran, *Bridges of God*; McGavran, *How Churches Grow*; McGavran, "Institute of Church Growth"; McGavran, *Church Growth in Mexico*; McGavran, *Church Growth and Christian Mission*; McGavran, "Wrong Strategy"; McGavran, "Church Growth Strategy Continued"; McGavran, *Understanding Church Growth*; McGavran, *Crucial Issues in Missions Tomorrow*; McGavran, *Ethnic Realities and the Church*; McGavran and Riddle, *Zaire*.

68. WCC Department of Mission Studies, "Growth of the Church" 195–99.

biography of McGavran.[69] These combine with Tippett's own writing in this vein which began with his *Integrating Gospel*[70] first written in 1958 and "His Mission and Ours,"[71] and which continued throughout his career.

The term "Great Commission" will be explained more in the definitions section, but the following description should provide clarity at this point in this chapter: In this study, the term Great Commission refers to the instructions Jesus gave to his disciples after his resurrection, defining their responsibilities to communicate the gospel and make disciples in the power of the Holy Spirit. The cluster of verses normally associated with the Great Commission are Matthew 28:18–20, Mark 16:15–16, Luke 24:46–49, John 20:21, and Acts 1:8.[72]

Missiological Theory

In a volume that anticipates examining the missiology and mission practice of Alan Tippett, the literature that drives the research is the theory that has practical application—"Theory of practice" was the way Kraft described it,[73] referring to the academic driving force at the Fuller Theological Seminary School of World Mission (FTS SWM).

There are others that aim for a reflective approach to missiological theory, one of the best known being David Bosch[74] in which he used his analysis of "paradigm shifts in theology of mission" as he describes it in the subtitle of his book. Others that aim for that big picture reflection are Verkuyl, in his broad ranging 432-page *Contemporary Missiology: An Introduction*[75] and Verstraelen's *Missiology: An Ecumenical Introduction*.[76] Another set of volumes add perspective to the study, namely Newbigin's *The Open Secret: Sketches for a Missionary Theology*,[77] Kraemer's *The Christian Message in a Non-Christian World*,[78] Hoekendijk's *The Church Inside Out*,[79]

69. McIntosh, *Donald A. McGavran.*

70. Tippett, *Integrating Gospel and the Christian.*

71. Tippett, "His Mission and Ours."

72. Tippett, *Church Growth and the Word*, 24.

73. Kraft, *SWM/SIS at Forty*, 69–70.

74. Bosch, *Transforming Mission.*

75. Verkuyl, *Contemporary Missiology.*

76. Verstraelen, *Missiology.*

77. Newbigin, *Open Secret: Sketches for a Missionary Theology.*

78. Kraemer, *Christian Message.*

79. Hoekendijk, *Church Inside Out.*

and the volume compiled by Whiteman and Anderson, *World Mission in the Wesleyan Spirit*,[80] as they examine different but related aspects of the field of mission and missiology. Two unique resources are Maurier's *The Other Covenant; A Theology of Paganism*[81] and Cavalcanti's *Human Agency in Mission Work: Missionary Styles and Their Political Consequences*.[82] These are noteworthy due to the quite different aspects of mission and the mission task to which they draw attention. Furthermore, *Perspectives on the World Christian Movement: Fourth Edition*[83] and the *Evangelical Dictionary of World Missions*[84] demonstrate the multifaceted nature of missiological study and reflection. It is also valid to highlight a range of literature that refers to Tippett in a fleeting way, but which does not engage with his key concepts. Some examples are Daniel DeLoach, John Roxborogh, and Charles Forman.[85] The focus on missiological theory in this section highlights the need for further research into theories of missiology, while asking if that research can also blend with a "theory of practice" considering the end goal of missiology and mission practice as demonstrated in Tippett's writing.

Practical Great-Commission-Focused Missiology

Under the heading of Great-Commission-focused missiology, a number of areas need to be explored. The first area of reflection, one of the twentieth century's major breakthrough areas in the study of mission has been an understanding of people movements through the writings of Pickett,[86] McGavran,[87] Tippett,[88] and Gary Trompf.[89] Until the late 1800s, people movements were not recognized as a separate social phenomenon.[90] Since they have been identified though, when understood and examined

---

80. Whiteman and Anderson, *World Mission*, 44.

81. Maurier, *Other Covenant*.

82. Cavalcanti, "Human Agency in Mission Work."

83. Winter et al., *Perspectives on the World*.

84. Moreau et al., *Evangelical Dictionary of World Missions*.

85. DeLoach, "Knowing God in Melanesia"; Roxborogh, "Missiology after 'Mission?'"; Forman, "Study of Pacific Island Christianity."

86. Pickett, *Christian Mass Movements in India*.

87. McGavran, *Bridges of God*.

88. Tippett, *People Movements in Southern Polynesia*.

89. Trompf, *Melanesian Religion*, 212.

90. Hesselgrave, "People Movements," 743.

retrospectively, it can be seen that they have been occurring since New Testament times. This is as people have come to Christ using their normal multi-individual decision-making procedures.[91] Recognizing and understanding people movements has allowed scholars such as McGavran,[92] Tippett,[93] and Hesselgrave[94] to reflect on what has occurred historically and also to strategize more effectively for the future.

The second area of reflection was raised in 1960, when Tippett raised the topic of animism in the context of ministry[95] Since then other scholars have contributed to this area in books and articles including Dan Shaw,[96] Paul Hiebert,[97] Gailyn Van Rheenen,[98] Jaime Bulatao,[99] Douglas Hayward,[100] David Burnett,[101] Charles Kraft,[102] Wonsuk and Julie Ma,[103] and Kenneth Nehrbass.[104] This material joins Tippett's extensive material on the topic.[105] Clinton Arnold adds biblical and archeological research in his two volumes.[106] On the other hand, some scholars have opposed the use of the term animism, for example, Tite Tiénou[107] and Michael Rynkiewich.[108] While the concept of animism has been the source of contention,

91. Malina, *New Testament World*.

92. McGavran and Wagner, *Understanding Church Growth*.

93. Tippett, *Introduction to Missiology*.

94. Hesselgrave, "People Movements."

95. Tippett, "Probing Missionary Inadequacies."

96. Shaw, "Every Person a Shaman."

97. Hiebert, "Flaw of the Excluded Middle."

98. Van Rheenen, *Communicating Christ in Animistic Contexts*.

99. Bulatao, "Split Level Christianity."

100. Hayward, "Evangelization of Animists"; Hiebert, *Understanding Folk Religion*.

101. Burnett, *World of the Spirits*.

102. Kraft, "Three Encounters in Christian Witness"; Kraft, "Power Encounter."

103. Ma and Ma, *Mission in the Spirit*.

104. Nehrbass, *Christianity and Animism in Melanesia*.

105. Tippett, *Solomon Islands Christianity*; Tippett, "Evangelization of Animists"; Tippett, *Introduction to Missiology*; Tippett, "Meaning of Meaning"; Tippett, "Christo-paganism or Indigenous Christianity"; Tippett, *Deep-Sea Canoe*; Tippett, *Slippery Paths in the Darkness*.

106. Arnold, *Ephesians, Power and Magic*; Arnold, *Powers of Darkness*.

107. Tiénou, "Invention of the 'Primitive'"; Tiénou, "Reflections on Michael A. Rynkiewich's."

108. Rynkiewich, "Do Not Remember."

this study makes a contribution by providing clarification regarding Tippett's original research.

Third, the topic of indigenous Christianity, contextualization, appropriate Christianity and insider movements is also an area that has produced much scholarly reflection. Tippett illustrates this well from the beginning of Christianity in Fiji in a number of his writings.[109] William Smalley's article, "Cultural Implications of an Indigenous Church"[110] seemed to provide a watershed in evangelical missions, extending past the earlier Henry Venn three-self concepts of indigenous church.[111] Since then, books and articles have abounded, positioning Christianity for more appropriate impact worldwide: Examples are Charles Kraft,[112] Tetsunao Yamamori,[113] Glenn Schwartz,[114] Darrell Whiteman,[115] and Dan Shaw.[116] Insider movements are represented embryonically by scholars such as Herbert Hoefer and H. L. Richard[117] with the volume edited by Harley Talman and John Jay Travis[118] providing recent broad reading on the topic.

The acceleration of urbanization and the concomitant elements of migration are seen with alarm by some in the missiological community.[119] Others would encourage further reflection, pointing out that migration has been a part of the world for all of Christian history.[120] Some scholars are concerned that the ways that the world's population has been grouped for purposes of analysis and strategy in missiology in the past, using terms like

---

109. Tippett, *Integrating Gospel and the Christian*; Tippett, *Oral Tradition and Ethnohistory*.

110. Smalley, "Cultural Implications."

111. Warren, *To Apply the Gospel*.

112. Kraft, "Dynamic Equivalence Churches"; Kraft and Wisley, *Readings in Dynamic Indigeneity*; Kraft, *Anthropology for Christian Witness*; Kraft, *Culture, Communication, and Christianity*; *Christianity in Culture*; Kraft and Gilliland, *Appropriate Christianity*; Kraft, *Worldview for Christian Witness*; Kraft, *Issues in Contextualization*.

113. Yamamori and Taber, *Christopaganism or Indigenous Christianity?*

114. Schwartz, *When Charity Destroys Dignity*.

115. Whiteman, "Contextualization."

116. Shaw et al., "Contextualization, Conceptualization, and Communication."

117. Hoefer, *Churchless Christianity*.

118. Talman and Travis, *Understanding Insider Movements*.

119. Rynkiewich, "Do Not Remember."

120. Tiénou, "Reflections on Michael A. Rynkiewich's"; Rynkiewich, "Do Not Remember."

"people groups," etc.[121] Stephen Pavey however, uses an alternate perspective, saying, "urban lives are lived in 'small social worlds,'"[122] with Smart adding, "where these spheres of lived experience are profoundly influenced by their location within the larger urban place and regional, national and global systems."[123] In Tippett's *Solomon Islands Christianity*[124] and in my own *Before All Else Fails*,[125] both include chapters that link our rural analysis into the urban scene. Other scholars have focused their research to especially serve the burgeoning urban centres of Africa and Asia, for example, Tereso Casiño (et al).[126] David Boyd on the other hand reflects on the strategy of ministering to the diaspora (students, migrant workers, etc.) in international cities like Sydney, with the plan of having those people return to their homelands transformed by the gospel.[127]

Writings about Alan Tippett

Although Tippett wrote so much, little has been written about him and his material. This can be illustrated by listing the items that have been written about him under a series of headings: (1) Three tributes to Tippett written after he passed away overview his life and achievements in one article each;[128] (2) A historical PhD on Tippett by Colin Dundon, completed in 2000. This is a well researched volume focused on the history of his life, but as part of that, it does highlight some aspects of his missiology;[129] (3) The December 2014 edition of the *Australian Journal of Mission Studies*[130] comprised ten articles relating to the person and material of Alan Tippett. It was compiled from the "Alan Tippett Symposium on Mission and Cross-Cultural Ministry" convened by Alphacrucis College in Sydney, Australia,

121. Rynkiewich, "Do Not Remember," 100–1.

122. Pavey, *Theologies of Power and Crisis*, 100–1.

123. Smart, *Political Economy of Street Hawkers*, 61.

124. Tippett, *Solomon Islands Christianity*.

125. Hovey, *Before All Else Fails*.

126. Casiño et al. *Reaching the City*.

127. Boyd, *You Don't Have to Cross*.

128. McGavran, "Missiologist Alan R. Tippett," 261–67; Kraft and Priest, "Who Was This Man?," 269–81; Whiteman, "Legacy of Alan R. Tippett," 163–66.

129. Dundon, "Raicakacaka."

130. This was compiled from the "Alan Tippett Symposium on Mission and Cross-Cultural Ministry" convened by Alphacrucis College in Sydney, Australia, in September 2013, conducted on the twenty-fifth anniversary of his death.

in September 2013, on the 25th anniversary of Tippett's death. This volume is useful, but is not intended to be comprehensive, as authors chose their own topics related to Tippett;[131] (4) Subsequently Richard Hibbert expanded his paper in "Negotiating Identity: Extending and Applying Alan Tippett's Model of Conversion" published in *Missiology*.[132] So while each of these documents have been significant in their own way, there has not been an extended document with the focus on mission and missiology, to be representative of that foundational aspect of Tippett's writing.

Having outlined the above material, it is clear that this study focusing on this missiology in particular fills a gap in the literature concerning Alan Tippett in two ways: First of all, it spells out Tippett's own missiology with its various components, something that has not been done before, either due to the brevity of the articles or the different focus of Dundon's dissertation. Furthermore, this study demonstrates Tippet's unique contribution in relation to each of these fields to which other scholars have contributed, thus adding to that body of knowledge. I contend that many of Tippett's insights into the theology, research, theory, and practice of mission were significant for Great-Commission-focused mission in his era, while it is discernible that his insights have laid foundations for contemporary Great-Commission-focused mission. Considering all that Tippett wrote and the time that has lapsed since he wrote it, there is a need for comprehensive reflection on Tippett's material and analysis of its contribution to mission theory and practice, a need which this study aims to partially fill.

DEFINITIONS

When aiming to define key terminology used in this study, succinct definitions from Tippett's own writing would be useful, but are hard to find. He had the tendency to "develop" his key subject areas as he wrote, rather than defining them precisely. At the same time, there is the danger of providing other scholar's definitions, because they may not define the specific topics being addressed in a comparable way. Therefore these definitions are

---

131. Hovey, "Guest Editorial"; Dundon, "Tippett Library"; Phillips, "Tippett Missiological and Anthropological Collection"; Reeson, "Wednesdays with Alan Tippett"; Priest, "Genesis of the Missiology"; Hovey, "Alan Tippett"; Hibbert and Hibbert, "Expanding and Applying Tippett's Model"; Kraft, "Power Encounter"; Humble, "Tippett for Today and Tomorrow"; Priest, "Vintage and Vantage"; Whiteman, Review of *The Ways*; Pruett, Review of *Fullness of Time*.

132. Hibbert, "Negotiating Identity."

intended to be helpful, but will be elucidated more when they are dealt with in more depth.

Great Commission: As noted earlier, the term Great Commission refers to the instructions Jesus gave to his disciples after his resurrection, defining their responsibilities to communicate the gospel and make disciples in the power of the Holy Spirit. The cluster of verses normally associated with the Great Commission are Matthew 28:18–20, Mark 16:15–16, Luke 24:46–49, John 20:21, and Acts 1:8,[133] Tippett observes that the Great Commission is intentionally placed at the end of the gospels. By then Jesus was the victorious, risen Lord of all who gave these instructions to his disciples,[134] thus signifying the priority of seeing those instructions fulfilled. Similarly, conversion will be used to refer to the act of people receiving salvation by turning to the Lord in repentance and faith. It is a vital term within mission and missiology and needs to be understood from a biblical, psychological, and sociological point of view.[135]

Mission: Mission, in response to an understanding of the Great Commission and conversion, is the act of declaring the gospel in word and deed and in seeking a response from the people ministered to in this way. Typically, but not exclusively, the word denotes a corporate response to this responsibility and carries a cross-cultural emphasis.[136]

Missiology: In simplest terms, missiology is the study of mission as defined above. Furthermore, over the last fifty years, with the increase in emphasis on the fulfillment of the Great Commission, this area of research has come to be a discipline in its own right.[137]

Great-Commission-Focused Missiology: Great Commission missiology, or Great-Commission-focused missiology, the cluster of terms I am using in this volume, then, is the study of the theories and activities of the church in carrying out the Great Commission.[138] For Tippett, that included the key components of the "biblical origin, the history . . . the

---

133. Tippett, *Church Growth and the Word*, 24; Moreau et al., *Evangelical Dictionary of World Missions*, 412–13.

134. Tippett, "Objectives of World Mission," 5.

135. Moreau et al., *Evangelical Dictionary of World Missions*, 231.

136. Tippett, *Introduction to Missiology*, 66.

137. Moreau et al., *Evangelical Dictionary of World Missions*, 633; Tippett, *Introduction to Missiology*, xiv.

138. Tippett, *Introduction to Missiology*, xiii.

anthropological principles and techniques and the theological base of the Christian Mission."[139]

Colonialism: Colonialism refers to the political and economic domination of Western nations over many non-Western nations, especially in the nineteenth and early twentieth centuries.[140] The philosophy behind this was ethnocentrically Western, with other nations being considered "primitive."[141]

Colonial Mission: Colonial mission was missions in that same era, which, while often driven by Christian motives, was typically still culturally ethnocentric. Tippett describes some of their actions based on that philosophy as "irresponsible missionary activity."[142]

Post-colonial Missiology: As time progressed, post-colonial missiology was the term that Tippett used to describe his culturally informed, church-growth-focused understanding of mission along with its models, theories, strategy and practice.[143] In that context, indigenous, contextually appropriate, and outreaching were three of his key words to designate the results of post-colonial missiology.[144] Tippett felt that much of this was formalized in the 1974 Lausanne Congress on World Evangelization and the "Lausanne Covenant." that it produced.[145]

Animism: Reflecting on specific contexts and ministry approaches, animism speaks of the societies living with active spirit-world beliefs and practices. In many ways, animism, thought of this way, represents the one religious universal in the context of which mission operates.[146] Therefore, for field missionaries, animism is as important to understand as the systems of the major world religions.

Indigenous Church: Another universal concept relating to the contexts in which mission operates is the concept of the indigenous church.[147]

139. Tippett, *Introduction to Missiology*, xiii.

140. Moreau et al., *Evangelical Dictionary of World Missions*, 633.

141. Tiénou, "Invention of the 'Primitive.'"

142. Tippett, *Verdict Theology in Missionary Theory*, 165; Tippett et al., *No Continuing City*, 476, 93.

143. Tippett et al., *No Continuing City*, 239, 377.

144. Tippett, "Task and Method," 23.

145. Tippett et al., *No Continuing City*, 401.

146. Tippett, "Probing Missionary Inadequacies"; Tippett, "Evangelization of Animists"; Van Rheenen, *Communicating Christ in Animistic Contexts*, 20; Hovey, *Before All Else Fails*, 127.

147. Terry, "Indigenous Church," 483.

Borrowing the concept from botany, an indigenous church is one that fits so naturally into its cultural environment, that to people of that society, it feels like it belongs. Of course, the church that "fits" in this way must still maintain integrity with biblical Christianity. In this instance, Tippett does provide a succinct definition, saying, an indigenous church,

> while maintaining a fixed faith in Christ as Saviour and Lord, and the Bible as norm for faith and practice, will need to be the most flexible with respect to the forms in which or through which the faith is practiced and transmitted. To be indigenous a Church has to belong to a culture, to be in it and to speak to it. It has to be the body of Christ ministering to that world which is its very own and we as missionaries must be prepared to let the church be itself.[148]

In mission, the term indigenous can also be used to refer to the movements of national churches that have been planted by using these principles.

METHODOLOGY

Having identified a gap in the literature, it is necessary to explain the methodological basis for this study which is suited to the analysis of the vast volume and breadth of Tippett's material.

Selecting a Construct: Tippett's "Three Sermons" as Life Themes

To achieve the goals of this study, there had to be a construct that enabled the volume and breadth of Tippett's writing to be encapsulated concisely yet without significant distortion. In doing so, I was aware that the danger in developing such a matrix is that the mechanism that is meant to illuminate can artificially influence the conclusions. With that danger in mind, I developed and evaluated a number of constructs by which to organize his material, such as: 1) Conceptual Themes: Documenting the development of Tippett's insights as they occurred; 2) Extended Timeline: The flow of Tippett's concepts suggest the validity of using his life transition points for the outline of his concepts, especially when he talks about his life using van Gennep's rites of passage.[149] However, while following these potential methods, it was discovered that the concern of illumination influencing conclusions was in fact occurring. In each of those cases, the historical and sequential nature of the process tended to distort the understanding of

148. Tippett, *Verdict Theology in Missionary Theory*, 175.
149. Van Gennep, *Rites of Passage*; Tippett, "Liminal Years," vii–x.

Tippett's concepts. It became obvious that there was a need to get beyond Tippett himself to be able to view Tippett with sufficient perspective. It was in that context that Richard Halverson's comment, "I've known some of the best preachers in the world, and the very best had only three sermons in them"[150] provided the inspiration for the approach that will be used. Namely, identifying and examining Tippett's "three sermons," to use Halverson's statement as an analogy, that is, to identify Tippett's essential life themes. Once those themes are identified, the goal will be to examine Tippett's missiology through the perspectives of those life themes. As will be seen below, five life themes have been identified. This study will demonstrate the value of this approach, as it places the focus on the broad brush strokes of Tippett's concepts. In doing so, it temporarily puts aside the terms by which he described himself such as missionary, anthropologist, ethnohistorian, and missiologist, and allows the postponement of the focus on his key conceptual breakthroughs. Using this minimalist perspective from Halverson, I believe that the following five life themes represent a meaningful distillation of Tippett's writings. Furthermore, the fact that it is only five chosen forces a prioritization of his material that makes his material manageable:

- Theme 1: Centrality of a relationship with God

- Theme 2: Centrality of the Church

- Theme 3: The Importance of Appropriate Research Methodologies

- Theme 4: The Importance of Strategic Missiology and Strategic Missionary Practice

- Theme 5: Guidelines for Mission Boards and Field Missionaries

These five life themes were chosen after extensive personal engagement with Tippett's concepts leading to this study and the research for this study. I first engaged with some of his published material starting in 1974 while I was a missionary on the Sepik River in Papua New Guinea. In that context I was able to implement many of Tippett's approaches as I read about them. In addition to that, I was a student in a two week block course on "The Development of Missionary Anthropology" that Tippett taught at Fuller SWM in 1979 and attended a 1986 mission consultation in Sydney where he was one of the keynote speakers. There was also personal time while driving him to second hand book shops in Los Angeles in 1979 and additionally in his library office in Canberra later that year. This was then

150. Miller and Goetz, "Finding the Eye," 26.

amplified by the research of his material for this study. It is on the basis of that diachronic and in-depth engagement with his insights that I have chosen these themes.

The following brief comments will explain each theme as part of the introduction to this study, while the various research methodologies that are employed will assist in the elucidation of these themes as the sections and chapters unfold:

Theme 1: Centrality of a relationship with God: Tippett lived his relationship with God, and it is also observed through his writings as he made a relationship with God through Christ available to others within their cultural worlds.

Theme 2: Centrality of the Church: Tippett's church growth emphasis is quickly evident in his writings, however seeing the church as a reason for so much of what he researched and wrote became clearer through the in-depth research for this study.

Theme 3: The Importance of Appropriate Research Methodologies: Tippett did research using standard and unique research tools. The goal of this research was to produce data to guide the development of effective mission strategies.

Theme 4: The Importance of Strategic Missiology and Strategic Missionary Practice: Strategic missiology and strategic missionary practice comprises reflection on mission by which missionary practice is selected in order to be effective in fulfilling the Great Commission.

Theme 5: Guidelines for Mission Boards and Field Missionaries: Tippett observed ripe harvest fields across the globe, but noted that mission leaders frequently failed to strategize to reap those harvests. Both Tippett and McGavran were outspoken about the responsibility to take those opportunities seriously. A classic example of this harshness in McGavran's case can be seen in his correspondence with David Barrett in 1963, in which he uses terms like, "mal-administration, criminal negligence, bumbling bureaucracy" to describe church structures not getting involved in mission. Tippett held a similar view.[151] This overall theme of guidelines for Mission Boards and Field Missionaries will be threaded through the other chapters seen in key application points compiled as lists, some prepared by Tippett and some distilled by me in writing this volume.

151. Tippett, "Task and Method," 22.

Triangulation of Methodologies

By utilizing a number of different methodologies to engage with different parts of this analysis, there is the benefit of triangulation of methodologies, each lending strength and balance to the other, with Jick's overview article demonstrating the benefits of such an approach from the perspective of a number of scholars.[152] In analyzing Tippett's contributions to twentieth-century missiology, different research methodologies were used depending on the goal of each chapter in this study. For example, chapters two, three, and four provide the background of Tippett's life. For those chapters, historical methods especially suited for autobiographical sources were used[153] to research the material.[154] Additionally, due to the range of external factors that need to be considered while documenting the decline of Tippett influence in chapter 4, ethnohistorical tools were used informally to understand the deeper external factors that contributed to his declining influence.[155]

Tippett's life theme four, the importance of strategic missiology and strategic missionary practice, provided the background to researching and writing chapters 7, 8, and 9. As such, the method that I used was to select and research key issues that Tippett wrote about extensively that have a significant bearing on effective mission strategies and practice.[156] This led to the selection of societal decision-making for chapter 7, ministry in animistic contexts for chapter 8, and the cultural fit of Christianity for chapter 9. Tippett wrote extensively on each of these, his insights on each went beyond many of his peers at the time. Furthermore, they were issues with which most cross-cultural missionaries needed to engage while aiming for their mission effectiveness.

The exercise of applying a set of identified cultural differences while engaging with a series of cultures different than one's own, when examined as a methodology, was in many ways similar to the research methodology described in Fons van de Vijver and Kwok Leung's article "Methods and Data Analysis for Cross-cultural Research,"[157] which is also similar to

152. Jick, "Mixing Qualitative and Quantitative Methods."

153. Stephenson, "Living History, Undoing Linearity."

154. Stephenson, "Living History, Undoing Linearity."

155. Whiteman, *Missionaries, Anthropologists and Cultural Change*; Pavey, *Theologies of Power and Crisis.*

156. Duriau et al. "Content Analysis"; Dayton and Fraser, *Planning Strategies for World Evangelization.*

157. van de Vijver and Leung, *Methods and Data Analysis.*

the approach described in Richard Brislin's article "Comparative Research Methodology: Cross-cultural Studies."[158] Their approach was to find cross referencing themes between cultures, then to observe the effect of the similarities or differences of those themes in their interplay between the cultures. So, using Vijver's and Brislin's perspectives, in chapters 7, 8, and 9, the alignment and misalignment of those key concepts can be observed as they played out. Therefore the sort of training that Tippett was developing and advocating would have been the key factors in overcoming those cross-cultural differences and positioning missionaries for effectiveness.

While researching Tippett, there are a number of factors that can be observed that are unique. Among the positive, helpful things he wrote, there is also an "anti" element that can be seen in his anti-establishment attitudes, and his opposition to what he considered to be inappropriate colonialism, and the like. At the same time, there was a counterbalancing lack of self-confidence. Regardless of whether this complexity can be understood, his tendency to "think outside the box" of the standard approaches of people around him are worth noting. Furthermore, the fruitfulness of those alternative approaches provide a lot of the data for this study. The functionally designed curriculum he developed in Fiji to train local leaders specifically for their own homeland roles, while providing a pathway for internationally recognized training for advanced participants, and internationally, for leaders from the perspective of their worldview[159] are two such examples.

Glenn Adams'[160] emphasis on decolonizing research methodology illuminates the strengths that are evident in Tippett's approach outlined above. Adams, in his African studies, is concerned that research structures themselves have an in-built "coloniality of knowledge"[161] as he describes it, which limits genuine research and limits the ability to gain genuinely new information drawn from the situation itself. So, stated bluntly, he aims to move the power base away from Western (or Western trained) research. Adams sees that "coloniality of knowledge" to be the natural result of scientific research procedures, due to those procedures assuming that they are "an identity-neutral tool . . . yield[ing] relatively unbiased readings of objective reality."[162] His approach is to identify the unrecognized bias in the

158. Brislin, "Comparative Research Methodology."
159. Tippett et al., *No Continuing City*, 428.
160. Adams, "Decolonizing Methods."
161. Adams, "Decolonizing Methods," 467.
162. Adams, "Decolonizing Methods," 467.

supposedly unbiased readings. Linda Tuhiwai Smith[163] addresses similar concerns and approaches in her book, *Decolonizing Methodologies: Research and Indigenous Peoples*. Adams' description of the problem, and his suggested solution, articulate key strengths found in Tippett's writing. To begin with, one of Adams' recommended approaches for decolonialization is "accompaniment," that is, immersing oneself in the life of the community being researched. This fits well with Tippett's emphasis on being on patrol in order to spend time in villages with local people, or in his continual use of personal interviews as a key part of his research methodology.

In this study, subsequently there will be references to key indicators that will demonstrate that Adams could have used Tippett's approaches as illustrations in his article. For example, Hollenweger refers to Tippett as an "independent thinker."[164] Taber describes Tippett as an "anthropologist of breadth and sophistication."[165] Shaw (et al) highlight his coming into the academic field after twenty years' experience on the field.[166] I have pointed out that he was not always writing on popular topics. While none of these items individually say that much, taken together there is an element of the decolonialization of method, to use Adams' term. Established as a significant tendancy, this is again illustrated in the following examples seen in detail in other parts of this study: his pointed 1962 evaluation of the Methodist work in the Pacific that was "lost" before publication, his remonstrating with the World Council of Churches regarding their Barbados Declaration, the fact that his board secretary eventually closed dialog with him regarding their Methodist strategy and deployment approaches in Papua New Guinea in 1962. All of this demonstrates that he felt bound to good research and the findings coming from that research, rather than the politically correct status quo that may have been organizationally beneficial to him.

Limitations of This Study

Clearly, there are limitations with the methodological approaches chosen. First of all, due to the volume and detail of Tippett's writings, it is not possible to cover every document or every concept in one study. Another

---

163. Smith, *Decolonizing Methodologies*.

164. Hollenweger, "Oral Tradition and Ethnohistory," 519.

165. Taber, *World Is Too Much*, 131.

166. Shaw et al., "Contextualization, Conceptualization, and Communication," 97.

limitation is the small numbers of scholars who have directly interacted in-depth with Tippett's material. However, in the study other scholars' points of view have been considered as they look at the same issues that Tippett was addressing. Hence the limited direct interaction with Tippett's concepts is complemented by this sort of academic third party interaction.

Another potential limitation in this study is the fact that Tippett has been my "teacher" since I first started reading his material in 1974. As described above, this was followed up in a two week course at Fuller School of World Mission in 1979, and other brief face-to-face time with him. While the danger of this insider approach is acknowledged, this is balanced by the fact that I was not simply reading his material but was intentionally putting some of his concepts into practice. That provided the opportunity to demonstrate the validity or otherwise of his concepts as they were implemented. Furthermore, we were from different generations and denominations, so there was no personal obligation to use his insights unless they proved to be beneficial. It was his ability to explain the cross-cultural world in which I lived, and his ability to provide me with ministry tools that increased my effectiveness.

Where possible, these limitations listed above are overcome by cross-referencing, triangulation, and researcher judgement. This work can also provide a foundation for further exploration at a later date.

STRUCTURE OF THE STUDY

In this study, I argue that Tippett made a vital contribution toward the development and dissemination of twentieth-century, Great-Commission-focused missiology. His missiological insights spoke to a number of areas: a clear theological basis for his missiology, research methodologies to provide accurate data for reflection and cultural insights especially geared for effective mission in non-Western environments. This included his unique insights in relation to societies that are propitious for innovation, societies where multi-individual mutually interdependent decision-making is the norm, leading to the potential for people movements, approaches that lead to indigenous Christianity along with the opportunities, challenges and appropriate ministry approaches in animistic contexts. The study is divided into three sections: Section 1—Alan Tippett's Life Journey; Section 2—Tippett's writings—Theological Basis and Research Methodologies; Section 3—Tippett's writings—Strategic Missiology and Strategic Mission Practice.

Section 1—Alan Tippett's Life Journey

The first section of the study comprises chapters 2, 3, and 4, relating to Alan Tippett's life journey. These will, first of all, overview his life story, then document the significant increase in his influence during his time in the United States of America (USA), and finally will analyze the decline of his influence, especially examining that decline in relation to the significance of his key mission concepts. Chapter 2 is a brief biography of Tippett's life that will especially demonstrate aspects of the development of his life themes and how they were expressed, while providing an overview of the major periods of his life. Chapter 3 traces the remarkable escalation of his influence beginning with his departure from Fiji until his retirement from Fuller School of World Mission, thus demonstrating the significance of his compounding insights. Chapter 4 examines the precipitous decline of his influence that coincided with the period of his retirement from Fuller SWM, USA to Canberra, Australia. This informal ethnohistorical reconstruction will show that, to a marked degree, factors other than the significance of his insights contributed to this decline of his influence.

Section 2—Tippett's Writings:
Theological Basis and Research Methodologies

Three of Tippett's life themes are examined within chapters five and six. The first two themes, elucidating Tippett's theological basis for mission comprising one chapter while his theme of the priority of appropriate research methodologies is served in its own chapter.

Chapter 5 is the first chapter devoted to in-depth examination of Tippet's life themes as they have been deduced from Tippett's writings. As such, this chapter will discuss the life themes of (1) the centrality of a relationship with God, and, (2) the centrality of the church. This will, in effect, provide the basis of Tippett's theology of mission. Chapter 6 is the second chapter examining Tippett's life themes with this chapter focused on his life theme of the importance of appropriate research methodologies.

Section 3—Tippett's Writings:
Strategic Missiology and Strategic Mission Practice

The trilogy of chapters in this section demonstrates the importance of strategic missiology and strategic missionary practice in Tippett's writings. Tippett placed an emphasis on recognizing opportunities for effective

Great Commission focused mission endeavours. Once recognized, he advocated the application of resources commensurate to those opportunities. Therefore his writings relating to this particular life theme are extensive and cover a wide range of topics.

Chapter 7 analyzes Tippett's life theme of the importance of strategic missiology and strategic missionary practice regarding societal decision-making. Societal decision-making is a key strategic area when recognizing opportunities for effective Great Commission mission and in seeing strategy, activities, personnel and resources dedicated to take advantage of those opportunities. Chapter 8 analyzes Tippett's life themes of the importance of strategic missiology and strategic missionary practice in relation to ministry in animistic contexts. Equipping Christian workers to understand the opportunities and challenges related to ministering in animistic contexts is a key strategic area. Tippett's insights show the positive results that could occur if such situations are approached appropriately, the pitfalls that could prevent that happening, and the seriousness of not taking such backgrounds into account.

Chapter 9 explores Tippett's life theme on the importance of strategic missiology and strategic missionary practice in relation to the cultural fit of Christianity. The cultural fit of Christianity into any culture on earth is important when it comes to effectively implementing Great-Commission-focused mission. It was through this process that the gospel could even be rejected without being heard, simply because of poor cultural fit in its presentation. Similarly, the impact of the gospel on a community and the strength of the church coming from that ministry could be enhanced or impeded by the degree of cultural fit. A brief conclusion chapter is added, to confirm the theoretical argument that Tippett's insights were seminal for effective missiology and mission practice in his era.

CONCLUSION

Due to the complexity and volume of material to be handled in this study, this introductory chapter establishes a basis for the study and for the individual chapters that follow. The overarching framework I have chosen is focused on his "life themes" in order to extrapolate his main contributions to Great-Commission-focused missiology and mission practice. This approach demonstrates some of the unique aspects of Tippett's writing that make his concepts difficult to access. Literature in the field was reviewed, key terminology was defined, and research methodologies were established.

Having noted Tippett's five life themes, the following three chapters will provide an overview of his life as a dynamic backdrop to the insights that will be deduced, analyzed, and applied in the subsequent chapters.

2

Alan Tippett's Life Journey

But, really, the tragedy of it all is that most of it should have been
available to me in training, before I ever went to Fiji. I had lost 14/15
years of direction because of the shortcomings of our training program.
At 45 years of age I was starting a game where I should have been at
30. When I knew the time had come to check out of Fiji I knew that
somehow I had to communicate that truth to the home Church.[1]

This was Tippett's own evaluation, having spent a year studying for
his Master's Degree.

CHAPTER 1 EMPLOYED THE question, "What were Tippett's three sermons?"
as a way of condensing Alan Tippett's life, calling, and material succinctly,
while staying close to his underlying concepts and philosophy. In doing so
it looked past the terms by which he described himself, such as "missionary," "anthropologist," "ethnohistorian," and "missiologist," and provided a
prioritization that makes his material manageable. In order to understand
Tippet's "three sermons," it is important to critically examine the development of his personal spirituality and professional career as seen in his life
journey. This chapter argues that Tippett's early formation in a godly home
contributed to who he became. His focus on the centrality of a relationship
with God can be traced back to that. His ministry call and experience, combined with his study and research, cemented a strong commitment to the

1. Tippett et al., *No Continuing City,* 251.

centrality of the church. Furthermore, his field ministry and subsequent specific research provided the framework for his missionary research and methodologies and through that, his strategic missiology and strategic missionary practice.

EARLY FORMATION:
CENTRALITY OF A RELATIONSHIP WITH GOD

Centrality of a relationship with God was Tippett's foundational life theme which was shaped through his formative years. Although never an absolute, Leslie Andrews[2] argues, the spiritual formation and family influences of missionaries play a crucial role in their long-term success. In Tippett's case it was a positive factor. Tippett was born on 9th November, 1911, in St. Arnaud, Victoria, Australia.[3] His parents, Will and Carrie Tippett (née Caroline Dower),[4] were ministering at the Cohuna Wesleyan Methodist Church at the time.[5] During his childhood years, the pastorates his father served were mostly in rural Victoria. By his teenage years, his father pastored in Geelong and a "mission" work in North Melbourne.

Loving Learning and God through Family Influences

Tippett's father's contagious love of knowledge infected his son.[6] Whether this was flora and fauna that they encountered in his early rural life, or the wonders of his father's library, with its seeming ability to answer so many of his questions, or his father's preaching that he found so engaging, it all contributed to his thirst for knowledge. His father encouraged him to read books of significance, and to be around books.[7] These factors converged with his own interest to stimulate him to write, including poetry, fiction, and particularly nonfiction material even during his school years.[8] Tippett's report of an experience he had while a high school student at Geelong College illustrates the quality of his nonfiction writing. "I was assigned an essay topic on Australian wildflowers and had handed in

---

2. Andrews, "Spiritual, Family, and Ministry Satisfaction," 107.

3. Tippett et al., *No Continuing City*, 21.

4. Tippett et al., *No Continuing City*, 18.

5. Tippett et al., *No Continuing City*, 19.

6. Tippett et al., *No Continuing City*, 488–90.

7. Tippett et al., *No Continuing City*, 488–90.

8. Tippett et al., *No Continuing City*, 27, 34.

a careful analysis, all botanically correct. The teacher had flicked it back to me ungraded. 'I wanted your own work, not something out of a book,' was his curt verdict and I was upset."[9] His father's commitment to God, people, and learning were probably the greatest influences on his life, including his own deep devotion to God. Two weeks after his father died in February 1940,[10] when Tippett was twenty-nine years old, he said of his father that, "He had opened my eyes to see the glory of God around me: he had opened my heart to the love of man to man: he had opened my soul, to see the love of God for me as a person."[11] He also described the complementary role of his mother as, "Our family devotional life was built round mother, the organ and Wesleyan hymnody and a selection of hymns she taught us."[12] These formative influences on Tippett during his early life were inextricably centred on the importance of developing a strong relationship with God in which the church was central and with a deep call to serve in church ministry. This became a defining aspect of his entire life.

Developing Perfectionism through School Experiences

In reading Tippett, there seems to have been some negative experiences from his schooling years that significantly impacted him for the rest of his life, resulting in his perfectionist compulsions and his pre-emptive strikes against would-be critics. This was also mentioned in his classroom lectures and in personal conversation in 1979, indicating that it had had a major impact on him. One aspect of this was the negative experiences he had with two of his teachers at the Geelong High School. As he described it,

> If Miss Lightfoot—my Ugly Witch, frustrated me, Mr. Charles, my Big Bad Wolf, infuriated me. I never forgot his superior lack of empathy. For years I remembered him, and whenever I had any success, I'd shake my fist at space and laugh at his ugly memory: "Eat your heart out, Charles." Nobody could treat a Cornish lad that way and get away with it.[13]

9. Tippett et al., *No Continuing City*, 26.

10. Tippett et al., *No Continuing City*, 451.

11. Tippett et al., *No Continuing City*, 99.

12. Tippett et al., *No Continuing City*, 29.

13. Tippett et al., *No Continuing City*, 33.

Observing the perfectionist[14] and workaholic tendencies of his adult life, which in fact contributed so much to the care taken in his research and writing, along with the proliferation of his writing, these experiences, while negative for Tippett, could be argued to have contributed to the legacy he left for Great Commission mission.[15]

Another of those negative influences that shaped Tippett was the schoolyard bullies he encountered, especially in North Melbourne. He described his tactics in dealing with them, and their influence on his later life with the statement,

> I went in with all I knew on the principle that the first well-aimed blow can determine a fight . . . In later life, I learned that there is an ilk of this type [schoolyard bullies] even in the academic life who love to 'take it out' on parsons and their children, especially if they have missionary connections. As a degree candidate in anthropology, as a footballer parson, and as a Christian in the academic world, I utilized a strategy I had learned under these unhappy schoolboy circumstances.[16]

As Tippett did encounter many challenges in his life which he termed "battles," a certain element in this schoolyard wisdom can be observed in the approaches he used in dealing with those challenges. Examples of these "battles" for Tippett would be such things as maintaining the priority of the Great Commission within mission and missiology, establishing the church growth perspective with the World Council of Churches, and having anthropology accepted within missions while establishing the credibility of missionary anthropologists within anthropology.

MINISTRY CALL, MINISTRY FORMATION: CENTRALITY OF THE CHURCH

There were several factors in Tippett's ministry call, formation, and experience that developed and demonstrated a strong commitment to the work, and church of God.

After leaving school at age eighteen, Tippett had four years in employment in Melbourne as a junior clerk with the Orient Steam Navigation

---

14. Tippett et al., *No Continuing City*, 370.

15. Tippett, "Task and Method," 8.

16. Tippett et al., *No Continuing City*, 25.

Company.[17] It was during this time, while listening to an evangelistic program at the Victoria Market, he "experienced a vigorous conversion of the
Wesleyan type" in 1929.[18] Several years later, feeling called by God into
full-time ministry, he resigned employment in November 1931 to enter
ministry training, his first year in an academically oriented Arts program
at Queens College, Melbourne. His subsequent two years of training were
in the more ministerially oriented Licentiate in Theology (LTh) program
at the Melbourne College of Divinity (MCD).[19] After completion of his
studies in 1934, he probationed for the Methodist ministry for three years.
Normally candidates probationed for two years, but because Tippett failed
Hebrew in his LTh, thus not immediately graduating, he was asked to serve
as a probationer for three years. Later he completed his LTh when other
subjects were able to be substituted, in his case, "Intertestamental Studies."[20]
His early pastorates were small, remote, poor, and mostly challenging, the
town of Manangatang in the Mallee region of northern Victoria, with its
population of 400 being the first of these.[21] Subsequently, he was ordained
as a minister on 3rd March, 1938.[22]

Support of Wife and Children

Tippett's marriage to Edna (née Deckert) on the 6th April 1938[23] was for
both of them, embedded in the context of two lives dedicated to God in the
service of the church. While Edna actively participated in the pastoral ministry in Australia, she was also deeply involved in their work as Methodist
missionaries in Fiji from their arrival on 6th May 1941[24] to the end of their
term of service in 1961,[25] as well as freeing Alan for his ministry. Claudia
Knapman in *White Women in Fiji 1835–1930: The Ruin of Empire?*[26] notes

17. Tippett et al., *No Continuing City*, 38.
18. Tippett et al., *No Continuing City*, 43–44, 492.
19. Treloar, "Towards a Master Narrative," 33; Dundon, "Raicakacaka," 27.
20. Dundon, "Raicakacaka," 27, 30.
21. Tippett et al., *No Continuing City*, 67.
22. Dundon, "Raicakacaka," 32.
23. From an electronic copy of the Certificate of Marriage, State of Victoria Certificate Number 8225, showing Alan as twenty-six years of age and Edna as twenty-three
years of age; Kraft and Priest, "Who Was This Man?," 171.
24. Dundon, "Raicakacaka," 38.
25. Tippett et al., *No Continuing City*, 252–53.
26. Knapman, *White Women in Fiji*.

that reductionist views of the contributions of missionary wives in Fiji must be challenged, in order to fully understand the broader perspectives. While this book was particularly examining women external to mission and church structures while looking at the century prior to Tippetts entering Fiji, the positive role for church and society that missionary wives played in Fiji is another variation that needs to be taken seriously. Edna Tippett certainly provided an important role model for church and society, playing a pivotal part in the success of her husband's endeavours.

While still a field missionary in Fiji, Alan took the 1955–56 school year to complete a Master's degree in history at the American University, Washington DC, aided by a Reynolds Fellowship grant.[27] During that time, Edna stayed in Australia, taking care of the family with support from their Mission Board until he returned 12 months later. After completing their field service in Fiji, Alan returned to the USA in 1961 to study and lecture at the Institute of Church Growth. On this occasion, the separation stretched to two and a half years (Dec 61—May 64) as Tippett completed his PhD in anthropology at the University of Oregon (1961–1964). Once again, Edna remained in Australia, this time taking a job to support the family.[28] In 1964, during the Solomon Islands research project for the World Council of Churches' (WCC) Department of World Mission and Evangelism (DWME), Edna's airfares were paid by the WCC so she could formally be part of the team as secretarial assistant.[29] Later she was employed part time in an office assistant role to Alan during his time as a faculty member at the School of World Mission (SWM) at Fuller Theological Seminary (1965–1977) with special significance during his three years as editor of *Missiology: An International Review*,[30] while proof reading the journal added voluntary hours to her role. This was expanded by her secretarial support for Alan on so many occasions such as his sabbatical research in the Pacific.[31] Edna's investments in these ways contributed so much to Tippett's academic and ministerial work, and his development of Great Commission missiology. Charles Kraft, knowing both of them well,

---

27. Tippett et al., *No Continuing City*, 236.
28. Tippett et al., *No Continuing City*, 264.
29. Tippett et al., *No Continuing City*, 293.
30. Tippett et al., *No Continuing City*, 426.
31. Tippett et al., *No Continuing City*, 293, 355.

observed that Edna intentionally supported Tippett in many ways in order to contribute to his development as a missiologist.[32]

His daughters, Lynette, Joan, and Robyn, maybe less intentionally, nevertheless contributed to Alan Tippett's life journey. At key points in their lives, they were deprived of their father so that he could be free for his research and writing,[33] and his daughter Joan delayed her wedding, waiting for her father to complete his PhD.[34] Tippett describes their lot as "Each one had a rough row to hoe," and then reflects, "Perhaps I should have given my girls more of my time."[35] It is clear from Tippett's own family life, shown in what they did and how they did it, that centrality of the church was of paramount importance.

FIELD FORMATION:
FIELD MINISTRY AND RESEARCH METHODOLOGIES

The third major theme of Tippett's life was a focus on the importance of appropriate research methodologies, this being evident even in his childhood, and expanded further through the methodologies he gleaned from his experience on the mission field. During his years of service as a Methodist missionary in Fiji,[36] he served in various roles and locations. His postings were at Nadroga (1941–1944), Kadavu (1944–1947), Rewa Division (Suva) (1948–1952), Bau Division (1953–1956), and the Theological Institution, Davuilevu (1957–1961).[37]

Those roles and activities, although varied according to location, could be summarized in a list as:

- Circuit missionary using extensive itineration as his mode of operation, while advocating for a new constitution for the national church as a result of what he was observing in this missionary role;

- Circuit ministry plus conducting a mission station Bible School, while preparing the churches and their leaders for the new constitution;

32. Kraft and Priest, "Who Was This Man?," 270.
33. Tippett et al., *No Continuing City*, 345.
34. Tippett et al., *No Continuing City*, 286.
35. Tippett et al., *No Continuing City*, 345.
36. Dundon, "Raicakacaka," 38.
37. Tippett et al., *No Continuing City*, 551.

- Acting Chairman of the whole mission in Fiji while based in an urban setting and coordinating relief work after a cyclone;

- An appointment to the Bau Division, as requested by the Fijian church leadership. This position had to particularly relate to the chiefly structures on the island of Bau, with its required protocol and ceremony, and Tippett was seen as the best missionary to fulfill these roles for the benefit of the church;

- His concluding period from 1957–1961 was in the role of Principal of the ministry training institution at Davuilevu. While there, he developed his own material in ways he felt were most appropriate for the benefit of his Fijian students. He also developed proposals for the future of ministry training in Fiji, taking into account the anticipated development of their denomination and of Fiji as a nation.[38] Interestingly enough, an educationally orieinted article written in 2003 demonstrated the wisdom of a future oriented approach such as he had advocated so many years before.[39]

- Additionally, from 1951—1955, he was the contributing editor of the Fijian language monthly church journal, *Ai Tukutuku Vakalotu*.[40]

These varied roles and responsibilities added together provided a significant breadth of experience that influenced him and his understanding of mission, and fitted him for his later roles of equipping others.

However, it is important to note that alongside all these primary missionary roles during his time in Fiji, Tippett also researched history and culture, albeit initially without a structure for doing so until he gained that through his Master's degree studies. Yet even without that structure, his research was of sufficient detail and accuracy that some years later, aspects of that research became the basis for his PhD dissertation without needing further field research. As a result of his historical research, he came to be regarded as the "resident historian" amongst the field team of both missionaries and nationals. This is seen in the books and articles he wrote during this period, whether or not for publication, for example, *The Christian, Fiji 1835–67*,[41] since republished as *The Integrating Gospel and The Christian*,

---

38. Tippett et al., *No Continuing City*, 244–46.
39. White, "Historicizing Educational Disparity."
40. Tippett, "Bibliography 1934–1988," 7.
41. Tippett, *Christian (Fiji 1835–67)*.

Fiji 1835–67,[42] and "The Road to Bau,"[43] since published as *The Road to Bau and the Autobiography of Joeli Bulu*.[44] Similarly it is seen in the people who were referred to him for historical insights[45] and the fact that he was asked to edit the manuscript of Birtwhistle's *In His Armour; The Life of John Hunt of Fiji*.[46] Tippett's years in Fiji provide a crucial lens through which he developed significant research methodologies.

Determination in Language and Culture Learning

One aspect of research that Tippett engaged in with determination was language and culture learning. On arrival in Fiji, both his own priority on his initial language and culture learning in his role as a missionary as well as the circumstances of his deployment at Cuva (near modern Nadi) meant that he developed his own language learning techniques and committed five hours a day to this activity. This determination may have been stimulated by another negative education experience which he described as, "My professor (at Queens) said . . . that I did not have the capacity for a language. He said that when he heard I was bound for the mission field."[47] The Fijians were also very cooperative. The end result, as told by Tippett is that,

> Kini, my Fijian senior minister, arranged for me to preach somewhere each Sunday that the people might get to know me. I was using a Court translator but within a couple of months I knew enough to follow him and I became dissatisfied with his efforts, more particularly because of his failure to get ethical distinctions. It was a vocabulary list on which I had concentrated and I figured that the sooner I can do my own translating the better. I wrote out a few short sermons and had Kini go over them and after 8 or 9 weeks I preached in (or rather read) my first short sermon in Fijian without a translator.[48]

Progressively, Tippett participated in Fijian village and Christian life at a deep level.[49] In doing so, he discovered how well Christianity had been con-

42. Tippett, *Integrating Gospel and the Christian*.

43. Tippett, "Road to Bau."

44. Tippett, *Road to Bau*, 227–28.

45. Tippett et al., *No Continuing City*, 234.

46. Birtwhistle, *In His Armour*.

47. Tippett et al., *No Continuing City*, 53.

48. Tippett et al., *No Continuing City*, 123.

49. Tippett, "Parallaxis in Missiology," 124, 42; Tippett et al., *No Continuing City*, 252.

textualized into Fijian culture. This was almost a shock, because the church in Fiji that he was now participating in was very different than the impression of that church he had gained from the stories told by field missionaries on deputation. He came to see it as,

> people who had taken over the gospel and translated it into terms of their own life-style, and when I heard its songs and rhythms, and ceremonials, its prayer and praise, I suddenly found myself in the Old Testament. So the transformation of my view of both the Old Testament and the Fijian worldview began at Tuvu, Bemana in the Nasaucoko Circuit section of my first Fijian appointment.[50]

From the perspective of missionary deployment around the world, these experiences sound very positive. Yet Tippett's own evaluation of how much could have been achieved had he been better trained is worth noting. As noted in this chapter's opening quote, having spent a year studying for his Master's Degree after being in Fiji for fifteen years, Tippett was concerned the significant insights that he leaned should have been available to him in his training, thus enabling him to arrive on the field at age thirty, with a skill set commensurate to his task. However he felt that because this was not the case, he was starting at forty-five where he should have been at thirty.[51] Tippett's determination to proactively engage with language and culture, is commendable, but the waste of human resource he identifies in the quote above is an issue that needs to be taken seriously by mission leaders as well as their field teams even today.

Culture learning was also a major emphasis of Tippett. He was aided in that by his understanding that the formal herald role was very important in traditional Fijian society. When used well by the missionaries, and especially if the herald was at least empathetic to their cause, that person positioned the missionary's message for at least serious consideration, if not acceptance. At the same time, this process also placed the missionary in a positive proactive mentor/mentoree environment with the herald as a culture broker that most missionaries in other countries would envy. It seems that Tippett had the wisdom and disposition to learn from his heralds, and as a result of learning from their insights, predisposed himself to be able to learn from other Fijians around him as well.[52] While language and culture learning were in themselves research techniques, they also placed him in

50. Tippett et al., *No Continuing City*, 130.
51. Tippett et al., *No Continuing City*, 251.
52. Tippett et al., *No Continuing City*, 213.

a position to be able to have deep understanding of the culture and the impact of Christianity within it.

Mission Organizational Approaches in Fiji as a Barrier to Mission

Tippett was not only concerned about finding positive ways of engagement in mission. He was equally, and sometimes more passionately concerned about externally induced barriers to mission. Simply stated, he was shocked by his first experience of the colonialism of the mission organization as he adjusted to life as a missionary in Fiji.[53] He described one aspect of this colonial system as "placing such authority and decision-making demands on a new worker who could not even speak the language was manifestly wrong."[54]

Another aspect of colonial mission that Tippett always felt uncomfortable with, and eventually fought against, was the high administrative expectations placed on missionaries that could so easily keep them from the real task of mission. This pressure could inhibit initial language and culture learning, and subsequently ministry to local people within their own local world. His feelings about this are clear when he says of a missionary,

> a man may become so involved with this kind of administration that it takes possession of his whole life and hinders his language learning and thereby his witness. A missionary at everyone's beck and call, however patient and loving his service, if he never learns the language to speak the things of the Spirit, is a pathetic figure. In my missionary research the wide world over . . . I have met this person. How sad![55]

This is such a telling statement relating to mission activities of his era, however it also has implications for those who would "speak the things of the Spirit" in any era.

Negative Implications of "Colonialism"

Although not clearly defined, Tippett often refers to "colonialism" and the new era of "post-colonialism," for example, in his foreword to Darrell Whiteman's *Melanesians and Missionaries: An Ethnohistorical Study*

---

53. Tippett et al., *No Continuing City*, 106.

54. Tippett et al., *No Continuing City*, 109.

55. Tippett et al., *No Continuing City*, 119.

of Social and Religious Change in the Southwest Pacific.[56] This issue is not unique to Tippett, as illustrated by Beidelman's comment in his introduction to his ethnography from East Africa,

> Yet before considering colonial life in Ukaguru, I need to provide some account of the issues that have been raised in the study of colonialism. This is not easy, since even the meanings of terms such as "colony" and "colonialism" are disputed. Given the complexity of the disagreements about these, I focus on only a few key points in this huge scholarly literature.[57]

Similarly, in the academic examination of colonialism, there is debate, not only about what is meant by "colonialism," but, as argued by Olufemi Taiwo in *How Colonialism Preempted Modernity In Africa* there is confusion about the role played by the different foreign agents during the time of colonization. Some authors would group all European agents such as traders, administrators, and missionaries as equal players in colonization. Taiwo summarizes V. Y. Mudimbe's[58] and A. J. Christopher's[59] perspective on this as,

> . . . the missionary's objectives had to be co-extensive with his country's political and cultural perspectives on colonization, as well as with the Christian view of his mission. With equal enthusiasm, he served as an agent of political empire, a representative of a civilization, and an envoy of God.[60]

Taiwo counters this while drawing on comments from Delavignette,[61] by saying,

> Delavignette described the Christian ideal: "The ontology of Christianity does not distinguish, does not separate its external expansion from its internal life. Colonization is defined by the fact that it presupposes a mother-country, but Christianity does not need a mother-country in the colonial sense of the term. It has the Cross, which is the same everywhere. 'Go and teach all nations.'" (15) . . . I submit that Christianity also could not, without more evidence, be convergent with colonialism. If the phrase "the

---

56. Whiteman, *Melanesians and Missionaries*, xviii.

57. Beidelman, *Culture of Colonialism*, 2.

58. Mudimbe, *Invention of Africa.*

59. Christopher, *Colonial Africa.*

60. Taiwo, *How Colonialism Preempted Modernity*, 54.

61. Delavignette, *Christianity and Colonialism.*

Church universal" has any meaning, a Christian who denies the humanity of a prospective convert or that of a fellow Christian must be deemed to have sinned. Similarly, a Christian who privileges his nation as if it were a favorite in God's eyes could in certain contexts be deemed guilty of having blasphemed.[62]

With these statements as background, Tippett's lack of precision in describing colonialism is still reflected in current analysis of colonialism. At the same time, Tippett can be seen as writing about two different periods that could be marked by the quotes above. In his research of early mission work in Fiji, the missionaries uniquely fitted the perspective subsequently described by Delavignette, because for the first forty years of their work (1835–1875), no colonial power ruled Fiji. After 1875, there was the possibility of their roles being confused, but by then, the prior establishment of the role of missionaries and the role of the church long before British colonialism was introduced minimized this danger.

The issues of colonialism that Tippett describes function at a different, and maybe more insidious level. In "Parallaxis in Missiology—To use or abuse,"[63] Tippett uses the term "parallaxis" to describe the phenomenon he simply lived with in his training and early deployment to Fiji. As he saw it,

> Our conflicts, our politics, our strategies, our acceptance and rejection of innovation, etc. may all be traced back to different points of viewing. Our most bitter battles come from two parties standing left and right of some object or system, and seeing themselves as wholly right with the others as wholly wrong . . . Wherever we stand to make our observations we manifest a parallax error. Within every community, in every cross-cultural exercise, we find this route of ethnocentricity.[64]

It was this cultural distortion of perspective, which, when combined with what could be called the "gun boat diplomacy" attitude of the ascendant Western nations of the previous century or two that allowed colonialism to occur in the first place and then to continue unchallenged.

To discover Tippett's understanding of colonialism and to feel the style of Tippett's writing, several slightly condensed quotes from his observations on the topic will make the point and will demonstrate his attitude to what he was observing:

62. Taiwo, *How Colonialism Preempted Modernity*, 54.
63. Tippett, "Parallaxis in Missiology."
64. Tippett, "Parallaxis in Missiology," 93.

Our view of Christian mission was colonialist, paternalistic, and ethnocentric. Our foreign mission protégés were treated as children. The fields were regarded as "primitive." The tribal lifestyle was said to be "static." To be progressive was to civilize. Neither church nor university offered any anthropology to correct this error or even to test it. Neither the "fathers of the church" or I myself were even aware of the need for correction.[65]

... missionary perspectives ... were shaped by three forces, ... First there was colonialism. Second there was the intellectualist approach to religion. Third there was the continuing historical denominationalism beyond its time. All of these were over-developed side-effects of the post-Darwinian transfer from biological to social and religious phenomena, which left the Westerner at the pinnacle of the evolutionary series. Therefore in Christian mission tribalism had to give way to civilization, the primitive child mentality had to be exposed to western education (and that in the English not the native language), and western forms had to replace the traditional in every field from music to house-building.[66]

All this led to a highly debatable theory of mission that in turn determined mission policy and strategy. It left us with such presuppositions as: "Primitives must first be civilized to be properly evangelized," "Tribal society, being static must be westernized to become progressive," or again "Convert the authority figure (priest, medicine man, chief) and the rank and file will follow automatically." All these have been demonstrated as erroneous ... We clad evangelism with western garments. I could go on ... Even in my college days I was beginning to question it.[67]

The long-term result for Tippett of his growing understanding of colonialism and its negative implications for effective mission were articulated by him as,

I went to Fiji as a missionary with high idealism and spiritual expectation, and I found a remarkably indigenous Church, yet it was 'light years' away from independence. I soon became utterly disillusioned about Christian mission as a system, its vested interests, its control from the home base, its missionary strategy and

---

65. Tippett et al., *No Continuing City*, 492–93.

66. Tippett et al., *No Continuing City*, 493–94.

67. Tippett et al., *No Continuing City*, 494.

academic theory of mission, and above all its paternalism. Within two or three years I was a rebel and became more and more rebellious as the years went on. For seventeen more years my rebellion against the system and its home control drove me more and more deeply into the mores of the society and modified my personal value system, and I gave myself completely to the achievement of independence. My straight talking to the home church was officially rejected.[68]

The insights he gained from his local involvement provided him with a significantly emic, or insider view of life and ministry in Fiji. That included identifying positive actions that should be engaged in as well as inappropriate approaches that should be avoided.

To this point, through Tippett's upbringing, training, field deployment, ministry, and research, the foundations of his life themes, (1) centrality of a relationship with god, (2) centrality of the church and (3) the importance of appropriate research methodologies have been evident. This lays the foundation for the strategic aspect of his life themes and the significance of the insights he developed.

Facilitating Incarnational Ministry through Missionary Itineration

In Tippett's missionary life, and subsequently in his writing, he continually emphasized missionary itineration.[69] He found he learned much through the informal relationships that prevailed while trekking with local people: he came to understand them by living in their communities and received much helpful feedback on the appropriateness of his ministry by opening himself to them for these extended periods. Having found these benefits for himself, he wanted all missionaries to make this a key part of their missionary program. He emphasized this for others because he realized that in a missionary's busy program, it is not just possible, but almost inevitable to disconnect from local people unless a proactive mechanism like this is utilized.[70]

For himself at a later stage, even in his busy program as principal of the theological institution at Davuilevu, he used term breaks for itineration, regarding a focus on itineration as "the most important decision I ever

68. Tippett, "Retrospect and Prospect," 35.

69. Tippett, *Peoples of Southwest Ethiopia*, 287.

70. Tippett, *Peoples of Southwest Ethiopia*, 287; Tippett et al., *No Continuing City*, 163–69.

made in Fiji."[71] Subsequently, Colin Dundon's historical PhD dissertation about Tippett used the Fijian word *Raicakacaka,* "walking the road," as part of the title, describing this type of missionary itineration, thus reflecting the priority that Dundon saw itineration playing in Tippett's life and ministry.[72] It was how he carried out his ministry, how the open relationships it engendered aided in reviewing his ministry, while proving to be invaluable for research.[73]

Study of Missionary Predecessors

As well as progressing well with language and culture learning himself, Tippett quickly became aware of the strength of his ministry forebears in Fiji, both in commitment and in understanding of Fiji and Christian ministry. In studying the missionaries and Christians in Fiji around 100 years before his time,[74] he came to see the process by which the Christian message had been communicated, accepted and assimilated in Fiji.[75] He documented this in his unpublished manuscript, *Road to Bau: The Life and Work of John Hunt of Viwa, Fiji.*[76] Tippett did not pursue publication because he had been asked to edit another "official" history[77] just as he finished his own work, so felt it would lack integrity to publish his own under those circumstances.[78] Thankfully Tippett's volume has now been published by William Carey Library.[79] John Hunt had ministered in Fiji[80] from 1838–1848. Hunt may have been the positive archetype of a great missionary, but he was in fact a great missionary amongst a team of great missionaries. To illustrate, this team of early missionaries had developed and documented

71. Tippett et al., *No Continuing City,* 182.

72. Dundon, "Raicakacaka."

73. The style of research that he would later discover in anthropology as "participant observation."

74. Tippett, *Christian (Fiji 1835–67),* subsequently republished in a combined volume, Tippett, *Integrating Gospel and the Christian.*

75. Tippett, *Oral Tradition and Ethnohistory.*

76. Tippett, "Road to Bau."

77. Birtwhistle, *In His Armour.*

78. Tippett et al., *No Continuing City,* 229.

79. Tippett, *Road to Bau.*

80. Other volumes written about John Hunt's ministry that Tippett was familiar with were: Rowe, *Life of John Hunt;* Nettleton, *John Hunt;* Birtwhistle, *In His Armour.* More recently Thornley, *Inheritance of Hope,* was written, then translated into Fijian by Tauga Vulaono.

a scheme to consistently Fijianize Bible names and terms so as to fit with the Fijian language.[81] Similarly, they handled the musical side of worship to make Christianity feel comfortable to Fijians long before the science and tools of ethnomusicology and ethnodoxology came into existence. This is documented under Tippett's heading, "Epic Chants and Christian Hymns" in *Oral Tradition and Ethnohistory: The Transmission of Information and Social Values in Early Christian Fiji, 1835–1905.*[82]

Such was Hunt's influence on Tippett, that in his introduction to that manuscript, he referred to the fact that it would be difficult to not write himself into the text, seeing he had spent so much time with the Hunt material in his research and had been so deeply influenced by him, as Paul influenced Timothy.[83] Other volumes that drew on his study of this period were *The Christian* (Fiji 1835–67),[84] the now published *The Road to Bau and the Autobiography of Joeli Bulu,*[85] "The Dynamics of Church-Planting in Fiji (Ono, Viwa, Bau, Kadavu, Vanua Levu and the Hill Tribes of Viti Levu)",[86] *The Integrating Gospel*[87] and *Oral Tradition and Ethnohistory: The Transmission of Information and Social Values in Early Christian Fiji, 1835–1905.*[88]

His Master's degree studies especially exposed Tippett to historiography, anthropology, and archival science, but also to his "greatest discovery"; "the existence of inter-disciplinary fields of research and study" like ethnopsychology, ethnolinguistics, and later, ethnohistory. He felt that these were important in his "new missiology for the post-colonial era,"[89] providing him with a greater ability to process the material from past missionary endeavours that he had already been researching.

At this point, a picture of Tippett's development is emerging: Tippett, who through nature and nurture had an insatiable hunger for information, having had the benefit of being brought up in a parsonage followed by

---

81. Tippett, *Road to Bau*, 58–59.

82. Tippett, *Oral Tradition and Ethnohistory*, 22–30.

83. Tippett et al., *No Continuing City*, 229.

84. Tippett, *Christian (Fiji 1835–67).*

85. Tippett, "Road to Bau."

86. Tippett, "Dynamics of Church-Planting in Fiji."

87. Now published as a consolidated volume, Tippett, *Integrating Gospel and the Christian.*

88. Tippett, *Oral Tradition and Ethnohistory.*

89. Tippett et al., *No Continuing City*, 239.

several years in ministry himself in his home country, became a field missionary. Once on the field, his development was enhanced by empathetic, insightful Fijians with whom he ministered. Additionally, he had access to the archives of his missionary forebears who were extremely effective despite the difficult and harrowing situations they ministered amongst, but who left ample records about the methods of evangelism and the result amongst the Fijians themselves.

TIPPETT'S DEVELOPMENT AS A MISSIONARY STRATEGIST

The result of Tippet's early life and missionary career was the development of his thinking about mission along with an understanding of the practical implications of those insights in his developing missiology. An example of this, as will be examined in-depth in subsequent chapters, is his in-depth understanding of how a society's decision-making processes could open the door for large numbers of people to come into Christian faith in people movements especially among animists. Tippett's development as a field missionary and as a missiologist in the field meant that his focus was on the development of effective missionary strategies, and with this focus, he provided an invaluable resource for others through his writings.

Joining Forces with Donald McGavran and the Institute of Church Growth

Drawing on the insights he had gained about key issues relating to ministry in Fiji, Tippett wrote his article "Probing Missionary Inadequacies at the Popular Level."[90] This article articulated the importance of an understanding of animism in order to have effective ministry in so many contexts in the world. This was published in the *International Review of Missions*. Through that he came to the attention of Donald Anderson McGavran who was establishing the Institute of Church Growth (ICG) at Northwest Christian College, Eugene, Oregon in the United States at that time.[91]

Ultimately, McGavran was to become integral to Tippet's formation as an internationally renowned missiologist. Therefore, it is valid to briefly meet McGavran who was born to missionary parents in India in 1897 and grew up in India. After his education in the USA he returned to India as a missionary in 1923, where he served in a wide range of roles for over

90. Tippett, "Probing Missionary Inadequacies," 411–19.
91. McGavran, "Missiologist Alan R. Tippett," 262.

thirty years. His biographer, Gary McIntosh, summarizes his life and its significance as,

> . . . a foremost educator with a Ph.D. in Education from a highly respected university, an evangelist who personally led over 1000 people to faith in Christ, a church planter who established 15 churches in the span of 17 years, a linguist who translated the Gospels into a new dialect, an administrator who directed the work of a mission agency in one of the world's largest countries, a world-renowned mission strategist, and a well-known author whose books and articles have changed the course of his discipline.[92]

The death of McGavran's six year old daughter in India left him with an intense feeling of the frailty of life, which stimulated his passion for evangelism.[93] For McGavran, this passion increased to include research into the growth of the church and the possibility of people movements. In this he was influenced by, and did joint research with Bishop Waskom Pickett.[94] In 1955, McGavran wrote his own volume, *The Bridges of God* [95] specifically about people movements,[96] a book that Tippett read in Fiji.

McGavran's plan in founding the Institute of Church Growth was to provide an opportunity for experienced field missionaries to come for a year of study in which he could train them in his understanding of church growth. On the basis of those studies, they would research the fields in which they were serving thus gaining and publishing a clearer picture of what existed already. This would also enable them to develop better strategies for the ongoing growth and development of the church movements in those locations. McGavran read Tippett's article, "Probing Missionary Inadequacies at the Popular Level"[97] just as he was launching the Institute of Church Growth. It was these strands coming together that resulted in McGavran offering Tippett "a fellowship to do his courses and write a study of Christian mission in the islands, and maybe help a little with the

---

92. McIntosh, *Donald A. McGavran*, 17.

93. McIntosh, *Donald A. McGavran*, 84–86.

94. For additional information on Pickett, see Seamands, "Legacy of J Waskom Pickett," which is a beautifully written, brief account of Pickett's amazing life.

95. McGavran, *Bridges of God*.

96. By that time, "people movements" was the term McGavran was using instead of the term "mass movements."

97. Tippett, "Probing Missionary Inadequacies."

teaching"[98] at the Institute of Church Growth. Tippett's title was "Research Fellow," to which a monetary amount was designated, that was primarily to be used for publication.[99] Tippett accepted this offer, understanding that it would provide him with a Master's degree in mission studies. This was important to Tippett because he felt it would make him a candidate for a missionary training post in Australia.[100] However, this Master's degree was only aspirational at that time, as reported by McIntosh,

> The brochure that many missionaries had seen promised a master's degree in missions upon completion of 30 credit hours and the writing of a thesis... Unfortunately, the accreditation committee only approved the granting of a bachelor's degree, ... Tippett was greatly annoyed and confronted McGavran about it. In his directive manner, Donald put it aside, telling Tippett to go ... to the University of Oregon and work instead on a Ph.D. in anthropology ... Once he (Tippett) resigned himself to having been, as he expressed it, "hoodwinked into a doctoral program," Tippett decided to make the most of the opportunity.[101]

Missiologist to the Whole World

Following the completion of his PhD in 1964, when a teaching post in Australia did not eventuate, he became a missiologist "to the whole world."[102] After a research project in the Solomon Islands for the World Council of Churches in 1964, he rejoined McGavran in the United States, but this time as the first faculty member invited to join McGavran as he launched the School of World Mission and Institute of Church Growth at Fuller Theological Seminary in 1965. Tippett served there until his retirement in 1977.[103] George M. Marsden's *Reforming Fundamentalism: Fuller Seminary and the New Evangelicalism* positions Fuller Theological Seminary within "new evangelicalism." This perspective suited Tippett's theological leanings even though it was not representative of his background,[104] and he prospered in this Great-Commission-focused environment. Tippett devoted his life

98. Tippett et al., *No Continuing City*, 265.

99. McIntosh, *Donald A. McGavran*, 158.

100. Tippett et al., *No Continuing City*, 265.

101. McIntosh, *Donald A. McGavran*, 155–56.

102. Tippett et al., *No Continuing City*, 269.

103. Kraft, *SWM/SIS at Forty*, 133; McIntosh, *Donald A. McGavran*, 269.

104. Dundon, "Raicakacaka," 199–200.

to the academic research and facilitation of mission, focused on effective fulfillment of the Great Commission and thus provided a major contribution to the field.

Formation of Tippett's Missiology

In analyzing the development of Tippett's research methodologies and missiology, there are several key factors that aided in their formation. The four book length missiological manuscripts that he wrote in English while still living in Fiji are: *The Christian: Fiji 1835–67*,[105] "Road to Bau: The Life and Work of John Hunt of Viwa, Fiji,"[106] "The Integrating Gospel,"[107] and "His Mission and Ours."[108] In a personal note which he wrote as he bound the unpublished "The Integrating Gospel" in 1970, Tippett commented, "This was written before I met McGavran. The manuscript represents the raw material of my cross-cultural experience." Additionally there was his master's thesis[109] which broadened his knowledge of the region and its history yet it is excluded because it is not directly missiological. However, it was his article "Probing Missionary Inadequacies at the Popular Level"[110] that brought him to the attention of McGavran. Tippett seemed to regard the latter three of those book length manuscripts as a "trilogy" representing his thinking prior to meeting McGavran. "The Integrating Gospel" and "His Mission and Ours" were written after he had completed his Master's degree in the USA, and bear the marks of the heightened research and organizational skills that he learned while doing those studies. They also evidenced the benefits of the interdisciplinary studies that impacted him so much from his time in the USA.

However conceptually these works are still classic Tippett pre-McGavran. In a lecture at the School of World Mission at Fuller Theological Seminary in 1979,[111] Tippett referred to the fact that for eleven years, he dedicated one day per week to study the history of Christianity in the Pacific. In Hunt's biography, he refers to that sort of research over fourteen

105. Tippett, *Christian (Fiji 1835–67)*.
106. Tippett, "Road to Bau."
107. Tippett, "Integrating Gospel."
108. Tippett, "His Mission and Ours."
109. Tippett, "Nineteenth-Century Labour Trade."
110. Tippett, "Probing Missionary Inadequacies."
111. "Emergence of Missionary Anthropology," March 1979. This observation was recorded in my class notes of this course.

years.[112] Those who have read his material, and sat in his lectures, and been mentored by him are grateful for the work he invested, the foundations he developed, and the insights that he gained at both an academic level and from his ministry experience.[113] He passed these insights on to people in cross-cultural ministry and those in the academy. While his protracted research resulted in the books and manuscripts referred to above, additionally that research laid the foundations for his books published as *Fijian Material Culture*,[114] *People Movements in Southern Polynesia*,[115] *Aspects of Pacific Ethnohistory*,[116] and *Deep-Sea Canoe*,[117] as well as influencing everything that he subsequently wrote missiologically. This demonstrates the benefit of the meticulousness of his research and the research methodologies that he implemented.

After twelve fruitful years at Fuller School of World Mission but still having the desire to influence Australia with strategic missiology,[118] Tippett retired to Australia in 1977, basing himself in Canberra. With the merger of the Methodist Church of Australasia, the Presbyterian Church of Australia, and the Congregational Union of Australia, Tippett maintained his ordination within the newly formed Uniting Church of Australia. On the 27th September 1979, he was also made an Honorary Research Fellow at St. Mark's Library, the Ministry Training Institution of the Anglican Diocese of Canberra and Goulburn,[119] to which he donated his library as a research collection.[120] This period of retirement proved to be a very frustrating time for him, as his denominational network did not seem to be open to his evangelical or missiological perspectives. Without institutional financial backing, administrative assistance or denominational support, his international prominence diminished quickly. Without administrative assistance, it was difficult for him to take advantage of even the Australian opportunities that were afforded him. He passed away on September 16, 1988, hav-

112. Tippett, *Road to Bau*, 47.

113. Kraft, *SWM/SIS at Forty*, 303, 304, 306, 310; Reeson, "Wednesdays with Alan Tippett."

114. Tippett, *Fijian Material Culture*.

115. Tippett, *People Movements in Southern Polynesia*.

116. Tippett, *Aspects of Pacific Ethnohistory*.

117. Tippett, *Deep-Sea Canoe*.

118. Tippett et al., *No Continuing City*, 265, 467.

119. Tippett et al., *No Continuing City*, 509.

120. Tippett et al., *No Continuing City*, 467.

ing made a lifetime contribution to Great-Commission-focused mission through his research based anthropologically informed missiology.

CONCLUSION

So, was Tippett primarily a missiologist as he came to describe himself,[121] or one of the other designations that fit him so comfortably, such as; historian, anthropologist,[122] ethnohistorian,[123] biblical scholar,[124] writer, inquisitive person, perfectionist or workaholic? While this list of potential classifications is both arbitrary and hypothetical, it could be argued that he was all of the above. At the same time, Tippett believed that missiology is an interdisciplinary field of study that becomes powerful through the synergy that happens from the interplay of those fields—"syngenesis," to use Tippett's term.[125] Therefore it should not be surprising to see this syngenesis exhibited in Tippett himself. At the same time, McGavran's description is notable. "God the Father Almighty laid his hand upon Alan Tippett and made him one of the apostles of effective evangelism throughout the entire world."[126] This was McGavran's evaluation having worked closely with Tippett for fifteen years, and having known him well for twenty-six years. Darrell Whiteman, who was profoundly influenced by Tippett, says much the same thing but in different words: "Alan Tippett was a remarkable and complex man . . . He was that rare breed who combined the careful, meticulous eye of the scholar with the passion of a fiery evangelist."[127]

Through examining Tippett's upbringing, his focus on a relationship with God and the centrality of the Church have been identified. His ministry and missionary experience, building on his identified nature and nurture, helped him to develop his research methodologies that could be engaged in while doing ministry. This then contributed to the effectiveness of his ministry. Combining this with his studies, he developed his theories of mission that he came to refer to as post-colonial missiology that provided the reflective process for the development of field strategies for effective missionary practice.

121. Tippett et al., *No Continuing City*, 290.
122. Tippett et al., *No Continuing City*, 227, 265, 314, 331–33, 402–4, 407.
123. Tippett, *Jesus Documents*, 1.
124. Tippett, *Jesus Documents*.
125. Tippett, *Jesus Documents*, 5.
126. McGavran, "Missiologist Alan R. Tippett," 267.
127. Whiteman, "Legacy of Alan R. Tippett," 166.

This chapter has provided the life story that is essential background to observe and examine the development of Tippett's theory of mission as observed through his life themes. In particular, it has demonstrated the appropriateness and effectiveness of the components of his post-colonial missiology as seen embryonically in this chapter. This then sets the stage for the contribution of his missiology, as expanded in subsequent chapters.

3

Alan Tippett's Escalating Influence

In that three years we covered most of the aspects of missiology,
published material from every Continent, by missionaries and nation-
als . . . It was a middle of the road publication between Evangelical and
Conciliary emphases, though we were specific about standing on the
Great Commission and Scripture . . . I think we were truly the mouth-
piece of a large body of missionary opinion, which believed the day of
mission was not dead and that somehow mission would go on until the
end of the age.[1]

This was Tippett's own view of his three years as editor of Missiology.

THE GOAL OF THIS study is to determine the degree to which Tippett's insights into the theory and practice of Great-Commission-focused mission
influenced the world of mission and missiology in his era, especially examining his unique contributions. While it is noted that many twenty-first-
century missiologists typically integrate mission and evangelism together
with ministries of justice and mercy, Tippett had a unique way of balancing
these, while keeping a priority on fulfillment of the Great Commission.
Therefore, in this study, that Tippett perspective will be pursued while
examining its relevance. As noted in chapter 1, Tippett's insights will be
examined through his life themes. The previous chapter documented the
development of the first three of his life themes through his life story. This

1. Tippett et al., *No Continuing City,* 426.

chapter will focus on crucial aspects of his life story pertinent to examining his life themes three and four: (3) the importance of appropriate research methodologies and (4) the importance of strategic missiology and strategic missionary practice. This will comprise an examination of some key historical and experiential factors that converged, resulting in the development and influence of Tippett's insights in the academic and practical fields of mission. As he concluded twenty years in Fiji, the following period of five significant years moved him on to the world stage and after that, operating from that platform for the following twelve years, he continued to have more and more influence.

FACTORS THAT CONTRIBUTED TO TIPPETT'S INFLUENCE

A number of factors are observable, that significantly contributed to Tippett's influence. While they did not all seem positive to Tippett at the time, with the benefit of hindsight it is possible to see how these factors contributed to his escalating influence.

Separation from Fiji: Convergence with Global, Field-Focused Missiology

Although Tippett could not have known it at the time, his departure from Fiji was a major step in a process that propelled him onto the world stage. Eventually this included his move to Fuller School of World Mission which positioned him to have a significant impact on strategic missiology and strategic missionary practice. With that in mind, it is interesting to note the experience Tippett had that he felt was a trigger point, showing him that his time in Fiji had concluded. Tippett's decision to leave Fiji, while potentially being influenced by a range of things including family needs and health challenges,[2] according to his autobiography was triggered almost mono-causally. This seems so extreme that it is valuable to include his own description,

> It was the synod of 1960. A rather short-sighted motion had been moved, and the discussion dragged on, quite one-sided, and clearly all would vote for it and it would be approved. But it really was a shortsighted proposal and would have caused unending trouble. I stood up and suggested that perhaps before voting we ought to look at its implication and the things that would happen

2. Tippett et al., *No Continuing City*, 252.

because of it—1 . . . 2 . . . 3 . . . which I enumerated in only one sentence each, and sat down. There was an awkward pause for a moment. No one else wanted to speak. The motion was put and lost—almost unanimously.

Frankly, I was staggered. What had I done? I had done the very thing I had criticised the Board for, and certain Chairmen. I should have let it pass. True it was shortsighted, but how do we learn except by our mistakes? How could I, in four sentences turn the whole synod round and impose my ideas on them? How could I be so overbearing? Had I been long enough in Fiji, and achieved a power and authority that could let me turn the decision-making like that? One by one they passed before my mind . . . James Calvert . . . Frederick Langham . . . Arthur Small, the men who in my history book stayed too long. There and then in the synod of 1960 I broke my own heart and announced that I had come to the end of the road.

I knew my men could carry on. I knew they could do it better than I could myself. I knew I had given them the tools. I knew they were creative in their own ways. I knew the time had come for them to go forth alone, and be themselves in the new Fiji. I now had to leave. Oh how it hurt to go, but I knew it had to be. I had no continuing city. I could only seek one to come.[3]

Considering the next steps that Tippett took, in contrast to what had been his expressed plan for ongoing ministry in Fiji, it clearly required a significant intervention, or as he saw it, divine leading, to redirect him. As he evaluates it in a personal note as he bound his unpublished "The Integrating Gospel" in 1970, "The hardest truth I ever had to accept in my life was to admit that my service in Fiji was finished."[4] Or, as he states in his autobiography, "I had really become so Fijian in my outlook that it took the notion of mission itself to take me home."[5] This is worth highlighting, because many missionaries before and after Tippett would have evaluated their "success" by noting the degree of influence they had over the local leaders. Tippett however was so deeply committed to a post-colonial view of the church and its local leaders that the thought that he was somehow overriding decisions they were empowered to make was abhorrent to him.

3. Tippett et al., *No Continuing City*, 252–53.

4. Tippett, "Integrating Gospel," iii. This quote has also been included in the published version Tippett, *Integrating Gospel and the Christian*, xi.

5. Tippett et al., *No Continuing City*, 253.

As he left Fiji, Tippett's convergence with McGavran, whose own influence was also on the rise,[6] was seminal in positioning Tippett for maximum global influence. To begin with, it is worth noting how unlikely this connection was. As Tippett describes it, his article, "Probing Missionary Inadequacies at the Popular Level" that was focused on effective missionary evangelism in the context of tribal religions, was published in the more liberal *International Review of Missions*, the journal of the World Council of Churches. It was,

> written in Fiji, sent to America then from America to England (at K. S. Latourette's suggestion), published there, was read in America by Dr. Donald McGavran, who wrote to me in Fiji about it from America, and we two got into correspondence on the matter of mission at the popular level.[7]

Their common interests that led to their convergence were described by Tippett as the,

> Realization that better missionary strategy could never be developed for the new age without solid research which exposed why our predecessors succeeded and failed drew me to McGavran. His institute provided the facilities for this kind of work, and the body of experienced missionaries with whom to interact, compare and test one's ideas.[8]

Talking of their relative strengths as they joined forces, Tippett says,

> McGavran's *Bridges of God*, . . . I read it in Fiji. I knew it was basically right, but I knew also it would be rejected. McGavran needed a sociological or anthropological input of some kind to gain a hearing. I know no-one in the world in my day with finer intuition in missionary strategy than Donald McGavran, but neither policymakers nor theologians buy intuition by itself.[9]

Tippett, in an ambivalent statement, describes how he saw it; "McGavran had realized that he needed an anthropologist's support at selling a number of his ideas. He knew the evangelical Christians in America at that time saw anthropology as anathema.[10]

6. Pinola, *Church Growth*; McIntosh, *Donald A. McGavran.*

7. Tippett et al., *No Continuing City*, 265.

8. Tippett, *God, Man and Church Growth*, 35.

9. Tippett et al., *No Continuing City*, xiv.

10. Tippett et al., *No Continuing City*, 265.

The range of points mentioned above may have brought them to-gether initially, but as will be observed in this study, their working together took them much farther than that. Tippett joining McGavran, unlikely as it was, occurred at the time when McGavran's own influence was increasing and focusing through his founding of the Institute of Church Growth. That institute provided input and expression for Tippett, but eventually became the link that brought Tippett into the heightened influence of Fuller Theological Seminary.

Added to Tippett's synergy with McGavran, there was the positive interaction of the first group of four researchers with each other and with McGavran as they came together at the Institute of Church Growth,[11] at Eugene, Oregon, that McIntosh refers to as a "powerful encounter."[12] The group comprised Alan Tippett, a Methodist with experience in Fiji, Bill Read, a Presbyterian with experience in Brazil, Roy Shearer, a Presbyterian with experience in South Korea, and Jim Sunda with experience in West New Guinea, (today, Papua Province, Indonesia), where he served with the Christian and Missionary Alliance[13] The positive influence of this group on each other, and on the concepts they were developing was something Tippett referred to a number of times,[14] and was reported also by McIntosh.[15] It was seminal that each of them came from fields where people had come to Christ in people movements.

Tippett originally hoped that by joining McGavran at Eugene he could enroll in the Master's degree in mission studies that would fit him to lecture in the Australian scene. However, upon arrival he discovered that the Master's degree was a goal for the program rather than present reality.[16] Tippett, while discussing this with McGavran was told, "No! No! You have to do a PhD."[17] That meant just over the road at the University of Oregon which had an outstanding library and faculty, especially in Anthropology and the Pacific. However, he questioned some of the anthropology program requirements, such as language exams. Furthermore, he was forced to write a dissertation in an area that, although it was within his competencies,

11. McGavran, "Institute of Church Growth"; McIntosh, *Donald A. McGavran.*

12. McIntosh, *Donald A. McGavran,* 155.

13. McIntosh, *Donald A. McGavran,* 155.

14. Tippett, "Parallaxis in Missiology," 120; Tippett et al., *No Continuing City,* 272.

15. McIntosh, *Donald A. McGavran,* 155.

16. McIntosh, *Donald A. McGavran,* 154.

17. Tippett et al., *No Continuing City,* 274.

was not what he wanted to do. His supervisor wanted him to complete his program, but knew that Tippett's preferred topic on "religious dynamics" would not be acceptable to the university's anthropology department.[18] Subsequently, his PhD dissertation was published by the prestigious Bishop Museum Press of Honolulu as *Fijian Material Culture; A Study Of Cultural Context, Function and Change*.[19] It was a breakthrough in its field, and was written without having to undertake specific or fresh field research, confirming the depth and detail of Tippett's informal research into Fijian culture while he was a field missionary. However, being a local case study, its insights have not been noticed by the wide range of people who potentially could have been helped by it.

There was another significant connection which would influence and underscore Tippett's strategic teachings and practices. In the process of his doctoral studies at the University of Oregon, he studied under Dr. Homer Barnett. Barnett (1906–1985) was professor of anthropology at the University of Oregon from 1939 to 1974. In Evon Vogt's review of Barnett's book on innovation[20] he recognizes Barnett "as one of the outstanding workers in the field of culture change" having done field work amongst North American Indians, in Palau, Micronesia, and Netherlands New Guinea (today, Indonesian Papua Province). He concludes his review by saying, "Dr. Barnett has certainly proved himself an exciting innovator in cultural theory in a stimulating book which should be read by all social scientists seriously interested in culture change."[21] Obviously this recommendation proved to be true in Tippett's case. Conceptually, Tippett saw Barnett's input as crucial, seen in this evaluation,

> Barnett's work on innovation was the most influential book on my life, with the exception of the Bible. It gave me a methodological frame of reference for the conceptualization of all my business in Christian mission and the terminology for its scientific analysis—advocates, acceptance or rejection and so on. It provided the machinery for examining processes of decision-making and models for depicting the components of the process. It provided me with perspectives for seeing acceptances as over against rejection and thus spoke to the relevance or otherwise of our advocacy of the gospel. It dealt with situations propitious for innovation—the

18. Tippett et al., *No Continuing City*, 286.

19. Tippett, *Fijian Material Culture.*

20. Vogt, Review of *Innovation*, 721.

21. Vogt, Review of *Innovation*, 722.

> "ripening of the harvest for reaping," if you like. It gave me the models and theoretical tools for analyzing the process of the people movement. It was the most exciting thing I ever found in academia.[22]

This seems to have been a significant academic relationship, summarized as having "utterly transformed my whole approach. He gave me an overall system for observing the dynamics of cultural (including religious) change."[23] That relationship was such that Tippett was able to conceptually draw Barnett as a secular anthropologist into the theory explorations that were taking place at the Institute of Church Growth.[24] This included the development of their replacement term for the ill-chosen term "mass movements" of 1930s publications on the topic of people movements, e.g. *Christian Mass Movements in India: A Study with Recommendations.*[25] "Multi individual" decision-making was Barnett's contribution,[26] which has been used ever since.

Although Tippett looked back on the PhD as seminal to all that he did later as an "anthropologist," including positioning formal studies in anthropology within missionary training, at the time the two and a half year process, including separation from his family, was difficult and painful, draining both his physical and emotional reserves. In fact, on the day he had successfully defended his dissertation his friends wanted to celebrate with him before he flew out for Australia the next day, but Tippett reflected,

> . . . it was no celebration. It was no achievement. It was one long, painful ordeal. I had never sought it. I had never wanted it. And I was utterly torn apart lest I had hurt those whom I loved more than life itself.[27]

With the perspective of time, it is evident that Tippett's life themes three and four, relating to missiological research, missiological reflection and missionary practice were being worked out even though this took such a toll on Tippett.

22. Tippett et al., *No Continuing City*, 283.

23. Tippett et al., *No Continuing City*, 335; This note is from the original typescript autobiography, which is not included in the published version.

24. Tippett, "Parallaxis in Missiology," 121.

25. Pickett, *Christian Mass Movements in India.*

26. Tippett et al., *No Continuing City*, 277.

27. Tippett et al., *No Continuing City*, 286.

From Rebel to Reformer:
World Council of Churches Iberville Consultation

An event that added to Tippett's influence while he was at the Institute of Church Growth at Oregon was the 1963 consultation hosted at Iberville, Canada by the Department of Missionary Studies (DMS)[28] of the World Council of Churches (WCC) to which Donald McGavran, J. Waskom Pickett, and Alan Tippett with twenty-six other men were invited.

Although Tippett was never sure of the reason behind the consultation,[29] he saw it as a watershed in two ways. First, it gave the Church Growth men an opportunity to share their perspectives first-hand with key WCC DMS people in a context where their concerns could be discussed and addressed. Kraft further explains the significance of the result of this consultation, and Tippett's part in procuring that result when he says, "The result, however, was a positive demonstration of the ability of McGavran, with Tippett's considerable help, to not only advocate but to effectively defend his position"[30] on the church growth emphasis.

Second, the document coming from that forum gave the Institute of Church Growth a statement about mission that they agreed with that also had World Council of Churches (WCC) endorsement. According to Tippett, the WCC seemed to back down from their early enthusiasm, thus delaying the publication of the statement that was developed at Iberville in their own journal for a number of years. Others had published it by that time, for example, the *Ecumenical Review* published it in 1964, much closer to the date of that meeting,[31] and it was well used by McGavran and Tippett by then.[32] Later, in a "deal" done with McGavran,[33] the WCC did eventually publish it in their journal, *International Review of Missions*.[34] However, by the time the statement from the consultation was published in

---

28. Tippett consistently refers to the sponsoring body as the Department of World Mission and Evangelism (DWME), and other scholars drawing on his material follow Tippett's usage. The WCC published documents, however, refer to the sponsoring body as the Department of Missionary Studies. McGavran also uses the WCC's DMS designation. See McGavran, "Missiologist Alan R. Tippett," 263.

29. Tippett et al., *No Continuing City*, 279.

30. Kraft, *SWM/SIS at Forty*, 19.

31. WCC Department of Mission Studies, "Growth of the Church."

32. Tippett et al., *No Continuing City*, 281.

33. McGavran, "Church Growth Strategy Continued."

34. WCC Department of Mission Studies, "Growth of the Church: A Statement."

the *International Review of Missions*, it is evident that the WCC enthusiasm for the statement had waned. It was placed along with a McGavran article, "Church Growth Strategy Continued"[35] and a number of other articles that were critical of the church growth perspective. Within the published consultation report itself, it included the disclaimer, "This text, drawn up by a special consultation convened by the WCC Department of Missionary Studies at Iberville, Quebec, July 31—August 2, 1963, represents only an initial statement, arising from a particular concern, and makes no attempt to cover other special contemporary situations, such as those in America or Germany.[36] It is worth noting Kraft's perspective on this consultation,

> It is likely that the underlying (and unspoken) issue leading to the calling of this consultation was McGavran's intransigence in advocating his positions rather than the positions themselves. The result, however, was a positive demonstration of the ability of McGavran, with Tippett's considerable help, to not only advocate but to effectively defend their positions. This, of course, lead to some further animosity on the part of those who were unable to effectively counter McGavran.[37]

This is important to notice while observing Tippett's influence, because McGavran had been able to have some level of meaningful dialog with the WCC constituency through the International Review of Mission until that time. That included publishing his promotional article entitled "The Institute of Church Growth"[38] as the ICG was initially being formed.

The Institute of Church Growth was still new at this time, and it had many detractors. In was in this light that Tippett saw the Iberville consultation as sufficiently significant regarding core concepts of Church Growth theory that he described it as a, "battle came to an end at Iberville" when writing for his own Board in Australia, in "Australia's Missionary Outreach in Our Time."[39] The influence of the Institute of Church Growth was increasing, as was Tippett's influence. Or to feel it even more, in his autobiography he said,

35. McGavran, "Church Growth Strategy Continued."

36. WCC Department of Mission Studies, "Growth of the Church: A Statement," 330.

37. Kraft, *SWM/SIS at Forty*, 19.

38. McGavran, "Institute of Church Growth."

39. Tippett, "Australia's Missionary Outreach," 1.

For the first time we had a document, a specific Statement, a quotable set of 12 affirmations [that is, affirmed by the WCC's Department of Missionary Studies]. Briefly stated they were:

The mandate for mission
The sin of introversion
The call for renewal
The existence of fields open for evangelism
The uniqueness of each situation
The work of the Spirit in the work of His agent
Deployment and watching
Incorporating converts in churches, themselves missionary
Quantitative and qualitative growth correlatives
Recognition of past mistakes
Discipling and nurturing both essential
Need for scientific research to improve strategy

This was a tremendous achievement as the provision of a springboard for working out a new missiology. For me personally it gave me a feeling of more freedom. Now I could say to my board that I was a reformer rather than a rebel.[40]

Having declared himself a "rebel" against colonialism and paternalism by the end of his first term in Fiji, there was obviously a strong sense of self-justification in re-labeling himself as a "reformer," using a WCC document for endorsement. To see this clearly, his own statement about his response to his early mission field experience in Fiji needs to be noted, in which he described his response as, "I soon became utterly disillusioned about Christian mission as a system, its vested interests, its control from the home base, its missionary strategy and academic theory of mission, and above all its paternalism. Within two or three years I was a rebel and became more and more rebellious as the years went on."[41]

Expanded Influence through WCC
Solomon Islands Research and Publication

Tippett's influence on strategic missiology and strategic missionary practice was substantially expanded through another set of seemingly negative circumstances. As he was concluding his PhD, he was further frustrated by the lack of interest in his skills back in Australia. His own Board leaders,

40. Tippett et al., *No Continuing City*, 402.

41. Tippett, "Retrospect and Prospect," 35.

through Mr Gribble,[42] had in fact told him to take a job in USA if one was offered.[43] While this seems negative as far as Tippett's life goals are concerned, it contributed positively to his influence during the next fourteen years. This positive process began with another long term result from the Iberville consultation. At Iberville he met Victor Hayward, former chief executive of the Baptist Missionary Society, London,[44] who at that time was quite involved in WCC research and writing projects, and in representing the ecumenical aspects of missions at various conferences. In discussing the 1969 *Third Latin American Protestant Congress* (III CELA) Hayward is mentioned as a participant while he was the Research Secretary of the International Missionary Council and produced the report, "Third Latin American Evangelical Conference" (Buenos Aires: Secretariat for Relationships with Christian Councils, 1969). He represented a WCC point of view, and made recommendations to the WCC for greater participation in Latin America.[45] His writing included *African Independent Church Movements*,[46] *Christians and China*,[47] and other articles in the *International Review of Missions*. He had earlier been in correspondence with Tippett[48] regarding publishing the second half of "The Integrating Gospel."[49] This time he invited Tippett to do the Solomon Islands research for the World Council of Churches' Department on Studies in Mission and Evangelism (DSME) in 1964–1965. The result of that research was *Solomon Islands Christianity: A Study of Growth and Obstruction*.[50] Somewhat characteristically, Tippett was surprised when he sent the manuscript of his study to Hayward of the WCC for inspection and comment, but it was immediately sent to press.[51] Tippett's view of one of his documents being ready for publication was consistently different from the view of many of his colleagues.

42. Dundon, "Raicakacaka," 181.

43. Tippett et al., *No Continuing City*, 284.

44. McGavran, "Missiologist Alan R. Tippett," 263.

45. Salinas, *Latin American Evangelical Theology*, 69.

46. Hayward, *African Independent Church Movements*, 11.

47. Hayward, *Christians and China*.

48. Hayward, Correspondence to Tippett, 28th October 1960. St. Mark's Library, Canberra, ref TIP 70-38- Vol 1–10.

49. Tippett, "Integrating Gospel."

50. Tippett, *Solomon Islands Christianity*.

51. Tippett et al., *No Continuing City*, 314.

As will be seen later in this study, *Solomon Islands Christianity* is Tippett's best known individual book providing one of the best examples of the utilization of anthropological missiological research to address field ministry problems. Its initial circulation would have been aided by its World Council of Churches imprimatur recommending it to the conciliar mission world followed by the reprint edition published by William Carey Library similarly recommending it to the evangelical mission world. Therefore Hayward's interaction with Tippett over a number of years was significant in making the benefit of Tippett's research and writing available to the church globally, positively enhancing Tippett's influence. In his editorial foreword to *Solomon Islands Christianity*, Hayward wrote about the significance of this book and the series as,

> It would be an entire misunderstanding of the significance of this book, and of the purpose of this series, to think that its relevance is confined to the Pacific. Not only is it pertinent to the churches' life in any region of the world where people are moving from tribal communities into modern society, but it will be found to have a bearing on problems of church growth in many kinds of more sophisticated areas.[52]

Subsequently it stimulated Darrell Whiteman's PhD research in the Solomon Islands, leading to the publication of his *Melanesians and Missionaries: An Ethnohistorical Study of Social and Religious Change in the Southwest Pacific*,[53] comprising 559 pages, in which Tippett wrote the foreword.

The immediate confidence building effect of the Solomon Islands project on Tippett was also significant, as he felt that it ideally suited his developing abilities as a missiologist. Having completed his PhD and now having completed this field study in another context, he expressed his own feelings as, "I felt now that I could face my fellow anthropologists and McGavran himself as a peer."[54] This is important to note, as it indicates that although his research and writing was having influence, there was still a confidence issue for Tippett. He also said, "now I had decided to be a professional missiologist. I was much better prepared mentally for the new role."[55] This seemed a similar transition to the one he described in a letter to Edna enroute to the USA after leaving Fiji to initially study with

52. Tippett, *Solomon Islands Christianity*, ix–x.

53. Whiteman, *Melanesians and Missionaries*.

54. Tippett et al., *No Continuing City*, 314.

55. Tippett et al., *No Continuing City*, 314.

McGavran, in which he wrote, "I know now we belong no-where except to the world church."[56] As a published study, *Solomon Islands Christianity: A Study in Growth and Obstruction*[57] brought Tippett on to a broader stage, especially owing to its World Council of Churches platform. Furthermore, even though it was still a Pacific study, it was of a field other than Fiji.

ENHANCED INFLUENCE THROUGH FULLER THEOLOGICAL SEMINARY'S SCHOOL OF WORLD MISSION

Fuller Theological Seminary was not quite twenty years old when they established their School of World Mission. However, in that relatively short time, the seminary had impacted evangelical academic scholarship and seminary training. In 1965, Fuller Seminary enhanced its own influence by the addition of two new schools, the School of Psychology and the School of World Mission.

Fuller Theological Seminary School of World Mission

The next dimension that increased Tippett's influence was joining McGavran as he founded the School of World Mission and Institute of Church Growth at Fuller Seminary. During the first half of 1965, as the influence of McGavran's Institute of Church Growth in Oregon was increasing, Fuller Theological Seminary asked McGavran to consult with them regarding their plan for a possible mission school. The founding of the School of World Mission came from Charles E. Fuller's vision for a mission school embedded within their seminary.[58] The eventual fruit of the McGavran consultations was that he was invited to become their Professor of Mission, commissioned to start their School of World Mission (SWM). As part of those arrangements, as described by McIntosh, "Donald (McGavran) was not interested in coming to Pasadena unless Fuller was willing to take over the entire Institute of Church Growth, which included both himself and Tippett as professors."[59] Or similarly, as reported by Kraft, McGavran assumed that Tippett would be coming with him.[60] McGavran explains that his agreement with David Hubbard, President of Fuller Theological Semi-

---

56. Tippett et al., *No Continuing City*, 269.

57. Tippett, *Solomon Islands Christianity*.

58. Kraft, *SWM/SIS at Forty*, vii–viii.

59. McIntosh, *Donald A. McGavran*, 177.

60. Kraft, *SWM/SIS at Forty*, 58–60.

nary was that he could add one new faculty member per year for the first seven years of its operation. "I told President Hubbard that the first man I would call would be Alan Tippett, the Australian Methodist missiologist."[61] This was agreed to, Tippett was invited, and, despite what seemed like an insurmountable problem that would have delayed his visa by several years, Tippett joined McGavran on opening day, September 28th 1965, and served there until his retirement in 1977. The fact that McGavran insisted that Tippett join him in the move to Fuller indicates that McGavran valued his missiological insights and research.

The background story to Tippett arrival on time is important for this story; McGavran wanted him there for the beginning of class on September 28th 1965. If that goal could be achieved, one of the sensitive points regarding relocating the Institute of Church Growth from Northwest Christian College, namely the Church Growth Research in Latin America (CGRILA) project for which $54,000 had been provided from Lily Endowment, Inc. would be able to be handled smoothly.[62] The United States Consul in Melbourne told Tippett that, as an Australian, he would not have been able to get a visa until 1968 due to the quota system in use at that time. But a week after that meeting, on 14th September, the Consul asked Tippett to visit his office again. As described by Tippett, "He said 'I don't know how you did it. Does this post require that you be a minister?' . . . I was given a ministerial non-quota visa on a case presented to the USA President Lyndon B. Johnson by Billy Graham."[63] He landed in Los Angeles at 6.40 am on 28th September, the first day of class; and was in class for the second session that same day.[64]

Placing the Tippett-McGavran dynamic on the strong organizational and reputational platform of Fuller Theological Seminary took Tippett's influence to a higher level, as another synergistic relationship developed. This time it was between Fuller Theological Seminary and the School of World Mission. The Seminary contributed its prestigious reputation, its profile in the Evangelical community and its reputation for Evangelical scholarship, while the School of World Mission added a dimension of relevance to real life ministry issues, and gave it global exposure through the missionaries and national leaders who studied there. This connection with Fuller

61. McGavran, "Missiologist Alan R. Tippett," 264.
62. McIntosh, *Donald A. McGavran*, 185.
63. Tippett et al., *No Continuing City*, 316.
64. Kraft, *SWM/SIS at Forty*, 49.

increased Tippett's global impact and is vital to understanding Tippett's thinking, development and influence. Documented as a list for brevity, the benefits that came from Tippett's involvement with Fuller Theological Seminary and the School of World Mission can be summarized as:

1. There was the organizational convergence with Charles E Fuller's goal of having a a missionary training institution. This was demonstrated by him providing US$75,000 per year for the first seven years.[65]

2. Tippett's involvement contributed to the academic status of the SWM at Fuller.[66]

3. His published material added to Fuller's mission credibility.

4. The Fuller platform allowed Tippett to develop areas of his own interest that may have been stifled if the Institute of Church Growth under McGavran was his only platform, anthropology being a good example.

5. The fact that some of his views were different from McGavran's meant that together they added breadth and depth that enhanced the School of World Mission program.

6. The breadth and needs of the School of World Mission allowed Tippett to develop Anthropology as a servant of mission, and mission as Applied Anthropology.

7. His lecturing and mentoring, with the pedantic detail and enormous reserves of material[67] was useful for the development of SWM's reputation through its students.

    a. His supervision of graduate writing was always meticulous and demanding on his students.

    b. His research emphasis and groundbreaking methodologies contributed to SWM's credibility.

8. Their limited faculty initially forced Tippett to work very broadly. His *Church Growth and the Word of God*[68] is an example of this, being an embryonic form of Church Growth Theology.

65. Kraft, *SWM/SIS at Forty*, vii–viii, 54.
66. Tippett et al., *No Continuing City*, 339.
67. Whiteman, "Legacy of Alan R. Tippett," 5.
68. Tippett, *Church Growth and the Word*.

9. He was vocal about the need for other faculty, especially History and Theology, resulting in Dr. Ralph Winter and later, Dr. Arthur Glasser joining the team.

10. After his retirement, his return visits contributed to the SWM, but to a lesser degree each visit,[69] until the big re-visit in 1986, which was well planned with a lot of celebration and nostalgia.

As another way of illustrating the strength of the convergence of Fuller and the School of World Missions as it developed, it is valid to focus for a moment on the appointment of Ralph D. Winter as the third faculty member. Although trained as a civil engineer, linguist, cultural anthropologist, and Presbyterian minister, from his ten years as a Presbyterian missionary to Guatemala, he was known in the mission world for the development of Theological Education by Extension (TEE). At SWM, he contributed (1) his unique History of Expansion of Christianity course following Kenneth Scott Latourette's perspective,[70] (2) semi-logarithmic graph paper to map growth rates, not just growth in church growth studies, along with (3) his continual stream of creative ideas.[71] In 1969, he founded William Carey Library Publishers to ensure they could publish the new books that were being written focused on Great Commission mission.[72] In 1972 he was part of the team that founded the American Society of Missiology with its journal, *Missiology* which launched in 1973 with Tippett as its editor. In 1974, his paper "The New Macedonia: A Revolutionary New Era in Mission Begins"[73] presented at the International Congress on World Evangelization in Lausanne, Switzerland, was a watershed for global mission. In 1976, he left Fuller SWM to found the US Centre for World Mission (renamed to Frontier Ventures in 2015), although he continued in an adjunct lecturing role at the SWM for some years. In 1981, his *Perspectives on the World Christian Movement*[74] became the published foundation for Perspectives Courses that are conducted around the world.[75] In 2005, Time Magazine included Winter on their list of "The 25 Most Influential Evangelicals in

---

69. Tippett et al., *No Continuing City*, 445.

70. Latourette, *History of the Expansion*.

71. Kraft, *SWM/SIS at Forty*, 89–97.

72. McIntosh, *Donald A. McGavran*, 212.

73. Winter et al., *Perspectives on the World*, 347–60.

74. Winter and Hawthorne, *Perspectives on the World*.

75. Parsons, "Celebrating the Work of God," 6–12.

America" (Time Staff, Monday, Feb. 07, 2005). In May 2009, one of the last pieces he wrote was his "Series Foreword" for the *Missiology of Alan R. Tippett Series* published by William Carey Library.

So for Tippett to have had significant influence in a wide range of areas in a school as influential as Fuller Theological Seminary definitely enhanced his influence as well.

Ambivalence in the Tippett-McGavran Relationship

Tippett's joining McGavran did much to enhance Tippett's worldwide influence and in the process contributed to McGavran's program. By looking at the record, one could argue that without McGavran, Tippett would not have gained the profile that he did. The same could actually be said about McGavran, but for very different reasons.[76] While exploring their relationship, differences and tensions between them become evident in what could be described as an ambivalent relationship. Tippett did not write about this very openly, but it was obvious to those who knew him and can be perceived subtly in his writings.

At the beginning McGavran saw the need for someone like Tippett to cover areas that were not his strength. Furthermore, owing to his aggressive style, McGavran had his detractors, so when he made some of his more grandiose statements, sometimes without sufficient data to support his view, he was an easy target. As described by Kraft, "both McGavran and Church Growth Theory needed Tippett. With all of his vision and insight, McGavran was quite limited in his understanding of cultural things."[77] But Tippett's detailed research and his growing influence in anthropological circles often meant that McGavran was saved from the full influence of his detractors, because those areas were covered more carefully by Tippett.[78] One example of this is referred to by Tippett as, "I do not think the W.C.C. had much time for any theology that came out of Fuller. They were always having a go at McGavran, but for some reason or other they left me alone. Once or twice they asked me in when they wanted an anthropologist to speak on something."[79] The process was described by Tippett as, "McGavran saw in his experience by observation, the underlying structures by which people make decisions and took action, and I had to establish them

76. Kraft, *SWM/SIS at Forty*, 116–17.

77. Kraft, *SWM/SIS at Forty*, 85.

78. Kraft, *SWM/SIS at Forty*, 85.

79. Tippett et al., *No Continuing City*, 402.

with credibility."[80] While Tippett saw that his role was to serve McGavran in this way, and sometimes noticed the "second-fiddle" aspect of this,[81] he was willing to contribute his growing expertise, and in doing so, coincidentally contribute to his own influence.

Another area of difference was in their goals for the theses and dissertations they supervised. Tippett observed this process as,

> McGavran and I had different ideas on the thesis. He had a master pattern and wanted every man to do his study on that pattern, so that in time he could bring them all together and obtain a world comparison. This was a good idea from that point of view, but it had two shortcomings. It robbed the candidate of his academic freedom . . . Second it meant that once you had read one you had read them all . . . For my part I resolved that no two theses would be the same, and they never were all the same to my retirement.[82]

So one could say that Tippett's goal was to have the data as accurate as possible, both his own and his students. This was in contrast with McGavran's goal to get things in print as quickly as possible.

Tippett saw McGavran as being narrow in his concepts over the long term, thus diminishing the respect given to the "Church Growth men" by others outside their immediate network. Therefore, when Tippett edited *God, Man and Church Growth*,[83] a festschrift in honour of McGavran, he compiled it in such a way as to show the breadth of the Church Growth scholars. Kraft describes this volume as "one of Tippett's major accomplishments while at SWM.[84] As Tippett described the dialog after publishing it,

> I felt I was saying to any evangelical reader: 'Now say that McGavran's writing is narrow if you dare!' I wish I had kept a record of the number of readers who told me that they were amazed at the width of his coverage. More still, it showed that McGavran's graduates and colleagues were ready to expand out from his stimulations.[85]

80. Tippett et al., *No Continuing City*, 319.

81. Kraft, *SWM/SIS at Forty*, 82.

82. Tippett et al., *No Continuing City*, 334.

83. Tippett, *God, Man and Church Growth*.

84. Kraft, *SWM/SIS at Forty*, 86.

85. Tippett et al., *No Continuing City*, 423.

Nevertheless, the differences between Tippett and McGavran did not diminish the stature of either of them. In fact, in Tippett's case it provided freedom for him to pursue areas of his own strength that may have remained fettered if he had been in locked step with McGavran. For example, although McGavran initially wanted Tippett's help in selling anthropological concepts to a skeptical evangelical world[86] and encouraged him to do a PhD in anthropology in Oregon,[87] McGavran did not take anthropology as seriously as Tippett. As the Institute of Church Growth was subsequently incorporated into Fuller Seminary's School of World Mission, Tippett saw anthropology as a field of study that had to be at the forefront of their academic programs because it was an essential tool for field missionaries and a foundational research tool for their church growth studies. For McGavran it was a useful background tool that in fact he did not understand well.[88] This can be illustrated with two examples: The first was the structure of the program of the School of World Mission as Tippett saw it, to maintain their credibility and to benefit their students in their interface with the academic world of anthropology;

> So I resolved that our basic course coverage had to be in line with university credits. I had difficulty with Dr. Mac in the modification of the course names. I wanted Anthropology and Mission to be Anthropology I, not to change its character, but to make it transferable. I never found any aspect of social or cultural anthropology which did not speak somehow to mission. Likewise I wanted my own title to be Professor of Anthropology, rather than Missionary Anthropology, not to change the emphasis but to give me credibility with my secular peers.[89]

The second illustration is that Tippett decided that the School of World Mission needed to be represented at anthropological conferences. Tippett described their differing priorities;

> Dr. Mac agreed that my going was a fair charge on the institute, but when I submitted my very small account afterwards (It was a meeting at San Diego, quite close to Pasadena.) he so haggled over the pennies that I never asked again.[90]

86. Tippett et al., *No Continuing City*, 265.
87. Kraft, *SWM/SIS at Forty*, 39; Tippett et al., *No Continuing City*, 274.
88. Tippett et al., *No Continuing City*, 332; Kraft, *SWM/SIS at Forty*, 17–18.
89. Tippett et al., *No Continuing City*, 332.
90. Tippett et al., *No Continuing City*, 342. This is quoted from the original typescript

Another example of Tippett's acknowledgement of the differences that existed between them is that, having completed his PhD and the Solomon Islands field research, Tippett said, "I felt now that I could face my fellow anthropologists and McGavran himself as a peer."[91] This indicates that until then he was aware that McGavran didn't treat him as a peer. Tippett's oft used term "Dr. Mac" for McGavran possibly implies a distance in the relationship.[92]

Thus, Tippett and McGavran, by being two very different individuals, but working together, committed to the same ultimate purpose, were able to mitigate each other's weak areas by contributing their areas of strength. Tippett's influence was significantly increased through this phenomenon. A quote from Tippett's autobiography further demonstrates the symbiosis yet tension to a marked degree,

> In 1970 the appearance of Understanding Church Growth was exciting because it gave us a bed-rock statement from which so much of our research was proceeding. The 'revision' of 10 years later must be regarded as disappointing because the revisions are selective and its shortcomings are not corrected. The graphing is still the old McGavran, and vulnerable. The terminology (Eurica and Africasia &c) so unacceptable to the anthropologists is more deeply ingrained. He recognizes anthropology and comes to term with it by his own rationalization; but when he speaks of 'relativism,' 'culture' 'holism' etc. he gives his own meaning (not always the same). He virtually passes the anthropological 'buck' off on to me with one reference. He draws only two or three aspects from me, cites Glasser once in an edited quote, and Kraft's contribution is not mentioned at all. He ignores the whole region of interdisciplinary material, ethnohistory (so essential for reconstructing church growth time depth studies), ethnotheology and ethnolinguistics do not have any mention. It is still the same old McGavran, still insightful, but very selective, fighting the same old battles and not altogether recognizing that the battle fronts are changing all the time . . . I mention it firstly to agree that it was the core of church growth, but also to point out that that its general acceptance actually depended on other church growth writing beyond that of McGavran himself.[93]

autobiography, but is not included in the published version.

91. Tippett et al., *No Continuing City*, 314.

92. Tippett et al., *No Continuing City* 277, 285.

93. Tippett et al., *No Continuing City*, 424.

Missiology Journal and Conferences

As the Fuller School of World Mission continued to shape post-colonial missiology, there was a growing sense that, to be regarded as its own valid field of study, it needed its own academic society and its own journal. This was important, because for many, especially in the areas influenced by European theological categories, missiology was considered to be a subset of theology. This view can be seen in the following quote from Gerben Heitink "Toward the end of the nineteenth century missiology emerged from practical theology,"[94] while post-colonial missiologists held the view that what they were involved in was its own field of study. A working definition from Tippett's *Introduction to Missiology* illustrates the point that missiology is its own field of study, and definitely not a sub-set of theology, the reverse being true in the case of missiology,

> Missiology is defined as the academic discipline or science which researches, records and applies data relating to the biblical origin, the history (including the use of documentary materials), the anthropological principles and techniques, and the theological base of the Christian Mission. The theory, methodology and data bank are particularly directed towards:

1. the process by which the Christian message is communicated,

2. the encounters brought about by its proclamation to non-Christians,

3. the planting of the Church and organisation of congregations, the incorporation of converts into those congregations, and the growth in relevance of their structures and fellowship, internally to maturity, externally in outreach as the Body of Christ in local situations and beyond, in a variety of culture patterns.[95]

Tippett was in favour of the formation of the society and the journal, but was not at the "American Society of Missiology" meeting where this was implemented. As a result, he was surprised and did not appreciate the way Ralph Winter "manipulated affairs" in his absence to have him appointed as the editor of the new journal *Missiology: An International Review* while also arranging that it would be launched in 1974. Part of the plan in what

---

94. Heitink, *Practical Theology*, 109.

95. Tippett, *Introduction to Missiology*, xiii.

Tippett saw as "Winter's manipulation" was to have *Missiology* ready to take over as the journal *Practical Anthropology*, a journal for missionaries and mission scholars, came to a close. That way it would have an established reader base before it started. Tippett would have liked to launch it the following year, so was hurt by criticism of the errors that had crept into the first edition in the rush for its release.[96]

Tippett carried the role of journal editor for three years, which made his name and concepts much more widely known. Darrell Whiteman commented about Tippett in this role as, "he was ideally suited for this role because of his anthropological background and breadth of missiological acumen."[97] Tippett's own view of the content and approach in the three-year period when he was the editor of *Missiology* was that the journal had covered key aspects of missiology, was representative of all continents while the views it represented were both evangelical and conciliar, while standing on the Great Commission and Scripture. In doing so they represented a broad spectrum of missionary opinion.[98] It is noteworthy that once again, something that greatly enhanced Tippett's expression and influence, while using his expertise for the sake of mission, was not something that he would have chosen for himself. But through the situation, he found himself in a position and role that enhanced his influence.

1974 Conferences of Significance

In the years that Tippett lived in the USA, he participated in many missiological and anthropological conferences all of which contributed to his influence. However, in 1974, two of these were seminal in contributing to and or confirming his influence. These were: Milligan, Tennessee—April 1974,[99] and Lausanne, Switzerland—July 1974[100] with its follow-up consultations; Pasadena on Homogeneous Units (1977),[101] and Willowbank on Gospel & Culture (1978).[102]

96. Tippett et al., *No Continuing City*, 426.

97. Whiteman, "Legacy of Alan R. Tippett," 5.

98. Tippett et al., *No Continuing City*, 426.

99. Tippett, "Parallaxis in Missiology," 97; Tippett et al., *No Continuing City*, 321–22; Yamamori and Taber, *Christopaganism or Indigenous Christianity?*

100. Tippett, "Parallaxis in Missiology," 130; Tippett et al., *No Continuing City*, 405.

101. McIntosh, *Donald A. McGavran*, 266; Lausanne Committee for World Evangelization, *Pasadena Consulation*, 1.

102. Lausanne Committee for World Evangelization, *Willowbank Report*, 2; Tippett

MILLIGAN SYMPOSIUM ON *CHRISTOPAGANISM* OR *INDIGENOUS CHRISTIANITY?*

In April 1974, the William S. Carter Symposium on "Christopaganism or Indigenous Christianity" was convened at Milligan College, Tennessee. This brought together 500 missiologists and students of mission, with papers presented by Donald McGavran, Johannes Hoekendijk, Peter Beyerhaus, and Alan Tippett.[103] Tetsunao Yamamori and Charles Taber compiled these papers into the book *Christopaganism or Indigenous Christianity?*[104] Tippett, writing in his autobiography in the 1986–1988 period, rates this as the most significant missiological event he ever attended in the United States, especially in regard to the platform engagement, as two papers were presented by each of the four speakers, and then were formally responded to by the others.[105] That comment had the time perspective of being written twelve to fourteen years later to substantiate this evaluation. A by-product of the Milligan Symposium was the consultation on missionary training that was coordinated as a prelude to the main program. Tippett was particularly pleased with the statement that was developed at that time, with its emphasis on anthropology in missionary training, as published in the *Milligan Missiogram*.[106]

INTERNATIONAL CONGRESS ON WORLD EVANGELIZATION, LAUSANNE, SWITZERLAND

Just three months after the Milligan Symposium, the International Congress on World Evangelization[107] took place at Lausanne, Switzerland, arranged by Billy Graham. Jacques Matthey's "From 1910 to 2010: A Post Edinburgh 2010 Reflection" from the International Review of Mission, highlights one possible motivation for the calling of the International Congress on World Evangelization. It is pertinent to other aspects of this study, so is included to gain the perspective of his whole quote,

> After the Willingen conference of the IMC in 1952, ecumenical missiology became strongly influenced by the missio Dei theology.

---

et al., *No Continuing City*, 475–76.

103. Tippett et al., *No Continuing City*, 321.

104. Yamamori and Taber, *Christopaganism or Indigenous Christianity?*

105. Tippett et al., *No Continuing City*, 321–22.

106. Tippett, "Report on the Curriculum Committee."

107. Douglas, *Let the Earth Hear*; Hunt, "History of the Lausanne Movement."

There are at least two major approaches to missio Dei. The first is the classical emphasis found in systematic theologies based on the following sequence of sendings: Father—Son—Spirit—Church—world. In such a sequence, the church faces the world with a message to deliver from God. The alternative missio Dei approach turns the argumentation upside down. It affirms that the Trinitarian God is present and active in the secular and multireligious world. The church's agenda is to discern God's activity and presence through reading the 'signs of the times' and join God in the struggle for justice, peace, liberation, and humanization, or in one term, for 'shalom.' This second version of missio Dei gained much influence within ecumenical institutions and provoked a strong reaction from mainly American and European evangelicals. Organizing themselves under the leadership of Billy Graham and his association, they convened several conferences up to the 1974 congress on world evangelization in Lausanne, Switzerland. By adopting a Covenant, that congress stated what it believed to be a correct biblical understanding of mission and evangelism priorities, in opposition to affirmations of WCC conferences such as Geneva, Uppsala or Bangkok and the creation of the Programmes to Combat Racism and on interreligious dialogue.[108]

Of the 3,000 delegates, Tippett estimates that 160 to 170 were Fuller faculty or graduates. As he points out, this was a small proportion, but he was satisfied that it was a vocal and active minority whose perspective was well accepted. However, considering this was a global conference, to have more than 5 percent participation from just one institution was significant numerically as well, especially when that institution had been in operation for less than ten years. He was even more satisfied that the Lausanne Covenant represented, on an even broader platform, much that they had fought so hard to protect and develop.[109]

His own involvement was to present his paper "The Evangelization of Animists."[110] but he also considered that one of his long term contributions in those forums was in preparing the Statements and Resolutions that emerged from them.[111] He rates this as a watershed in missiology.[112]

108. Matthey, "From 1910 to 2010," 266–67.

109. Tippett et al., *No Continuing City*, 405.

110. Douglas, *Let the Earth Hear*, 844–56.

111. Tippett et al., *No Continuing City*, 405.

112. Tippett et al., *No Continuing City*, 406.

There were follow-up consultations on topics like *The Homogeneous Unit Principle, Gospel and Culture,* etc.,[113] which Tippett attended.[114] Although he was not as comfortable with the way some of those sub-units were conducted, he was comfortable with the statements that came from them, recognizing John Stott's skill in the accepted documents.[115]

Tippett's view was that finally mission leaders had substantive documents that could guide them in strategic mission. This was a good resource for them, but left them accountable if they did not use them. "No one has an excuse anymore"[116] was his view. The fact that these statements aligned well with Tippett's perspectives indicates that there was general agreement amongst key leaders regarding the validity of the perspectives that Tippett held and proposed for others. However on Tippett's statement about no one having an excuse, there seems be an issue of over-optimism here. He is assuming that mission executives, missionaries, and others involved in the task of mission will actively seek out such material and actively implement their findings. Tippett's assumption on this matter could be a contributing factor in these key insights not being utilized even in his era or in the years since then.

CONCLUSION

The story of the increase in Tippett's influence, as observed in the list of contributory items in this chapter, is quite remarkable. The era begins as an Australian Methodist missionary to the Fiji islands returns to Australia, having suddenly decided that his time in Fiji had concluded. He describes the sense of isolation and frustration he felt as having "no continuing city."[117] However less than five years later, he has a PhD, and is senior faculty at the recently founded School of World Mission at the cutting-edge Fuller Theological Seminary. From that role, he continued to influence mission around the world for the following twelve years until he retired in 1977. In all of the aspects examined above, it must be noted that Tippett's written observations were not only prolific but were generally based on meticu-

113. Lausanne Committee for World Evangelization, *Willowbank Report*, 2.

114. McIntosh, *Donald A. McGavran*, 266–67.

115. Tippett et al., *No Continuing City*, 476.

116. Tippett et al., *No Continuing City*, 476.

117. Tippett et al., *No Continuing City*, 253, 255.

lous research. The breadth of the knowledge this gave him when combined with his own unique insights and wisdom made his written material very valuable.

4

Alan Tippett's Influence

Analyzing the Decline

If I had made any worthwhile contribution to missiology for the post-colonial era, it has probably been in the area of the theoretical base, the development of research methodology, the application of anthropological principles positively to church growth, and the exploration of research models for pin-pointing matters for concentration of evangelistic thrust and pastoral care.[1]

EXAMINING TIPPETT'S LIFE THUS far, and observing the increasing significance of his insights and material, it could be assumed that, even though Tippett passed away in 1988, the influence of his insights and material would continue, whether field focused or in the academy. At the same time, some decline in influence is understandable as a result of Tippett's retirement and return to Australia, but as will be seen in this chapter, the decline was particularly marked in Tippett's case.

Looking on the positive side, some of his books are readily available and some have occasionally been reprinted.[2] Those who know his material continue to use it in course work or in developing field strategies, while much of his material has remained unpublished until recently. Thankfully,

---

1. Tippett et al., *No Continuing City,* 428.

2. For example, Tippett, *Deep-Sea Canoe,* was reprinted again by William Carey Library in 2006.

starting in 2012, a number of titles have been published for the first time by William Carey Library in a project endorsed by the late Dr. Ralph Winter and coordinated by Doug Priest as *The Missiology of Alan R. Tippett Series.* Priest, while a student at Fuller SWM in the mid-1970s had been a teaching assistant to Tippett. Furthermore, a number of his concepts have become so commonplace in missionary parlance that they are employed within missiology without the users being aware of their source. Examples of this would be the internal dynamics of people movements, multi-individual mutually interdependent decision-making,[3] animism concepts, functional substitutes, power encounter,[4] etc.

In this chapter it will be important to investigate whether the long term decline of Tippett's influence was due to the lack of significance and relevance of his insights. The argument of this chapter is that his ideas and concepts were indeed relevant and significant for his era of mission and that the decline of his influence was due to factors external to the perceptiveness and relevance of his concepts and insights, thus validating the task of exploring his insights.

ONGOING SIGNIFICANCE, BUT DIMINISHED INFLUENCE

I will argue in this chapter that there were a range of things that converged to diminish Tippett's influence on his retirement, even though his insights were still valid. They can be categorized into five areas: (1) Personal, (2) Situational, (3) Organizational, (4) Strategic, and (5) Contextual within mission and church growth missiology.

PERSONAL FACTORS

Personal—Writing Style

While the content of Tippett's writing is noted as one of his key strengths, his writing style diminished his influence. In summary, the following list emerges:

1. The labourious detail of his writing that one could term "unabashed particularism" made his material difficult to read, even though well worth the effort. An example of this is the fact that while writing this

---

3. McGavran and Wagner, *Understanding Church Growth*, 231.
4. Wimber and Springer, *Power Evangelism.*

volume, it has been extremely difficult to find succinct definitions for many of his key concepts.

2. Much of his best theory was encapsulated in local case studies and therefore was not noticed by people interested in mission in other locations. Or else, for those who did read them outside of their own context, the labourious detail made it difficult to distill the applicable insights.

3. He was willing to write about other people's issues, both positively to support and negatively to critique. This sometimes made it difficult to identify who Tippett really was while making it especially difficult to identify his areas of strength because most of what he wrote was well researched.

4. He saw writing and publishing as two separate functions, so was willing to write numerous book-length manuscripts without any guarantee of publication. Being unpublished limited their influence in the broader world of mission study and research, even though it is worth noting the significant number of libraries and private collections that have copies of at least some of Tippett's unpublished volumes.

Personal—No Specialization Textbook

The fact that Tippett left no published textbook or otherwise unified documents within his areas of strength allowed his influence to diminish quickly. His book *Introduction to Missiology*[5] comes closest to being a book covering his areas of strength. But it was originally written, then compiled, then bound by Tippett as a "hobby project" under the title of "Adventures in Missiology: Picture of a Growing Discipline."[6] As it was published, it retained much of the character of a series of articles and chapters of significance, but lacking the force of a cohesive textbook. Even so, its publication would have enhanced his influence on the world stage, however it was published a decade after his retirement, and just the year before he passed away, so was too little too late, and even then his name was misspelled as "Tippet" on the cover and spine of the published book.

---

5. Tippett, *Introduction to Missiology.*
6. Tippett, "Adventures in Missiology."

As a result, anyone wanting to understand his insights had to read a lot of his material to gain an aggregated understanding of his concepts. This was particularly challenging when his key concepts covered such a wide area of mission understanding and were spread across so many volumes. Also, because many of his key insights were unpublished at the time of his retirement, in the academic world his influence would have quickly moved from centre stage when he left his formal roles.

Personal—Public Speaking Style

Outside of the academic circles at Fuller where his insights were valued, the style of his verbal presentations were a liability for him. Even at Fuller where he was known and respected there were challenges. Using a personal example, when I took a class with Tippett at the School of World Mission on his return visit in 1979, his lecturing style was definitely not gripping, and there was a tendency to digress into other areas of his vast reserves of material. For me, the diversions were all interesting and generally helpful, but for students who were relying on the advertised course topic for perspectives towards their theses and dissertations, it was very frustrating.

This was exaggerated more as he retired to Australia and had to establish himself in what was virtually a new environment for him. A personal experience again makes the point: I had the privilege of listening to Tippett present two papers at an Assemblies of God mission consultation in Sydney in 1986. His knowledge of his material was encyclopedic, but in an auditorium full of Pentecostal preachers, with their preference for a gripping oratorical style, Tippett's presentations felt laboured to say the least. This factor of his speaking style, when multiplied across various speaking opportunities led to rapid decline of influence. Return invitations amplify influence, however return invitations are based on the impression made with each previous presentation. When Tippett was not invited for a second or third time due to the above factors, his influence was diminished, as well as the phenomenon being personally discouraging for him.

TRANSITION FROM USA TO AUSTRALIA

Situational—Decision to Leave Fuller

As has already been noted, when Tippett went to study at Oregon, his goal was to get a Master's degree in mission studies so he could lecture at the Methodist college of Queens in Melbourne or some other missionary training institution in Australia. This had eluded him during his life of active ministry and teaching, so he decided to retire at sixty-five years of age, move to Australia, locate his library in Australia as a research collection, and to use the freedom this gave him to work on his writing projects. This was part of his estimation that Australia was twenty years behind the rest of the world,[7] especially in its understanding of theology and mission at that time. This was something he obviously hoped to change. But in choosing to retire from Fuller and return to Australia, unknowingly Tippett chose to submerse himself in a situation that was not necessarily open to his influence, be it through apathy, ignorance or resistance.

On closer analysis, it appears that for many people in church and mission leadership in Australia, Tippett was largely unknown. This similarly applied to many within the world of anthropology. In his autobiography he refers to some invitations to speak as someone who had attended the International Congress on World Evangelization at Lausanne, Switzerland, and also some teaching opportunities in Bible colleges.[8] But this was limited. So, while it appears that he was rejected or ignored, in fairness, for most it was just that they did not know about him or the significance of his material, or how to avail themselves of his material. For the few who did know him, there was too much respect, assuming that a person as important as Tippett would not have been interested in lecturing or consulting for them. I remember two examples from within my own denomination. In 1981, talking to the academic dean of our Bible college, I suggested they utilize Tippett, who lived just four hours' drive away, to provide input to enable them to develop a mission program. His profile was one of the reasons given as to why that would not be feasible. Then in anticipation of the 1986 Assemblies of God Missions Consultation in Sydney referred to above, the Mission Director of AOG World Missions asked my opinion about the likelihood of being able to secure Tippett as a speaker for that event, again assuming his profile was such that he would not be available. As it turns out, the consultation did go ahead, Tippett was invited and he presented two papers.[9]

Tippett's retirement from Fuller was earlier than his colleagues there thought was wise. They suggested that he stay on and to keep his library there where it would be used. The President, David Hubbard, tried

7. Tippett et al., *No Continuing City*, 464.
8. Tippett et al., *No Continuing City*, 464–66.
9. Tippett, "Objectives of World Mission"; Tippett, "Frontiers of Evangelism"

to persuade him to "stay on after retirement, deciding just one year at a time."[10] However he went ahead with his decision to retire with his departure even taking some of his closest colleagues by surprise, with Kraft reporting, "he began packing his books . . . catching me off guard in my attempt to copy . . . the yearly bound volumes . . . I had to copy them later in Australia."[11] One reason Tippett gave at the time was that he wanted to write three or four textbooks, a book on animism being one of them. He said that students were taking too much of his time at the School of World Mission so leaving was the only way to facilitate the writing. He retired to write, but that did not happen. The three missiological works that he published in his retirement were his seventy-page *Oral Tradition and Ethnohistory: The Transmission of Information and Social Values in Early Christian Fiji, 1835–1905*,[12] his forty-page "Parallaxis in Missiology—To Use or Abuse"[13] prepared for the *Symposium on, Missionaries, Anthropologists and Culture Change* coordinated by Darrell Whiteman, and the update and release of his 1972 compilation "Adventures in Missiology"[14] as *Introduction to Missiology*.[15] This was implemented at the behest of Charles Kraft and his friends from the School of World Mission ten years after his retirement.[16]

So, Tippett's publication of new missiological research virtually stopped. In the move to Australia, and especially to Canberra, he seemed to underestimate the power of the stimulus he had found initially at the Institute of Church Growth and subsequently at the School of World Mission. Charles Kraft also comments on Canberra as a location, and St. Mark's as an institution, as far as the stimulus that it provided, having visited him in Canberra numerous times in that period.[17] By contrast, Tippett described his USA experience as, "His [McGavran's] institute provided the facilities for this kind of work [research and writing], and the body of experienced missionaries with whom to interact, compare and test one's ideas."[18] While regarding Australia, he wrote, "David Hubbard's prediction of my dying

10. Tippett et al., *No Continuing City*, 434.

11. Kraft, *SWM/SIS at Forty*, 133–34.

12. Tippett, *Oral Tradition and Ethnohistory*.

13. Tippett, "Parallaxis in Missiology."

14. Tippett, "Adventures in Missiology."

15. Tippett, *Introduction to Missiology*.

16. Kraft, *SWM/SIS at Forty*, 84.

17. Kraft, *SWM/SIS at Forty*, 134.

18. Tippett, *God, Man and Church Growth*, 35.

from lack of collegiality was suddenly tragically meaningful."[19] He confided in Kraft a month before his death, "I think I retired too soon." a sentiment Kraft agreed with.[20] Had he continued his missiological writing, especially published writing, regardless of where he was based, he would have maintained greater influence, while the lack thereof contributed to his decline in influence.

On looking at the archivist's summary of correspondence of his early retirement period, there were,

> . . . letters from McGavran and Kraft and other colleagues at Fuller and A.R.T. [Alan R. Tippett] to the Dean on the possibility of an annual visit [to SWM]; from various individuals and organisations relating to A.R.T.'s return visit to the States in 1979, a number of individuals in mission situations round the globe, seeking advice . . . training colleges and societies, sometimes relating to possible visits, consultancy work, seminar or workshop participation, the preparation of articles, or supervision of individuals in training; publishers on . . . publication of "The Ways of the People."[21]

Clearly, there were significant opportunities for Tippett. In the first year of his retirement this resulted in him being quite busy, with visits to Pasadena, Bermuda, Bali, New Zealand, and Papua New Guinea with very full programs in each location. However he used the expression of, "my role as an internationalist was terminated"[22] to describe this new era of his life. This may also relate to a statement he made in his autobiography ten years after his retirement, when he observed, "Looking back now I realize I myself suffered considerably from culture shock respecting Australia, my retirement and the Church itself."[23] He seemed to have underestimated the effects of that culture stress on him. The outcome was that he still wrote, but it was on his family biographies and his beloved stamps. Beyond those activities, he prepared individual lectures, organized his older material, and wrote an occasional book review and engaged in some seminar and field consultations when opportunities afforded him. In that same era, he comments about taking opportunities for personal witness.[24] Somehow however, due to the

19. Tippett et al., *No Continuing City*, 441–42.

20. Kraft, *SWM/SIS at Forty*, 134.

21. St. Mark's National Theological Centre, "Guide to the Tippett Collection," 68.

22. Tippett et al., *No Continuing City*, 473.

23. Tippett et al., *No Continuing City*, 439.

24. Tippett et al., *No Continuing City*, 447.

impact of all of these factors in the move to Australia, he lost confidence in new missiological writing. This lack of confidence is evident in the paper *Task and Method: How Anthropology and Theology need to Integrate in Post Colonial Missiology* that he presented to the faculty and students at Bible College of Victoria.[25] His insights in it were significant, but in the section where he tried to apply the concepts to the Australian situation, which is what a non-mission audience would have been looking for, his statements are insightful but were stated in very tentative ways.

Situational—Exit from the Conference Circuit

Due to the prohibitive cost of travel from Australia, an unintended consequence of retiring to Australia was that Tippett was taking himself out of the vital conference circuit in the USA, and also the less frequent international conferences. During his first two years back in Australia, both the School of World Mission and Lausanne Committee assisted him to attend events. Even then, the USA based anthropological conferences were no longer accessible to him.

Subsequently, when "financial and institutional sponsorship" was no longer available, especially as Lausanne changed their policy on sponsoring travel for attendees,[26] he was out of the circuit and his ongoing influence at that level ceased. This was compounded by the fact that during his lifetime, any spare money he had was predominantly spent on buying books for his library; "kept me poor" was his term;[27] which meant that on retirement he did not have reserves to independently fund travel.

Organizational—Strained Relationship with Australian Mission Board

While investigating ways in which his missiological influence diminished on his retirement and subsequent return to Australia, it is worth noting that there was a growing distance between Tippett and his Australian denomination,[28] and its Mission Board, the *Methodist Overseas Missions*[29]

25. Tippett, "Task and Method."
26. Tippett et al., *No Continuing City*, 445.
27. Tippett et al., *No Continuing City*, 433.
28. Wood, *Overseas Missions*.
29. Tippett and Priest, *Fullness of Time*, 112, 115.

long before his retirement.[30] The short description of this phenomenon is to say that he became more and more mission, cross-culturally, and missiologically oriented, while his denomination maintained its colonial view of mission while eventually losing the evangelistic zeal that Tippett had known during his upbringing. He summarized his feelings of this by saying, "Deputation was often a destructive and infuriating experience."[31] On his return from his time as a field missionary, and then as a missiologist at the School of World Mission, he described this issue as he discovered it as,

> I was terminating my life within an overseas academic institution and returning to ordinary church life in my homeland . . . It was even more difficult to envision because of the recent union of the Churches to form the Uniting Church. I hoped it would retain enough of its Wesleyan character to be still the situation into which I wanted to settle. I was not at all comforted when re-establishing myself with the Connexional Secretary and commenting that changes had taken place, he responded. "Yes, John Wesley is no more!" I was dismayed.[32]

Surveying the process from the beginning, on arrival on the field he came to see that the theory of mission he was asked to labour under was not appropriate, so he became a "rebel" whose "views were officially rejected by the church."[33] As time went on, the growing rift between Tippett and his sending agency, the Methodist Overseas Missions[34] of which Mr. Gribble[35] was the General Secretary in Australia[36] can be seen in various ways. Tippett, in his twelve-page response to an unexpected letter of appreciation from Gribble in 1959 wrote, "Please forgive me. I write to you about once in 5 years and put 5 letters in one."[37] Tippett was very open in his letter, including a statement explaining that it may have been necessary for him to leave the field for family reasons. The reply from Gribble said, "I can imagine that your retirement from the District would be a dreadful loss

30. Tippett et al., *No Continuing City*, 284.

31. Tippett et al., *No Continuing City*, 258–60.

32. Tippett et al., *No Continuing City*, 462.

33. Tippett, "Retrospect and Prospect," 35.

34. Tippett and Priest, *Fullness of Time*, 112.

35. Dundon, "Raicakacaka," 152–53.

36. Tippett et al., *No Continuing City*, 295.

37. Letter Tippett to Gribble, TIP 70/38 Vol 6, St. Mark's Library, 26th September 1959, marked personal

to the District at this stage. You would be warmly welcomed in Australia, however, your suggestion about U.S.A. is also one that should be given serious consideration."[38]

In that era, for an Australian mission leader to be agreeable for one or their field teams to be taking a USA post seems to indicate that there was something abnormal in the relationship, as does Tippett's "one letter in five years." Later, while working on his PhD, again he was advised to take a position in the USA or a position that the World Council of Churches might offer him. Tippett interpreted that to mean "Either he did not want me personally, or he did not want a missionary training specialist,"[39] further indicating tension in the relationship.

Another example of this relates to Tippett's time at the Institute of Church Growth in Oregon. In response to a request for an article, he wrote *Australia's Missionary Outreach in Our Time*[40] of which he later said, "The writing shows me as influenced considerably by McGavran at the time and also by Barnett. However I was following a much wider orbit than either of them."[41] He described an intriguing situation that occurred in relation to that article that illustrates the point being made. Tippett says the analyses it contained were,

> written for the missionary supporters of the Australian Methodist Church and were accepted for publication by the editor of "The Spectator."[42] One of the Board members . . . wanted them circulated to the Australian Church at large, rather than in the denominational paper. Thus the manuscript passed to and fro and between them they lost it, and were never able to give me an adequate explanation. I have never been convinced that other members of the Board could not take the frank appraisals.[43]

This further indicates a breakdown of his relationship with his Australian Board, with McCaughey's article illustrating well the mood and issues of

---

38. Letter from Gribble to Tippett, TIP 70/38 Vol 6, St. Mark's Library, 2nd November 1959, marked personal

39. Tippett et al., *No Continuing City*, 285.

40. Tippett, "Australia's Missionary Outreach."

41. Tippett, "Australia's Missionary Outreach," 1.

42. A Methodist weekly for Victoria and Tasmania.

43. Tippett, "Australia's Missionary Outreach," 1.

this era for Tippett's denomination and why his advocates and adversaries would have found themselves in difficult situations.[44]

Then there was the publication of his research into the Methodist work in the Solomon Islands in what became part of *Solomon Islands Christianity*.[45] He researched the Anglican mission and church as part of that same volume. The Methodist ministry in the Western Solomons that he researched, began in 1902,[46] with the early stages carried out under the direction of the Wesleyan/Methodist movement in Australia, with New Zealand leadership continuing similar patterns of ministry after they took over in 1921.[47] On the basis of his 1964 research, Tippett was most critical of the ministry patterns they employed, indicating that they seriously impeded the growth and development of the work there.[48] He saw this as being in contrast with the effective Wesleyan/Methodist ministry in Fiji and Tonga, and, to make a point, he even contrasted their work with the Roman Catholic mission in the Solomon Islands. In 1964, this contrast with a Roman Catholic missionary's activities would have been a much bigger issue than it would be in today's ecumenical world. Then there was his extended analysis of Etoism, the syncretistic "Christian Fellowship Church." In that he pointed out the weaknesses in missionary practice that were seminal to the formation and eventual strength of this movement.[49] He drew the conclusion that the Methodist approach in the Solomon Islands, whether from Australia or New Zealand, was a major factor contributing to this schism. Noting Tippett's observations, it is reasonable to assume that when *Solomon Islands Christianity*[50] was published by the World Council of Churches (WCC), giving a global platform to his evaluation of a Methodist strategic weakness, this would have caused additional tension between him and his Australian leaders.

Similarly, while pointing out that initially the WCC were more open to his input than they were to McGavran's, he then referred to an alienation that occurred at that level, when he said, "Once or twice they asked me in when they wanted an anthropologist to speak on something . . . I took them

44. McCaughey, "Church Union in Australia."
45. Tippett, *Solomon Islands Christianity*.
46. Tippett, *Solomon Islands Christianity*, 55.
47. Tippett, *Solomon Islands Christianity*, 68.
48. Tippett, *Solomon Islands Christianity*, 54–76.
49. Tippett, *Solomon Islands Christianity*, 219–66.
50. Tippett, *Solomon Islands Christianity*.

to task on their 'Barbados consultation' and since then have not been called on again."[51] His own statement, "Unfortunately my Church in Australia takes many of its initiatives from the W.C.C."[52] would help explain some of the ambivalence of his Australian mission agency leaders towards him in the circumstances analyzed here. That was evident at later stages of his time away from Australia, and especially on his retirement. Tippett expressed the growing tension quaintly by saying, "I had the strong feeling that with the Board and its High Priest the urim and thummim were loaded against me,"[53] The "high priest" reference was not included in the published version of his autobiography, but it is included here to illustrate Tippett's perception of the situation—and his dry sense of humour. Thus, even before Tippett retired from Fuller, these factors were combining to undermine the influence that had been building in other ways, especially his influence in Australia and with his own denomination and sending agency.

Strategic—Tippett's Goal for His Library to Influence Mission in Australia

In reading Tippett's autobiography, it is clear that by the time he retired he particularly pinned his hopes for influencing the future of mission in Australia on the availability of his library.[54] He described his intent as, "Having been denied such resources in my own missionary training I intended making it available somewhere in Australia, where it could be open for use by any researcher who cared to use it."[55]

Converging with this goal, as Tippett was anticipating his retirement to Australia, Rev. David Durie from St. Mark's Library in Canberra visited Tippett at the School of World Mission and suggested placing his library at St. Mark's Library, that belonged to the Anglican Diocese of Canberra and Goulburn.[56] His reason to invite Tippett to locate his library at St. Mark's Library was because he felt that the Church Growth perspective was the only chance for the future of mission in Australia.[57] Tippett did propose a

51. Tippett et al., *No Continuing City*, 403.

52. Tippett et al., *No Continuing City*, 403.

53. Tippett, "No Continuing City", 299.

54. Tippett et al., *No Continuing City*, 481.

55. Tippett et al., *No Continuing City*, 433; also 467, 471–72, 496–99.

56. Tippett et al., *No Continuing City*, 509.

57. Tippett et al., *No Continuing City*, 441.

way for his own denomination to have the benefit of his library, utilizing some of the buildings that had become surplus to their needs through the process of merging into the Uniting Church. When they were not open to his proposal[58] he agreed to St. Mark's Library's proposal. As he arrived in Australia, individuals associated with St. Mark's Library assisted the Tippetts in moving from Springvale, Melbourne and settling in Canberra.[59] At the time, St. Mark's Library was progressive enough to build a whole new wing to house his collection in "compactus" shelving. Tippett had an office desk in this wing, and both before and after his death, I was one of many who experienced Tippett's dream of having his library available as a resource.

The shape of Tippett's plan was honed by several factors. First, he wanted to make his resources and information available to others. In fact, this was one thing he had given his life to, as seen in his statement that it was his library that had kept him poor.[60] Also, even though he did not publish much of his own material (compared to the extensiveness of his writing), he willingly made copies of his material available, for example, 100 single spaced foolscap pages of notes per person for the presentations he made on his last visit to Fuller in 1986.[61] Second, when his father died in February 1940[62] his father's library was sold piecemeal to free up money needed by his mother.[63] At that time Tippett made a commitment that whatever library he accumulated would be kept as a total collection when he died. The way he stated it was, "I was determined to see that it (my library) did not suffer the same tragic fate of my father's library after his death . . . [it] had kept me poor, and I had no intention of letting it be dismembered," and "I resolved . . . that my library would not be dismembered when the time came."[64] So that became a non-negotiable condition in donating his resource library to St. Mark's Library forty-four years later, as he formally handed over his library to St. Mark's in 1984.

Regarding the ongoing influence of Tippett's library, there are several aspects to consider: The first and predominant one is location. By the end

58. Tippett et al., *No Continuing City*, 441.

59. Tippett et al., *No Continuing City*, 442–43.

60. Tippett et al., *No Continuing City*, 433.

61. Tippett et al., *No Continuing City*, 517.

62. Tippett et al., *No Continuing City*, 451.

63. Tippett et al., *No Continuing City*, 490.

64. Tippett et al., *No Continuing City*, 433, 490.

of 1975, Tippett was considering three possible locations for his retirement in Australia:[65] Springvale, Melbourne, where he owned a home, Armidale, NSW, and Canberra, ACT. St. Mark's Library in Canberra was the only institution to demonstrate a willingness to accommodate Tippett's library at the time that he needed to make his decision about his retirement location, and Tippett, having seen the transition into Canberra proceed smoothly, felt that this location was God's will for him.[66]

However, strategically, it was hardly the best location from the point of view of Tippett being noticed and having influence in the halls of mission organizations or in missionary training institutions during his retirement, let alone in the long term influence of the library now that Tippett is no longer a part of it. Canberra is a long way from the centre of mission organizations, mission leadership and mission studies in Australia. There is not even a school with a major mission program in Canberra and the majority of evangelical mission organizations have their head offices in either Melbourne or Sydney. Strategically, Melbourne and Sydney, probably in that order, would have been the best choice.

Another aspect to consider when asking about the ongoing significance of this library is that of physical and structural changes at St. Mark's Library since Tippett donated his research collection. At the time of this writing, the Tippett collection is housed in a Rare Books Collection, with no unsupervised public access allowed. St. Mark's Library staff have indicated that the condition of no unsupervised access is to fulfill contractual obligations they accepted on other collections that were given as "rare book collections" and so applies to the Tippett Collection while it is housed there. It seems that it is housed in the Rare Books Collection instead of in its own wing as was arranged with Tippett, due to the need for additional library space at a time when resources were not available to physically extend the library. So Tippett's goal of having the presence of his library communicate something to the Australian Christian public, and to allow bona fide researchers to browse its shelves is difficult to fulfill. That is despite the St. Mark's Library team making every effort to assist me in this current research project. An ancillary factor is the reality that St. Mark's Library, which in itself is a significant resource, at the time was the facility of one progressive Anglican diocese, and as such did not even represent the missionary training arm of the Anglican denomination, let alone the broader

65. Tippett et al., *No Continuing City*, 357.

66. Tippett et al., *No Continuing City*, 441–42.

spectrum of missionary training in Australia. In making this point, it must be understood that this statement is intended to be a comment "about" St. Mark's Library and the influence of the Tippett Research Collection, and definitely not a comment "against" St. Mark's Library. At least St. Mark's had the progressive vision to facilitate Tippett's research collection when no one else in Australia did. That fact should not be forgotten.

Contextual—SWM, USA and Church Growth Missiology

In continuing to explore factors that could have contributed to the marked decline of Tippett's influence, it is essential to investigate what was happening in the context of the Fuller School of World Mission and in church growth missiology in that era. The findings could be summarized as delegation, decline, diversion, and dissipation because of the way that differing emphases entered the SWM program under the leadership of subsequent deans. Others would no doubt use words like, maturing, development, fulfillment, and broadening, thinking that the new programs and emphases were evidence of a maturing and developing school. But from the point of view of the impact on Tippett's specializations, the former descriptors are fitting.

Some of the factors that contributed to this decline and diversion can be seen in other stories for which Kraft's *SWM/SIS at Forty* provides important insights. After Peter Wagner graduated from the School of World Mission, he had taken those insights and saw how it revolutionized his effectiveness in Bolivia. Then in "1971 . . . Wagner came on as McGavran's understudy, a second person in Church Growth . . . moving more and more over the years into a primary focus on American church growth."[67] Wagner's perspective was that, once he was based at SWM, God had placed him in the USA, so now he should use those insights to facilitate effective ministry in the USA.[68] Through this process, church growth became a victim of its own success, as it became popularized, with key concepts that would have been important to Tippett and McGavran often being diluted through this process. As well as the church growth teaching that emanated from the SWM, Fuller Theological Seminary's Doctor of Ministry program, Win Arn's Institute for American Church Growth and many other Pastor's seminars were using the church growth nomenclature. However, some of

67. Kraft, *SWM/SIS at Forty*, 112.
68. Kraft, *SWM/SIS at Forty*, 113.

them had little or no contact with the McGavran-Tippett insights of church growth.[69] The effect of this can be seen in Kraft's observations,

> "Though McGavran also gave some of his attention to church growth in America, he was disappointed that Wagner no longer gave his major attention to church growth in nonwestern contexts . . . the stream of nonwestern church growth studies published . . . at Eugene and in the early years at Fuller began to taper off."[70]

While all this was happening, opponents continued their attacks. Books continued to be written against the church growth movement, Peter Wagner reporting five such volumes within a few weeks of each other in 1978, which McIntosh saw as "at least acknowledging . . . the church growth school."[71]

To illustrate the impact of the new courses and programs on SWM, when I studied at SWM in 1978–1979, students took the fixed SWM core courses of Church Growth, History, Theology, Anthropology, and Animism and then sat their comprehensive exams. This showed the original focus of SWM (and ICG). Subsequently, under later deans, new subject areas were introduced into the School of World Missions: A Chinese ministry program under Glasser,[72] leadership plus Bible Translation under Pierson.[73] Then the spiritual dimensions of church growth became an emphasis. By the time I returned to SWM in 1983, students could elect to replace some of these core courses with either leadership or Bible translation subjects. The by-product of this was that the focus shifted from Tippett's key areas.

Kraft's summary of the impact of the leadership program was,

> . . . we hired him (J. Robert "Bobby" Clinton), . . . in . . . 1981 with Leadership as his field . . . As it turned out. Leadership soon became one of our most popular concentrations so that by 1985 . . . we . . . hire[d] a second person . . . to teach in the

69. McIntosh, *Donald A. McGavran*, 271.

70. Kraft, *SWM/SIS at Forty*, 114.

71. McIntosh, *Donald A. McGavran*, 279–80. The volumes were Newbigin, *Open Secret: Sketches for a Missionary Theology*; Verkuyl, *Contemporary Missiology*; The Trinity Forum (Olson 1978); The Other Side (Crass 1978) and The Christian Ministry (Armstrong 1978).

72. Kraft, *SWM/SIS at Forty*, 166.

73. Kraft, *SWM/SIS at Forty*, 163.

leadership area . . . students we attract either are, or expect . . . to be leaders.[74]

As a result, "Church growth (at SWM) became just one of five core curriculums . . . By the mid-1980s church growth could no longer be viewed as the integrating force in the curriculum. With McGavran's retirement, Wagner became the sole professor of church growth on the faculty."[75] Increasingly, those looking specifically to SWM and church growth as their point of reference inadvertently found that they were not looking at Tippett's insights as reference points for their reflection or action. Kraft devotes a whole section of his book *SWM/SIS at Forty* to describe and critique this very phenomenon.[76] He identifies the significant focus that resulted from only having the core courses of Church Growth, Theology of Mission, Anthropology, Animism, and History. At the same time, he also acknowledged the strengths that have resulted from the expansion of faculty, from seven faculty in 1976 to twenty four in 2004. The expanded faculty provided offerings in Leadership, Islamics, Urban Mission, Translation, Spiritual Dynamics, Communication, Ethnomusicology, Mission to Contemporary Culture, Distance Learning, Children at Risk,[77] etc. With the breadth of the perspectives and experience these specialists bring, he also cautions against dissipation, and offers practical suggestions.

CONCLUSION

Having documented and analyzed the range of factors that contributed to the sudden decline of Tippett's influence, it is evident that there were many factors that contributed to that decline that were not directly related to the question of whether his insights were in themselves, relevant and significant. Therefore, the door is open for this study to critically analyze his insights, interfaced with the writings of other scholars. This will facilitate an evaluation of the significance of his insights for mission, be it field focused or in the academy.

In concluding this section of Tippett's life story, his own evaluation at the beginning of this chapter of his contribution to missiology for the postcolonial era included theories, research methods and models with which to

74. Kraft, *SWM/SIS at Forty*, 156–57.

75. McIntosh, *Donald A. McGavran*, 303.

76. Kraft, *SWM/SIS at Forty*, 260–80.

77. Kraft, *SWM/SIS at Forty*, 264.

focus evangelism and pastoral care, all of this with the aid of anthropology.[78] As he continues reflecting,

> this, I think, was my greatest contribution to post-colonial missiology. I was able to harness for Christian mission a century of the history and developing research method and the discovered principles of anthropology . . . I put the biblical models into anthropological terms without changing them and showed that missiology was both a theological and scientific discipline . . . That I have tried to do. To that end I have exhausted my physical and mental energies.[79]

So the world Alan Tippett left behind was very different from the world he was born into in so many ways as was the world of mission that he left behind significantly different than the world of mission he himself entered in 1941. As will be evident in this volume, Tippett himself was influential in a number of those changes. Tippett didn't hesitate to suggest that the future of missiology would need to be different due to the changes in the world situation[80] or what would be important for the future of missiology.[81] In this study of Alan Tippett, it will be beneficial to first of all understand his insights, and, coming from those perspectives, to be able to see the contribution his insights made to Great-Commission-focused mission.

78. Tippett et al., *No Continuing City*, 428.

79. Tippett et al., *No Continuing City*, 429.

80. Tippett et al., *No Continuing City*, 525.

81. Tippett et al., *No Continuing City*, 483–84, 517.

5

The Basis of Alan Tippett's Theology of Mission

But if you really breathe the spirit of the Saga of Jesus you do not come up with a religious system. Christian mission is bringing people face to face with a Person, and what emerges is a fellowship group of disciples around their Leader. This divine Person receives the worship of men— the wise men at the beginning (Mt 2:11), and the disciples at the end (Mt 28:17)—which would be contrary to Scripture itself internally, unless Jesus was indeed the Lord, and Divine Son, as the Spirit certifies (Mt 3:16–17).[1]

THE PREVIOUS CHAPTERS EXAMINED Alan Tippett's life story and his life themes as distilled from that life story. This chapter will analyze the first two of Tippett's life themes in detail, namely, the centrality of a relationship with God and the centrality of the church. In so doing, it will establish the basis of his theology of mission.

Advocates for the priority of the fulfillment of the Great Commission such as Tippett, recognize how central a relationship with God is to God's own purposes. Tippett held that a relationship with God is available through Christ and that this is the only way of salvation. Furthermore, the Bible as the word of God needed to be read contextually for maximum communication and understanding. Through prioritizing the Great Commission, others can be brought into this relationship with God.

1. Tippett, *Jesus Documents*, 57–58.

Additionally, Tippett's focus on the centrality of the church is evident in his writings. His interest in the nature, function, theology, and practice of the church is foundational to his missiology, and is in fact foundational to who he was. He saw: the nature of the church as Jesus' plan for mission; that the nature of the church caused it to grow; the theological basis of the church as indigenous; and that the practical outworking of mission is through evangelism and church planting. Through this process, it will be demonstrated that the concepts related to these two life themes provide the basis for Tippett's theology of mission, which thus provides the basis for his missiology, vision, and work.

THEME 1: CENTRALITY OF A RELATIONSHIP WITH GOD

Understanding Tippett's view of the importance of a relationship with God is like a heuristic device to unlock so many other aspects of his theology of mission, and in fact other aspects of his missiology as well. However, because he often assumed this relationship rather than writing about it, it is possible for a person researching Tippett to not notice this important aspect. His own personal relationship with God was very important to him, but so was his sense that others needed to have an opportunity to know about and enter into a similar relationship with God. The exclusive availability of this relationship through Jesus, the Bible as God's word conveying the information about this relationship, and the Great Commission responsibility to communicate that message to others, are all components that fit together in analyzing this first life theme.

Priority on a Relationship with God as the Goal of Mission

In Tippett's writings, as in his personal life, the centrality of a relationship with God is a primary goal of mission. According to Tippett, this relationship with God is only available through Christ and that is revealed to humanity through the Bible as the word of God. Tippett was involved in many things so that others could hear the gospel and have an opportunity to come into a relationship with God through Christ. A statement at the beginning of his autobiography written approximately fifty-five years after his conversion experience[2] illustrates well his feeling about the importance of his relationship with God:

---

2. Tippett et al., *No Continuing City*, 45, 492.

> In spite of all the "bogeys" of my boyhood and the humbugs of
> my Australian ministry the greatest thing in my life is the good-
> ness of God, his self-revelation in Jesus, the way in which the great
> Creator and Provider is also my Heavenly Father. It is in the con-
> viction that God is not dead, that His mission to sinful mankind
> continues "unto the end of the age" and that until that time we
> have His assurance of His presence with us. This is my testimony,
> the paradigm on which my life goes forward.[3]

When researching the centrality of this relationship with God in missiological literature, it is evident that many authors assume rather than state
the goal of people coming into and maintaining a relationship with God.
The means of them coming into this relationship with God is often discussed. The process of engaging communities towards this purpose is also
a frequent topic. Biblical material is similarly mined to identify God's priority for mission. So, it is interesting to notice that the specific purpose of that
mission in bringing humankind into relationship with God is not stated
so explicitly. An example of this is Gary McGee's article, "Assemblies of
God Mission Theology: A Historical Perspective,"[4] which discusses many
aspects of the Assemblies of God USA's theology of mission from their ear-
liest formal endeavours in mission after their formation in 1914 until the
last dated entry of 1985. Within all of that, there is no reference to the goal
of mission being to bring people into a relationship with God.

Salvation Only through Christ as the Foundation of Mission

By contrast to many other scholars, Tippett's statements about the exclusiveness of salvation through Christ are prolific and provide a foundation
for his more technical writing about the science of missiology. This is why
the following concept from *Verdict Theology in Missionary Theory* is so crucial, when he says,

> Not only does the Bible house the Great Commission which is the
> reason for the Christian mission, and the directives as to how the
> people of God are to go about it, but it also contains the Gospel
> message itself. The two are found together and stand with the same
> authority . . . The Gospel does not have to be made relevant. It is
> continually relevant, has been so since his resurrection and will
> continue to be so until he comes again. This means that when the

3. Tippett et al., *No Continuing City*, vi.
4. McGee, "Assemblies of God Mission Theology."

Bible makes a direct affirmation we can safely take that as true, and if we are told plainly that there is no other name under heaven whereby we may be saved, we are just not free to open the way for the theological possibility that the great religions may have other ways of salvation. *We just do not have this option* to vary our theology.[5]

In *The Jesus Documents*, Tippett further explains his view of the uniqueness of Jesus including the short and long term goals of Jesus' mission as seen in the Gospel of Matthew:

> This person (Jesus) is more than the typical hero of a typical saga, who perhaps by physical skill, remarkable insight, and under the favor of the gods, achieves great things. This Jesus is absolutely unique in his Person and his accomplishments. This special character and ministry is revealed to Joseph by the Holy Ghost before the birth of the Hero, when the name Jesus (Saviour) is specified (Mt.1:21), indicating his functional role on earth.
>
> . . . But if you really breathe the spirit of the Saga of Jesus you do not come up with a religious system. Christian mission is bringing people face to face with a Person, and what emerges is a fellowship group of disciples around their Leader. This divine Person receives the worship of men—the wise men at the beginning (Mt 2:11), and the disciples at the end (Mt 28:17)—which would be contrary to Scripture itself internally, unless Jesus was indeed the Lord, and Divine Son, as the Spirit certifies (Mt 3:16–17).[6]

At numerous other points, he refers to his understanding of salvation through Christ alone. Some samples would be: "Possessing the Philosophy of Animism for Christ" in *Crucial Issues in Missions Tomorrow*,[7] and *Verdict Theology in Missionary Theory*.[8] Tippett was adamant that the exclusiveness of salvation through Christ is central to missiological teaching.

People holding either pluralistic views or anti-Christian religious intolerance perspectives would have difficulty with Tippett's view that for any individual, a personal relationship with God is a priority, and that approaching God through faith in Jesus' sacrificial atonement is the only way that is possible. Patrick Cate's chapter, "The Uniqueness of Christ and

5. Tippett, *Verdict Theology in Missionary Theory*, xii–xvi.

6. Tippett, *Jesus Documents*, 57–58.

7. Tippett, "Possessing the Philosophy of Animism," 126.

8. Tippett, *Verdict Theology in Missionary Theory*, 17–24, 32–33.

Missions"[9] in *The Centrality of Christ in Contemporary Missions*[10] uses the terms exclusivism, inclusivism, and universalism to describe three positions that are common in Christian circles relating to whether salvation is available by any means other than through Christ.[11] While dividing the perspectives of all Christians into just three categories denotes a level of naivety, the real situation being much more nuanced than that, he does make the point over and over again that Christ is the only means of salvation. To emphasize this further, he also draws on the insights of a list of scholars, e.g. John Piper, Ronald Nash, R. C. Sproul, and Carl F. H. Henry.[12] If limited to Cate's three categories, Tippett would be more aligned with his exclusiveness category.

Tippett's view then appears to be in contrast with the perspectives of some well-known authors from the current era, such as Stephen Bevans, who, in *Models of Contextual Theology* writes "Jesus may not be the exclusive way by which men and women can encounter God . . . but Jesus is, to use the famous phrase of Edward Schillebeeckx, 'the sacrament of the encounter with God,'"[13] thus representing a post-Vatican II view of Catholic theology. In doing so, he includes a footnote referring to a number of authors in interaction with the view he presented.[14] Pinnock's discussion of "pagan believers" while examining the exclusive Christocentric way of salvation in *A Wideness in God's Mercy: The Finality of Jesus Christ in a World of Religions*[15] and his chapter on "Hope for the Unevangelized" would be important in this discussion. Tippett's personal and missiological view would have been uncomfortable with an extreme application of some of these positions, as they negate the need for the vital foundation of salvation through Christ. Paul Knitter's view sees interreligious dialog as a primary goal, which leads to his theocentric model, around which, other beliefs must adjust. For Knitter, "The problem . . . hinge[s] on . . . the claim for the superiority and normativity of Jesus Christ."[16] From reading Tippett on this subject, one could assume that Tippett would have a different

9. Cate, "Uniqueness of Christ and Missions."

10. Barnett and Pocock, *Centrality of Christ*.

11. Cate, "Uniqueness of Christ and Missions," 44.

12. Cate, "Uniqueness of Christ and Missions," 44.

13. Bevans, *Models of Contextual Theology*, 12.

14. Bevans, *Models of Contextual Theology*, 149n46.

15. Pinnock, *Wideness in God's Mercy*.

16. Knitter, *No Other Name?*, xiii.

view of the hinge of the problem. In contrast, the conclusions of Malcolm McVeigh's article, "The Fate of Those Who Have Not Heard? It Depends"[17] surveys in a cryptic way the views of Harold Lindsell, Donald McGavran, J. Herbert Kane and Norman Anderson to see their view of the eternal situation for those who have not heard the gospel. Lindsell considers not hearing the gospel as having the same eternal result as not receiving the gospel once heard. McGavran's view is similar. Yet for those who, through no fault of their own have not heard, McGavran suggests that because God is sovereign, he can do whatever he chooses to do. But McGavran makes the clear point that if this is on God's agenda, it is not revealed in scripture. Kane, thinking of those who have not heard the gospel points to the light of God in creation, in providence, and in conscience. He then suggests that judgement will depend on the degree of light the person has. Jews will be judged by the light of the law, heathen by the light of conscience, and those who have heard the gospel will be judged by the light of the gospel. Yet he points out that most do not live by the light of the revelation they have, therefore even Cornelius was unsaved before Peter presented the gospel to him. Anderson highlights God's self-disclosure in Jesus as not being just an epiphany. In contrasting the other types of revelation that are recorded in the Old Testament, he describes the contrast as them seeing the shadow of an image, compared with those who have heard the gospel seeing God's revelation face to face. Considering the Old Testament revelation, people don't live up to the light they have. Knowing Tippett's approach of reading scripture contextually, it would be meaningful if he was here to interact with these positions directly. From reading Tippett, I feel he would hold a position similar to Anderson, while strongly maintaining that the only way of giving those who have not heard the gospel a real hope of salvation is to take the gospel to them as effectively and as quickly as possible.

The Bible as the Word of God Providing a Contextualized Framework for Mission

Tippett's view of the Bible as the word of God can be represented in two aspects. First, using interpretive tools at his disposal, he endeavoured to read the Bible contextually so as to understand its meaning to the fullest possible extent. From that position, he treated God's word as a framework for life and ministry which was fundamental to his missiology. The second

---

17. McVeigh, "Fate of Those."

aspect was his understanding that the Bible was equally applicable to all other people in all other cultures, hence his efforts to make the Bible understandable to those of other cultures. An example of this would be the Fijian language pastoral publishing program that he was responsible for in Fiji. At the same time, he became aware that he could also learn biblical interpretation from the Fijians, as aspects of their culture were closer to biblical cultures, which they had been able to capitalize on. Tippett describes one of his early experiences of this as,

> What I discovered that week was this other world of adult people who had taken over the Gospel and translated it into terms of their own lifestyle, and when I heard its songs and rhythms, and ceremonials, its prayer and praise, I suddenly found myself in the Old Testament. So the transformation of my view of both the Old Testament and the Fijian worldview began at Tuvu, Bemana in the Nasaucoko Circuit section of my first Fijian appointment.[18]

The personal phenomenon that Tippett describes here is something that Randolph Richards and Brandon O'Brien describe in *Misreading Scripture with Western Eyes: Removing Cultural Blinders to Better Understand the Bible*[19] as a benefit that all Christians can experience cross-culturally. Tippett's ongoing engagement with seeing the Bible illuminated in this way is further illustrated in his writings, such as *Verdict Theology in Missionary Theory*[20] and *Introduction to Missiology*.[21]

Furthermore, the importance of the Bible as the word of God to Tippett is evident by the frequent references to scripture in his missiological writing as well as the fact that he wrote six book length volumes that expound on biblical and theological themes. These were "His Mission and Ours,"[22] *Church Growth and the Word of God; the Biblical Basis of the Church Growth Viewpoint*,[23] "Theological Encounters,"[24] *Verdict Theology in Missionary Theory*,[25] *The Jesus Documents* (first written in 1975),[26] and

18. Tippett et al., *No Continuing City*, 130.

19. Richards and O'Brien, *Misreading Scripture with Western Eyes*.

20. Tippett, *Verdict Theology in Missionary Theory*, xi, 177.

21. Tippett, *Introduction to Missiology*, 11, 14–15, 62, 241–42.

22. Tippett, "His Mission and Ours."

23. Tippett, *Church Growth and the Word*.

24. Tippett, "Theological Encounters."

25. Tippett, *Verdict Theology in Missionary Theory*.

26. Tippett, *Jesus Documents*.

The Deep-Sea Canoe: The Story of Third World Missionaries in the South Pacific.[27] This volume of writing underscores the importance of the Bible as foundational to his missiology and his personal life.

When it came to the importance and interpretation of the Bible he regarded himself as a conservative, but saw a clear distinction between being a conservative and a "literalist." This is seen in how he and McGavran saw their target audience in the Church Growth school, "We were not disposed to battle with the extreme liberals who rejected biblical authority, or at the opposite pole with the extreme fundamentalists who were biblical literalists."[28] Tippett's view was that scripture had to be interpreted in its context so as to gain a clear understanding of the biblical message. With his knowledge of New Testament Greek and his understanding of history, anthropology, and ethnohistory, he was well positioned to develop those contextual understandings as he needed them. In another context Tippett also makes a finer distinction to describe himself and some of the church growth scholars as "contextualists," however he did not put McGavran in this category.[29] In *Verdict Theology*, he articulates the internal and external principles he used;

> First there is a presupposition about the use of the Bible itself. The Bible is accepted as the word of God to man, the norm for discussion, and particular stress is laid on direct statements that do not need interpretation. Normally texts are not extracted from their context, unless they express some generalization which seems to be incontestable . . . I do not accept the 'parallelistic' procedure of many writers in the theory of mission, who seemed to me to build their theology on the "needs of the world" as they see them, and seek for some biblical idea that falls in line, regardless of the whole context from which they have extracted their material. I do not regard this as biblical theology . . . Therefore I take the Bible as it is, at the risk of being described as simplistic and naive. I differentiate biblical and "biblicoid" theology.[30]

This contextual approach to the interpretation of scripture is again seen clearly as he outlines his approach to each of the four Gospels in *The Jesus Documents*,

27. Tippett, *Deep-Sea Canoe*.
28. Tippett et al., *No Continuing City*, 278.
29. Tippett et al., *No Continuing City*, 475.
30. Tippett, *Verdict Theology in Missionary Theory*, xi.

> But the significant common points in the gospels are not merely
> formal and literary—they are, (1) the person of Jesus, (2) the eccle-
> siological and missionary intention of Jesus, and (3) his message.
> Each gospel writer has dealt with these in quite his own way.[31]

While many examples of agreement or disagreement could be cited, the
opening chapter of Arthur Glasser's, book *Kingdom and Mission*, entitled
"Revelation and Scripture: A Discussion of Presuppositions" succinctly
summarizes the issues. He recognizes the new data and perspectives on the
Bible that critical scholarship contributes, yet he states a foundation of his
whole book as being,

> The Bible—both Old and New Testaments—is the authoritative
> Word of God . . . this indicates our determination to focus atten-
> tion on the actual canonical text. This is the text that has been
> received and used as the authoritative Scripture—and treasured as
> such—by the community of faith.[32]

While Tippett was obviously aware that others held views that differed
from his own, gathering his own internal evidence while being bolstered by
the views of others, he held the position that contextualization of the word
of God was a fundamental key to successful mission and was foundational
to his theology of mission.

Priority of the Great Commission as the Fulfillment of Mission

Within his understanding of scripture, Tippett saw a biblical priority for
the fulfillment of the Great Commission,[33] in that "the Great Commission
has never been cancelled, and the Gospel has not been modified."[34] He saw
the responsibility of fulfillment of the Great Commission as primarily beginning with the proclamation of the Gospel of Jesus as the only way of
salvation.[35] Additionally, the person proclaiming that message should seek
a verdict for Christ from among those with whom the gospel was communicated. Those who respond should be formed into Christian churches
made up of and led by those so reached, while enabling those churches,

31. Tippett, *Jesus Documents*, 4.

32. Glasser, "Kingdom and Mission," 13.

33. Tippett, *Church Growth and the Word*, 8; Tippett, *Introduction to Missiology*, 4;
Tippett et al., *No Continuing City*, 318.

34. Tippett, "Parallaxis in Missiology," 95.

35. Tippett, "Possessing the Philosophy of Animism," 126.

over time, to be able to reach out to their own communities and beyond in evangelism and service.[36]

In "His Mission and Ours,"[37] his depth of feeling regarding the priority of the Great Commission is apparent as he explains,

> A few years ago a certain Commission on Ministerial Training published a text-book for ministerial students on the Christian World Mission, a symposium of experts. It was more concerned with modern aspects than with the Biblical roots. The article on Jesus suggested the universal Gospel was not at all clear in his preaching, and the passages for study left one uncertain. It suggested that Jesus' sense of world mission was indirect, and that it lay, not in his statements about it but in his conception of God, and his readiness to take sides with the under-privileged. Though he made it inevitable, he did not direct it.[38]

Tippett's response was to spend two hours before breakfast each day, over a twelve-month period, working over the four Gospels in Greek, using critical methods that he had developed for himself. This was despite his involvement in the busy program of the training institution at Davuilevu in Fiji at the time. He describes his analytical, grammatical, and deductive process as,

> I first considered the clusters of words related to the idea of mission—the sending forth, the witness-bearing, the preaching the gospel, the teaching, and so forth. I examined every sentence using these in noun, verb, [and] adjectival form. I eliminated the manifestly secular cases, and then I eliminated the cases of use by the evangelist, until I was left with a residue of the words regarded as Jesus own utterances. In each of these I worked on the context of passage and sentence to get as close as I could to what Jesus said and meant.[39]

36. Tippett, *Verdict Theology in Missionary Theory*, 76, 166; Tippett, *Introduction to Missiology*, 66–70.

37. Tippett, "His Mission and Ours."

38. Tippett, "His Mission and Ours," viii.

39. Tippett et al., *No Continuing City*, 261.

His conclusion was in sharp contrast to the "unnamed document" that stimulated his research, which Dundon[40] identifies as being William Anderson's *Christian World Mission*.[41] As Tippett says,

> The viewpoint of *His Mission and Ours* is quite different. I believe Jesus used a whole terminology of Mission, which reveals a clear universal Gospel. While it is quite true that this terminology was much developed by the early Church and by men like the Apostle Paul, its roots come from Jesus Himself; and indeed go back beyond Jesus to the Prophetic Tradition of Israel . . . Furthermore, as Jesus interpreted his Mission to mankind in terms of Prophecy, so he interpreted our Mission in terms of his own (John 17.16).[42]

This volume is labourious reading with compelling arguments advocating involvement in seeing the Great Commission fulfilled,[43] concluding with the statement, "from the human side, ultimately the Christian Mission becomes personal and individual . . . a Fellowship of surrendered wills, each knowing, as John Chrysostom put it, that Christ is really not valued at all unless he is valued above all."[44] One question the reader is left with is why did Tippett put that much time and effort into this volume without ensuring it was published? The answer, it seems, is twofold: first, as demonstrated in the theme of this section, he felt so strongly about the priority of the Great Commission that he had to settle the issue for himself and for others through this research and writing. As he summarized it in *No Continuing City*, "I had written up my . . . theology of mission in . . . 'His Mission and Ours.'"[45] Second, once it was complete, he did offer the manuscript to Epworth Press for publication, however it was rejected.[46]

This topic has stimulated major debate in both church and missiological circles, so among Tippett's "friends" it was not difficult to find those who agreed with his priority. His most outspoken friend is McGavran, who, in a 1968 article, used the following biblical references as a short list to support his Great Commission position: Matthew 28:19, Romans 1:5, John 14:6,

---

40. Dundon, "Raicakacaka," 135n74.
41. Anderson, *Christian World Mission*.
42. Tippett, "His Mission and Ours," viii.
43. Tippett, "His Mission and Ours," 22.
44. Tippett, "His Mission and Ours," 99.
45. Tippett et al., *No Continuing City*, 419.
46. Dundon, "Raicakacaka," 135.

Acts 4:12, 1 John 5:12, Romans 10:11–15, and 2 Corinthians 5:18–21. In the same article, he summarizes the situation as,

> Vatican II affirms that the purpose of mission is to win the world for Christ and His Church. Vatican II makes vigorous pronouncements on social justice, peace and other duties of the Christian and the Church, but does not substitute these for mission—for the redemption of sinful, unbelieving men. In the Protestant wing of the Church, too, an increasing number are turning from the comfortable doctrine that everything the Church ought to do outside her four walls is mission, and are concentrating their attention on the redemption of the two billion men and women who owe no allegiance whatever to Jesus Christ, and do not even know His name.[47]

Aimed to goad his World Council of Churches colleagues to Great-Commission-focused action, this is, in that sense, something that Tippett would have agreed with. However, the polemic nature of this statement is identified by David Bosch as being a significant breaking point in McGavran's relationship with the WCC.

> I believe Dr. McGavran was right when he charged the WCC for neglecting what you might call the "evangelistic mandate." But I would like to plead for a larger and broader historical perspective . . . if, in a given moment, the other does not see things the way I see them?[48]

Victor Hayward's fascinating article, "Call to Witness: But What Kind of Witness?"[49] was written in response to Robert Strachan's article regarding "Evangelism in Depth" in Latin America. Hayward uses many statements that align with those used by Tippett, such as, "All church members have to be concerned with the evangelization of the world. And the churches themselves, not missionaries from outside, must be the basic agency of mission."[50] As he proceeds however, his focus moves away from the primary need to call individuals to faith, saying instead that "The objective of witness is all creation, or all the nations. Surely this indicates that the Gospel is addressed, not to isolated individuals here and there, but essentially to men

---

47. McGavran, "Church Growth Strategy Continued," 337.
48. Bosch, "Church Growh Missiology," 14.
49. Hayward, "Call to Witness,"
50. Hayward, "Call to Witness," 201.

in their social and corporate structures of existence."[51] This then leads him to advocate social involvement because, to Hayward, that would indicate that the world is correctly our focus rather than the church. If that were done, then church members who are concerned for their societies would be able to stay in their churches while expressing their concerns.

By contrast with Hayward, Ralph Winter, in a similar way to Tippett, maintained that the church should hold the Great Commission as a central position in its activities, however it is crucial to see how this was outworked through their different perspectives. The special edition of "Mission Frontiers" that was issued soon after Winter's death in 2009 included Greg Parson's article that described the growing divergence between Winter and the team at the Fuller School of World Mission. In the decade that Winter was at the School of World Mission, the team including Tippett helped 1,000 missionaries who were returning from the field to do research into how to be more effective in the fields to which they were deployed. The teaching of the SWM team, combined with the research and writing of their students was aimed at seeing the Great Commission fulfilled. Winter however was asking a different question: As described by Parsons,

> But as Winter heard about . . . those 1,000 missionaries, he began to see a pattern. In Winter's classic style, he would say things like, "None of these missionaries came back from fields where no missionaries had gone." In other words, there were "fields" from which no missionaries could return, because none had been sent.[52]

Identifying and addressing this unmet need was then the thrust of the paper that Winter presented at the International Congress on World Evangelization at Lausanne, Switzerland in 1974 entitled "The Highest Priority: Cross-Cultural Evangelism,"[53] now known as "The New Macedonia: A Revolutionary New Era in Mission Begins."[54] Winter's concern to see the Great Commission fulfilled led him to the formation of the U.S. Centre for World Mission, now Frontier Ventures, an influential multifaceted institution focused on seeing the Great Commission fulfilled amongst the unreached, least-reached, most neglected people groups of the world.[55] It is obvious that Tippett and Winter shared a common concern to see the Great

---

51. Hayward, "Call to Witness," 207.

52. Parsons, "Celebrating the Work of God," 9.

53. Douglas, *Let the Earth Hear*, 226–41.

54. Winter et al., *Perspectives on the World*, 347–60.

55. Kraft, *SWM/SIS at Forty*, 133.

Commission fulfilled, even though their responses to this concern were expressed in quite different ways.

Tippett's life theme of the centrality of a relationship with God is encapsulated in his teaching that a relationship with God is the goal of mission, with salvation through Christ alone as its foundation. The contextualization of the Bible as the word of God provides the framework for this task. Advocates for the priority of the fulfillment of the Great Commission, such as Tippett, recognize how central a relationship with God is to God's own purposes.

THEME 2: CENTRALITY OF THE CHURCH

Tippett's interest in the nature, function, theology, and practice of the church is foundational to his missiology, in fact, foundational to who he was. As he states it, "my whole vision of the world as my field of service and witness springs from the encounters I have had with my Lord within the Church, its fellowship, its instruction, and its means of grace."[56] Therefore the centrality of the church in his thinking, planning, and strategizing can be identified as another one of Tippett's "three sermons," and as such, helps to understand him and his written material. The centrality of the church for Tippett was not only theoretically central. It was theologically central. Not only was it theologically central, but it was practically central. Furthermore, not only was it practically central from the etic point of view of the missionary church planter or an outside observer, but it was emically central in every way to the life and culture of the society in which it was planted. For Tippett, this was not just an idealist's dream. He had observed the places where this had been achieved to a significant degree, and the places where it had not. He gave his life to equip people to see these grand goals achieved.

The Individual and Corporate Nature of the Church as Jesus' Plan for Mission

In this section, the nature and essence of the church will be clarified. This includes its internal and external functions as well as the individual and corporate aspects of the church. For Tippett, the centrality of the church in his thinking comes directly from his understanding that the intention of Jesus was to leave the church on earth embroyonically in the loyal group of his disciples in fellowship with each other and in fellowship with him by the

---

56. Tippett, *Verdict Theology in Missionary Theory*, 53.

Spirit.[57] The church as his body was to continue to grow from there. Tippett's own process of discovery can be summarized from comments in his autobiography *No Continuing City* relating to his experience in his first parish at Manangatang, Victoria, Australia. As he entered pastoral ministry, he came to see that the institutional church was not related as it should be to the role of the body of Christ in the world. He felt this problem began with inadequate ministry training, where the focus, while limited, was primarily on the sacramental nature of the church. That issue came from a lack of a doctrinal perspective of the church as the body of Christ in the world. In church life, he saw that there was a lack of a sense of the church being a called out group of people and a lack of understanding of the church being a group of people called together.[58] In summary, he lamented that in his experience in Manangatang he learned "that being loyal to one's Church and loyal to one's Lord were not necessarily the same thing. That realization came as a shock."[59]

The corporate nature of the church was a key area of Tippett's understanding. In *The Jesus Documents* while discussing Matthew's Gospel as the "Saga of Jesus," he says, "The Christian mission not only needs the Key Personality, who is the Mediator of salvation (1:21) and the Divine Presence in our midst (1:23), but it requires also the loyal fellowship group—call it what you will, a band of disciples or the Church."[60] This insight was further fueled as he read Bowman's book, *The Intention of Jesus* (1943).[61] Suddenly the difference between the form and the idea of the church became clear for him. He states the result for him as, "I saw the corporate aspect of Christian mission." For Tippett, this occurred appropriately as he saw, "the Church as the body of Christ, speaking his mind, ministering his love, and engaging in his encounters in the world." This brought him to another resounding conclusion, that, "There cannot be a Christian mission without the emerging fellowship group. This is a corporate business. Mission means planting

57. Tippett, *Jesus Documents*, 61.

58. Tippett et al., *No Continuing City*, 70.

59. Tippett et al., *No Continuing City*, 71.

60. Tippett used the convention of capitalizing the word "Church" to indicate the church universal. When quoting from Tippett his convention will be followed. Otherwise, the more contemporary convention will be used, where the capitalized word "Church" will be used to refer to a specific church or denomination, e.g. the "Church of God" movement while the church universal will not be capitalized. See Tippett, *Jesus Documents*, 61.

61. Bowman, *Intention of Jesus*.

fellowships."[62] As time went on, through his informal and formal involvement with anthropology, his understanding of the significance of the group was enhanced. As this impacted his thinking about the nature of the church more and more deeply, it shaped much of Tippett's research, writing and practice.

He also documents his feelings about the importance of the doctrine of the church late in his career when, in his autobiography he says,

> If I was to continue in theology I felt it ought to be in the doctrine of the Church, . . . The immediately important issue for me was now working out the contours of the new missiology for post-colonial times, and that did require a better theology of the Church.[63]

In 1987, Arthur Glasser invited David Bosch to present an evaluation of the Fuller School of World Mission to their faculty, which Bosch published in *Missionalia* as "Church Growth Missiology." In that paper, Bosch reported, "I am pleased to learn . . . that the SWM is constantly strengthening its theological undergirding . . . I hope there will be even more . . . particularly in the area of ecclesiology."[64] Tippett's priority on ecclesiology in missiology is something that Bosch also emphasized, but was possibly not conversant with Tippett's interest and research. In fact, Tippett was putting this into practice by writing his "Let the Church be the Church: Ten Basic Theological Studies to Bring the Bible to Bear on the Mission of the Church at Home and Overseas" in 1988, up to a few months before he passed away.[65] St. Mark's Library had requested this volume and planned to publish it, however the final edit and publication did not eventuate.

In Tippett's editorial article "Florescence of the Fellowship" in *Missiology*,[66] while reflecting on the nature of the church, he uses the complex and abstract analogy of florescence in both flora (inflorescence—coming into flower) and chemistry (efflorescence—process of crystallization) to describe key elements of the nature of the church. He uses a series of headings to reflect on the confluence and significance that is the individual within the church and the church comprised of individuals.[67] Through

62. Tippett, *Jesus Documents*, 61.

63. Tippett et al., *No Continuing City*, 329.

64. Bosch, "Church Growh Missiology," 21.

65. Tippett, "Let the Church Be."

66. Tippett, "Florescence of the Fellowship," 131–41.

67. Tippett, "Florescence of the Fellowship," 133.

those headings he points out that experiencing the true life of the church: is a spiritual experience which is focused on worship; places demands on rigorous commitment and a high moral life while positioning the participant for fellowship in suffering and fellowship in service.[68] Meantime, all of this puts the individual (*koinonoi*) and the gathered church (*koinonia*) under an obligation for world mission. The local congregation is a microcosm of Paul's concept of the cosmic *koinonia*.[69] As such they have a part to play in God's purpose of challenging all humans with the Lordship of Christ. This is implemented by concentrating the forces of,

> the service ministry (*diakonia*), the loyalty of the *koinonoi*, the spiritual resources (the fellowship of the Son, the Holy Spirit, and the Gospel), the ritual of worship (especially the fellowship of the body and blood), the life of holiness and the missionary program of the outreaching Church.[70]

So, the local and cosmic *koinonia*, having burst into flower by the life force operating within it, has the resources to maintain the spiritual process and also has the "capacity to reach from Jew to Gentile,[71] and open their spiritual resources to be shared by the nations (Rom 15:27)."[72] The complexity of this article and its significant implications are hardly what one would expect in an editorial article in a missiological journal, however it illustrates his perspective of the priority of the church.

Reflecting on the nature of the church from a different perspective, Susan Liubinskas, in her article, "The Body of Christ in Mission: Paul's Ecclesiology and the Role of the Church in Mission"[73] analyzes a related mission question from the writings of Paul. That is, whether all Christians and all churches have a role in mission the way the Great Commission is spoken of, or whether these are distinct roles. She does this by contrasting views of biblical scholars, where two distinct schools of thought can be discerned. The metaphor she explores in depth to arrive at her conclusion is "the church as the Body of Christ" in Paul's writings.[74] She finds first of all that this metaphor is used by Paul with implications for the individual

68. Tippett, "Florescence of the Fellowship," 133.

69. Tippett, "Florescence of the Fellowship," 138.

70. Tippett, "Florescence of the Fellowship," 139.

71. Yoder Neufeld, "Koinōnia," 340.

72. Tippett, "Florescence of the Fellowship," 136–39.

73. Liubinskas, "Body of Christ in Mission," 406–10.

74. Liubinskas, "Body of Christ in Mission," 404–5.

and for the corporate body of the church. Then from Ephesians 4:11 she points out that because the gifts of apostles and evangelists, those who would primarily reach outside the church are included with prophets and teachers, those who would minister primarily amongst existing members, the church as the body of Christ, both corporately and individually by its nature is involved in mission. Although arriving at her conclusion by a method different than Tippett's, the convergence on the theme of the body of Christ and the convergence of her conclusion with Tippett is worth noting, seeing this was such an important component in Tippett's ecclesiology.

Tippett emphasizes the church as the plan of Jesus, giving the impression that, if ministry is being fulfilled, then churches will be the result. While continuing to reflect on that dimension, it is worth noticing Jonathan Campbell's chapter entitled "Mission in Postmodern Contexts." He is writing about the deconstructionist approaches of postmodernism, in Edgar J. Elliston's *Teaching Them Obedience in all Things: Equipping for the 21st Century*.[75] As he documents the deconstruction of a cultural view of the church and religion, one thing emerges organically, namely the church itself. In describing a key stage in the development of a church he had planted, he said, "The issue was . . . whether we could trust the Holy Spirit to guide a group of believers in community with one another. If they were functioning as churches, why not let them be churches? . . . The issue here was really about control."[76]

Growth as an Expression of the Nature of the Church

Tippett's missiological teachings also make it clear that to him the growth of the church occurs dynamically because of the nature of the church. Hence, while the term "church growth" arising out of the Institute of Church Growth, in both the Oregon and Fuller SWM eras, was the source of much heated academic debate, the church is something Tippett passionately believed in as God's idea. As such, the church, in its transformed state, is revealed in scripture as the bride of Christ of the book of Revelation.[77] Tippett saw the growth of the church as something that every Christian should give their utmost to see fulfilled. It is also why he was in no way comfortable with the popular concept that the only thing that Christians,

75. Elliston, *Teaching Them Obedience*.

76. Campbell, "Mission in Postmodern Contexts," 190–91.

77. Tippett, *Church Growth and the Word*, 60, 78; Tippett, *Verdict Theology in Missionary Theory*, 149–50.

ministers, and missionaries had to do was to be "faithful" where they were. That philosophy was used as an excuse to justify the placement of ministries when there was limited church growth. However, for Tippett, to the best of their ability, they needed to be effective.[78] It was to this end that he continued to research and write in order to make resources available for this to happen.

However, in using the term church growth, Tippett was not referring to denominational expansion—"denominational extensionism" to use his term.[79] This was the allegation of some critics of the church growth emphasis,[80] assuming that the growth they talked about was not new growth of the church, but at best was simply a means of promoting one's own denomination, or even transferring members from another denomination. Tippett counters this aspersion with the fact that the Institute of Church Growth had fourteen denominations represented while the School of World Mission had seventy.[81] He was also quick to refute the allegation, because he saw attempts at denominational expansion as potentially hampering the development of indigenous churches. When foreign ways, structures, etc. the essence of a foreign denomination, were unnecessarily forced on the new converts, their own ability to be a valid local expression of the body of Christ would potentially be inhibited. The point is, even positive denominational distinctives were unique aspects of the local expression of Christianity for another place and another time. Therefore, they are not necessarily suited to this new location or new era in which the church is being planted.[82] That is why Tippett's view was that denominational points of focus needed to be evaluated for their appropriateness to the new culture prior to introduction.[83]

78. Tippett, *Church Growth and the Word*, 40–42; Tippett, *Verdict Theology in Missionary Theory*, 139, 42–43, 51.

79. Tippett et al., *No Continuing City*, 279.

80. Tippett, "Holy Spirit and Responsive Populations," 79; Tippett, *Introduction to Missiology*, 71.

81. Tippett et al., *No Continuing City*, 283; Tippett, *Introduction to Missiology*, 71.

82. Tippett, *Peoples of Southwest Ethiopia*, 287; Tippett, *Verdict Theology in Missionary Theory*, 156; Tippett, *Introduction to Missiology*, 334–35.

83. Tippett, *Verdict Theology in Missionary Theory*, 146.

CASE STUDIES ABOUT CHURCH GROWTH

In contrast to Tippett's view that the church universal and individual churches should grow, Jay Childs' article in *Leadership Journal*,[84] aims to make the point that his no longer growing church of 1,500 people was normal. To do so, he suggests that McGavran's emphasis on church growth had somehow started a fad in which churches in the USA were now "fixated on numerical growth."[85] Although Childs is challenging McGavran's rather than Tippett's point of view at this juncture, Tippett's perspectives are similar to McGavran's on this point. Childs' concern was that, "If churches never stopped growing—ever—they would take over whole towns."[86] Childs draws on Bishop Lesslie Newbigin's[87] perspectives to strengthen his point:

> Reviewing the teaching of the New Testament, one would have to say, on the one hand, there is joy in the rapid growth of the church in the earliest days, but on the other, there is no evidence that numerical growth of the church is a matter of primary concern.[88]

Having established the fact of the joy in rapid church growth, whether one argues for ongoing growth or non-growth, the argument will be an argument from silence when it comes to actual statistics provided in the biblical record. That being the case, it would be at least as valid for Newbigin and Childs to use the argument from silence to show that because the growth was continuing to grow in the same way, there was no reason to comment on it. This is an approach that was used in the New Testament in relation to regular church attendance. There was no comment about church attendance until the practice was being eroded in approximately AD 64–65, thirty years after some of those churches began, at which time the corrective teaching was documented in Hebrews 10:25. If that same approach was used in relation to the growth of the church, it could be argued that growth was still occurring and was still a reason for joy, hence there was no need to comment.

A question that Childs is not asking however, is whether this is just a USA or even a Western church phenomenon. With the largest Methodist, Presbyterian, and Assemblies of God churches in the world being in South

---

84. Childs, "Church Growth vs Church Seasons," 39–41.

85. Childs, "Church Growth vs Church Seasons," 40.

86. Childs, "Church Growth vs Church Seasons," 39–41.

87. Newbigin, *Open Secret: An Introduction.*

88. Childs, "Church Growth vs Church Seasons," 39–41.

Korea, not to mention the mega-churches of other parts of the majority world such as India, Nigeria, Philippines, bustling cities like Singapore, and countries like Ukraine, it seems that others are asking and answering the question differently to Childs. Furthermore, considering the Christian movements in many countries that continue to grow exponentially despite the persecution they suffer, one finds oneself feeling more comfortable with Tippett's view than Childs', two such examples being Iran and China. As reported by Krikor Markarian in his article "Today's Iranian Revolution: How the Mullahs Are Leading the Nation to Jesus," numbers of believers in Iran went from virtually zero in the early 1960s to over a million by 2008.[89] Similarly, church movements in China; best estimates of China's Christian population in 1948 indicate between one and one and a half million divided equally between protestants and Catholics while the *Yearbook of International Religious Demography*[90] identify the number of Christians in China in 2015 as 123,019,000.

Eddie Gibbs however provides a link between McGavran-Tippett church growth research and Childs's USA church growth concerns in his chapter, "How Appropriate is the Church Growth Paradigm in Today's Mission Contexts?"[91] published in Kraft's *Appropriate Christianity*[92] while he occupied the McGavran Chair of Church Growth at Fuller's School of Intercultural Studies (formerly SWM). His chapter was particularly focused on the church growth movement in the USA, reflecting on its strengths and weaknesses, achievements, and deficiencies. He pointed out that as church growth seminars and courses proliferated across the country, the pastors who attended often assumed that on returning home, their churches would experience growth as obstacles were removed and achievable goals for growth were established. Yet on many occasions, this was not the result. Rather than relying on local contextual research specific to each church's situation, these seminars tended to use the truncated approach of looking instead at case studies of growing churches to identify causal factors. This approach often identified leadership as a key growth factor. Gibbs observed, "This simply inflated the egos of some ambitious pastors with disastrous consequences"[93] and caused other problems as a result of "the damaging

---

89. Markarian, "Today's Iranian Revolution," 9.

90. Grim et al. "Yearbook of International Religious Demography."

91. Gibbs, "How Appropriate Is the Church?," 293–308.

92. Kraft and Gilliland, *Appropriate Christianity*.

93. Gibbs, "How Appropriate Is the Church?," 302.

consequences of empowering the incompetent. It is perilous to empower without discipling."[94] This was so different to the research based approach to church growth that came from McGavran and Tippett. This led Gibbs to reflect that "one of the major challenges is to revive the field research focus of Dr. McGavran to discover as much as we can about the progress of the Christian movement around the world, including North America."[95] From all of this, it is clear that Tippett's strong emphasis on growth as the function of the church is in response to other currents of thought being generated at the time.

The Tridimensional Nature of Growing Churches

For Tippett, not only does the church have a unique nature, but by that nature it grows in three dynamically balanced dimensions: quantitative, qualitative, and structural or organic growth. He refers to these in a number of places. For example: *The Deep-Sea Canoe: The Story of Third World Missionaries in the South Pacific*,[96] *Verdict Theology in Missionary Theory*,[97] and *Introduction to Missiology*,[98] to name a few.

Quantitative or numeric growth, according to Tippett from *Verdict Theology*, must occur both biologically, as Christian families grow biologically and as children of those families are retained in the church.[99] At the same time, churches must grow through new conversions.[100] Transfer growth must be taken note of, as existing Christians join the congregation.[101] This is a unique aspect of numeric growth that needs to be measured, so as not to be confused with or seen as a replacement for conversion growth. At the same time, numerical shrinkage must be monitored, to ensure that migration is not mistaken for nominalism or reversion, for example. Looking at the bigger picture implications of a church not having a goal of conversion growth, Tippett's research suggests that this could be a precursor to other problems as well,

94. Gibbs, "How Appropriate Is the Church?," 303.

95. Gibbs, "How Appropriate Is the Church?," 305.

96. Tippett, *Deep-Sea Canoe*, 63–64.

97. Tippett, *Verdict Theology in Missionary Theory*, 148–49.

98. Tippett, *Introduction to Missiology*, 352–53.

99. McGavran and Wagner, *Understanding Church Growth*, 71.

100. McGavran and Wagner, *Understanding Church Growth*, 72.

101. McGavran and Wagner, *Understanding Church Growth*, 72.

If a Church has no evangelical outreach it is also likely to neglect its service outreach unless it uses this as a substitute for evangelism. In the former case a congregation becomes enclosed and shut off from the world, in the latter it becomes distorted in its impact.[102]

As illustrated in Tippett's *Deep-Sea Canoe*, the second type of growth, qualitative growth, "is one that focuses on the inner life of man. He grows in faith. He develops an ethic. He lives the Christian life. He helps those in need. He witnesses to those who do not know the gospel."[103] In *Verdict Theology*, Tippett points out that the term "qualitative growth" is utilized for this second type of growth to counter the allegation that the church growth scholars were only interested in quantitative growth. The standard mechanisms utilized to facilitate this important area of growth are "Christian education, Bible study, worship, fellowship (within the group), and by witness and service (without).[104] Without qualitative growth, quantitative growth can be short lived or tends to nominalism or syncretism. Copeland's "Church Growth in Acts," while documenting the numerical statistics of Acts to emphasize his point, also highlights the qualitative dimension of growth seen in Luke's carefully structured record.[105]

From *Verdict Theology*, Tippett's description of the function of organic or structural growth as the third dimension of growth, is,

> The moment a group or society comes into being some form of organization, however simple, is required. Thus from the very start of church-planting the Church is viewed as an organism. Organic growth includes the participation and roles of persons designated for group action, the structure within which they operate, their inner relationships, and outside contacts, so that the Church may be a living organism within an environment . . . in a form suitable to the world in which it lives.[106]

Summarizing problems that were evident in the mission world of his day, Tippett argued that these three areas of growth need to be kept in balance, or the result can be "a monstrosity—paternalistic structures, foreign patterns, monolithic excesses, home church domination, enclosed congregations are

102. Tippett, *Verdict Theology in Missionary Theory*, 149.

103. Tippett, *Deep-Sea Canoe*, 63–64.

104. Tippett, *Verdict Theology in Missionary Theory*, 149.

105. Copeland, "Church Growth in Acts."

106. Tippett, *Verdict Theology in Missionary Theory*, 149–50.

different forms of distorted growth."[107] Reflecting on these points while re-capping the theme of this section, it is obvious first of all that the planting and growth of churches should be planned utilizing best practice methodologies. However, because the churches being planned and grown are only ever part of the church that Christ is building, these actions can only be implemented with an attitude of servanthood and faith. Second, when growth is not occurring in a healthy way, those involved need to similarly be aware that the health and growth or otherwise of the churches they are involved with is a reflection on the nature of the true church, of which that congregation is a small part. Once again it can be seen that the key feature resulting from the nature of churches is growth, and that in three dimensions.

The Theological Basis of the Indigenous Church

Having established the priority and foundational nature of the church along with the importance and balance of its growth, another key area of Tippett's contribution to an understanding of the church in the context of Great-Commission-focused mission is his insights on "the indigenous church." The term "indigenous church" has mostly been replaced by terms like contextualized, and more recently, culturally appropriate churches.[108] However, in this section of the study Tippett's term "indigenous church" will be used because Tippett's insights can be initially seen more clearly by using his terminology. Once understood clearly, they are more readily translatable to the contemporary terms. This section will explore the theological issues of the concept of the indigenous church while the concepts relating to the strategic factors of the indigenous church will be examined in chapter 9.

Following Tippett's usage, the term "indigenous church" in this study will refer to two different aspects in relation to churches and movements. The first can be understood by using an indigenous/exotic continuum analogy from biology,[109] comparing how well the style and structure of a new church fits within the culture in which it was planted (although the term "exotic" is not used in church studies of this kind). The underlying assumption is that the more indigenous a church is, while still accurately portray-

---

107. Tippett, *Verdict Theology in Missionary Theory*, 149.

108. Kraft and Gilliland, *Appropriate Christianity*; Kraft, *Issues in Contextualization*.

109. Terry, "Indigenous Church," 483.

ing biblical Christianity, the better representation of biblical Christianity it will be in that culture.

Tippett's emphasis on "indigenous" was always a reminder to the missionary that the language, approaches, methods, and structures selected for the new ministry environment should not be those with which the missionary himself or herself felt comfortable, rather they needed to be approaches with which the local people in that community feel at home. There is a famous quote in William Smalley's 1958 article "Cultural Implications of an Indigenous Church" that speaks to this situation: "One (of the implications of an indigenous church) is that missionaries often do not like the product. Often a truly indigenous church is a source of concern and embarrassment to the mission bodies in the area."[110] Although Tippett never refers to this article, for him to think of a missionary doing things in a way that made the missionaries feel comfortable at the expense of the people to whom they went to minister, would have smacked of "colonialism," the cultural, political, and economic consequences of which he often spoke against. Tippett believed that the end result of his recommended approach, applied effectively, is that the person hearing the gospel will gain a clear understanding of the Christian message and its applicability to himself or herself within their own cultural world.

Tippett also believed that contextualization is not something we do for other people, rather it is something they must do for and by themselves as they search the Bible for guidelines on how to be a follower of Jesus in their specific cultural, historic, political, and economic context. This would of course include a realization that they cannot save themselves and equally a realization that it is only by their acceptance of the salvation that is available to them by grace through Jesus' vicarious death on the cross that they can be saved. When this is achieved, the only stumbling block for the acceptance of the Christian message would be, as Paul termed it, the "stumbling stone" (GNB), that is, the stumbling block of accepting that salvation had to be provided by God's grace demonstrated through the cross, and accepted by human faith in that finished work (Rom 9:32–33). Whiteman highlights an aspect of this when he says,

> Another function of contextualization in mission is to offend—but only for the right reasons, not the wrong ones . . . When the Gospel is presented in word and deed, and the fellowship of believers we call the church is organized along appropriate cultural patterns,

110. Smalley, "Cultural Implications," 56.

then people will more likely be confronted with the offense of the Gospel, exposing their own sinfulness and the tendency toward evil, oppressive structures, and behavior patterns within their culture.[111]

Andrew Walls in "The Gospel as the Prisoner and Liberator of Culture" identifies the challenge of the gospel in action as,

> Along with the indigenizing principle which makes his faith a place to feel at home, the Christian inherits the pilgrim principle . . . which . . . warns him that to be faithful to Christ will put him out of step with his society.[112]

The importance of a suitably contextualized communication of the gospel is highlighted by C. René Padilla when he says, "In order for the gospel to receive an intelligent response, either positive or negative, there must be . . . communication that takes into consideration the point of contact between the message and the culture of the hearers."[113] The underlying issues here align well with the situation addressed, and the decisions made at the Jerusalem Council, as recorded in Acts 15:28–29, in which it was decided that gentiles did not have to undergo Jewish cultural conversion in order to experience spiritual conversion as followers of Jesus within their gentile context.

Mission Practice: The Body of Christ in a Needy World

Tippett's view of the church was so extensive and comprehensive that he was not unsettled by the debate of his era that pitted the evangelism, church planting focus against the service, social justice priority in mission. Nevertheless, because this was swirling around in the missiological debates, he did engage in the interaction as they related to the practice of mission. For Tippett, however, the issues related to an understanding of ecclesiology rather than that of "mission" practice. His own view was not disturbed by the debates, even though he participated in these discussions for the benefit of others.

Through Tippett's breadth of understanding of the church, he believed that, even while thinking of society's needs, which others tend to address through service and social justice programs, for him it was appropriate to

111. Whiteman, "Contextualization," 3.

112. Walls, "Gospel as the Prisoner," 98–99.

113. Padilla, *Mission between the Times*, 109.

focus on fulfilling the Great Commission in evangelism and church plant-ing as the practical outworking of mission. His summary evaluation was stated succinctly as, "the church growth ideal is to plant a Church which then fulfills the service mandate in its own country."[114] This is because to him, a well-founded local indigenous congregation and well-founded na-tional/indigenous church movement functioned as the physical body of Christ in its own community. In the same way that the incarnate Christ ministered to the physical needs of those around him, those congregations and movements would therefore recognize and seek to meet the physical and social needs of the societies in which they were planted.

Sometimes this was done with foreign assistance, but it was normally done at the initiative of that local church. In *Introduction to Missiology*, Tip-pett describes the fulfillment of this using a simple statement, "Thus is the church always involved in the world about her. Her faith and teaching are of little value unless *applied* to the world."[115] Veli-Matti Kärkkäinen makes a useful point, when he says, "It is not right to say that Pentecostals have been totally inactive with regard to social concern; it is more accurate to say that they have had a distinctive approach to solving social problems as part of their missionary enthusiasm."[116] This was written much later and written about Pentecostal missions and social justice, so evidently was not talking about Tippett's point or his context. However, observing the phenomenon that Kärkkäinen is describing, it becomes a good example of Tippett's point in action; the church ministering to social needs, but doing it in its own community and in its own way.

George Hunter's statement in the 1977 *Church Growth Bulletin* adds a perspective to Tippett's point:

> Wherever, anywhere in the world over the last 19 centuries, when the Christian movement has emphasized disciple-making, two things have happened. Generally we have made some new disciples and planted churches and generally have had a social influence out of proportion to our numbers. But, whenever the Christian mis-sion has neglected outreach for disciple-making and simply con-centrated on the other facets of Christ's work, we haven't made any disciples or planted many churches and haven't had much social influence either! Why is this the case? Our social causes will not

114. Tippett, *Verdict Theology in Missionary Theory*, 76; Tippett, "Objectives of World Mission," 1.

115. Tippett, *Introduction to Missiology*, 239; italics his.

116. Kärkkäinen, "Are Pentecostals Oblivious?"

triumph unless we have great numbers of committed Christians. It is by evangelism that we bring people into the kind of commitment and empowerment that enables them to become involved in redemptive social service and reform.[117]

Some notable perspectives relating to the practice of mission that were evident in the era when Tippett served in the USA could be summarized as: (1) ministry with a focus on evangelism, gospel proclamation and church planting as an exclusive activity, or; (2) Tippett's perspective, which was, ministry with a focus on evangelism, gospel proclamation, and church planting, through which service, social justice, and social development ministry needs would be fulfilled, or; (3) service, social justice, and social development ministry as a priority in mission activity, or; (4) service, social justice, and social development programs as stand-alone activities.[118]

It appears that there were two separate but interrelated conflicts that raged around these sometimes-polarized perspectives that related to the Institute of Church Growth team and later, the School of World Mission. First there were those who misrepresented the emphasis of the Institute of Church Growth's and the School of World Mission's church growth perspective, saying that they were not concerned about social issues. Second there were those who emphasized service and social justice ministries separate from local churches, as if they were in competition with evangelism and church planting. In response to those opposing views being presented in a lot of publications, Tippett wrote at length around this area of debate to balance what he considered to be the incorrect views of others.[119] In the volume of what he wrote, he consistently comes out in favour of "proclamation for a verdict," church planting, etc.

To understand the broader issues here, it is important to clarify some parameters relating to the discussion. When Tippett was writing about these issues, he was particularly writing about foreign mission organizations and their personnel getting engaged in relatively unreached ministry locations, where the mission organization, as a parallel structure was still in process of establishing the national church movement. In such cases, when

117. Hunter, "Multi-individual Conversion," 117–18.

118. Tippett, *Church Growth and the Word*, 56; Tippett, *Introduction to Missiology*, 68–71.

119. Tippett, *Church Growth and the Word*, 54–57; Tippett, *Verdict Theology in Missionary Theory*, 66, 75, 76, 92, 103, 111, 149, 166; Tippett, "Florescence of the Fellowship," 138–39; Tippett, "Parallaxis in Missiology," 105; Tippett, *Introduction to Missiology*, 86.

funds and personnel are procured under the promotional name of "mission," it did not seem right to Tippett that the priorities would be focused towards service and social justice programs. By contrast, for Tippett this was quite distinct from the way an existing national church congregation or movement should be functioning as the body of Christ, meeting the needs of its own community both in evangelism and in service ministries. When reading material regarding these debates, they are often fueled by misunderstanding the difference between these two phases of ministry. However, when these two phases are clearly identified, the results of utilizing this best practice approach is evident.

In contrast to Tippett's view, Bishop Lesslie Newbigin's perspective, documented in *One Body, One Gospel, One World*, recommended that Christians should not prioritize evangelism over Christian service. His statement was,

> Our Lord was sent both to preach and to be the servant of all . . . Each of these two activities has its proper dignity within the wholeness of the mission, and neither should be subordinated to the other. If service is made merely ancillary to evangelism, then deeds which should be pure acts of love and compassion become suspect as having an ulterior motive.[120]

In the close interaction between Tippett and the Institute of Church Growth and in publishing the *Church Growth Bulletin*, McGavran represented the ICG view when he challenged Newbigin's view in his article "Principles and Policies Bearing on Church Growth" in *The Church Growth Bulletin*.[121] Using points similar to Tippett's, McGavran asks, "When our Lord stretched out his hand to heal the leper, is it conceivable that He intended to heal merely the man's body?"[122] He compares this to the evangelistic program that Jesus sent his disciples on, telling them "to fear not him who can kill the body, but him who can throw body and soul into hell" (Matt 10:28). McGavran similarly assumes from Jesus' declaration "He who believes in me has eternal life; He who does not obey me shall not see life, but the wrath of God rests on him" (John 3:36), that Jesus intended both physical healing for "the leper" and also the goal of eternal life. McGavran sees in Jesus' ministry, not two separate activities (service and evangelism),

120. Newbigin, *One Body, One Gospel*, 22

121. McGavran, "Principles and Policies," 153.

122. McGavran, "Principles and Policies," 153.

each with its own proper dignity, each of equal important [*sic*] with the other. In Him, we see that the salvation of the soul always had priority . . . Bishop Newbigin's statement begs the question. It makes "evangelistic strategy" something not quite "pure," something which defiles the "pure" act of love and compassion.[123]

While pointing out that this reflects the thinking of many, McGavran is concerned that this view makes it seem that to aim for a person to convert to faith in Christ is somehow a selfish act. He disagrees with this view on the basis that our values must be modeled on those of our Lord. As he states the priorities, "the Christian today must within himself always think, 'education, literacy, housing, food, agricultural know-how—all these good things are nothing compared with eternal life in Christ.'"[124] Tippett however never refers to this particular interchange, and elsewhere refers to Newbigin in a positive light.[125]

In reality, in Tippett's theology of mission and in his view of the practice of mission, he sees the issues of evangelism, church planting/service ministries as being a both-and instead of being an either-or situation. However, he still prioritizes evangelism, gospel proclamation and church planting, because that is the means of implementing the service and social justice programs through the lives so changed and the churches so planted.

This perspective leads to a broader dimension of his understanding of global mission strategy. From his broader point of view, it is always possible to find ripe harvest fields where gospel proclamation and church planting are productive, so they should be prioritized and targeted. Because those ripe harvest fields will not remain ripe forever, they must therefore be prioritized in mission deployment and strategy. As he describes it,

> This does not mean that he (the missionary) fails to recognize the validity of the service mandate (of scripture). It means that as God alone has brought the field to ripeness, it is his duty as steward to regard this as the time for harvesting, and, in missions policy, this means deployment of funds and personnel into this aspect of the Church's program.[126]

As he points out, when these priorities are followed correctly, "the development of good churches which attend to their service projects is part of

123. Newbigin, *One Body, One Gospel*, 22.

124. Newbigin, *One Body, One Gospel*, 22.

125. Tippett, "Let the Church Be," 64.

126. Tippett, *Verdict Theology in Missionary Theory*, 76.

organic church growth."[127] However, when not, "wrong types of foreign aid" can "hinder the emergence of the indigenous church."[128]

At the same time, thinking of long term evangelism and church planting opportunities, using the mission frame of reference of this section, Tippett is quick to point out that resistant fields should not be left empty. Rather, personnel should be deployed to carry out the service mandate, anticipating that that type of loving service may lead people to enquire about the way of Jesus.[129] "We do not expect a field to yield a great harvest until the Lord brings it to ripeness."[130] Gary L. McIntosh's biography of McGavran notes that McGavran was also willing to concede the wisdom of some involvement in service ministry amongst those totally isolated from the gospel, "that his [God's] saving knowledge may be made known to all these who lie in the darkness of ignorance and sin."[131] But then a key difference between Tippett's view presented above and McGavran's view is highlighted as McGavran's statement quickly moved back to his standard position of seeking deployment amongst the receptive,[132] with the brisk statement, "Gospel-accepters have a higher priority than Gospel-rejecters."[133]

To those who advocate service without proclamation, Tippett reserves a special indictment. In *Verdict Theology*, using concepts from Linnenbrink,[134] he points out that "service that is not missionary can 'thus be self-justification and self-worship' because we act as if we are ourselves the source of what we give instead of being the channel of what has been given to us."[135] In *Church Growth and the Word of God*, he again addresses this sharply when he says,

> When mission becomes a mere demonstration of our supposed virtue in service projects, it is a form of self-righteousness which obstructs real gospel proclamation. It is humanistic in that it directs the observer to man instead of to God, to the good works

127. Tippett, *Verdict Theology in Missionary Theory*, 76.
128. Tippett, *Verdict Theology in Missionary Theory*, 76.
129. Tippett, *Verdict Theology in Missionary Theory*, 76.
130. Tippett, *Verdict Theology in Missionary Theory*, 76.
131. McIntosh, *Donald A. McGavran*, 113.
132. McIntosh, *Donald A. McGavran*, 187, 338.
133. McIntosh, *Donald A. McGavran*, 187.
134. Linnenbrink, "Witness and Service."
135. Tippett, *Verdict Theology in Missionary Theory*, 66.

which we can do instead of to the salvation which we as men cannot effect.[136]

Tippett held a both/and approach to the question of evangelism for a verdict, combined with church planting along with the responsibility of the church to be the functioning body of Christ in its community. So whether the statements above are actual indictments depends on the heart attitude and overall strategy of the mission leaders, missionaries, national leaders along with supporters who facilitate the approaches being used. The point is, done in an effective way, these activities can precipitate people making a decision to follow Christ, thus having positive eternal consequences. However, these quotes are most telling when, referring to overseas organizations raising funds and personnel for community development under the banner of "mission," but implementing those projects with the name of Jesus hidden. Jesus himself said that people would see the good works of his people and glorify their heavenly father (Matt 5:16). That predicted result promised by Jesus is difficult to achieve when the children of the father do not make that paternity obvious.

CONCLUSION

This chapter has established key components of Tippett's theology of mission by examining the first two of his life themes, namely, the centrality of a relationship with God and the centrality of the church. The emphasis on a relationship with God brings an emphasis on the person of Jesus who provides the means for that relationship and on the Bible as the source of the information on which this is based. The same message that tells Tippett and his readers that that relationship with God is available is the same message that propels Jesus followers to take that message to others, seeing them formed into discipling communities, contextually interfaced in their own culture. Furthermore, Tippett held that, as Jesus called the original disciples to be a community of his followers, the package in which Jesus intended this to be lived out as his disciples is in the called out and called together community of the church, which then serves its community both within and without its own family of faith. He also revealed quantitative, qualitative, and structural or organic growth as three dimensions of church growth. As recognized by others, his engagement with and expansion of the concept of the indigenous church laid a great foundation that others have

---

136. Tippett, *Church Growth and the Word*, 39.

continued to build on. Finally, Tippett's practical insights into the church as the body of Christ in a hurting world provided much needed clarity that facilitates community service and social justice through a strong evangelism and church planting priority.

As observed through the eyes of others in earlier chapters, in many areas of Tippett's life, he was plagued with a sense of low self-esteem. However, an analysis of the basis of his theology of mission, utilizing his material in interaction with others, shows his advanced ability to make his points clearly, and to engage with others, even if they held a view different than his own.

6

Alan Tippett's Research Methodologies in Relation to Mission

Homer Barnett . . . gave me the model of his recombination thesis. F.B. Jevons gave me the notion of imposing a set of personal relationships on the symbol of a triangle for critical analysis. A.F.C. Wallace supplied his structure of crisis situations for which I created my own model, and his cognitive maps. From . . . Arnold van Gennep on rites of passage I prepared a processual model, which I developed more and more as I researched conversion in animist society. I diagrammed my version of world view from the inspiration of Malinowski . . . it became an essential tool to me for explaining . . . the nature of cultural voids and functional substitutes.[1]

Tippett reflecting on what he learned from secular anthropologists

THIS CHAPTER WILL EXPLORE the third of Tippett's life themes, that is, the importance of appropriate research methodologies. The fields of history, anthropology, and ethnohistory were the three areas in particular where this was applied, and proved to be one of his significant contributions to world mission. His careful use of historical material provided insights for the future. This combined with his own anthropological field and library research to help shape the newly emerging discipline of missiology, while

1. Tippett et al., *No Continuing City,* 428.

131

establishing boundaries within that discipline. He utilized both formal and informal ethnohistorical methodologies to further enhance these insights. As a result, these research methodologies and his writings coming from that research significantly informs Great-Commission-focused mission.

THE CENTRAL IMPORTANCE OF VALID
AND VERIFIABLE RESEARCH DATA

To a unique degree, Tippett's life was a life of research, as his continual quest for valid and verifiable information is clearly demonstrated in his life story. He was always concerned lest he or other people would come to conclusions for which there had been no verifiable research.[2]

Tippett's Preferred Research Style

Library and archival research suited him, because it was data that was already documented, and therefore did not change. Furthermore, this material could be applied across his key research interests; history, anthropology, and ethnohistory. This meant that any time he spent in a library, a set of archives or a second-hand book shop was time well spent, as illustrated in his comments about the bonus Pacific material he discovered while undertaking his focused research on the distorted information in Michener's[3] novel.[4] Yet even when working from published material, his quest for verifiable data meant that he was cautious about secondary sources, realizing the potential distortion that can occur through the eyes of an interpreter. This delayed the publication of *People Movements in Southern Polynesia* from its original writing in 1962 until 1971, much to McGavran's frustration. McGavran wanted such studies published quickly as part of a global project. Tippett delayed because he was concerned with the "feel" of some published information from a secondary source that he was using in a footnote. He later discovered the original source on a visit to New Zealand, and found that his secondary source had distorted the original information to fit with specific points which that author was trying to make.[5] Once the footnote was corrected, the book was quickly sent to press.

---

2. Tippett, *Peoples of Southwest Ethiopia*, xi; Tippett, *Verdict Theology in Missionary Theory*, 143, 61; Tippett, *Introduction to Missiology*, xiii, 95, 396.

3. Michener, *Hawaii*.

4. Tippett et al., *No Continuing City*, 380.

5. Tippett, "Parallaxis in Missiology," 118.

With verifiable data as a goal, he was pleased with the new field research methodologies he developed for his Solomon Islands research resulting in *Solomon Islands Christianity*,[6] and later, the special interview techniques he developed for the Church Growth Research in Latin America (CGRILA) project which resulted in the publication of *Latin American Church Growth*.[7]

Thesis and Dissertation Supervision

Regarding his goal of producing verifiable data, of the dissertations he supervised Tippett said, "I prided myself that every one of my graduates produced a thesis which was distinctly his own, and could stand on its own merits."[8] In tracing the "three sermons" of his life themes, the research methodologies which he discovered, developed, used, and refined are of significant interest. It was from these that his missiological insights flowed. Initially Tippett's own informally structured observations in Fiji equipped him with a good understanding of Fijian social, ceremonial, and material culture, which provided a great basis for his later areas of research.

Throughout his life, Tippett used three predominant research methodologies: historical research utilizing archives, library research, and interviews; anthropological research including field data collection, structured and informal interviews, participant observation, ethnographical research and questionnaires; and ethnohistorical research which primarily gained its data from history and anthropology, but then used ethnohistorical methods such as upstreaming,[9] along with synchronic, diachronic and synchronic-diachronic research[10] to come to the insights that such research provides.

RECOGNIZING THE IMPORTANCE OF HISTORICAL RESEARCH

Tippett was most comfortable when dealing with history and believed strongly that historical research could provide missiological insights for future mission. He describes his bent for history and historical study as,

---

6. Tippett, *Solomon Islands Christianity*, xiii–xv.

7. Read et al., *Latin American Church Growth*.

8. Tippett et al., *No Continuing City*, 334.

9. Fenton, "Ethnohistory and its Problems."

10. Tippett, *Aspects of Pacific Ethnohistory*, 2.

History was my first love in grade school, and I owe that love to my early history teacher, and to the other history teachers along the way. But it was Dr. Ernst Posner, Professor of Archives in Washington DC, who opened up to me the fascination and the methodology of archival studies."[11]

Describing how his study of history shaped his anthropology and missiology, he said "I came out of history. It was therefore natural that my anthropology should have a historical flavor to it."[12] Furthermore, Tippett the historian demonstrated a penchant for discovering a seemingly unlimited supply of historical archives and resources. This can be seen in the writing of his insightful *Church Planting in New Guinea and Papua*[13] more than a decade before his first visit to Papua New Guinea or in his unpublished *Distribution and Use of Documents in Oceania*[14] comprising 283 pages which he developed during his 1969 Pacific sabbatical. As part of this sabbatical, Tippett was in Hawaii for the sesquicentennial celebrations commemorating the arrival of the first missionaries in 1819.[15] His expertise in the identification and research of historical material was well placed amongst his peers for his own research. Nevertheless, he wanted the benefits of this important field to be readily available to their students at Fuller SWM, therefore he pressed to have a historian appointed to the faculty.

The Future through an Historical Lens

As well as a bent for history, he felt that any valid understanding of the present, let alone projections for the future, had to be based on a thorough understanding of the past. At the Institute of Church Growth in Oregon and then at the Fuller School of World Mission in Pasadena, he and the team supervised many researchers who were learning lessons from the past to envisage more effective strategies for the future. He advised those involved with these church growth case studies to ensure they were researched and written over sufficient time to allow ethnohistorical interaction with primary resources. If this was done, Tippett believed that such ethnohistorical engagement with primary resources would then be evident in the

11. Tippett and Priest, *Fullness of Time*, 345.

12. Tippett, "Anthropological and Ethnohisorical Pilgrimage"; Tippett and Priest, *Fullness of Time*, 345.

13. Tippett, "Church Planting in New Guinea."

14. Tippett, "Distribution and Use of Documents."

15. Tippett and Priest, *Fullness of Time*, 101.

documentation of the research, and, by implication, in the quality of their findings. Using Tippett's own words

> The weakness of most of our church growth case studies lies in their inadequate documentation from primary sources . . . Probably this is because we write our studies in too short a period of time. Historical, and especially ethnohistorical research is a time-consuming matter. In the footnotes, or end notes, of a book we can discover whether . . . it is a genuine ethnohistorical reconstruction.[16]

In this regard, Tippett was not alone in his view of the importance of the study of history for the sake of the furtherance of the cause of mission. Kenneth Scott Latourette's multi-volume sets, including his seven volume *A History of the Expansion of Christianity*,[17] *A History of Christian Missions* by Stephen Neill and Owen Chadwick,[18] and Andrew Walls' *The Missionary Movement in Christian History: Studies in the Transmission of Faith*[19] are additional examples. Furthermore, most schools that teach mission subjects include the history of mission as part of their curriculum.

Predictions without Historical Research

In analyzing Tippett's writings it becomes evident that historical information, in providing fixed data to work with, suited his way of thinking. When forced to give predictions and projections without specifically researched data to work with, Tippett, although highly qualified to venture opinions, became quite uncomfortable, while still arriving at good conclusions. As noted previously, in 1987 he presented a paper at the Bible College of Victoria, Australia, entitled "Task and Method: How Anthropology and Theology Need to Integrate in Post Colonial Missiology."[20] While saying it is hard to predict the future, he does venture some projections about Australia saying,

> I believe in our evangelical program for Australia we greatly need a great theologian who will give us a constructive Christian theology for our times, a theology biblically and anthropologically whole that speaks to the Australian scene as it is today: . . . the

16. Tippett and Priest, *Fullness of Time*, 346.

17. Latourette, *History of the Expansion*.

18. Neill and Chadwick, *History of Christian Missions*.

19. Walls, *Missionary Movement in Christian History*.

20. Tippett, "Task and Method"; Tippett et al., *No Continuing City*, 526.

theology of a Person in the middle of human events . . . May God raise for us a theology which will stand the test as they say proverbially "where the rubber meets the road." . . . To go with this may I also express the hope for something musical to go with it.[21]

In that paper, because he was projecting rather than reporting on specific research, there was an uncharacteristically tentative tone to what he wrote. Nevertheless, his comments were insightful, in that much of this has occurred since this 1987 presentation, albeit in ways different from what he would have anticipated. In my article, "Alan Tippett, Australian Missiologist" in the *Australian Journal of Mission Studies*, I respond to these projections as:

Tippett talks about the need in Australia for a theologian: However, due to our "tall poppy syndrome," possibly it will need to be a process of theologizing that we need, with a number of voices that separately but together raise a theological platform. Even the format will change. Some will primarily write, some will primarily lecture while others will primarily popularize a process of theologizing with their preaching across broad and influential platforms. But if we broaden the phenomenon we are looking for in this way, again we would say that this has occurred to an unprecedented degree in the past 25 years.[22]

One other area that I commented on in my article, was,

Tippett also advised us in advance that revival in Australia will have to have its own music: How much locally developed worship music has impacted Australia, including even the secular Aria charts, and from here, has influenced worship music around the world during the past two decades? When we combine that fact with the statistical increase of the Pentecostal and Charismatic churches in Australia during this time, we are not left with the question of whether Tippett was correct. Rather we are left with the "chicken and egg" question of which came first?[23]

21. Tippett, "Task and Method," 11.
22. Hovey, "Alan Tippett," 32.
23. Hovey, "Alan Tippett," 33.

ANTHROPOLOGICAL FIELD RESEARCH
PROVIDING AN INFORMATION BASE

Field research that Tippett did himself, or that he supervised, was approached with the same attention to detail that he applied to his library and archival research, highlighting the importance of forming an information base as a starting place for reflection. In those cases it was the research techniques themselves that were key to producing the verifiable data.

Solomon Islands Research Models

With verifiable data as a goal, in three chapters of *Solomon Islands Christianity*[24] he described how he used surveys of hymns, biblical readings, and church attendance in two different village churches to provide verifiable and comparable data to examine the virility of church life. He summarizes the procedure as,

> I kept a complete record of every hymn used and every biblical text used in each village. It served as an index to so many aspects of the religious life, and was open for some degree of scientific measurement. It also permitted comparisons between the Methodist village of Rarumana and the Anglican village of Fouia.[25]

From his hymn and biblical text data he was able to statistically plot theological patterns, presentation styles, etc., in the worship and preaching of those churches. This enabled him to analyze the appropriateness or otherwise of these components for the cultural background of the congregation. Or, by logging the church attendance of individuals as a research instrument he describes the process as,

> To the extent that church attendance indicates a degree of piety I developed a tool for measuring this in Solomon Island villages. I remembered work done on an American southern parish by the Roman Catholic sociologist, Fichter, and figured out a modification for my own purposes . . . which raised some serious questions for the missions concerned. I found a drift from marginality to nominality in the church life in places where the social life demonstrated a capacity for a much better state of affairs. Research turned up a number of shortcomings in the second generation . . . I found myself going back into mission history and looking at things like

24. Tippett, *Solomon Islands Christianity*, xiii–xv, 286–318.
25. Tippett et al., *No Continuing City*, 297.

Bible translation and the scope of theological emphasis given in the mission evangelistic program over the years.[26]

The following diagram[27] (see figure 1) and description demonstrates the use and usefulness of the attendance analysis as Tippett saw it. The percentage axis represents the number of people in the potential pool of attendees, while on the A-E axis, A indicates as a person who is diligent in church attendance while E indicates indifference.

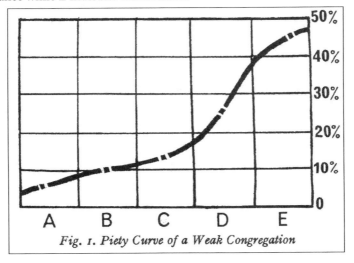

Fig. 1. *Piety Curve of a Weak Congregation*

Figure 1. "Piety Curve of a Weak Congregation" from *Solomon Islands Christianity*.[28]

This provides a way of grouping individuals for purpose of analysis, which Tippett describes as,

> Figure 1 represents a weak congregation with a small nucleus of pious persons and a great deal of indifference among the majority. Two types of situation can produce this kind of curve. It could be either *(a)* a young cause just emerging in a pagan village, or *(b)* in the case of a second generation Christian village, a static cause in which the congregation has become enclosed or sealed off from the unconverted remainder of the village. In the former, the category "E" represents the pagan reservoir or residue, and this represents an open door for evangelism, so that although the

26. Tippett et al., *No Continuing City*, 301.

27. Tippett, *Solomon Islands Christianity*, 309.

28. Tippett, *Solomon Islands Christianity*, 309.

Christian cause is statistically weak, the situation is dynamic. In the latter, the cause is static and new spiritual insights are required by the nucleus. The field for evangelism is still there, although it may well have hardened and become more resistant. Both these types appear to exist in the Solomon Island scene, and could be studied by persons prepared to collect six or eight week samples of statistics for examination.[29]

So, from a statistical basis compiled over time, he had a database, the analysis of which was able to suggest questions to be asked by the church and mission leaders, and to project possible answers.

Research Models: From Simple to Complex

While these instruments are in themselves simple, the projections that can be made from the data they provide is significant. This is reminiscent of Joseph Grimes "Ethnographic Questions for Christian Missionaries" published in *Practical Anthropology*[30] and the research section of Viggo Søgaard's *Everything You Need to Know for a Cassette Ministry: Cassettes in the Context of a Total Christian Communication Program.*[31] Søgaard's more recent *Research in Church and Mission*[32] took his research concepts much further. However, when compared to the detailed questionnaires of volumes like *Notes and Queries on Anthropology*[33] that dates back to 1874, or Pertti and Gretel Pelto's *Anthropological Research: The Structure of Inquiry,*[34] some of the research methods used by Tippett hardly seemed profound. However, they were effective in providing the key information needed for his mission-focused research, and were usable by other missionaries who were less experienced in field research than Tippett.

A key aspect of Tippett's field research was personal interviews. For the Church Growth Research in Latin America (CGRILA) project, he developed and trained the research team in special interview techniques, which he and the team members used experimentally in Mexico prior to the team using them for the balance of their project, as seen in his unpublished

29. Tippett et al., *No Continuing City*, 308–9.

30. Grimes, "Ethnographic Questions for Christian Missionaries."

31. Søgaard, *Everything You Need to Know*, 45–76.

32. Søgaard, *Research in Church and Mission.*

33. Royal Anthropological Institute of Great Britain and Ireland, and British Association for the Advancement of Science, *Notes and Queries on Anthropology.*

34. Pelto and Pelto, *Anthropological Research.*

autobiography[35] An abbreviated version of this research experience can be found in the published autobiography, while his notes from the two weeks comprised 200 pages of single spaced research notes.[36] This included sample worksheets, the goal of which was to get the key information from the greatest number of people as accurately as possible in the least amount of time. One such form could cover twenty interviews and minimize notetaking. Speaking to the team about the benefit of another of his forms, he says, "If during 3 months in Chile you check off a thousand answers to this one question, you have a great deal of valuable data . . . use different coloured pens for different races you can record a comparative racial count also."[37] A year's coordinated research using the methods Tippett had developed for the team resulted in the publication of *Latin American Church Growth*.[38] This was the first major Fuller School of World Mission project. While talking about the finished product, he was keen that his readers know that McGavran had edited the text before it was published. Tippett had written that it was "research in progress." McGavran changed that to "a definitive study." To Tippett, no one study covering all of Latin America could be "definitive."[39]

APPLYING ANTHROPOLOGICAL RESEARCH TO MISSION

Tippett's writings leave no doubt about his view of the importance of the social sciences, especially "social anthropology" and "applied anthropology." He was passionate when he was handling anthropological theory, insights, and perspectives. He often referred to himself as an anthropologist,[40] and worked hard to see missionary anthropology recognized in secular anthropology as a valid field within "applied anthropology."[41] As part of his effort to have Christians see the benefits of anthropology to enhance their ministry, he pushed hard to encourage the formation of an association of Christian anthropologists in the USA,[42] a dream which was subsequently

35. Tippett, "No Continuing City," 345–54.

36. Tippett et al., *No Continuing City*, 341–43.

37. Tippett, "Experiment in Data Collecting, Mexico," 169.

38. Read et al., *Latin American Church Growth*; Tippett, *Introduction to Missiology*, 401–2.

39. Tippett et al., *No Continuing City*, 422.

40. Tippett, *Peoples of Southwest Ethiopia*, 274; Tippett, *Jesus Documents*, 1.

41. Tippett et al., *No Continuing City*, 339.

42. Tippett et al., *No Continuing City*, 338.

fulfilled by the Network of Christian Anthropologists formed in 1989 by Darrell Whiteman.

Putting Tippet's work in perspective, although his role at the Institute of Church Growth at Oregon and Fuller SWM added to the influence of anthropological insights in mission training and reflection, he was not alone in that pursuit. Prior to him taking any formal courses in anthropology, the mission oriented journal, *Practical Anthropology* had been launched in 1953, to which he subsequently contributed articles. Covering some of the same time period, although working from psychology as a base, Jesuit Jaime Bulatao was researching some similar areas to those covered in *Practical Anthropology*, so in effect contributing to the anthropological data available regarding Catholic mission in the Philippines. A significant sample of his work has been published in *Phenomena and Their Interpretation: Landmark Essays, 1957–1989*.[43] Two books that were very influential in the early days of missionary anthropology were Eugene Nida's 1954 *Customs and Cultures; Anthropology for Christian Missions*[44] and Louis Luzbetak's 1963 *The Church and Cultures: An Applied Anthropology for the Religious Worker*.[45] Of course, more recently, many others such as Paul Hiebert, Charles Kraft, Daniel Shaw, Darrell Whiteman, and Michael Rynkiewich have contributed significantly to this field in numerous books and articles.

Using Anthropology to Understand Cultural Constructs

As a missiological anthropologist, Tippett was also able to learn and apply anthropological concepts and practices from secular anthropologists, and provided a number of cameos demonstrating how they contributed to his concepts. This was illustrated in the quote from Tippett at the beginning of this chapter, as he described the insights he gained from a list of these anthropologists: Homer Barnett, F. B. Jevons, A. F. C. Wallace, Arnold van Gennep, and Bronislaw Malinowski.[46]

Tippett's chapter on "Cultural Compulsives" in the McGavran festschrift *God, Man and Church Growth* that was edited by Tippett,[47] develops a concept that he borrowed from Calverton.[48] As he explains, "cultural com-

43. Bulatao, *Phenomena and Their Interpretation*.
44. Nida, *Customs and Cultures*.
45. Luzbetak, *Church and Cultures: An Applied Anthropology*.
46. Tippett et al., *No Continuing City*, 428.
47. Tippett, *God, Man and Church Growth*, 167–85.
48. Calverton, *Making of Man*; Hook, "Modern Quarterly."

pulsives made objectivity in the social sciences impossible; that one could only be objective in his collection of facts, not in their interpretation."[49] Looking back, it should be observed that while this was a breakthrough comment in Tippett's day, the advancement of philosophy of science and epistemology require the recognition that the collection of facts is also subjective. Tippett felt that without the use of anthropology, these problems would be unnoticed. The result would be, as he describes it earlier in that chapter, Western observers could easily feel that because "western civilized cultural constructs were the climax of the process [of linear evolution] then the idea of private ownership, of individualism, and monogamous marriage were validated as the most developed cultural forms"[50] simply because these values of their own culture would be used subconsciously and uncritically as benchmarks by which other cultures would be judged. All the while, the observer would not even notice his or her own bias in this process.

Tippett describes the extreme seriousness of the implications of this situation in his chapter "The Negative and Positive Value of Anthropology to the Missionary" in *Introduction to Missiology*,[51] as a missionary using inappropriate technique can actually lead to "*quench[ing] the Spirit* as Paul puts it."[52] He then briefly refers to five thematic mistakes that can be made when one is not culturally sensitized and sensitive. They are mistakes: *of misunderstanding; of offence; of causing opposition; of imposition; of void creation.* In contrast, he points out that cultural awareness through anthropology provides the following benefits:

- *Procedure*—the ability to see patterns in the society and so to be able to use them for positive ends;

- *Communication*—the benefits of understanding cultural communication channels, especially as would be used for such important information as the gospel;

- *Proficiency in the language*—anthropology helps the missionary see the absolute importance of language proficiency, and when the tools of ethnolinguistics are added in, the benefits are considerable;

---

49. Tippett, *God, Man and Church Growth*, 172.

50. Tippett, *God, Man and Church Growth*, 69.

51. Tippett, *Introduction to Missiology*, 125–27.

52. Tippett, *Introduction to Missiology*, 125; italics his.

- *Innovation*—in studying how cultures change, the missionary understands how the acceptance of the gospel changes a society, and what are the factors that predispose people towards such acceptance;

- *Methodology*—these tools of anthropology assist the missionary in observing and recording cultural data, understanding how cultures function, as observed in other anthropological case studies, etc.[53]

Furthermore, Tippett believed that the insights of anthropology also assist a missionary as their ministry matures. He argued that this was especially the case when multi-individual mutually interdependent decisions for Christ were utilized because at those times, change in the religious dimensions of the society would be rapid. In order that this not be unwittingly constrained, the foreign Christian worker must understand the cultural dynamics so they can guide and not hinder the development of churches that use the language, structures, and leadership approaches familiar to the people. Also, on the occasions when there is direct conflict between some traditional elements and biblical Christianity, the use of anthropological insights provides the missionary with the tools to empathetically guide in the development of functional substitutes, a key concept in Tippett's writing that will be discussed in depth in a subsequent chapter. These insights from anthropology are necessary to maintain the "moving equilibrium"[54] that is necessary to see such dynamic movements consummated into strong national church movements. Additionally, Tippett points out how missionary anthropology has contributed to the science of anthropology by its research and case studies that have documented such movements.[55]

Missionary Anthropology as a Specialized Discipline

Tippett's anthropological research in the Solomon Islands and Ethiopia broke new ground in missionary anthropology. This includes the breadth of what he distilled culturally considering the short periods of field research. Furthermore, those insights were already applied to mission, ready to be utilized by other missionaries. As well as his library and archival research for those projects, a key research method that enhanced his ability to acquire the required material in a limited time frame was his interview techniques that were referred to earlier. He provides an exposé of his "power

53. Tippett, *Introduction to Missiology*, 127–29.
54. Tippett, "Cultural Compulsives," 183.
55. Tippett, "Cultural Compulsives," 183.

interview techniques" in "Experiment in Data Collecting, Mexico" in which he answers the CGRILA research team's questions about interview problems they had experienced.[56] For himself, interviews provided a key part of the material for his two books *Solomon Islands Christianity*[57] and *Peoples of Southwest Ethiopia*.[58] Similarly, interviews were part of his methodology that led to his confidential reports and summaries on his research in what he calls Navaholand in the USA. These reports provide important insights into how to approach situations where significant acculturation had taken place, especially when such acculturation had occurred in unhealthy or at least unhelpful ways.[59]

Tippett's 1977 compilation, *The Ways of the People*, published in 2013 by William Carey Library,[60] combines ninety-three selections from Protestant missionaries who have served around the world over the previous 200 years. As a reader in social anthropology, he based its development on the presupposition,

> that before people go out as an evangelist into cultural systems or world views other than their own, they should have a general understanding that man and woman do live in homogeneous ethnic groups, and that these groups are extremely diverse in organization, values, and religion."[61]

The volume makes that point very well. Additionally, the anthropological problems that the missionary will confront he describes as: (1) the *problem of social organization*, (2) the *problem of social disequilibrium*, (3) the *problem of cultural voids and functional substitutes*, (4) the *problem of syncretism*, (5) the *problem of meaning*, and (6) the *problem of dynamic equivalence*.[62] His view is that anthropology will enable the missionary to get past these challenges on first arrival on the field, and also to move towards long term effectiveness. Further demonstrating Tippett's engagement with anthropology, his library includes a number of unpublished bound collections of his anthropological writings grouped by year, e.g. *Anthropological Writings*

56. Tippett, "Experiment in Data Collecting, Mexico," 155–70.

57. Tippett, *Solomon Islands Christianity*.

58. Tippett, *Peoples of Southwest Ethiopia*.

59. Tippett et al., *No Continuing City*, 388–91.

60. Tippett, *Ways of the People*.

61. Tippett, *Ways of the People*, x; also, 63.

62. Tippett, *Ways of the People*, 6.

Fiji 1944—1963, Anthropological Writings 1962—1971, Research and Writings—1973-74, etc.

It is evident that Tippett had a missiological cycle in his mind that could be described as: There needs to be more effective missionary strategy which comes from better missiology; a major contributor to missiology is anthropology with its various research methodologies including ethnohistory; the use of these tools helps missionaries to understand both the source of their message as it is encoded in the many different cultures in which the Bible message is written, the people to whom they plan to deliver that message along with understanding themselves as cultural beings involved in this complex cross-cultural communication task. For Tippett, the only safe way to do this was to use anthropology's research tools, models, and methods of classification, then to be able to inform one's understanding of the message and so to enhance the ability to deliver it.[63]

While advocating the use of anthropology as strongly and extensively as he does, Tippett wisely warns his readers to differentiate anthropology from Christian mission: Anthropologists, if they are doing their work well, simply observe and record culture and culture change. Missionaries on the other hand, having been informed by anthropology in how to do their work, endeavour to guide such culture change in a particular direction. Anthropology asks *why* of the culture, but a missionary *does things* with the people in the culture. Summarizing the relationship between the two, Tippett says that for a dedicated missionary, "anthropology offers tremendous resources, methods, and information that will aid in their church planting and building up of converts in the new faith."[64] Differentiating between anthropology and mission will continue to be important when proposing approaches for contemporary mission. A key part in this evaluation will relate to the changes that have occurred in anthropology itself in the last thirty years.[65] Tippett's view was that missiology was an academic discipline in its own right, which could therefore develop its own perspectives or borrow from other fields of study as it chooses. This means that missiology is not bound to take the turns that secular anthropology has taken, should these not prove helpful. This is especially the case because post-colonial missiology was focused on effective field strategies rather than the development of anthropology as a discipline.

---

63. Tippett, *Introduction to Missiology*, 307–9.

64. Tippett, *Introduction to Missiology*, 129.

65. Rynkiewich, *Soul, Self, and Society*.

The Boundaries of Appropriate Use of Anthropology

It is important to recognize that there are boundaries to the beneficial results of the use of anthropology. Anthropology can be used to further the cause of mission, or it can be used to hinder that same cause. This fact is highlighted by Tippett in two articles that he published about anthropology in *Evangelical Missions Quarterly*, "Anthropology: Luxury or Necessity for Missions?"[66] and "Taking a Hard Look at the Barbados Declaration."[67] These articles are particularly helpful in summarizing Tippett's view of the importance of anthropology, in essence providing the positive and negative poles of his thinking about anthropology.

At the positive pole, "Anthropology: Luxury or Necessity for Missions?" is structured around six basic questions representing virtual scenarios relating to the need and challenges of anthropology in missionary training. He then examines what a candidate should be able to expect in their training, and how a school and its faculty with limited resources could provide satisfactory courses in anthropology for missionary candidates. In asking about the adequacy of the training given to missionary candidates, he recounts his own experience where he believes that his learning curve on the field as a missionary would have been shortened from ten years to two years had he received anthropological training before he went to Fiji.[68] Reflecting on that experience, he briefly looks at the wisdom of utilizing the anthropology departments of secular universities to meet the need should the Christian training institution lack qualified faculty. While examining this option, he recognizes the weaknesses of the secular university approach he is suggesting. His concerns are: faculty who continue to criticize missionaries rather than helping to create the new day; a professor with a focus on just one discipline who is training people to work in the multi-discipline task of mission and the danger of utilizing faculty who don't share the missionary's sympathies for the Christian mandate of the missionary's task.[69]

Despite these disadvantages, he sees anthropological training of the right type, even though not providing the complete training a missionary would need, as still having advantages. Speaking of the new missionary, he points out that they will additionally need the natural and spiritual abilities of common sense, grace, and guidance. Furthermore, understanding

---

66. Tippett, "Anthropology."
67. Tippett, "Taking a Hard Look."
68. Tippett, "Anthropology," 8.
69. Tippett, "Anthropology," 11–12.

the culture of the people, including their motivations and values that are different from his/her own, can save the missionary from making serious mistakes. It can also help that person to see opportunities, and know how to work with those opportunities to assist in bringing "the growth of the church and the glory of God."[70] His other questions explore what preparation the indigenous church can rightfully expect people sent to them as cross-cultural missionaries and fraternal workers to have received. Tippett considers this preparation to be related to four essential dimensions: knowledge, attitudes, emphases, and methods. The question is, have the new missionaries been prepared to be able to learn and contribute in all of these areas, while motivated by the goal of seeing the development of the local indigenous church. In drawing together his reflection regarding anthropology in mission training, he proposed a specialized pre-field missionary training seminar combining new and experienced missionaries. This would assist the new missionary to quickly make contacts and build rapport on arrival on the field; to help them deal with the challenges that come from ministry in very different situations, which he highlights as "the pagan-Christian encounter, magic, polygamy, cross-cultural ethics, and the problem of meaning."[71]

At the negative pole of his examination of anthropology, Tippett's interaction[72] with the "Barbados Declaration" demonstrates his view of how anthropology should not be used. The description in Alison Brysk's book, *From Tribal Village to Global Village: Indian Rights and International Relations in Latin America* provides useful background to Tippett's interaction, when she says,

> . . . the first Barbados Conference in 1971, [was] organised by the World Council of Churches and the Ethnology Department of the University of Bern (Switzerland). In the Barbados declaration, 12 prominent anthropologists affirm their own professional responsibility for promoting the self-determination of the indigenous subjects and called for a moratorium on missionary work.[73]

In summary, Tippett sees the declaration as representing a group of anthropologists: (1) who have not respected their sponsoring organization (WCC on this occasion); (2) who criticized those who claim to speak for those

70. Tippett, "Anthropology," 16.
71. Tippett, "Anthropology," 17.
72. Tippett, "Taking a Hard Look."
73. Brysk, *From Tribal Village*, 64.

of other cultures at least without getting the specific input from members of those other cultures, and all of this while doing the very thing they are criticizing others for; as he points out, there are no Indian names in the list of the participants. (3) As professional anthropologists, they can only speak as far as their research data allows them. On this point, again he felt they failed by generalizing about Indian and missionary situations in ways that may have vestiges of truth for some such situations, while being untrue for many others. (4) He also saw them as breaching the boundaries of applied anthropology, which theoretically would have been their closest ally. He pointed out that if they had used an applied anthropology approach, they would have in fact found themselves close to many missionaries, who, in doing their work well in the language and culture of the people, are, whether formally or informally, following those principles. (5) Having pointed out the inconsistencies in the Declaration, Tippett's most telling concern was their call for the cessation of the activities of mission organizations and missionaries. As he points out, that decision is outside the anthropologist's field. The Great Commission is theological, so that call is made by someone outside the social science of anthropology, in fact, someone beyond human authority (Matt 28:18–20).[74] At this negative pole, Tippett's evaluation has provided a telling cautionary list regarding the use of anthropology.

USING ETHNOHISTORICAL RESEARCH TO UNDERSTAND CULTURE AND CULTURE CHANGE

While Tippett continued to value all of the interdisciplinary areas that he discovered, ethnohistory, which he became aware of a little later, was to him the best way of using his expanding historical and anthropological knowledge to penetrate more deeply into the inner workings of cultures. Having gained a greater understanding of where a culture had come from, he found that he gained the insights needed to trace culture change forward through time to the present day situation that he and his protégés were researching.

It is useful to compare two overview articles on ethnohistory, Kelly Chaves' "Ethnohistory: From Inception to Postmodernism and Beyond"[75] in the journal *Historian* and Robert Carmack's "Ethnohistory: A Review of Its Development, Definitions, Methods, and Aims"[76] in the *Annual Review*

74. Tippett, "Taking a Hard Look," 293–94.

75. Chaves, "Ethnohistory."

76. Carmack, "Ethnohistory."

of Anthropology. As overview articles, both examine the anthropological and the historical inputs into the development of ethnohistory, while the timeline in both provides a reminder that ethnohistory was still developing in method and definition at the time that Tippett began using it and saw so much benefit from it. One contrast Chavas makes is that of "upstreaming" and "downstreaming."[77] The anthropological use of "upstreaming" referred to in this study progresses from the known present into the unknown past. Historians use "downstreaming" by beginning with what they consider to be a known point in the past from which they document forward to the present. While Chavas approached the topic from within history, Carmack approached it from within anthropology, the nuanced differences in their perspectives are useful in observing ethnohistory's development as a method or technique rather than being itself a discipline.[78] In particular, Carmack highlights anthropologies' goal of ahistorical recording of cultures in the past, while he provides extensive lists of cultures whose histories have been reconstructed by the use of ethnohistorical tools, including an evaluation of their effectiveness.[79]

Engaging Ethnohistorical Methodology for Mission Research

Tippett used ethnohistorical method informally while learning Fijian culture and history, then later, formally, finding it to be a very useful method. While continuing to think of effective strategies for church growth, Tippett could see that even radical growth of the church at a certain point in time needed to be put in the context of its antecedents if lessons were going to be learned to contribute to its quantitative, qualitative, and structural or organic growth in the future. Ethnohistory provided him with the tools to be able to do such diachronic studies of the cultures he worked with, tracing them through time. This was in contrast to his frustration with both anthropologists and historians who, using the exclusive tools of their respective crafts, were limited at best to synchronic studies in which the researcher looks at a culture or historical situation at just one point in time. Tippett's major concern with these synchronic studies was that they didn't sufficiently compensate for the bias of the researcher. His chapter on "Cultural Compulsives" in *God, Man and Church Growth*[80] spelt this out very

77. Chaves, "Ethnohistory," 496.
78. Carmack, "Ethnohistory," 230.
79. Carmack, "Ethnohistory," 239.
80. Tippett, "Cultural Compulsives."

clearly.[81] His frequently expressed concern with "salvage anthropologists" is an example of this.[82]

Using Dark's[83] terminology Tippett describes the ethnohistorical tools that are used for cultural reconstruction, "(1) *Cross-sectional* (2) *Institutional,* and (3) *Culture Continuum.* In the first type the synthesis is synchronic; in the second it is diachronic and in the third it is both spatial and temporal (synchronic-diachronic)."[84] Then he moves on to another form of ethnohistorical reconstruction known as "upstreaming," quoting Fenton's description as "against the tide of history going from the known present to the unknown past."[85] Tippett saw two advantages of upstreaming. First, it is easier to accurately understand a culture at a given point in time as one has reconstructed it step by step from the present back into history. Second, new insights into the culture are often gained when a known culture trait suddenly disappears as one goes backward in the reconstruction process.[86] While reflecting the usefulness of the tools of ethnohistory, it becomes obvious that the analysis of Tippett's decline in influence in chapter 4 of this study was an informal ethnohistorical reconstruction. As would have already been noticed, the analysis carried out in that way brought insights to light that would otherwise have been obscured behind the basic reality of the decline of his influence. This could have resulted in a lack of appreciation of the significance of his insights, that this study has subsequently analyzed.

In describing ethnohistory, Tippett counters misunderstandings while highlighting the strengths of ethnohistory as he talks about the symbiotic union of historical and anthropological techniques, rather than the simple addition of the two. As they are united in this way, both fields add their respective strengths while correcting the other's weaknesses. He points out that while history and anthropology are disciplines, ethnohistory is a methodology. The end result is more than just symbiotic, as he first described it.

---

81. Chaves, "Ethnohistory"; Carmack, "Ethnohistory."

82. Tippett, *Fijian Material Culture*; Tippett, *Aspects of Pacific Ethnohistory*; Tippett, *Introduction to Missiology*, 88.

83. Dark, "Methods of Synthesis in Ethnohistory."

84. Tippett, *Aspects of Pacific Ethnohistory*, 2; italics his.

85. Fenton, "Ethnohistory and its Problems," 12.

86. Tippett, *Aspects of Pacific Ethnohistory*, 4–5.

Rather it is "syngenetic," as the two are put together resulting in something new being created.[87]

Demonstrating the usefulness of ethnohistory, but from a negative example, in "The Dynamics of Church-Planting in Fiji" Tippett tells the story of Henderson writing a history of Fiji, working from original documents, namely Thomas Williams' journal.[88] Tippett explains his concern that a historian could still come to incorrect conclusions even though using original documents. He questions, "whether a historian should ever write history outside his own culture without a deep appreciation of anthropological principles." In this case, because Henderson didn't understand the cultural and ceremonial issues of the situations he was describing, he consequently misinterpreted the information.[89] In *Oral Tradition and Ethnohistory: The Transmission of Information and Social Values in Early Christian Fiji, 1835–1905*, Tippett gives more detail of the errors of interpretation that Henderson had fallen into. He then goes even further, to indicate that these errors are virtually inevitable to a historian, unless the natural tendency to interpret other people's situations on the basis of one's own, is buffered by such research methodologies as ethnohistory.[90]

The Importance of Ethnohistory as a Method in Tippett's Missiological Research

Tippett had come to value ethnohistory since he first discovered it by name, and used it on many occasions. However, in *No Continuing City*,[91] he reports that in the process of researching *Aspects of Pacific Ethnohistory*[92] in 1969, that he came to see "the significance of ethnohistory for missiology . . . I realized the place it had to be given in our curriculum."[93] This indicates that he saw a vulnerability in missiological research if ethnohistory was not one of the research tools used.

Ethnohistory, both formally and informally, was very much a part of the way Tippett did his research. This can be seen in the following list of

87. Tippett, "Contour of Ethnohistory," 405–6.

88. Williams and Henderson, *Journal of Thomas Williams*.

89. Tippett, "Dynamics of Church-Planting in Fiji," 101, 103–4, 113, 121.

90. Tippett, *Oral Tradition and Ethnohistory*, 7.

91. Tippett et al., *No Continuing City*, 385.

92. Tippett, *Aspects of Pacific Ethnohistory*.

93. Tippett et al., *No Continuing City*, 385.

Tippett's books, manuscripts, and articles which use ethnohistory to establish a significant part of the database from which he is writing. As a way of demonstrating Tippett's development with the tools of ethnohistory, the list is compiled according to the date of first writing, rather than by publication date. It is worth noting that the first two books were written before he had formally discovered ethnohistory:

- *The Christian (Fiji 1835–67)*[94]
- "Road to Bau"[95]
- "The Integrating Gospel"[96]
- *Fijian Material Culture*[97]
- "Church Planting in New Guinea and Papua"[98]
- *People Movements in Southern Polynesia*[99]
- *Solomon Islands Christianity*[100]
- *Aspects of Pacific Ethnohistory*[101]
- "The Cultural Dynamics of Fijian Cannibalism"[102]
- *The Jesus Documents*[103]
- *Oral Tradition and Ethnohistory: The Transmission of Information and Social Values in Early Christian Fiji, 1835–1905*[104]
- "Parallaxis in Missiology—To Use or Abuse"[105]

94. Tippett, *Christian (Fiji 1835–67)*, republished as Tippett, *Integrating Gospel and the Christian*.

95. Tippett, "Road to Bau," since published as Tippett, *Road to Bau*.

96. Tippett, "Integrating Gospel," since published as Tippett, *Integrating Gospel and the Christian*.

97. Tippett, *Fijian Material Culture*, initially written from 1962–1964.

98. Tippett, "Church Planting in New Guinea."

99. Tippett, *People Movements in Southern Polynesia*, initially written in 1963.

100. Tippett, *Solomon Islands Christianity*, initially written in 1964.

101. Tippett, *Aspects of Pacific Ethnohistory*.

102. Tippett, "Cultural Dynamics of Fijian Cannibalism."

103. Tippett, "Jesus Documents," since published as Tippett, *Jesus Documents*.

104. Tippett, *Oral Tradition and Ethnohistory*.

105. Tippett, "Parallaxis in Missiology."

- Sections of *Introduction to Missiology*[106]

Tippett could see internal and external factors where ethnohistory would be an advantage to missiologists. Internally, he wanted missionaries to use strategies that had the greatest possible potential for the planting and development of local culturally appropriate churches and movements in fulfillment of the Great Commission. He was concerned however because he felt that this was often undermined by missionaries and missiologists simplistically viewing historical examples of people turning to Christ and attributing the movement and the resultant culture change, and societal transformation to a single cause.[107] As a result, these unfounded assumptions would provide no firm basis on which to build better strategies for the future.[108] Externally, he was concerned about a process he observed with secular anthropologists and historians, similarly engaging synchronically with situations where churches have been planted, then from that limited database of genuine information, forming their own constructed opinions about what they assume happened. Those opinions were subsequently published as if well-established fact, and in doing so, damaged the cause of mission. Tippett observes that when researching cases of the long-term impact of radical Christianity, "one usually discovers (1) a whole complex of specific events, (2) a significant number of key persons, and (3) a set of distinct and precise relationships between them."[109]

ETHNOHISTORY'S USEFULNESS SEEN IN CASE STUDIES

Regardless of ethnohistory's importance to Tippett's research, this study will demonstrate that it is not a common research tool today. For that reason, there is value in using a series of case studies focused on different perspectives to ensure the reader has an effective understanding of its potential usefulness.

Triangle of Personal Relationships: Making Personal Journals Useful for Research

While theorizing about the use of ethnohistorical tools from his Pacific research, Tippett points researchers to an additional and important database

106. Tippett, *Introduction to Missiology*, written between 1962 and 1987.
107. Tippett and Priest, *Fullness of Time*, xxviii.
108. Gibbs, "How Appropriate Is the Church?" 302–3.
109. Tippett, *Aspects of Pacific Ethnohistory*, 106–7.

for their research and analysis that would have otherwise been disregarded. In this case he is referring to the personal journals, correspondence, reports, etc. of individuals who lived in the field situations during the early contact and early church planting phases of mission on those fields. Often the scientific community considered these documents to be "too biased" to be of value. However, Tippett points out that the rejection of those documents produced another problem, because, in many cases, these documents are the only documents that describe the endemic culture including religious practices before and during contact with the outside world and before and during contact with the gospel. Similarly, they are the only documents that could help explain why individual situations were predisposed to accept the advocated culture change referred to as the gospel while other situations were resistant.[110] To make valid use of these documents, Tippett uses F. B. Jevons'[111] simple model that enables a researcher to recognize and compensate for the bias of the author. In his N-A-M triangle of personal relationships (see figure 2), the triangle represents the whole situation, while each point reflects the point of view or the perspectives of the players in the situation being observed. In his Pacific studies, his codes were; N = Nationals, A = Foreign Adventurers (e.g. slavers, whalers, sandalwood traders) and M = Missionaries.[112]

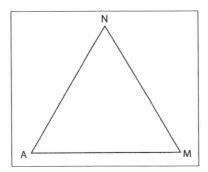

Figure 2. **"The triangle of personal relationships,"** from *Fullness of Time: Ethnohistory Selections from the Writings of Alan R. Tippett.*[113]

110. Tippett, *Aspects of Pacific Ethnohistory*, 106.

111. Tippett et al., *No Continuing City*, 428.

112. Tippett and Priest, *Fullness of Time*, 136.

113. Tippett and Priest, *Fullness of Time*, 136.

Demonstrating its usefulness, Tippett uses this model to analyze a missionary journal in the New Hebrides in the days of early evangelism. At that time, slavery and the sandalwood trade were both very active. The Europeans involved in those trades were also outsiders as the missionaries were, but they advocated very different cultural change than the missionaries did. All of this complexity makes it difficult to understand such a situation by "looking at a distance" as it were. Yet using an ethnohistorical approach aided by the N-A-M diagram, data from that era in the journal of a missionary, or a colonial administrator, for example, becomes useful data. Without this tool, those documents would otherwise have been unacceptable. As the bias in the document is recognized and compensated for, they become invaluable to readers in a totally different era.[114] He uses a similar approach to understand the issues behind the assassination of Bishop Patteson in the Solomon Islands (1871) in the same era.[115]

With characteristic vigor, having established the usefulness of this model, Tippett additionally applies it to enable missionary evangelists to see the complexity of their task in a focused way. Still using Jevons's diagram, he highlights the danger of a missionary focusing exclusively on the MN advocate relationship on the basis of the Matthew 28:18–20 directive. Tippett argues on the basis of John 17 that the apostles are sent into the world so that implies that MA and NA relationships will also have a bearing on the MN advocate relationship. It speaks of Tippett's breadth in this description, because there was no one who should be excluded from the purview of ministry responsibility.

Ethnohistorical Case Studies: Fiji and Australia

It is significant to observe Tippett's use of ethnohistorical case studies and the insights that the method produces. He identifies his PhD dissertation, later published as *Fijian Material Culture*,[116] as primarily an ethnohistorical study. The process in that book was to begin with several categories of artifacts, using local language terminology to trace them in their cultural context along with the function they fulfilled within that context. Using that as his foundational data, he then looked at the people who related to those artifacts—the craftsmen, the warriors, the sailors, etc. and from there to the cultural institutions and occasions in which their roles were carried

114. Tippett, *Aspects of Pacific Ethnohistory*, 106–8.

115. Tippett and Priest, *Fullness of Time*, 48–49.

116. Tippett, *Fijian Material Culture*.

out, and the "relationships and values the artifacts brought into focus."[117] This approach brought fresh light to cultures long since past, and to the display and description of such artifacts within historical collections such as museums.[118]

His unpublished article *The Cultural Dynamics of Fijian Cannibalism*[119] is an example of his use of and the benefits of ethnohistory as a research methodology. Without ethnohistorical research, the fact that cannibalism ended in Fiji about the same time that Fiji was ceded to British rule (1874), it is easy to assume that British administration resulted in the end of cannibalism. However using the ethnohistorical method of upstreaming to find the roots of the change, Tippett takes his audience back 100 or so years before that, as Tongans traded with and started to settle in Fiji,[120] bringing about subtle but influential culture change.[121] Then, beginning in 1809, the sacred nature of cannibalism began to be corrupted by Western men—escaped convicts, adventurers, etc.—hiring themselves out to Fijian chiefs as marksmen and gunsmiths, and as the sandalwood traders offered firearms for sandalwood.[122] As a result of these new methods of warfare being employed, death became so prevalent to the communities being attacked by their now better armed enemies, that they were looking for new solutions.[123] Change was also occurring amongst those who were victorious. In their communities, the ready availability of bodies meant that cannibalism was becoming a secular instead of a sacred activity.[124] That brought about a change in the motivation for cannibalism.[125] Added to that was the influence of the gospel and the contrasting lifestyle of its messengers compared with the other outsiders now frequenting Fiji. This contrast became evident commencing with the arrival of the first Western and Island missionaries in 1835. The accumulating result of all of this, including the conversion of

---

117. Tippett and Priest, *Fullness of Time*, xxiv–xxv.

118. Tippett et al., *No Continuing City*, 339.

119. Tippett, "Cultural Dynamics of Fijian Cannibalism."

120. Tippett, *Deep-Sea Canoe*, 19.

121. Tippett, "Dynamics of Church-Planting in Fiji," 7–13; Tippett, *Oral Tradition and Ethnohistory*, 33.

122. Tippett, *Road to Bau*, 9, 12; *Deep-Sea Canoe*, 26–27; Tippett, "Ethnolinguistics and Bible Translation," 67.

123. Tippett, *Deep-Sea Canoe*, 27–28.

124. Tippett, *Road to Bau*, 76–77.

125. Tippett, *Road to Bau*, 74.

the greatest cannibal chief, Ratu Cakobau in 1854, was the eventual death of cannibalism itself, coincidentally about the time of the 1874 Cession to British rule. Following the same morbid theme of cannibalism and cannibals in Fiji in another case study, Tippett uses ethnohistory to analyze the ethnopsychology of the individual within his culture using the Ruth Benedict's topic of the relativity of normality. From the insights of this ethnohistorical case study, he demonstrates why the first forty years of the development of the Methodist church in Fiji was so effective. The missionaries had been able to see beyond cannibalism to the cannibal himself as a person and then to see in that person their potential as a Christian leader in his own setting. Furthermore, the society was gradually changing as a result of changed individuals, "innovators" in the context of culture change, to use Barnett's term. This in turn opened the way for larger multi-individual people movements to Christ, so the church was able to be more indigenous because people were converted within their social structures.[126]

In another case study, Tippett uses ethnohistory to address the allegation that the Methodist mission and church in the early days of the white settlement of Australia had not been effective in Aboriginal ministry due to neglect of that ministry. Using historical information, he clearly makes the point that the alleged non-involvement is not true, even though the churches and Christian leaders could have done more. Additionally, using ethnohistorical methods to probe the early contact period, he was able to ask a much more important question about the seeming failure of the work. He concluded, with reasonable confidence, that there were several contributing factors. However, the most important one was the fact that the offer of Christianity was almost always linked with the requirement of residential settlement in place of a nomadic lifestyle. Because of the sensitivity of this topic in an Australian context, and the lack of published availability of Tippett's writing on this topic, the following quote will give a more complete sense of Tippett's findings on this matter and what he felt could have occurred if the messengers in that first contact period could have seen past their sedentary culture to engage in this ministry:

> To what extend did the failure of missionary work among the Australian Aborigines arise from the form of religion the Church attempted to give them? This is an anthropological question. It is relevant today, and will continue to be so as long as the Church seeks to evangelize nomadic peoples . . . To what extent should

126. Tippett and Priest, *Fullness of Time*, 176.

missions try to break the nomadic habits of a people and bind them to a station? Now the answer to that question in Australia today, may be very different from what it should have been a century ago. Today it is a case of saving a perishing people, and giving them a stability without which they cannot hope to exist in the face of competition. I am not dealing with that question. We are dealing with beginnings. All the missionaries felt lost in the face of nomadism. Yet there were moments for Walker and Tuckfield and others when they got close to the people—they were moments when they too became nomads. I have yet to be convinced that the God who called the nomadic Abraham could not call the wanderers of the Australian Continent also. I can well imagine what an obstruction our institutional religion would be to a nomadic people.[127]

Ethnohistory Assisting Biblical Study

For Tippett, ethnohistory was not only a tool to help missiologists, anthropologists, and subsequently historians, but for biblical scholars as well. As he stated it in his 1975 typescript volume "The Jesus Documents" that was subsequently published in 2012, "if we could achieve the breakthrough of more acceptance by the critical theologians, the ethnotheologians could offer tremendous methodological resources for biblical interpretation."[128] In his introduction he describes the issues that are at stake,

> It is certainly not that I would usurp the research field of another discipline, but rather that I believe that all our disciplines are merely convenient abstractions for purposes of analyzing our data, and setting up the criteria necessary for our evaluations . . . The tools of any discipline frequently go beyond their immediate purposes of analysis and classification and force an academic rigidity of the discipline on scholars, with two very unfortunate effects—they make the discipline meaningless to ordinary people, and render the academicians closed against other methodologies. The value of interdisciplinary research is that we have a two-way process—a symbiosis of both giving and receiving.[129]

127. Tippett and Priest, *Fullness of Time*, 325.

128. Tippett, *Jesus Documents*, 5.

129. Tippett, *Jesus Documents*, 1.

Thus, he wrote *The Jesus Documents* as an ethnohistorical study of the four gospels, which is a significant contribution to biblical scholarship that has thankfully now been published by William Carey Library.[130]

The conceptual tools that Kenneth Bailey used for analysis of some of the Lukan parables of Jesus, in his joint volume, *Poet & Peasant; and, Through Peasant Eyes: A Literary-cultural Approach to the Parables in Luke*[131] provide another example of the power of this sort of analysis. That is, he combined a number of aspects to illuminate his understanding of these parables using what he calls "Oriental Exegesis,"[132] which combined: his experience in living amongst twentieth-century Middle Eastern peasants; insights of ancient texts, ancient near culture translations of ancient texts and modern scholarship from a range of perspectives (historical, aesthetic, etc.).

Perseverance vs. Productivity in Using Ethnohistory as a Mission Research Tool

For Tippett, the major use he saw for ethnohistorical studies was in gaining in-depth understanding of existing patterns of growth and non-growth of the church, and through that to assist in developing strategies to position the Christian message for maximum impact both in places where the church exists and where it is yet to be planted. Tippett's goal for missiologists in particular was that ethnohistory would continue as a primary missiological research tool. He also saw its significance for anthropologist more generally. This was aspirational on his part for two reasons. In his mind, the benefit of ethnohistory as a research methodology stood out. However, he was aware of the painstaking research it required, but felt that the results were well worth the effort. At the same time, he did notice how few researchers followed his lead in using ethnohistory.

One example of his fruitful use of it was to understand the sub-recent past in order to enhance ministry in current field situations as he did with the John Hunt biography *Road to Bau*.[133] He also said he would like to see it applied to researching the historical and cultural dynamics of the people movements by which Christianity initially spread and developed around

---

130. Tippett, *Jesus Documents*.

131. Bailey, *Poet & Peasant*, 29–32.

132. Bailey, *Poet & Peasant*, 29.

133. Tippett, "Road to Bau," 3 (now published as Tippett, *Road to Bau*).

the Mediterranean and across Europe, including their continuation into the Middle Ages. In saying that, he was confident that such a study would be in a position to dispense with the designation of *The Thousand Years of Uncertainty: A.D. 500-A.D. 1500* that K. S. Latourette used for the title of the second volume of his *A History of the Expansion of Christianity* series.[134] Tippett's research led him to the conclusion that this was an inaccurate understanding of the situation of the time. His view was that progress was being made in the expansion of Christianity during that period, however our modern Western individualistic view of decision-making hides that phenomenon from modern observers. Furthermore, he was disturbed at Latourette's stated unwillingness to unravel the dynamics of those situations as a historian bound by the skills of their own craft,[135] a position that could be remedied by the tools of ethnohistory. As Tippett explained, it is not so much that a missiologist would discover new data but rather, with ethnohistorical tools would have new perspectives on the culture change dynamics that made those situations propitious to cultural and religious change.[136]

While Tippett highlights the use of missionary records as crucial databases from which to do very productive ethnohistorical reconstructions as part of the science of missiology, he doesn't under-estimate the challenge of doing this level of research. This includes statements about how widely scattered the necessary documents are, and the need for familiarity with the language and culture of the situation being researched. However, he points out that there is academic precedence for the use of such resources, as documented by Kluckhohn.[137] The detail with which Tippett wrote his ethnohistorical studies[138] and the labour entailed in using ethnohistory as a research methodology is impressive. For Tippett, it was a disadvantage that he was aware of, but treated it as a "cost versus benefit" equation, with the painstaking time producing benefits that made it worthwhile and that could not be achieved in any other way. To help overcome the problem for others, he compiled both lists and examples of approaches in his unpublished

---

134. Latourette, *Thousand Years of Uncertainty.*

135. Latourette, *Thousand Years of Uncertainty*, 2:14.

136. Tippett, *Introduction to Missiology*, 254–55.

137. Gottschalk et al., *Use of Personal Documents*, 79–173; Tippett, *Aspects of Pacific Ethnohistory*, 197.

138. Tippett, *Aspects of Pacific Ethnohistory.*

manuscript "The Distribution and Use of Documents in Oceania,"[139] and more of his compiled material has now been published as *Fullness of Time: Ethnohistory Selections from the Writings of Alan R. Tippett.*[140]

He was enthusiastic about the potential for ethnohistorical studies to provide understanding of existing patterns of growth and non-growth of the church, and through that to aim for maximum impact using better strategies. In his enthusiasm he predicted that studies of cultures and the impact of Christianity around the world would be much more accurate and useful by the end of the twentieth century because of the availability of interdisciplinary areas of study, especially ethnohistory. In fact, he sees those areas of study as so important that he muses,

> One of the features of the next generation of missiologists will certainly be the development of that currently vague area covered by terms like ethnohistory, ethnotheology, ethnolinguistics, ethnopsychology, and ethnobiblical studies. If I am still alive at the end of the century I expect to see a large body of literature along these lines, and I think it will transform the character and quality of missiology in this Post-colonial Age . . . If we do not develop these interdisciplinary methods missiology will perish and become no more than a historical experiment of the 1970s and 80s, an unsuccessful attempt to deal with the anomie of the 1960s.[141]

While highlighting the importance of these types of studies, he was apprehensive at the same time as to whether they would be used by others. Regarding ethnohistory he notes in *Introduction to Missiology*, despite its importance, "nobody wants to teach it."[142]

Having seen the benefits of ethnohistorical research methodologies from Tippett's perspective, the current situation in missiological writing does not reflect the enthusiasm that Tippett exuded: The late Lloyd Kwast contributed an ethnohistorical chapter to *God, Man and Church Growth: A Festschrift in Honour of Donald Anderson McGavran*;[143] Darrell Whiteman's 559-page, extensively footnoted *Melanesians and Missionaries*[144] was researched in the Solomon Islands and was described by Alan Tippett as "a

139. Tippett, "Distribution and Use of Documents."
140. Tippett and Priest, *Fullness of Time.*
141. Tippett, *Introduction to Missiology*, 246.
142. Tippett, *Introduction to Missiology*, xviii.
143. Tippett, *God, Man and Church Growth.*
144. Whiteman, *Melanesians and Missionaries.*

truly significant piece of work . . . in ethnohistory,"[145] and Stephen Pavey's *Theologies of Power and Crisis: Envisioning/ Embodying Christianity in Hong Kong*[146] is fascinating reading, making good use of the tools of ethnohistory in a modern city, and once again, arrives at some surprising and useful conclusions. The last major work is Doug Priest's compilation of Tippett's writings on the topic, *Fullness of Time: Ethnohistory Selections from the Writings of Alan R. Tippett.*[147] While being able to list individual works that have used ethnohistorical insights, it is obvious that this research methodology that Tippett considered to be the most useful in missiology has not been utilized by others in mission and missiology to the degree that he thought was warranted. That does not necessarily mean that ethnohistory is not a valuable research tool. It does mean that it has not been used significantly.

This leaves the question of why ethnohistory has not entered the mainstream of missiological research? It seems to be all but forgotten by contemporary missiologists. I suggest the following six factors may have contributed to its demise in missiological research. (1) While it has been demonstrated that Tippett was very engaged with ethnohistorical research, however, for other researchers, professional tenure and advancement in the academic world places requirements on them to do their own research and to maintain a publication schedule coming from that research. This induces an automatic tendency to leave other people's perspectives and to work on one's own perspectives and priorities. (2) Economic rationalism tends to limit missionary research, particularly at the level of research that Tippett did and advocated, especially ethnohistorical research. From the point of view of a mission board, ethnohistorical research requires a large investment of time for the personnel involved. For leaders to approve this type of research, they would need to understand it well, including the benefits that would come from it. However, as shown in this study, this has seldom been the case. (3) Often the findings of such research were not popular with the mission boards that had to give their approval for the research to take place. (4) The direction of mission activity was also a barrier. For some mission organizations, church growth and the focus on unreached people groups quickly became unpopular because they were either implemented naïvely so long term fruitfulness was not achieved, or were too threatening to the status quo or vested interests of mission boards and missionaries. (5) The

145. Whiteman, *Melanesians and Missionaries*, xviii.

146. Pavey, *Theologies of Power and Crisis.*

147. Tippett and Priest, *Fullness of Time.*

neo-colonial approaches typical of contemporary mission activities, which are predominantly focused around short term mission, do not provide the reflective process to even notice that this sort of research should play a part. Furthermore, (6) there is a general sense that the twenty-first-century world is changing so fast that there is not only no time for such research, but also the thought that its findings would be invalid by the time that they were documented. While acknowledging these six elements, they do not fundamentally diminish the importance of the types of research that Tippett did, or the in-depth reflection coming from that research that was the essence of his missiological writings.

CONCLUSION

This chapter has explored the third of Tippett's life themes, namely, the importance of appropriate research methodologies. Having identified Tippett's life as a life of research, the chapter showed conclusively that Tippett saw the research methodologies of history, anthropology, and ethnohistory as seminal to provide the verifiable data that would provide the basis of missiology and guide effective mission. The importance of historical research was recognized. Furthermore, the usefulness of historical study when focusing on the future was also identified, thus aiding in the study of Great Commission missiology. Anthropological field research was shown to be useful in developing a valid and verifiable information base to understand the people and cultures amongst whom missionaries were serving. That information base yielded insights to enhance the task of mission while buffering possible negative influences that could come from inappropriate utilization of the tools of anthropology. Ethnohistory, as an anthropological research method, was identified as a very fertile research methodology that was especially important to Tippett. The reasons for this were demonstrated in an extended series of case studies. It was shown that the painstaking work required to carry out ethnohistorical research richly rewarded the researcher with the insights gained. So much so that in this study there was a sense of loss in realizing that ethnohistorical methods are seldom used in missiological anthropology today. In summary, there was so much that Tippett developed in each of these areas of research that was a great resource to those who chose to use it in his era. The same could be said for those who choose to utilize those insights for contemporary mission.

7

Alan Tippett's Strategic Missiology 1

Societal Decision-making

Barnett's book on Innovation[1] provided him [Tippett] with,

terminology for its scientific analysis [of the task of mission]—advocates, acceptance and rejection and so on. It provided the machinery for examining processes of decision-making and models for depicting the components of the process . . . It gave me the models and theoretical tools for analysing the process of the people movement.[2]

THIS CHAPTER WILL EXAMINE the societal decision-making aspect of Alan Tippett's fourth life theme regarding the importance of strategic missiology and strategic missionary practice. The concept of people movements will be researched from a societal and mission point of view, utilizing Tippett's extensive insights. This will focus on people movements as a social and religious phenomenon, documenting key concepts regarding precipitating and caring for people movements. Societal receptivity to the gospel will be investigated through Tippett's writings to show mission leaders and field missionaries the importance of continually evaluating the most fruitful areas for mission deployment and involvement. Meanwhile, Tippett's perspective on the two related concepts of discipling and perfecting provide the means

1. Barnett, *Innovation*, 283.
2. Tippett et al., *No Continuing City*, 283.

for significant ministry impact as quantitative and qualitative growth of individuals and movements are facilitated and monitored for maximum long term growth. These technical areas provide Tippett's insights into how to see the greatest number of people and societies impacted by the gospel.

SOCIETAL DECISION-MAKING

In numerous ways, Tippett highlighted why it is so important to understand societal decision-making processes and structures, because he realized that the degree of understanding and utilization of that knowledge can help or hinder the communication of the gospel.[3] When reflecting on the fact that a part of the task of mission is to bring people to faith in Christ, it is obvious that decision-making plays a key part in seeing that task fulfilled. However, while reflecting on this task, decision-making terminology is often used without noticing the societal issues of the way those decisions are made. For example, both the evangelical Christian term "decision for Christ" to identify the process by which a person formalizes their new-found faith, or the anthropological term of "cultural innovation," relate to the process of decision-making.[4] Asamoah-Gyadu's "Your Body is a Temple: Conversion Narratives in African-Led Eastern European Pentecostalism" highlights decision-making in a meaningful way for his context, as does McGavran's *Bridges for God*[5] for other multi-individual contexts. The point is, each society has its own decision-making norms, and therefore people in those societies assume that important decisions will be made following their cultural rules. Conversely, they tend to suspect decisions made in other ways.

These decision-making approaches can be quite different from society to society. Sample decision-making terminology and structures from various societies will illustrate this point: Individualistic decision-making is particularly familiar in contemporary urban Western society. The term "multi-individual, mutually interdependent decision-making" was developed by the Institute of Church Growth team while in Oregon to describe the decision-making processes in societies where decision-making is multi-individual in nature. The point of interest here is that such societies, therefore, have the potential for people movements to occur. Bruce Malina, in his *The New Testament World: Insights from Cultural Anthropology* describes the, "psychological orientation (of people in the New Testament era)

3. Tippett, *Verdict Theology in Missionary Theory*, 124, 166.

4. Asamoah-Gyadu, "Your Body Is a Temple."

5. McGavran, *Bridges of God*.

as 'dyadism' (from the Greek word meaning a pair, a twosome), as opposed to 'individualism.' The dyadic person is essentially a group-embedded and group-oriented person."[6] This study will explore the societal dimension of decision-making that is central to the fulfillment of the Great Commission, using several key concepts from Tippett's missiology for practical application in mission, namely people movements, societal receptivity, discipling, and perfecting.

PEOPLE MOVEMENTS

In this section, people movements will be investigated as one important aspect of societal decision-making that is part of the strategic outworking of Tippett's missiology.

Defining People Movements

People movements is the term given to the phenomenon of people making decisions for Christ utilizing the multi-individual decision-making procedures that were common through much of human history and are common in many parts of the world today. This is known technically as multi-individual mutually interdependent decision-making, a term that will be explored further.[7] People movements is a term that has been attributed to McGavran,[8] which he describes as,

> A people movement results from the joint decision of a number of individuals all from the same people, which enables them to become Christians without social dislocation, while remaining in full contact with their non-Christian relatives, thus enabling other segments of that people group, across the years, after suitable instruction, to come to similar decisions and form Christian churches made up exclusively of members of that people.[9]

Hesselgrave's more restrictive definition is, "People movements is the phenomena of a significant number of people of one tribe, class, or cast converting to Christ together."[10] While Tippett, in his chapter "The Holy Spirit

---

6. Malina, *New Testament World*, 62.

7. Tippett, *Introduction to Missiology*, 175, 260.

8. Tippett, *Introduction to Missiology*, 253.

9. McGavran and Wagner, *Understanding Church Growth*, 223.

10. Hesselgrave, "People Movements," 743.

and Receptive Populations" in *Crucial Issues in Mission Tomorrow*,[11] uses the word "populations" from his title to direct attention to people of non-Western background where the decision-making processes of ethnic and extended family realities mean that "such groups may elect to turn from animism to Christianity as total units at one precise point of time,"[12] with the term "animism," as used by Tippett in this quote being addressed in a subsequent chapter.

Referring again to McGavran's description above, one phrase however requires additional comment, that is, "form Christian churches made up exclusively of members of that people." Often this statement has caused reaction, due to the fundamental theological assumption that the church as both the biblical body of Christ and the bride of Christ is intended to be inclusive rather than exclusive. One could explain this by saying that McGavran was writing from his Indian experience, where caste was a religiously sanctioned social reality. In that context, where many people movements had occurred, they had swept horizontally across individual castes, with new cross-cultural ministries being required to start new movements in different castes. McGavran uses the image of "mosaic" to describe this social dynamic. However, McGavran continued to feel that this concept still applied in situations far removed from the structured Indian context. His view was that wide sweeping movements of people coming to Christ are more likely to occur when the group dynamics of "one kind of people" are utilized rather than inviting people to become part of conglomerate congregations as the only alternative.[13] As McGavran observes, addressing some of his opponents, the Galatians 3:28 oneness in Christ "is a fruit of the Spirit, not a prerequisite of salvation."[14]

Importance of People Movements

People movements will be shown to be an important aspect of societal decision-making in Tippett's missiology, as seen historically and as was demonstrated in his era. People movements are important for five essential reasons. First of all, because the decision for Christ is made in a multi-individual way which feels natural to people in such a society, there will be

11. Tippett, "Holy Spirit and Responsive Populations," 77–78; Tippett, *Introduction to Missiology*, 46.

12. Tippett, *Introduction to Missiology*, 46.

13. McGavran and Wagner, *Understanding Church Growth*, 261.

14. McGavran and Wagner, *Understanding Church Growth*, 169.

a stronger sense of local ownership in the churches that result. The second reason comes from the first, in that the natural/local ownership element means that more people will consider becoming Christians as part of such a movement. The third reason relates to the strength of the churches that come into being in that way, as the joint decision-making encourages all participants to continue to be involved in the decision that they have made. The fourth reason is the degree of social and cultural integration that naturally occurs because of the sense of identity with the community that individual members feel.[15] The fifth reason is in the form of a reality check. In societies where their societal decision-making would naturally lead to people movements, if such movements are not strategized for and encouraged, or are even discouraged by only providing people with opportunities to turn to Christian faith in a strictly individualistic way, then the benefits above will potentially be reversed to become barriers to effective evangelism and church planting in that society. Hence, people movements need to be understood, strategized for, barriers removed, and ministry carried out in such a way as to facilitate people movements whenever possible.

Tippett's Initial Research of People Movements in the Pacific

Tippett's understanding of people movements initially came from his research of how Fijians progressively turned to Christian faith following the arrival of the first missionaries in 1835. Reflecting on the initial impact of Christianity on Fiji, Tippett says,

> One does not get far along the track of pondering the data before he comes up against the problem of the individual and his community. We are not dealing with an isolated individual convert over against his social group, which would make his conversion idiosyncratic or abnormal. Unfortunately many Christian missions have tried to grow this way. But this was not so in Fiji, where waves of conversion swept through localities and lineages by group decision or consensus. People were converted together within their groups, and new group normalities emerged at the same time, in the totality of the multi-individual conversion movements.[16]

What Tippett was researching in the initial movements in Fiji informed his reading of the Bible (e.g., Acts 11:13–14; 16:13–15; 16:33; 18:8), where people movement dynamics are also evident, in extended-household-wide

15. McGavran and Wagner, *Understanding Church Growth*, 225.
16. Tippett and Priest, *Fullness of Time*, 168.

movements. He refers to this in *Church Growth and the Word of God*,[17] and *People Movements in Southern Polynesia*.[18] This was well developed in his knowledge base and crystallized in his thinking by 1949–1950[19] and was documented, using other terminology, in *The Christian (Fiji 1835–67)*[20] and *Road to Bau: The Life and Work of John Hunt of Viwa, Fiji*,[21] volumes that have subsequently been published.[22] Later, Tippett's informal ethnohistorical reconstructions of the arrival and impact of the gospel in Fiji were enhanced by his studies at the American University in 1956. This included his first anthropology course, his archival studies courses combined with the research and writing of his Master's thesis, "The Nineteenth-Century Labour Trade in the South West Pacific: A Study of Slavery and Indenture as the Origin of Present-day Racial Problems."[23] This study and research added to his understanding of people movements and their strategic significance. About this time, he read McGavran's *The Bridges of God: A Study in the Strategy of Missions*.[24] This study of people movements helped Tippett with terminology including the term *people movements*.

Early Missiological Research into People Movements

In the twentieth century, much of the initial writing about people movements related to spontaneously occurring people movements in India. Since the 1930s, "mass movements" was the term that had been used to describe those movements, starting with J. Waskom Pickett's important work *Christian Mass Movements in India: A Study with Recommendations*.[25] From McGavran's continued research on the topic, he had developed the term "people movements" by the time he wrote his book, *Bridges of God*.[26] Tippett had researched the phenomenon extensively in Fiji using other terminology, "revival" being one of the terms he used, drawing on the journals of the missionaries of the time. The outward dramatic demonstration of

17. Tippett, *Church Growth and the Word*, 31–33.

18. Tippett, *People Movements in Southern Polynesia*, 85, 199–206, 262.

19. Tippett, "Dynamics of Church-Planting in Fiji," ii.

20. Tippett, *Christian (Fiji 1835–67)*.

21. Tippett, "Road to Bau."

22. Tippett, *Integrating Gospel and the Christian*; Tippett, *Road to Bau*.

23. Tippett, "Nineteenth-Century Labour Trade."

24. McGavran, *Bridges of God*.

25. Pickett, *Christian Mass Movements in India*.

26. McGavran, *Bridges of God*.

some individual conversion experiences within these people movements would align with the usage of that term in that era.[27] Later he accepted the term "people movements" from McGavran's *Bridges of God*[28] usage.[29] As people movements came to be understood more, this provided better tools to subsequently research and document the phenomenon of multi-individual mutually interdependent decision-making, that was the basis of people movements.[30]

The terminology used to describe people movements has practical as well as theoretical importance. As Pickett reported from his India studies,[31] he studied 100 reports of historic people movements, but didn't find an attempt to identify them by a special name until 1892. Hence, because of lack of terminology to describe the phenomenon they were largely ignored or incorrectly named. When the outsider ministering in a people movement situation does not recognize the internal dynamics, the tendency is to describe the large numbers turning to Christ as a "revival," or by some other terminology that they may be familiar with.[32] When that occurs, it causes serious misunderstanding because they do not realize that what they are observing and ministering to is a normal but unique phenomenon. Because it is normal, there is no need for concern. However, because it is unique, it will require special follow-up procedures to bring it to full fruit and stability; "consummation," to use Tippett's term.[33] Either way, when people ministering in those people movement contexts did not understand the phenomenon, they were less likely to be able to respond appropriately. McGavran illustrates this phenomenon in a chapter entitled "Halting Due to Redemption and Lift."[34] He refers initially to the naturally occurring redemption and lift that occurs as people come to faith in Christ.[35] However he also points out that mission organizations can become involved in social development programs such as education and medical in a way that is un-

27. Tippett, *Integrating Gospel and the Christian*, 180.

28. McGavran, *Bridges of God*, v, 13.

29. Tippett, "Dynamics of Church-Planting in Fiji," ii.

30. Tippett et al., *No Continuing City*, 277; McGavran and Wagner, *Understanding Church Growth*, 231.

31. Pickett, *Christian Mass Movements in India*, 21.

32. Hesselgrave, "People Movements," 743.

33. Tippett, *Verdict Theology in Missionary Theory*, 149.

34. McGavran and Wagner, *Understanding Church Growth*, 209–20.

35. McGavran and Wagner, *Understanding Church Growth*, 210.

healthy for the ministry in that situation.[36] Later, while examining people movements, he takes this a step further, highlighting that mission organizations need to be even more cautious. First of all, due to the unprecedented number of new converts involved, community strength and community resources can take on those challenges without relying as extensively on external assistance compared with the situation when only a few people convert to Christianity. At the same time, if the missions involved do get involved in social programs, no matter how well intentioned they are, due to the large numbers of new converts, it will be difficult for them to assist people equitably. Therefore the attempt to do good runs a high risk of producing conflict. Furthermore, the institutionalization of such a large scale program would undermine the indigenous nature of the people movement that it was intended to serve.[37] The nature of people movements means that when they are not responded to appropriately, their positive potential is seldom maximized.

To illustrate this point, when it comes to evangelistic ministry in a multi-individual society, social coherence needs to be taken into account due to the strong sense of social responsibility felt by the individuals. If it is ignored, it can result in a culturally truncated conversion process that will leave a sense of loss for the people. To lose their sense of identity with and within the group is serious. Also, previously, conforming to their responsibility within and for the group was part of their definition of a "good person," so loss of face issues were involved as well.[38] That sense of loss will very likely make the option of Christianity seem unattractive to others in that society while leaving a sense of vulnerability for those who convert away from their social group. This potential vulnerability is described well by Malina, focusing on the societies of New Testament times, when he says,

> Such a group-embedded, collectivistic personality is one who simply needs another continually in order to know who he or she really is. The person . . . is not an individualistic but collectivistic personality. Such persons internalize and make their own what others say, do, and think about them because they believe it is necessary for being human to live out the expectations of others. Such persons would conceive of themselves as always interrelated with

---

36. McGavran and Wagner, *Understanding Church Growth*, 211–14.

37. McGavran and Wagner, *Understanding Church Growth*, 231–32.

38. Tippett, *Verdict Theology in Missionary Theory*, 139–42; Tippett, *Introduction to Missiology*, 332.

other persons while occupying a distinct social position . . . horizontally . . . and vertically.[39]

Using a similar point of view, it was obvious to Tippett that, in those types of societies, people either come to Christian faith in people movements, or, if by individual decisions away from their decision-making group, then in small numbers at best. Furthermore, if it was in small numbers, there would be a tendency to vulnerability or even instability as they endeavour to follow through on their decision for Christ.[40] There are also limited possibilities of an indigenous church to be formed according to Tippett's definition, because that also occurs most naturally when significant numbers of the group become Christians together. They, as a decision-making group, are then able to adapt their new faith into their functioning society. The positive potential of all of this is captured by Latourette when he says, "More and more we must dream in terms of winning groups, not merely individuals . . . Experience . . . shows that it is much better if an entire natural group . . . can come rapidly over into the faith.[41]

Tippett's Broadening People Movement Research: Conceptually and Geographically

Tippett researched people movements in a more formal way as he joined McGavran at the Institute of Church Growth in 1962. It was while writing his PhD at the University of Oregon that he developed the term "multi-individual" in interaction with Homer Barnett.[42] This more processual term has developed to be "multi-individual mutually interdependent decision-making."[43] After the terms "people movement" and "multi-individual mutually interdependent decision-making" were developed, when Tippett mentions the term "mass movements," he often does so with an explanation of why it had been such a poor choice.[44] Homer Barnett was the leading applied anthropologist in America, whose concepts aided Tippett in a num-

39. Malina, *New Testament World*, 62.

40. Tippett and Priest, *Fullness of Time*, 168.

41. Latourette, *Missions Tomorrow*, 159.

42. Tippett et al., *No Continuing City*, 277.

43. McGavran and Wagner, *Understanding Church Growth*, 231.

44. Tippett, "Holy Spirit and Responsive Populations," 78; Tippett, *Verdict Theology in Missionary Theory*, 139; Tippett, *Introduction to Missiology*, 47; Tippett et al., *No Continuing City*, xiv, 275.

ber of ways, including in understanding and describing people movements as seen in the quote at the beginning of this chapter. Writing about Barnett's book on *Innovation: the Basis of Cultural Change* Tippett said that it had influenced him more than any other book other than the Bible. Areas where he felt Barnett[45] benefitted him were key terminology for analysis, such as the missionary as an advocate, with acceptance and rejection being possible responses from the people. It included ways examining the processes people's decision-making. In particular, it provided him with the tools to understand and analyze people movements.

As Tippett explains it, the key decisions being made in a people movement are being made by people who live in mutually interdependent communities, so it is only natural and normal for them to make important decision in a multi-individual way.[46] This is why J. Waskom Pickett says that people movements ("mass movements," as he described them at that time) "constitute the most natural way of approach to Christ."[47]

Having come to see the concept of people movements, Tippett wrote extensively about their phenomenology, as he researched them in many eras in history and in many different parts of the world: The New Testament record,[48] the Middle Ages,[49] Fiji,[50] Southern Polynesia,[51] Papua New Guinea,[52] Solomon Islands,[53] etc. Behind these historical reconstructions, Tippett was highlighting the fact that the phenomena was still occurring, due to the multi-individual decision-making structures in many societies around the world as he knew it.

45. Barnett, *Innovation*, 283.

46. Tippett, *Verdict Theology in Missionary Theory*, 139–42; Tippett, *Introduction to Missiology*, 47; Tippett et al., *No Continuing City*, 277; McGavran and Wagner, *Understanding Church Growth*, 231.

47. Pickett, *Christian Mass Movements in India*, 330.

48. Tippett, *Church Growth and the Word*, 23–33.

49. Tippett, *Introduction to Missiology*, 240, 254–63.

50. Tippett, *Integrating Gospel and the Christian*; Tippett, "Road to Bau"; Tippett, "Dynamics of Church-Planting in Fiji."

51. Tippett, *People Movements in Southern Polynesia*.

52. Tippett, "Church Planting in New Guinea."

53. Tippett, *Solomon Islands Christianity*.

PEOPLE MOVEMENTS AS A MINISTRY FOCUS

People movements are much more than just a concept. They are a significant approach for ministry to multi-individual societies. For that reason,
reflecting on key ministry-related issues becomes an important second part
of this study on people movements.

Implications of Understanding People Movements

Looking back at the experience of Western led mission organizations,
people movements have not always been recognized or welcomed, let
alone sought after. Colin Dundon documents a conflict that occurred in
1962 between Tippett and Mr. Gribble, the Board Secretary of Methodist Overseas Mission, Australia, regarding a situation in the highlands of
Papua New Guinea. Tippett's research indicated that a people movement
was possible, in fact, likely. Gribble however declined to adjust their field
strategies or deployment policies to take this into account, and eventually
formally closed the correspondence with Tippett on the topic.[54] In another
example with a similar beginning point, but with a very different outcome,
Philip Hogan reports that, as Executive Director, Foreign Missions Department, Assemblies of God USA, he had heard of people movements but was
skeptical. However as some of their missionaries came to better understand
the culture of the people group they were ministering to, they realized they
were using an individual decision-making approach while those people
were multi-individual in their decision-making. When they realized this,
they were able to remove some of the barriers previous ministry attempts
had created. This opened the door for people to respond to the gospel in
a people movement, even though they had previously been regarded to
be resistant. Hogan's article reporting on this people movement was enthusiastic as he observed the difference a people movement approach had
made,[55] with the result that the Christian message became a viable option
in the minds of the people of that society because of that decision-making
approach.

54. Dundon, "Raicakacaka," 176–79.
55. Hogan, "Multi-Individual Conversion," 415.

The Individual in Multi-Individual, Mutually Independent Decision-making

People brought up in an individualistic society often have difficulty understanding the role and responsibility of an individual in a society where multi-individual mutually interdependent decision-making is the norm. Therefore, it is hard to comprehend the role of the individual within a people movement. When a person who is brought up in a society where individual decision-making is the norm, first encounters people movements, it is understandable that they could be skeptical of what they see. Such a person, say for example, a Westerner from a major city, having been influenced by the individualistic decision-making style of their own culture, would assume that individual decision-making is normal. For that reason, it is easy to become concerned about the group dimension they observe.[56] It can seem to them as if it is just a "follow the leader" situation. Thus, they do not notice the role of the individuals within the group.

A poignant example of this misunderstanding can be seen in the following story: In the highlands of Papua New Guinea in 1977, a long serving elderly missionary, when hearing about people movements for the first time as I shared at a conference, was astounded. He then told the story of how, in the early stages of his ministry in that area, he had seen family groups come as a group to confess their faith in Jesus. However, until he heard about people movements that day, he had been quite proud of the fact that he had sent them home again, telling them, "You don't become a Christian that way." Observing that missionary's response to the teaching about people movements that day was humbling to me as a younger missionary. He was so concerned that he had misunderstood the situation and was thankful to me for helping him understand these cultural dynamics. The point is, in a multi-individual society, individuals are not ignored. Rather they are noticed in the group context which is normative for them. The very fact that decision-making in these contexts can take extended periods of time is due to the time it takes to allow a consensus of individuals to develop.[57] This is in contrast to "majority rule" decision-making more familiar to Westerners, in which, in reality, potentially the desire of 49 percent of the decision-making group can be overridden by the determination of 51 percent.[58]

---

56. McGavran and Wagner, *Understanding Church Growth*, 227.

57. Hovey, *Before All Else Fails*, 210–11.

58. Tippett, *People Movements in Southern Polynesia*, 166.

It is interesting to look at this issue from both sides of the "multi-individual" divide. A person from a multi-individual society feels a sense of vulnerability if somehow they have to make decisions separate from their group. However, a person from an individualistic background would find it hard to imagine that vulnerability. Similarly, a person from a multi-individual society feels a sense of strength when they make decisions within their group. Once again, this sense of strength is foreign to a person of individualistic background. This of course will have very significant implications for contemporary mission, when thinking of the large groups of non-Christians today who fit Malina's category of "group-embedded, collectivistic personality."

Using some modern examples, this would apply to family members in many contemporary societies of Asia, where decisions are made as family units. Similarly, members of a religious community that requires uniformity, such as Muslims or Hindus in a community that relate to a particular mosque or temple, who observe each other to ensure uniformity. There are examples of whole communities coming to faith in Jesus by progressively making decisions as a group. This would fit the community by community phenomenon that McGavran refers to when he observes, "The great ingathering from Islam, for example, will come by people movements to Christ."[59] Another expression of this would be the peer groups of Generation Y/Millennials in Western society who make decisions as peer groups.[60] Decisions for Christ have been observed in high schools in Australia and Japan, as church youth ministries suddenly see an influx of students from the same class into their youth groups. On hearing those stories, I am always left thinking how much more could be achieved if the people involved in those ministries were undergirded by an understanding of the phenomenon of people movements. Reporting from yesteryear, Tippett documents age-grade people movements,[61] which would have some similarities.

As Tippett aims to remove conceptual barriers that might hold mission organizations back from a positive response to the potential for people movements, he stresses the significance of this for today by highlighting the historical fact that, "most parts of the world where Christianity is solidly

---

59. McGavran and Wagner, *Understanding Church Growth*, 224.

60. Carver and Cockburn, "Online Skill Development"; McGlynn, "Teaching Millennials."

61. Tippett, *Introduction to Missiology*, 46, 332; Tippett, *Peoples of Southwest Ethiopia*, 61.

entrenched were originally won from paganism in the first place by people movements,"[62] thus providing the Christian community the strength to impact its whole society. His point is that we don't question the fruit of these historic people movements, so why should we question the significance of contemporary people movements.

At the same time, while highlighting the strategic significance and strategic responsibility of the potential for people movements, Tippett repeatedly pointed out that there are other advocates vying for influence in those situations, such as other religions, materialism, etc. Therefore, Christians cannot simply relax knowing of the potential for people movements. Instead they are responsible to make the most of that potential for the sake of the fulfillment of the Great Commission. There are opportunities, but they imply urgency.[63] Furthermore, when combined with appropriate follow up, have the potential to see significant church growth, both in a quantitative and qualitative dimension.

Ministry Using People Movement Approaches

In addition to the spontaneously occurring people movements referred to above, missionaries, national pastors and other Christian workers informed by the phenomenology of people movements have been able to use the underlying decision-making approaches to enhance the effectiveness of their ministry. When this is done intentionally it sets the stage for groups to come to Christ using the decision-making methodologies most familiar to them, as documented in McGavran,[64] Hesselgrave,[65] Hovey,[66] Ma and Ma,[67] etc., often with large numbers of people coming to faith in these movements.

From Tippett's writing about people movements, it is possible to deduce a set of guidelines that would assist in future involvement with people movements:

- Worldwide, large numbers of "populations" are open to the gospel if approached as multi-individual groups;

---

62. Tippett, "Holy Spirit and Responsive Populations," 77–78.

63. Tippett, *Verdict Theology in Missionary Theory*, 76, 124.

64. McGavran, *Understanding Church Growth*, 296–334.

65. Hesselgrave, *Planting Churches Cross-Culturally*, 251–52.

66. Hovey, *Before All Else Fails*, 203–26.

67. Ma and Ma, *Mission in the Spirit*.

- When ministering to individuals, always remember their social context and aim to reach their group as well;

- The churches planted by people movements must be appropriate to the culture of the people, especially in such aspects as leadership, religious expression, etc. This leaves the door open for the people movement to penetrate as widely as possible within that social group;

- Do not hold back in the harvesting of a people movement for such things as "consolidation," leadership development, etc. They must continue simultaneously.[68]

- Leadership structures, roles, and individuals in society must be taken into account in stimulating and in consummating people movements;

- The energizing role of the Holy Spirit must be recognized as part of the people movement strategy.[69]

In the world of mission analysis and reflection, it is interesting to observe what other people have done with the people movement concept that Tippett considered to be such a strategic concept in his Great-Commission-focused missiology. First of all, there are those who have learned of the concept from Tippett and McGavran, adapted its implementation for their own situation and typically have seen increased fruitfulness as a result. As has been found in this study, if such a person has been following Tippett's missiology, they would also have been very aware of other factors that would need to be considered in the goal of seeing people movements occur. While not endeavouring to give the impression of fruitfulness in ministry being mono-causal, having an understanding of and setting a goal towards people movements has been significant in quite a number of cases.

My own experience is an example of this. The effectiveness of the ministry I was involved in on the Sepik River in Papua New Guinea increased significantly as I used people movement approaches such as advocated by Tippett and McGavran with people movements occurring in a number of villages and language groups. Looking back, the approach I used almost seemed to follow Tippett's script, when he said,

> Church growth studies demonstrate that responses to the gospel
> had been more effective when missionary advocates have directed

68. Tippett, *Solomon Islands Christianity*, 132; Tippett, *Introduction to Missiology*, 373.

69. Tippett et al., *No Continuing City*, 282.

their appeals to autonomous decision-making groups, who have power to act, rather than to individuals who have to rebel against the group to act alone winning converts out of, or against, or in spite of their families may build a few strong individual Christians, but it throws up tremendous group barriers against the Christian appeal.[70]

The results of my own direct approach to the community decision-making structures is documented in several chapters of my book, *Before All Else Fails, Read the Instructions*.[71] This came about from reading Tippett/Mc-Gavran material while on-field, at the very time that I was seeking insights that would make my ministry more effective.

The second approach is that of people who have their own ministry emphasis, who have claimed people movements that had already been documented but renamed them to suit their model of ministry. Don Richardson's entry in the *Evangelical Dictionary of World Missions* on the topic of redemptive analogies is a case in point. Having described redemptive analogies, he then adds, "Most writers on people movements miss the role of redemptive analogy as the cultural catalyst God uses to trigger such movements. Missionaries who . . . employ redemptive analogies . . . are more likely to experience the mass response a people movement brings."[72] This is an interesting claim when there is so little evidence joining the two concepts or the statistics in the way that Richardson has juxtaposed them. From my research of people movements over many years, experience with them in my ministry in Papua New Guinea, and now in researching this volume, I have not become aware of any material that would substantiate Richardson's statement, although he must have some examples that he is aware of in order to make his statement. In a similar way, people writing about church planting movements as a current phenomenon often assume that church planting movements are a new phenomenon that therefore replace people movements. Such a view is articulated by Wolfe in in his dissertation entitled, "Insider Movements: An Assessment of the Viability of Retaining Socio-Religious Insider Identity in High-Religious Contexts," even going so far as to state that ministries that emphasized people movements did not have a focus on planting churches.[73] Of course, as document-

70. Tippett, *People Movements in Southern Polynesia*, 200–1.

71. Hovey, *Before All Else Fails*, 203–26.

72. Richardson, "Redemptive Analogies," 813.

73. Wolfe, "Insider Movements," 35–37.

ed in many parts of this study, that position is unable to be substantiated, as seen in the many references to church planting in chapters 5, 6, 7, and 9 in this study.

A third approach is represented in those who have opposed the concept of people movements. Hesselgrave's artful brief article summarizes their areas of concern as: 1) use of the term "mass movements"; 2) political and social phenomenon of the Middle Ages being a) not understood well, and b) being too broadly branded as people movements; 3) biblical issues applied from a Western individualistic point of view, thus interpreting the biblical text as seeming to speak against people movements. Having outlined their concerns, Hesselgrave presents historical people movements and the potential of future people movements in a positive context.[74]

Caring for People Movements

For Tippett, the distinction between the quantitative and qualitative dimensions of church growth was very important in the context of people movements, because there are examples of people movements in various parts of the world that have not resulted in the sort of long term stable church growth that the church growth scholars like Tippett and McGavran saw as an achievable goal. When looking at the instances where this has not been the result, critics of people movements have often assumed that the problem is the fact that those people came to Christ in a people movement. Yet Tippett's research demonstrated this is more often due to the fact that the follow-up has not been carried out effectively, especially in the specialized way that people movements require.[75]

I provide a list covering this specialized follow up in my book *Before All Else Fails, Read the Instructions*,[76] which highlights three particular areas: 1) The need for the missionaries to accept and to learn to understand and work with multi-individual mutually interdependent decision-making in their involvement with the people generally as well as in ministry; 2) Learn to recognize and work with existing leaders, while facilitating the development of other long term leaders as would be needed for the well-being of any movement; 3) The missionary should anticipate the need for revival and do all within their power to precipitate such a move of the Holy Spirit. As well as the renewing and refining of the Holy Spirit's works at

---

74. Hesselgrave, "People Movements," 743–44.

75. Tippett, *Church Growth and the Word*, 62.

76. Hovey, *Before All Else Fails*, 213–14.

such a time, the fresh impetus of a such a renewal movement provides a new opportunity for the review and ongoing alignment of their culture in the light of their growing understanding of biblical Christianity.

Appropriate follow up was also a key point coming from Pickett and McGavran's research, as articulated by McGavran,

> Much of the failure in people movements is wrongly ascribed to the multi-individual nature in which they have decided for Christ. It should be ascribed rather to the poor shepherding they have received, both before and after baptism . . . Pickett's studies published in 1933 show conclusively that the motives from which unbelievers turn to Christian faith play a smaller part in developing Christian character than good postbaptismal care.[77]

Being Ready for People Movements

Being ready for people movements is a key to being able to see the maximum fruitfulness result from a people movement if and when one does occur. A missionary on the field, when observing the beginning of a people movement, can be overwhelmed by either the euphoria about what is occurring or by the ministry demands of the increased number of converts. Either way, unless the people movement has been prepared for in advance, the above factors can lead to ineffective follow-up. That is why missionaries need training in how to precipitate and care for people movements as part of their training and deployment to the field. That way they can be aware of the specialized follow-up approaches required for people movements and so be ready to implement those strategies in a timely manner. This potential lack of preparation is amplified when the people movement occurs in situations that have seemed to be resistant until then. In those cases, often there has not been sufficient preparation of follow-up materials prior to the beginning of the people movement. This can result in a lack of resources with which to disciple the large numbers of new converts. This is in contrast to what Tippett found in his research of early Fiji. The Hunt and Lyth families had used their virtual house arrest in Somosomo to prepare material in preparation for a major movement should it ever take place. As a result, discipleship materials were ready before the major people movements did eventually occur.[78]

---

77. McGavran and Wagner, *Understanding Church Growth*, 248.

78. Tippett, "Dynamics of Church-Planting in Fiji," 110; Tippett, *Road to Bau*, 58–60.

Tippett's understanding of responsive harvest fields and his research into people movements, left him with a positive sense about the future. That optimism however was contingent upon two things: First that these concepts would be taken up by those in mission leadership, and second, that field personnel would be trained to be effective in such situations. His main areas of concern were that the individualism that pervades so much of modern Christian thinking, coming from Western influences, will continue to make people, especially leaders, insensitive to the opportunities of, or skeptical about the validity of people movements. Tippett's concern was exaggerated when he saw the way that people movements which had experienced difficulties were cited as reasons to not encourage people movements as a major part of mission strategy. Rather, better research would have shown that mostly the problem was with the need for better follow up rather than with the fact of the people movements.

SOCIETAL RECEPTIVITY

While focusing on societal decision-making, Tippett and McGavran, through their several and combined areas of research were very aware that not all societies were equally receptive to the gospel at the same time. Therefore, being able to gauge and respond appropriately to societal receptivity was a key part of their strategic missiology. Tippett, especially through his anthropological and ethnohistorical research was able to see that some societies and situations were propitious for innovation.[79] In such a situation, it was as if they were looking for change, as if there were leaders willing to lead change while the society was willing to experiment with a new set of norms. In the previous chapter, it was observed that Tippett saw his research methodologies as providing the tools to be able to understand such situations, and be able to reasonably predict such openness on some occasions. As well as the anthropological "situations propitious for innovation" terminology, ripe harvest fields, and responsive populations[80] were terms that were also used to describe this phenomenon, with ripe fields,[81] being the shorthand terminology that will be used in this section.

---

79. Tippett, *Verdict Theology in Missionary Theory*, 175; Tippett et al., *No Continuing City*, 283.

80. Tippett, *Introduction to Missiology*, 59; Tippett, *Peoples of Southwest Ethiopia*, 286; McGavran, "Church Growth Strategy Continued," 342.

81. Tippett, *Introduction to Missiology*, 177.

Focus Ministry on Ripe Harvest Fields

Tippett's emphasis on the concept of people movements was complemented by the concept of ripe harvest fields.[82] Tippett's understanding of *ripe harvest fields* was a key concept in his strategic missiology[83] which he felt strongly about from his reading of the Bible,[84] his study of history,[85] and from his anthropological, ethnohistorical, and church growth research.[86] This was also an area where he and McGavran were in strong agreement even though Tippett used anthropological terms to describe the phenomenon more so than McGavran.

It is important to explore the potential for significant church growth that occurs when multi-individual decision-making procedures co-exist in a society with the characteristics of "open for culture change"/"ripe harvest fields" as examined in this section. Tippett sees the openness to religious change producing a psychological responsiveness. At such a time, if the gospel message is made available to the right people in the right way, there is the strong possibility of many people in such a community coming to faith in Christ.[87] Illustrating the implications of ministering to responsive peoples in *Peoples of Southwest Ethiopia*, Tippett points out that when people feel that their traditional religious systems are not meeting their needs as they expect them to, this situation indicates that a religious alternative could be presented without what he terms "too much social dislocation."[88] At such a time, a fear of being "godless" is the one reason they cling to their former practices. This provides such a wide open opportunity that, as Tippett says, "If Christianity cannot win converts under these conditions then there must surely be something wrong with her methods of communication."[89]

82. Tippett, *Introduction to Missiology*, 223.

83. Tippett, *Introduction to Missiology*, 177.

84. Tippett, *Church Growth and the Word*, 52–54, 56–57.

85. Tippett, *Road to Bau*; Tippett, *Integrating Gospel and the Christian*.

86. Tippett, *Solomon Islands Christianity*, 54–76; Tippett, *Peoples of Southwest Ethiopia*; Tippett, "Holy Spirit and Responsive Populations," 81.

87. Tippett, "Dynamics of Church-Planting in Fiji," 98; Tippett, *Introduction to Missiology*, 223, 92.

88. Tippett, *Peoples of Southwest Ethiopia*, 283.

89. Tippett, *Peoples of Southwest Ethiopia*, 283.

Understanding Responsive Populations

Of the numerical implications of ministering in ripe harvest fields, Tippett says, "When we speak of 'responsive populations' we are thinking of large homogeneous units of people who, once they have made the decision act in unison."[90] At the same time, he points out in his article "Parallaxis in Missiology—To Use or Abuse," in *Missionaries, Anthropologists, and Cultural Change*, "Any idea of a 'Group Mind' we reject. Communal groups are multi-individual."[91] This establishes the process and the numeric potential for people movements in the context of ripe harvest fields.

However, not all responsive peoples are responsive to the degree referred to above, nevertheless Tippett's example demonstrates the importance of being aware of the level of responsiveness of the people being ministered to, or in deciding who should be ministered to. In *Introduction to Missiology*, Tippett gives two historical examples that show the underlying factors that influenced such receptivity, thus illustrating the process of arriving at a state of receptivity. That was the mood-attitude complex that played a part in the acceptance or otherwise of Christianity in the period of AD 50—800. He provides a number of positive and negative examples, such as the Ephesian Acts chapter 19 account of the mood-attitude of the guild of magicians and sorcerers, who, it seems, were predisposed to accept Christian faith. However, at the very same time and place, the mood-attitude of the guild of the silversmiths was negative as they saw the potential for economic harm brought about by the actions of the guild of magicians and sorcerers. Consequently they reacted negatively by persecuting the Christians.[92] He further illustrates this from Indonesia's Batakland, where he explains how ethnic cohesion had held back widespread acceptance of Christianity. However, over time, the "demonstration of Christianity by a few families"[93] combined with other factors to "contribute to a growing conviction that the new religion was better,"[94] eventually opening the way for large numbers of people to come to Christ in a people movement.

Ramseyer however, questions the assumption that "open for change" necessarily means "openness to the gospel."[95] His point does have some

90. Tippett, *Introduction to Missiology*, 46.

91. Tippett, "Parallaxis in Missiology," 113n47.

92. Tippett, *Introduction to Missiology*, 227–31.

93. Tippett, *Introduction to Missiology*, 291.

94. Tippett, *Introduction to Missiology*, 292.

95. Ramseyer, "Anthropological Perspectives," 73.

theoretical value if there was any sense that Tippett and McGavran were making absolute statements about gospel receptivity. From a strategic point of view however, it is safe to say that people who are open to change are more likely to be open to the gospel than those who are not open to change.

In contrast to the positive potential for people movements in ripe harvest fields examined so far, in his chapter "The Holy Spirit and Responsive Populations" in *Crucial Issues in Missions Tomorrow*, Tippett uses the word "tragic" five times as he describes how the experience of non-growth in resistant mission fields had influenced vocal theologians and many mission policy makers to assume that this factor of non-growth therefore applied to the whole world. While opposing that view, in the early 1970s, Tippett observed many situations around the world that were open to religious change, and were in fact already turning to Christianity in large numbers.[96] He obviously did not want that "tragic" view to blind mission leaders to the ripe harvest fields of the world in his day.

As noted when discussing people movements, Tippett emphasized the importance of reaching the ripe harvest fields of animistic people while they are reachable still in their tribal situation and before they are exposed to more of the world scene including globalization, urbanization or other major world religions.[97] As the advances of the kingdom of God on earth since Tippett was writing about the ripe harvest fields of people of animistic backgrounds, there have been numerous other groups who have demonstrated amazing and unexpected openness to the Christian message. To use examples already referred to, Iran went from almost no evangelical Christians in early 1960 to one million by 2008.[98] China was estimated to have one to one and a half million at the time of the communist takeover of China in 1949, equally divided between Protestants and Catholics, although Yu's estimate is lower at half a million.[99] In 2011, calculated estimates indicated 70 million Christians, that is 5 percent of the population, according to "Counting China's Christians" by Stark et al. of Baylor University,[100] while 2015 research indicates 123,019,000 Christians.[101] Although these situations may have had some influence coming

---

96. Tippett, "Holy Spirit and Responsive Populations," 80–84.

97. Tippett, "Task and Method," 3, 5.

98. Markarian, "Today's Iranian Revolution."

99. Yu, "China's Christian Future," 49.

100. Stark et al., "Counting China's Christians," 16.

101. Grim et al., "Yearbook of International Religious Demography."

from the broader understanding of the spirit world that will be referred to in the discussion of animism in a subsequent chapter, they were hardly the tribal animists that formed Tippett's primary database. The focused openness of those situations indicates that there is validity in the concept of ripe harvest fields and responsive populations.

Homogeneous Unit Principle

Considering the volume of Tippett's missiological writing, his use of the terminology and concepts of homogeneous units is relatively minor. Yet when he does refer to homogeneous units, it is more as a statement of anthropological fact than in the more polemic style that came to be associated with McGavran's use of the term. For example, as referred to while talking about people movements, Tippett explains that the term "responsive populations" often refers to "large homogeneous units of people" who make decisions together then implement those decisions in unison.[102] The best articulation of his understanding of homogeneous units is in "The Evangelization of Animists," where he says,

> Most animist societies are communally orientated; they tend to operate in homogeneous groups. These groups, of course, do not ignore the individual; he is always an individual within a group context, however groups are multi-individual. Discussions of important issues for decision go on and on until a consensus is reached. This may take a long time . . . These communal societies have a high degree of social responsibility, and often the individualistic foreign evangelist has trouble with group decision-making. Groups exist at different levels of social organization, and authority for decisions may lie at different levels—for example, decision-making in domestic affairs, agriculture, religion, politics, and war may be the responsibility of household, extended-family, village or clan. It is important for the evangelist to identify these because the manifest behavior of the multi-individual group in turning from heathenism to Christ will have the appearance of 'group movements:' households, villages, age-grades, extended families or clans, according to their normal social organization. Unless it is so, it will not be meaningful to the people.

> There is nothing strange or unbiblical about this. The Apostles found that the rural villages and townships of Palestine often

"turned to the Lord" as whole communities, like Sharon and Lydda (Acts 9:35), whereas, in other cases, like that of the centurion at Philippi (Acts 16:30–34) and Crispus, the chief of the synagogue at Corinth (Acts 18:8), the groups became Christian as households. They were acting within the regular operative social mechanisms of daily life.[103]

So to Tippett, the homogeneous unit was a fact that needed to be taken seriously while engaging in ministry. However even the homogeneous unit itself had a fluid dimension to it. A family group, for example, that may have turned to the Lord as a household, could have similarly come to the Lord as part of a village wide movement if the situation was propitious for a wider movement. When it came to preparing missionaries to work in such societies, in "The Ways of the People", Tippett writes, "before people go out as evangelists into cultural systems . . . other than their own, they should have a general understanding that man and woman do live in homogeneous ethnic groups, . . . are extremely diverse in organization, values and religion."[104]

Yet because of Tippett's more measured tone, and his good understanding of McGavran, he understood the issues well yet was able to nuance them in a more helpful way. When the Lausanne movement conducted their follow-up consultation on Homogeneous Units at Pasadena,[105] Tippett was there as a consultant. He was pleased with the report agreed to by the meeting on their final day, that Tippett identifies as having been salvaged from a very difficult meeting by the editing skill of John Stott as the chairman. His observation at that time was that there were many people there with entrenched views that made it difficult to hear the views of the others. While he does not include McGavran in that category, he did observe that McGavran was fighting the same old battles in his characteristic way, when in fact the battle ground had moved.[106] Even René Padilla's article, "The Unity of the Church and the Homogeneous Unit Principle,"[107] whose title indicates an ongoing battle ground was in fact being negative to some extreme positions relating to homogeneous unit approaches, rather than directed against McGavran's main teaching.

---

103. Tippett, *Introduction to Missiology*, 333.

104. Tippett, "Ways of the People," x; Tippett, *Ways of the People*, 63.

105. Lausanne Committee for World Evangelization, *Pasadena Consulation*, 1.

106. Tippett et al., *No Continuing City*, 476.

107. Padilla, "Unity of the Church."

Persistent Proclamation in Contexts of Persecution

While drawing insights from Tippett's writings about appropriate strategies aiming for positive church growth, it is important to note what he has written from his study of the persecution that was part of the early spread of the gospel in Fiji. Tippett recognizes that there is an experiential and faith challenge in anticipating deployment of field personnel to places that don't seem immediately fruitful. He considered that Christians have a responsibility to make the gospel available as part of their role in fulfilling the Great Commission. That included being prepared to take risks to ensure the gospel is available to people in non-responsive regions of the world. Nehrbass, in *Christianity and Animism in Melanesia: Four Approaches to Gospel and Culture* describes how this challenge worked out on the Island of Tanna, Vanuatu in a period of twenty years beginning in 1842.[108] Reflecting on these challenges, Tippett recognizes the fine line that mission executives have to negotiate, as they distinguish between courageous deployment of their teams for the sake of the gospel amongst the unreached/least reached people groups, and foolish bravado that could be unwisely and unnecessarily detrimental to those teams. I can vouch for the difficulty of making such decisions, from my experience as Field Leader of the Assemblies of God in Australia New Guinea Mission, and then later in my role as Director of Assemblies of God World Missions in Australia. In the context of such challenges, Tippett admits the difficulty of determining,

> how much persecution should be endured. To what point of time is persecution and martyrdom the 'seed of the Church' and at what point does it become just stubbornness . . . At what point is it justifiable to discontinue a fruitless mission and turn to a more promising field nearby?[109]

One thing that has changed since Tippett raised these questions is the ubiquitous access to information using such technologies as radio, television, satellite TV, internet, and data-enabled smartphones, etc. This opens the possibility for initial pre-evangelism using gospel nuanced media programs carefully prepared with the culture and situation of the particular unreached people group in mind, aided by the insights of people like Viggo Søgaard in his book *Media in Church and Mission: Communicating the Gospel.*[110]

---

108. Nehrbass, *Christianity and Animism in Melanesia*, 102–5.

109. Tippett, "Dynamics of Church-Planting in Fiji," 99.

110. Søgaard, *Media in Church and Mission.*

By using these types of delivery systems, the information provided in that pre-evangelism can predispose those accessing that material to be more receptive to incarnational face-to-face ministries at an appropriate time. That way, it is possible to delay the on the ground deployment of personnel until the gospel information that has been made available by these means has brought that society to a greater degree of receptivity. These statements could be seen as authorization for missionaries and mission organizations to make pre-evangelism, as referred to here, an "excuse" to not have face-to-face contact with potential followers of Jesus. This danger is heighted because of the emphasis that this approach seems to place on the information about following Jesus and not enough on the formation of disciple-making. Yet I have information directly from leaders of organizations that are using these "long-arm" pre-evangelism approaches through radio, satellite television, internet including mobile phone based applications, who are finding that these approaches are making a positive difference in resistant people groups as a process of preparation for face-to-face deployment. Conceptually, what I have written here is illustrated from the experience of some of my ministry colleagues involved in campus ministry in Thailand. As they spent time with students who had received Christ, they discovered that most of them had been listening to Christian radio broadcasts for some years before they pursued Christian faith through the campus ministry that was available to them. Also, in the example noted previously in Philip Hogan's *Church Growth Bulletin* article, he explains that one of their missionaries had radio broadcasts to communicate the gospel to a people group that had previously been identified as resistant, and that this radio broadcast was one of the keys to the beginning of the people movement.[111]

DISCIPLING AND PERFECTING

For Tippett, the topic of people movements and ripe harvest fields had a natural link to the concepts of "discipling and perfecting." "Discipling" was seen to be the initial step as a person (or decision-making group) made a decision for Christ, and "perfecting" was the ongoing discipling and maturing process. This terminology, which Tippett borrowed from McGavran, was compatible with his Wesleyan theology,[112] and also with his research findings. He referred to these concepts as he reflected on his own significance,

111. Hogan, "Multi-Individual Conversion."

112. Tippett, *Integrating Gospel and the Christian*, 181, 193–94.

... this, I think, was my greatest contribution to post-colonial missiology. I was able to harness for Christian mission a century of
the history and developing research method, and the discovered
principles of anthropology. I showed how these can be applied to
the mission of God at the levels of discipling and perfecting.[113]

In *Church Growth and the Word of God*, Tippett aligns the concepts of
quantitative and *qualitative* church growth with McGavran's terms, *discipling* and *perfecting* respectively. He then examines many biblical passages
that address the maturing or perfecting process, Ephesians 4:11–16 and the
benedictions of many of Paul's letters being just a few such examples. He
also adds, "Discipling and perfecting then are different but related types
of growth—one the quantitative intake due to evangelistic outreach, the
other the qualitative development to maturity within the congregation."[114]
He illustrates how this balance was often misunderstood or distorted by
their critics,

> McGavran's emphasis on discipling (bringing people to Christ into
> a Master/disciple relationship as with conversion) and the follow-
> up of nurture or growth in grace (which was based on the New
> Testament Greek itself)—was frequently attacked as meaning dis-
> cipling without perfecting, which is nowhere found in McGavran's
> writings.[115]

The misunderstanding Tippett is referring to here is echoed by Wagner in
1978, when he told McGavran in a letter that theologians were at last starting to understand what they were saying about discipling-perfecting. At the
same time, he indicated that the controversy would continue, because when
understood, it is still confronting to people holding entrenched positions.[116]

CONCLUSION

This chapter, while analyzing Tippett's strategic missiology and strategic
missionary practice as seen in his fourth life theme, has shown societal
decision-making as one key component of his Great-Commission-focused
missiology. This has focused on people movements, societal receptivity, and ministry application phases of discipling and perfecting. People

113. Tippett et al., *No Continuing City*, 429.
114. Tippett, *Church Growth and the Word*, 63.
115. Tippett et al., *No Continuing City*, 279.
116. McIntosh, *Donald A. McGavran*, 279.

movements, it has been argued, because they utilize the normal multi-individual decision-making approaches of a given society, facilitate large numbers of decisions for Christ but do so in a way that has the potential to produce strong indigenous churches due to the multi-individual nature of the decision-making. This also reduces the foreign feel of Christianity. It was also shown that there are still opportunities for people movements today, while recognizing the challenge to ensure that they are discipled effectively.

The mood-attitude of societal receptivity to the gospel has been shown to open the door for major impact of the gospel in a society. The changes in community attitudes that result in ripe harvest fields can occur quickly. With that understanding and information available, decisions regarding the deployment of personnel and resources need to be made in the light of this ripe harvest field information.

This chapter's analysis of the way people make decisions, including multi-individually, fit well with Tippett's life theme of strategic missiology and strategic mission practice. The following chapter will continue that emphasis by looking at animism, and the strategic mission issues that come from that area of study.

8

Alan Tippett's Strategic Missiology 2

Animistic Contexts

There is much in the philosophy of animism which is in alignment with Scripture, and this should be possessed for Christ. Animist religion, on the other hand, is sadly misdirected towards deities who cannot save, and many of its offensive elements are perversions of ideas which could be good if redirected. The animists certainly needs Christ, for Christ alone can meet his needs. And this brings us back again to Romans 10:14.[1]

THE ABOVE QUOTE FROM Alan Tippett demonstrates his empathy with people of animistic backgrounds and his concern to see them in relationship with God, and then it alludes to his understanding of the challenges of ministry in those contexts, and provides a sense that this ministry was something in which the whole church should play a part.

Having examined Tippett's focus on societal decision-making in the previous chapter, this chapter will show the significance of another key area of the strategic missiology and strategic missionary practice of Tippett's fourth life theme, namely, Tippett's understanding of animism and ministry to people for whom spirit world beliefs and practices are a current reality. One important aspect of that—power encounter—will be examined in detail.

1. Tippett, "Possessing the Philosophy of Animism," 143.

Tippett's insights into the worldview of people of animistic background, plus his significant concepts relating to the opportunities and challenges for ministry arising from that understanding of animism, made him a key resource person in the missiological world. This occurred as his material became available through his writing and through his involvement on the world stage with McGavran in the USA. After providing a brief background regarding Tippett's experience of ministry in animistic contexts and the terminology he developed as a result, I will argue in this chapter that Tippett revolutionized the concepts available to analysists and practitioners regarding this topic. This was done by emphasizing the importance of an emic or insider perspective on animism, understanding biblical foundations of approach to animists, providing strategic points of practical application and outlining the key structural features of animism. More specifically, he revolutionized the field through his innovative and insightful teachings relating to effective ministry in animistic contexts, such as understanding the implications of *mana*, reading the Bible from an animistic perspective, and, in particular "power encounter." His concept of power encounter centred on: the cosmic supremacy of God; supernatural intervention in everyday life through the miraculous; and encounters of supernatural power precipitated by converts to Christianity, demonstrating their change in primary allegiance. Considering how many scholars have interacted with, adopted, and used the name of Tippett's concept of power encounters, it is clear that his teachings transformed the field of ministry in animistic contexts. In this study, I will show how Tippett's insights into ministry in animistic contexts have made a significant contribution to the effective strategies needed for Great-Commission-focused missiology.

BRIEF BACKGROUND: TIPPETT'S INSIGHTS INTO MINISTRY IN ANIMISTIC CONTEXTS

Tippett's upbringing was a long way practically, conceptually, and theologically from the animistic world that he came to serve as a specialist. Given Tippett's upbringing as a pastor's son in a Western society in the early twentieth century, his contribution toward the study of ministry in animistic contexts could not be a foregone conclusion. Nevertheless, he remains one of the most insightful and effective missiological anthropologists and strategists in the world of mission study and mission practice in relation to this area of ministry. This has been made available through the twenty-six articles and books he wrote addressing animistic issues, which include both detailed theoretical understandings and practical applications.[2] That practical emphasis in his writing can be linked to his initial engagement "on patrol," to use his term for his village-by-village circuit ministry in Fiji. As he trekked, canoed, and lived with Fijians, he came to understand their view of life, including the exposure to the spirit world that was a part of their life. Additionally, he was able to combine what he learned in that way with his research into the early impact of Christianity in Fiji and the response of the Fijians to that message. From that he was able to distill many insights to guide others ministering in animistic contexts. The implications of the insights that came from his Fijian ministry and research were published as "Probing Missionary Inadequacies at the Popular Level."[3] This article highlighted the importance of an understanding of animism for effective missionary ministry, even more so than the knowledge of other religious systems such are Hinduism or Buddhism, etc. As seen in chapter 2, it was this article that brought him into contact with Donald McGavran, and on to the world stage by joining McGavran in the USA, where, both at Oregon and Fuller SWM, animism was one of his teaching and research areas.

Tippett's initial Fiji research was followed by broader research on the topic reflecting different parts of the world, thus assisting many people in their ministry in animistic contexts. This started with his 1962 research for "Church Planting in New Guinea and Papua,"[4] his 1963 research for the book that became *People Movements in Southern Polynesia*,[5] his 1964

2. Tippett, "Probing Missionary Inadequacies," summarized the implications of the insights that came from his Fijian ministry and research, as seen in these later publications: Tippett, "Dynamics of Church-Planting in Fiji"; Tippett, *Solomon Islands Christianity*; Tippett, *Fijian Material Culture*; Tippett, *Peoples of Southwest Ethiopia*; Tippett, *Bibliography for Cross-Cultural Workers*; Tippett, *People Movements in Southern Polynesia*; Tippett, "Possessing the Philosophy of Animism"; Tippett, "Glossolalia as Spirit Possession"; Tippett, "Holy Spirit and Responsive Populations"; Tippett, "Adventures in Missiology"; Tippett, "Not-so-secular City"; Tippett, *Verdict Theology in Missionary Theory*; Tippett, "Suggested Moratorium on Missionary Funds"; Tippett, "Cultural Dynamics of Fijian Cannibalism"; Tippett, "Formal Transformation and Faith Distortion"; Tippett, "Evangelization of Animists"; Tippett, "Liminal Years"; Tippett, "Spirit Possession"; Tippett, *Deep-Sea Canoe*; Tippett, "Ways of the People" (since published as Tippett, *Ways of the People*); Tippett, *Oral Tradition and Ethnohistory*; Tippett, *Introduction to Missiology*; Tippett, "Slippery Paths in the Darkness" (since published as Tippett, *Slippery Paths in the Darkness*); Tippett, "No Continuing City" (since published as Tippett et al., *No Continuing City*).

3. Tippett, "Probing Missionary Inadequacies."

4. Tippett, "Church Planting in New Guinea."

5. Tippett, *People Movements in Southern Polynesia*.

research in the Solomon Islands resulting in the publication of *Solomon Is-lands Christianity*[6] which is Tippett's best known book. Therefore, to many, the numerous sections in that book that refer to animism, and the ministry approaches that such situations require spell out Tippett's understanding of animism. The following three chapter titles illustrate this point sufficiently without delving into the fertile detail of the text throughout the whole book: "Pre-Christian Religion"; "Problems of Encounter," and; "The Process from Animist to Christian Forms." However, his most read piece of writing on the topic is "The Evangelization of Animists,"[7] the paper he presented at the International Congress on World Evangelization at Lausanne in 1974. This was published with all of the conference papers in the 1975 compendium, *Let the Earth Hear His Voice*.[8] It was later included in Winter and Hawthorne's *Perspectives on the World Christian Movement*[9] so was read by tens of thousands of readers. It was included in the 1991 and 1999 editions, however, it was not included in the updated 2009 revision, when articles by a number of authors were revised or removed. By 2009 the Perspectives course in which this book is used had 80,000 graduates in the USA alone.[10] However, in such a large volume, he was just one author amongst many, so his name is not as well-known as a result of that book. That article was also published in Tippett's own *Introduction to Missiology*.[11] This volume uses page references from that publication. It was through these publications that utilize his insights into animism that he made his insights available to the mission world, be that missiologists, missionaries or church and mission leaders. He had additionally hoped to write a book specifically about animism during his retirement. That didn't happen and the mission world and missiology are the poorer as a result.

ANIMISM: DEFINITIONS AND APPLICATION

An important part of the analysis of animism is to define what is meant by the term animism in this study, including engaging with the debate about the use of the term. Similarly, it will be important to clarify the numerical

6. Tippett, *Solomon Islands Christianity*.

7. Tippett, "Evangelization of Animists."

8. Douglas, *Let the Earth Hear*.

9. Winter and Hawthorne, *Perspectives on the World*.

10. Parsons, "Celebrating the Work of God," 10.

11. Tippett, *Introduction to Missiology*.

application of such a term, when thinking of strategic Great-Commission-focused missiology and mission practice.

Phenomenological Definitions of Animism

Tippett's definition of animism in *Verdict Theology in Missionary Theory* reveals both biblically and experientially the importance he placed on an understanding of animism for Christian ministry:

> Animism exists in many forms—fetishism, totemism, ancestor worship, shamanism, and so forth. Sometimes, as in the Bible, it is spoken of as idolatry, a word about which there has been much theoretical debate. In the main we are concerned with the belief that the inanimate objects, trees or animals are the 'shrines' of spirits, which may influence the life and fortunes of mankind either for good or evil. Animism in some form or other is the belief of a huge percentage of the world's population—the very part which is undergoing the most rapid and dramatic culture change at the present time. This is why we have heard so much about people movements from the church growth missiologists. They speak especially (but not only) to this kind of people . . . The biblical attitude to the animist is that he remains in darkness until such times as he can distinguish between the Creator and the creature, the sacred and the profane.[12]

Tippett's definition has also been adopted and incorporated into other missiological writings, demonstrating the impact he has had on the field, with others providing similar but nuanced definitions. In *Communicating Christ in Animistic Contexts*, Van Rheenen defines animism as the, "belief that personal spiritual beings and impersonal spiritual forces have power over human affairs and, consequently, that human beings must discover what beings and forces are influencing them in order to determine future action and, frequently to manipulate their power."[13] In my book, *Before All Else Fails, Read the Instructions: A Manual for Cross Cultural Christians* I define animism as, "the deep awareness of the spirit world in everything, with this spirit world playing a real part in all of life."[14] Each of these statements were written as a result of field experience in Fiji, Kenya and Papua New Guinea respectively, combined with broader research. The comprehensiveness of

12. Tippett, *Verdict Theology in Missionary Theory*, 4.

13. Van Rheenen, *Communicating Christ in Animistic Contexts*, 20.

14. Hovey, *Before All Else Fails*, 127.

spirit-world involvement as represented in these statements demonstrates that Christian ministry will have to take animism seriously anywhere in the world where spirit-world beliefs and practice are endemic.

Numerical Definitions of Animism

Besides phenomenological definitions of animism, Tippett also referred to animism numerically using two descriptions. First, there was a broad global base of animism which he referred to as, "a huge percentage of the world's population."[15] However, even though global animism was an area that he knew well, he often referred to the hundreds of millions of tribal animists who, in his day, were on the cusp of embracing significant religious change. In *Verdict Theology*, he wrote of this urgency saying,

> change is going on all the time whether we like it or not, that no society can be static. This is especially so in animist communities, whether they are migrating to the urban areas or remaining in their traditional localities. This means the openness of millions of animists to new social and religious ideas, and the readiness on their part to accept innovations. It is doubtful if these doors will remain open for very long. Their new acceptances will tend to be permanent, at least for a generation or so.[16]

With that group in focus, Tippett appealed to mission leaders and missionaries to respond to the urgent opportunities that the tribal animistic world afforded. As he did that, he often referred to this segment of animists in the world as if they were the sum total of animists. It is while referring to this group specifically that he predicted that this degree of openness would be over in twenty years.[17] Gailyn Van Rheenen[18] and Paul DeNeui[19] have challenged Tippett's prediction. However, Van Rheenen and DeNeui's view that Tippett was unduly pessimistic regarding the time frame, does not draw the urgency factor into question. This is illustrated by the observable phenomenon that, since 1973, the tribal animists who have self-identified as Christian or Muslim have done so resolutely, regardless of the depth of their religious experience.

15. Tippett, *Verdict Theology in Missionary Theory*, 4.
16. Tippett, *Verdict Theology in Missionary Theory*, 178.
17. Tippett, *Verdict Theology in Missionary Theory*, 9, 95.
18. Van Rheenen, *Communicating Christ in Animistic Contexts*, 23.
19. DeNeui, "Typology of Approaches," 418.

The tribal animists that Tippett is referring to, number 267 million in 2017, as "ethnoreligionists."[20] However to Tippett, that was different from the "huge percentage of the world's population,"[21] those who believe in the active intervention of the spirit world in their lives and situations. Using numbers to add perspective to Tippett's statement, in 1970, Stephen Neill estimated that this number was 40 percent of world population.[22] Using the 2017 population figure of 7,515,284,000,[23] that would mean 3.006 billion. Commenting on Neill's figure, Van Rheenen says, "Because animism frequently hides behind the facade of other world religions, Neill's already high percentage is probably a low estimate."[24] In 1983, Phil Parshall estimated that 70 percent of Muslims are folk-Muslims.[25] Using that percentage with today's figures would mean 1.248 billion out of a total of 1.784 billion. Hiebert, Shaw and Tiénou observe that most Hindus, Buddhists and even Christians in numerous parts of the world are involved in folk beliefs and practices.[26] Consulting with one of the editors of the *Yearbook of International Religious Demography 2016*[27] while writing this volume, he said that they know of the fact of the large numbers animistic practitioners within the world religions, but make no estimate about the numbers themselves.[28] Considering the accumulated total of those actively involved in animistic practices, Tippett's "huge proportion" takes on very real significance. In *Christopaganism or Indigenous Christianity* Tippett referred to this broader scope of the term animism with the statement, "when I speak of the animist world, I am not confining myself to forest tribes, but include the great religions of Asia and the streets of the great American cities."[29]

Current Understandings of Animism

However, while looking at the definition of animism as used in this chapter, it is worth noting that in anthropological and some missiological studies,

20. Johnson et al., "Christianity 2017," 48.

21. Tippett, *Verdict Theology in Missionary Theory*, 4.

22. Neill, *Christian Faith and Other Faiths*, 125.

23. Johnson et al., "Christianity 2017," 48.

24. Van Rheenen, *Communicating Christ in Animistic Contexts*, 25.

25. Parshall, *Bridges to Islam*, 16.

26. Hiebert et al., *Understanding Folk Religion*, 77.

27. Grim et al., "Yearbook of International Religious Demography."

28. Email correspondence with Todd Johnson, 8 January, 2017.

29. Tippett, "Formal Transformation and Faith Distortion," 191.

"animism" is no longer used extensively to describe tribal religions such as exists in places like Papua New Guinea, let alone the broader aspects of spirit-world beliefs and practices subsequently referred to in this study. Using a statement from Michael Rynkiewich to make the point, "Few anthropologists talk any more about 'tribe' or 'chief,' let alone 'animism' or 'worldview,'"[30] a statement endorsed by Tite Tiénou in his response to that article,[31] and the fact that terms like primitive and animism ever did exist is a concern for Tiénou.[32] However, the term "animism" was the term Tippett used as the most acceptable terminology of his era, and as will be seen, used in quite a different way to the way Tiénou used it.

Tippett himself debated the use of the term animism in his chapter, "The Evangelization of Animists," showing that he was similarly aware of other terms, but chose to use the term animism. He resisted "tribal religion" and "primitive religion" as being too restrictive.[33] The three best-known terms for this concept in missiological circles have been "primal religions" (Harold Turner),[34] "animism" (many missiologists but especially Alan Tippett[35] and Gailyn Van Rheenen),[36] and "folk religions" (Paul Hiebert, Dan Shaw and Tite Tiénou[37] and many others), although Hiebert, Shaw and Tiénou frequently use the term animism throughout their book *Understanding Folk Religion*.[38] One of the objections to the term animism is that it globalizes religious expression that in fact is only ever local. Therefore, for people hearing their own tribal religion referred to as "animism" there can be a sense that this is a colonial putdown on their own traditional religion. This is especially the case for those who have been educated in a foreign context, with that education framed by an Enlightenment worldview. Some First Nations people themselves use terms like Indigenous Religious Experience,

---

30. Rynkiewich, "Do Not Remember," 309.

31. Tiénou, "Reflections on Michael A. Rynkiewich's," 319.

32. Tiénou, "Invention of the 'Primitive.'"

33. Tippett, *Introduction to Missiology*, 324.

34. Turner, "Further Dimension for Missions."

35. Tippett, "Evangelization of Animists."

36. Van Rheenen, *Communicating Christ in Animistic Contexts*.

37. Hiebert et al., *Understanding Folk Religion*.

38. Hiebert et al., *Understanding Folk Religion*.

or Indigenous Religion, for example, Richard Twiss.[39] Tippett infrequently but helpfully uses the term "animist religion"[40] as an alternative.

Therefore, using Tippett's frame of reference, animism takes many forms: "fetishism, totemism, ancestor worship, shamanism," idolatry, the belief that "objects such as trees or animals are the 'shrines' of spirits and may influence the life and fortunes of humankind either for good or evil." As such, it "is the belief of a huge percentage of the world's population."[41] Tippett's view was that Christian ministry anywhere in the world, whether directed towards the tribes of the tropical forest or the masses in the urban jungle, needed to take the presence and issues of animism seriously. As an update, it is interesting to note that the 2016 book *New Mana: Transformations of a Classic Concept in Pacific Languages and Cultures*[42] which is a compilation of the papers from a symposium on the topic published by Australian National University, Canberra, Tippett was not referred to in the text or bibliography.

TIPPETT'S CONTRIBUTION TO MISSION IN ANIMISTIC CONTEXTS

Tippett's prolific and insightful technical and practical writings regarding animism provide a vital contribution to mission studies by highlighting: the importance of an insider perspective; biblical foundations for this emphasis on animism; strategic points of practical application; and an examination of the structured features of animism. Furthermore, by making key animistic concepts understandable, and by highlighting the importance of key ministry approaches for animistic contexts such as power encounter, Tippett has made an outstanding contribution toward effective ministry amongst animists.

Gaining an Insider View of Animism

Tippett's chapter, "Possessing the Philosophy of Animism for Christ"[43] in McGavran's *Crucial Issues in Missions Tomorrow*[44] provides key informa-

39. Twiss, *Rescuing the Gospel.*
40. Tippett, "Possessing the Philosophy of Animism," 142.
41. Tippett, *Verdict Theology in Missionary Theory*, 4.
42. Tomlinson and Tengan, *New Mana.*
43. Tippett, "Possessing the Philosophy of Animism."
44. McGavran, *Crucial Issues in Missions Tomorrow.*

tion regarding an understanding of and ministry towards people of animistic backgrounds. At the same time, it provides a sense of Tippett's feel and empathy towards those people. His summary is classic for its brevity and clarity,

> Thus I believe that, despite the inadequacy of the animist gods and spirits and their inability to save, that the basic philosophy of animism demonstrates a capacity for the Christian gospel, if it can be adequately presented to them. The basic notions of this philosophy—the notion of the supernatural, the notion of right and wrong with a just penalty for the latter, the notion of salvation, and the notion of reconciliation between man and man—are the principles on which the gospel hope stands.[45]

The significance of Tippett's insights into animism comes from his understanding of animism from the point of view of those involved in such practices, and those who live in such societies. His article, "Mana" in *The Ways of the People*[46] is a good example of his "feel" for animism at the grass roots level. That is, where success or otherwise in all of life was dependent on the supernatural power that was used either for or against that person. This one key element of animistic understanding of supernatural power is often described in the literature, including in Tippett's writings, by the word *mana*. This is taken from its usage in some of the languages of the region of Melanesia in the South Pacific and was first introduced in the literature by Robert Codrington in *The Melanesians*.[47] Codrington served with the Melanesian Mission on Norfolk Island (1871–1888), where he had first-hand contact with many different converts from Melanesians tribes from the Solomon Islands and New Hebrides. These converts spent time on Norfolk Island to be trained as Anglican catechists before returning to their islands to carry on the ministry of the Melanesian Mission although he did visit their islands during his school breaks. It was in this mission context, more than formal anthropological research that led Codrington to write his famous book. Originally published in 1891 as Codrington left Melanesia, it has been regarded as a classic, resulting in it being reprinted in 1957, 1969 and 1972. In the African context the term often used to describe this phenomenon is "life force."[48]

45. Tippett, "Possessing the Philosophy of Animism," 139.
46. Tippett, *Ways of the People*, 379–83.
47. Codrington, *Melanesians*.
48. Tippett, "Formal Transformation and Faith Distortion," 172.

Tippett then describes *mana* and its operation as an "animistic belief in the supposed existence of a supply of *mana* or power which can be built up quantitatively and stored for good or evil intent, and this may be acquired by reciting certain magical formulae to a fetish."[49] So, it is with this understanding that Tippett described the socioreligious system of ancient Fiji, which, with variations, still represents so much of the world today, "The acquisition of mana was the most serious business of life. Without it there could be no fertility in the field of the cultivator or good favor for the lover, or victory in war. Without these the tribes could not survive."[50] Because "the animists have come from a world of power encounter,"[51] conversion and discipleship needed to take this seriously, which led to his development of the concept of power encounter, which will be examined later in this chapter.

Using that depth of insight in so much of what he wrote on animism, he was able to guide his readers to an understanding of animism from an emic, insider perspective as seen in an extended quote from "Possessing the Philosophy of Animism for Christ"[52] referred to above. Tippett demonstrates animism as a philosophy and as a religion from an emic perspective as he describes the process of a person or community of animistic background turning to faith in Christ. Although the simple sentences could seem to be an "ideal type," there is a strong resemblance of Tippett's description to many such cases around the world.

> The animist lives in a world filled with powers in a state of tension. Confronted with demons and the evil work of the sorcerer—often done through some evil spirit, he steers a perilous course among fears and demonic forces of all kinds. His gardening, his house-building, his personal relationships, his family encounters with sickness, and the enemy tribe, and many other things involve him in a complex of powers and counterpowers. He finds himself a victim of one magical practitioner after another and spends his days making costly but futile sacrifices. Then he hears the message of one who says, "All power is given unto me!" He discovers the evangelist has a Bible with a record of a life of amazing power, of a dramatic demonstration which speaks to his own situation. Here is a Lord who sends forth his servants with the promise of

49. Tippett, *Introduction to Missiology*, 8.
50. Tippett, "Liminal Years," 13.
51. Tippett, *Introduction to Missiology*, 331.
52. Tippett, "Possessing the Philosophy of Animism."

"power . . . over all . . . power" (Lk 10:19), the "Power with author-ity" (*exousia*) over all the powers (*dunamis*) of the enemy, and this is the kind of Saviour he has been seeking. He gathers together his charms and fetishes, and religious paraphernalia, which have always been too terrifying to handle (so that he has to carry them in baskets), and together with many others like him who comprise a socially structured group, they make a public bonfire or throw them overboard into the sea. The sacred, ornamented skulls, mana repositories that give them power in battle, are all now bur-ied in a common grave. The way of life for individual and group changes. The demonic fears vanish; people dying of sorcery crisis recover with amazing speed. I can document hundreds of cases of this kind of thing from Oceania alone. In my anthropological notebooks I also have records of interviews with nationals from Mexico, Guatemala and Navajoland to Taiwan and Indonesia, and Ethiopia, so much so that I am persuaded that the Christ of the animist-conversion experience is a Lord of power.

Thus there is much in the philosophy of animism which is in alignment with Scripture, and this should be possessed for Christ. Animist religion, on the other hand, is sadly misdirected towards deities who cannot save, and many of its offensive elements are perversions of ideas which could be good if redirected. The ani-mists certainly needs Christ, for Christ alone can meet his needs. And this brings us back again to Romans 10:14.[53]

The insider view described in the paragraphs above are a valid represen-tation of traditional life and subsequent conversion experiences in many parts of the world. It demonstrates the world as the animist sees it. It shows the animist's response to that world. It illustrates the fear that is endemic while living in a world of unseen powers and counter powers. It shows the underlying dissatisfaction with this status quo, yet a sense of helplessness in the face of it. As such, it also illustrates the sense of good news that they feel when they hear the gospel of a God of supreme power. The global im-plications of this type of thinking is illustrated, along with Tippett's distinct sense that animism has in fact prepared people for the gospel, as long as Christian messengers learn how to address the animist's issues. Having lived around communities like this over a thirty-one-year period in Papua New Guinea myself, this description has a ring of truth to it. However, one thing that is difficult to sense in these few paragraphs is the time depth that is usually part of the living and decision-making processes involved. This

53. Tippett, "Possessing the Philosophy of Animism," 142–43.

could have taken weeks, months, or even years, as a lot of the decision-making described above would include multi-individual aspects as well.

This section has focused on the challenges and opportunities of ministering to people for whom spirit-world beliefs and practices are very real. Therefore, while ministering to them, there is the possibility of them being open to solutions from the God of the Bible, that is, offering to pray for them, asking God to meet their needs. Subsequent sections will show Tippett's recommended ministry approaches that are appropriate to such situations.

Biblical Foundations for Ministry in Animistic Contexts

Tippett argues that examining the implications of animism for Christian ministry is not a new phenomenon but has biblical foundations, therefore should remain a priority. The opening chapter to his *Verdict Theology* is entitled "The Prophetic Attitude to Idolatry (Isaiah 44)"[54] and, in effect, provides a basis for the book's encounter with the world. It is in this chapter that he provides his definition of animism, and points out that the animistic world of his day was still an Old Testament world, meaning that the message of Isaiah 44 was still relevant. Tippett holds that, while much has changed in the world, the choice is still the same: to choose the sacred (God) or the profane—one of the other religions or materialistic options that are available to them. Further to that, Tippett traces the encounter between animism and Christian faith back to the New Testament period, such as Simon the sorcerer in Acts 8:9–10, Elymas the sorcerer of Cyprus in Acts 13:6–11, the girl possessed with a spirit of divination in Acts 16:16–18 and the bonfire of magical books in Acts 19:19 as well as references in the Epistles. Drawing on Barclay's research, Tippett points out that the religious and magical practices that set the stage for key concepts that Paul wrote about in his letter to the Galatians are quite similar to other animistic situations around the twentieth-century world.[55] He says similar things about the record of the Ephesian experience recorded in Acts 19 and Paul's subsequent letter to them.[56] The New Testament, as a guidebook for Christian ministry articulates factors relevant to animism that need to be factored into Christian strategies when ministering in communities where animistic beliefs and practices are present.

54. Tippett, *Verdict Theology in Missionary Theory*, 3.
55. Tippett, "Possessing the Philosophy of Animism," 128.
56. Tippett, "Possessing the Philosophy of Animism," 129.

Tippett's engagement with his peers demonstrates that this was an active field of investigation in which Tippett made an important contribution. In Tippett's book review of Maurier's *The Other Covenant; A Theology of Paganism*,[57] he admits that "Very few books have so stimulated this reviewer as Henri Maurier's attempt at a Theology of Paganism has."[58] Another perspective on the book, also referred to by Tippett,[59] is provided by Jean Daniélou. In the preface to the book, while commending Maurier's middle path approach, Daniélou states, "There is a real danger of failing to recognize inherent values in them [paganisms] or an even greater danger of minimizing the uniqueness of Christianity and thus falling into syncretism or relativism."[60] In Maurier's extremely detailed volume however, the emphasis on knowing the "pagan" personally is a theme that resonates with Tippett's approach. Having then described certain aspect of Maurier's goals and approaches, Tippett seems to be comfortable with his analysis of conversion. "Maurier sees the process of conversion as (1) *rupture* (a radical and total break), (2) crossing the threshold (open transition to something new), and as (3) bringing the whole man to God (the offering of the self to God being not just a pious formula: human life must still operate but be handed over wholly to God)."[61] A strength of Maurier's work is the way it provides significant surveys of both Old and New Testament material relating to animism. J. J. Burden's "Magic and Divination in the Old Testament"[62] goes further than either Tippett's or Maurier's Old Testament reflection, showing clearly how prolific the practices of divination and magic were in Old Testament times. It is apparent from these researchers that the biblical record of these practices is descriptive rather than prescriptive. These practices are reported, and understood culturally. However, they are condemned rather than endorsed as practices in which God's people should engage. Maurier, commenting on the extensive descriptions of the spirit world in the biblical text, makes the point that the Bible is the story of God seeking humans. As such, it is to be expected that the text will take the reader where those people are, in their involvement with those powers, making the biblical

---

57. Maurier, *Other Covenant*.

58. Tippett, "Other Covenant," 30.

59. Tippett, "Liminal Years," 2.

60. Daniélou, "Preface," xi.

61. Maurier, *Other Covenant*, 231; Tippett, "Other Covenant," 30.

62. Burden, "Magic & Divination."

text "eloquent for the peoples who are close to paganism."[63] Tippett's active engagement with other scholars shows the importance he placed on biblical foundations for ministry in animistic contexts.

"PAY ATTENTION TO THE PROBLEMS" OF ANIMISM: TIPPETT'S STRUCTURED POINTS

One of Tippett's most enduring legacies regarding ministry to those of animistic backgrounds is the detailed practical application he provides for his theoretical concepts. An example of this is his summary of "problems" that need "attention" in his article "The Evangelization of Animists."[64] In that article, Tippett provides a list of structured points of application which has immediate applicability to tribal animistic situations where the cross-cultural nature of ministry means that the problems he describes are more overt. Even though Tippett has chosen "evangelism" as his title, he points out that he aims his concepts at much more than just the initial evangelistic encounter. Therefore, due to the depth of Tippett's analysis behind each of his points, the article was applicable to ministry in the broader global and urban world where animistic beliefs and practices were active.[65]

These "pay attention" statements are listed here for convenience, yet are so crucial that it is important to explain briefly what Tippett meant by each of them, while one in particular will provide a stimulus for further analysis.

- *Pay Attention to the Problem of a Proclamation-only Gospel*

- *Pay Attention to the Problem of Motivation*

- *Pay Attention to the Problem of Meaning*

- *Pay Attention to the Problem of Social Structure*

- *Pay Attention to the Problem of Incorporation*

- *Pay Attention to the Problem of Cultural Voids*

- *Pay Attention to the Problem of Power Encounter*

---

63. Maurier, *Other Covenant*, 109.

64. Tippett, "Evangelization of Animists"; Tippett, *Introduction to Missiology*.

65. Tippett, *Introduction to Missiology*, 328–36; Tippett, "Formal Transformation and Faith Distortion," 191.

Pay Attention to the Problem of a Proclamation-only Gospel

While this statement about the problem of a verbal only gospel is not on Tippett's original list of sub-headings, I have added it to represent the essence of the following quote from within the article itself, thus showing that it is appropriate to add this sub-heading to his list while using the list as a guideline for ministry:

> The animists have come from a world of power encounter and presumably they, therefore, need a God who speaks and demonstrates with power. The preaching of a purely ethical Gospel is hardly likely to inspire such a people; but a life transformed by a God of power will lead to a new ethic.[66]

It should be noted that the emphasis in this sub-heading does not diminish the fact that the gospel message itself is a verbal message, the presentation of which can never be truncated or substituted with some other message. However, this "pay attention" statement relates to gaining the attention of a person of animistic background. Such a person has seen supernatural power validated by observable phenomena in the past. Therefore, when it comes to helping them to realize the significance of the verbal message, as reported in Mark 16:20, signs and wonders corroborating the verbal message are important. This becomes a demonstration of the reality of the Christian God of power, whose gospel message has the power in itself to transform lives from the inside. Similarly, as has been demonstrated many times in the history of the church, as Christian messengers and new converts have demonstrated the fruit of the Spirit in their lives, the transformed quality of their lives has often led non-Christians to request an explanation of what they have observed.[67]

Tippett makes an important point regarding life and ministry in the power of the Holy Spirit, when he says,

> So Jesus taught His followers to interpret His own mission to the world as a prototype for, and a prelude to, their mission. Quoting the Scriptures, He claimed the Spirit (Luke 4:18), and the gospel writers who reported what they remembered of Him certainly declared that the Spirit was with Him. *Thus for their mission to be built on the prototype He had provided, there had to be an event something like Pentecost.* The mission of the Apostles presupposes

---

66. Tippett, "Evangelization of Animists"; Tippett, *Introduction to Missiology*, 331–32.

67. Stark, *Rise Of Christianity*; Stark and Wang, *Star in the East*.

the *availability* of the Spirit as a source of power. An intellectual
or social Christian "mission" without the power of the Holy Spirit
is invalid because an essential ingredient is missing. When Jesus
gave his own model for mission it implied the power and activity
of the Spirit.[68]

This statement has implications for Christian life, witness, and ministry
anywhere in the world. Yet the implications of the statement for ministry in
animistic contexts are such that they must be taken seriously.

Pay Attention to the Problem of Motivation

Although using Papua New Guinea's experiences with Cargo Cults as his
more extreme example here,[69] Tippett's main point is that if people turn to
faith in Christ for any reason other than responding to a clear understanding of the gospel message and a sincere desire to repent and receive salvation through Jesus, there will always be longer term problems when their
expectations that were not part of the intended message are unfulfilled. For
detailed descriptions and reference material regarding cargo cults and cargoism, see chapters 13–15 in my book, *Before all Else Fails*.[70] Tippett cites
the example of Simon, the sorcerer of Samaria, as an example of a convert
that did not understand his own needs. Obviously, his motivations from
the deeper level of his own worldview had not been addressed. Therefore
discipling programs will need to provide opportunities for the converts, in
conjunction with their national church leaders, to evaluate their motivation
to ensure that such deficiencies are noticed and addressed, with the responsibility falling on the pastoral counselor, according to Tippett.[71] To illustrate
this point, in 1970, my second year in Papua New Guinea, my wife and
I had the privilege of hosting the National Superintendent of our church
movement in our home every second weekend over a period of months.
This facilitated some wonderful meal time conversations. On one occasion
our guest, an engaging story teller, told us of how he first responded to a
salvation altar call in a Sunday morning church service so that the missionaries would consider him as a candidate for part time employment. He
went on to tell of subsequent experiences he had with God as he later grew

68. Tippett, "Holy Spirit and Responsive Populations," 86–87.

69. Hovey, *Before All Else Fails*.

70. Tippett, *Introduction to Missiology*, 329–30.

71. Tippett, *Introduction to Missiology*, 330.

in faith. I then asked him when he considered he had really experienced salvation. Was it in that first response, or was it in one of those subsequent experiences? His answer has helped me in my ministry with people many times since, when he said, "No young man, I received salvation that very first time. I came for the wrong reason, but I came to the right person." As he continued to tell the stories of how the missionaries had maintained close contact him as he grew in faith, it was evident that they had enabled a good decision, based on problematic motivation, to blossom into a society transforming experience as he grew in his spiritual and leadership experience. The influence of his transformation on others is seen in his twenty years as the first National Superintendent of Assemblies of God of Papua New Guinea, during which time he led the movement in significant growth in number of churches, the number of provinces in which it operated, and the transition from missionary to national leadership.

Pay Attention to the Problem of Meaning

Tippett sees the potential for miscommunication as endemic in cross-cultural mission, especially when taking the gospel to people of animistic backgrounds. For example, he explains,

> Every cross-cultural missionary runs into this problem sooner or later. It is the problem of translation and of Scripture interpretation. Every word selected—the word for God, for the Spirit, for the Son of God, for sin, for love, for prayer, for forgive—comes from a non-biblical worldview, and is a potential for misunderstood meaning.[72]

Therefore, at that most fundamental level, it is impossible to avoid the problem if the very concepts that are to be conveyed have fundamental differences built in to them from the individual cultures represented. Instead, ways to work with the problem have to be devised. In particular, Tippett highlights three areas where the problem of meaning is likely to be the most volatile: (1) the way the listeners interpret the message using the filters and interpretational processes of their own culture and animistic worldview; (2) how the evangelist is perceived by the local people to whom that person is ministering; and (3) how the evangelist conceptualizes the message, remembering it will be filtered by the evangelist's own culture,

---

72. Tippett, *Introduction to Missiology*, 331.

including the culture of his or her denominationalism.[73] If the Christian worker assumes that the responsibility lies with him or her to remove as many endemic barriers as possible to allow for the effective communication of the Christian message, then each of those three areas will need attention. It could be helpful to subdivide each point into an informal research questionnaire, such as, "What filters of my own culture would make it difficult for me to understand the animistic worldview of the people?" "How am I perceived by the local people? That applies at a personal level, the level of my ministry organization, or the level of my ethnic background, etc." Having taken that exercise seriously, practically utilizing any new insights that become available, the next step is to prayerfully seek a pathway through the cross-cultural communication maze. By taking this challenge seriously, the problem of meaning can at least be mitigated as much as humanly possible, while the Holy Spirit is able to take the efforts of the Christian worker and use them to reveal Jesus (John 16:8–13). The insights of Randolph Richards and Brandon O'Brien in *Misreading Scripture with Western Eyes: Removing Cultural Blinders to Better Understand the Bible*[74] are significant in assisting a western missionary's adjustment from their own background and perspectives.

Pay Attention to the Problem of Social Structure

As seen in the previous chapter, social structure does have significant bearing on effective missionary strategy. This will prove to be true in animistic contexts as well. Social structure is a topic that Tippett refers to frequently in this writing. This was due to the way that social structure shapes/impacts the way people respond to and interact with ministry efforts. Therefore, knowledge of this topic will be important for ministry at many levels, from evangelism to power encounter. Whiteman defines society as being "composed of a group of individuals who in living and working together hold certain cultural elements in common, which enables them to organize and define themselves as a social unit, with well-defined limits."[75] So, it is the knowledge of these common cultural elements, plus the well-defined limits of this group of individuals living together that Tippett is focusing on. In

---

73. Tippett, *Introduction to Missiology*, 331–32.

74. Richards and O'Brien, *Misreading Scripture with Western Eyes*.

75. Whiteman, *Melanesians and Missionaries*, 27n26.

Understanding Folk Religion, Hiebert, Shaw and Tiénou, writing about the importance of rituals, define a society as,

> a structure of statuses and roles . . . differentiated and hierarchical . . . these structures become fuzzy and ambiguous, and the original order needs to be restored. Rituals reaffirm the roles, the relationships, power structure, and economic responsibilities of the society. At times, however, social structures need to change to conform to the changing world. Rituals are also used to mark transitions and to change people into new beings—children into adults, singles into married couples, and humans into ancestors.[76]

When reflecting on Tippett's statement about the problem of social structure through the prism of the above definition of a society in the context of ritual, a range of positive and negative possibilities come to the fore. People live in societies with predetermined roles. Ignore this in the evangelism process and societal conflicts are likely. Furthermore, societies have inbuilt structures for change and rejuvenation. If the evangelist pays attention to the problem of social structure, strategizing to work within that society, then there is the potential for wide-ranging transformation. Taking this a step further from Tippett's guidelines, one realizes that many of the people groups who are animistic in orientation use multi-individual decision-making. In chapter seven, this multi-individual decision-making procedure was shown to have the potential to produce people movements. If this is not included in the evangelist's strategy, and a very individualistically oriented invitation to become disciples of Christ is utilized, then this may seem unattractive or even subversive or demeaning to potential converts. Alternatively, when approaches are made to the group decision-making structures there is the potential for multi-individual movements to Christ and the potential for the transformation of society in the process. Furthermore, when the decision to follow Christ is deeply embedded in the group's decision-making, it affords two unique opportunities (1) the deep seated issues of animism are able to be addressed if approached in the right way, and (2) an appropriately indigenous or contextualized church is able to be established: one that follows the fundamental requirements of biblical Christianity, while either reflecting, or being compatible with existing ways of life, leadership, and related structures.[77]

---

76. Hiebert et al., *Understanding Folk Religion,* 293.

77. Tippett, *Introduction to Missiology,* 332–33.

Pay Attention to the Problem of Incorporation

Tippett argues that seeing people incorporated into the physical body of Christ for discipleship, fellowship, worship, and service is part of the task of fulfilling the Great Commission. He points out that evangelism that does not result in converts being a part of a fellowship group is deficient.[78] This has been examined in chapter 5 as part of Tippett's theology of mission. Furthermore, when it comes to practically implementing this, Tippett realizes that the communities that the majority of missionaries will be ministering amongst will comprise people of animistic backgrounds. The implication of that is his recognition that the church as people and structure in those contexts will need to be quite different from the model of church in the missionary's home country. In that context he asks, "How do they get their new experience of Christian *belonging*, so they become participating, worshipping, witnessing, and serving members of the Body of Christ *in their own kind of world?*"[79] In emphasizing "their own kind of world," he is highlighting the fact that he has just asked an open-ended question, the answer to which will have to be discovered anew from place to place as the church is planted.

Pay Attention to the Problem of Cultural Voids

In projecting his thinking to the prophesy from the book of Revelation (7:9), that heaven will include identifiable cultural and ethnically diverse people groups, Tippett asks what a Christian life should look like for those people groups here on earth? "How does the converted animist meet the physical and spiritual needs that spring from the tribal way of life—the problems of danger, of death, of sickness, or sorcery—and how does one discover the will of God for that person?"[80] His answer to that question will be analyzed in detail under the topic of functional substitutes in the next chapter where Tippett explores solutions to the problem of cultural voids. While researching that topic, there will be the need to look beyond the complex issues of "danger, of death, of sickness, or sorcery," to also engage proactively with the positive aspects of a Christian lifestyle in a very different world.

78. Tippett, *Introduction to Missiology*, 333.
79. Tippett, *Introduction to Missiology*, 334; italics his.
80. Tippett, *Introduction to Missiology*, 336.

Pay Attention to the Problem of Encounter

Tippett makes this the first item on his list, because he believes that when there is a problem at this level, there will be a problem at all the other levels as well. In this study I have placed it last for the same reason. That is, the following part of this chapter will expand on this concept from Tippett's writings. Biblically, for example, in Joshua's challenge to the Israelites in Joshua 24 and in Paul's challenge to the Corinthians in 1 Corinthians 10, becoming a follower of God in the Old Testament sense or becoming a Christian includes turning from certain things in order to turn to God. The positive side of the Christian sense of this is encapsulated in the Greek word *metanoia* which implies turning from one thing to another.[81] However, from the anthropocentric perspective of animism, this brings unique challenges because, within animism, adding more gods and accumulating more supernatural power was considered positive, if not the ideal. However, in turning to Christ, one has to turn from allegiance to those other gods and powers, and from reliance on them for any benefits. Without this realization, and without its implementation as part of the conversion and discipling process, the "Christian faith" of the "convert" can be quite tentative, even though that tentative position can be held for an extended period of time, and can even become an intergenerational lifestyle. Paul told the Corinthian Christians that you "cannot drink the cup of the Lord and the cup of devils" (1 Cor 10:21). As Tippett sees it, "it is precisely at this same point that the modern mission among animists becomes really Christian or just another kind of Animism."[82] This disturbing statement highlights why Tippett's insights into ministry to animists are so important. As a Christian worker, it is disappointing, if not devastating to acknowledge Tippett's suggestion that it is possible to commit one's life in service to God amongst animistic people, only to discover later on that such ministry had signally missed the mark. Yet Tippett reserves this statement for his topic of "pay attention . . . encounter" highlighting the importance of this item on his list.

Yet when analyzing Tippett's writing on encounter, one quickly discovers that he more frequently talks about it as power encounter. For the sake of articulating his contribution most clearly, this topic of power encounter will subsequently be engaged with in some detail.

---

81. Koranyi, "Mission as Call to Metanoia."

82. Tippett, *Introduction to Missiology*, 329.

THREE PHASES OF POWER ENCOUNTER:
ANALYZING A KEY CONCEPT OF MINISTRY TO ANIMISTS

Having concluded Tippett's "Pay Attention" list with his statement about encounter, this section focuses on what Tippett referred to as "power encounter," which is arguably a key application of his "pay attention to encounter" strategy. Tippett refers to power encounter and power encounters frequently in his writings, but for all of that, a cogent definition is hard to find.

Definition of Power Encounter

A summary statement defines power encounter as the ocular demonstration of allegiance change that is so necessary for effective Christian growth among people of animistic backgrounds. From *Introduction to Missiology*, the following condensed description, summarizes a number of the key issues:

> They are *power encounters* in which converts show their change of faith and demonstrate that they no longer fear the old gods . . . an encounter between their old and their new God. They have rejected the supernatural resources on which they relied and are challenging the old power to harm them . . . The forms of ceremonial cutting off . . . vary . . . These are symbolic acts, with their focus on the *locus of power* of the rejected religion. . . This cut off point may be a highly emotional and stressful experience, but until the battle is won here, their old gods will never leave them alone, and they will not be able to share the experiences of the Christian Fellowship. The conversion of animists is not a passage from non-faith to faith. It is a passage from wrong faith to right faith, from the false god to the true God.[83]

There is general agreement amongst scholars that Tippett coined the term "power encounter" with the following people directly attributing the term to Tippett: Gailyn Van Rheenen,[84] Edward Rommen,[85] Charles Kraft,[86]

83. Tippett, *Introduction to Missiology*, 82–83.
84. Van Rheenen, *Communicating Christ in Animistic Contexts*, 83.
85. Rommen, *Spiritual Power and Missions*.
86. Kraft, *Anthropology for Christian Witness*, 452.

Opal Reddin,[87] Peter Wagner,[88] and Wonsuk Ma and Julie Ma.[89] In ana-lyzing Tippett's writing on power encounter, I believe he uses the term in three related but separate ways although he simply used the term "power encounter" for each of these usages. In Tippett's own writing, the context he provided each time was sufficient to differentiate his usage, so there was no confusion when he used a single term to designate all three aspects.

However, in order to contribute to the discussion in a helpful way, I will articulate what I perceive as the three dimensions of power encounter as promulgated by Tippett as a heuristic device for the purpose of analysis and clarity. I have chosen to describe these three aspects of power encoun-ter observable in his writing as "three phases of power encounter." They are designated as "phases" (see figure 1) because, while they are interrelated, they are not hierarchical which the term "stages" would imply. The terms can be summarized as: (1) phase one encounter: God is supreme. This is the cosmic encounter of God demonstrating ultimate authority over Satan and Satan's forces. For a person of animistic background especially, hav-ing knowledge of God in this way provides a "safe place" from which to reflect on Christian faith; (2) phase two encounter: God is powerful. This is the demonstration of God's power at work in the form of supernatural intervention in the lives of or on behalf of humans, thus getting the atten-tion of a person of animistic background, and building their confidence as they reflect on and engage with Christian faith; (3) phase three encounter: Jesus is Lord. This is the conversion level encounter which takes place as the convert(s) to Christian faith, by an ocular demonstration, declare their conversion level allegiance change. This is done by destroying the power symbols of their former supernatural allegiances, trusting God to protect them, and thus demonstrating their absolute dependence on God within the context of their Christian faith and their society.

87. Reddin, *Power Encounter*, 3.

88. Wagner, "Missiology and Spiritual Power," 92.

89. Ma and Ma, *Mission in the Spirit*.

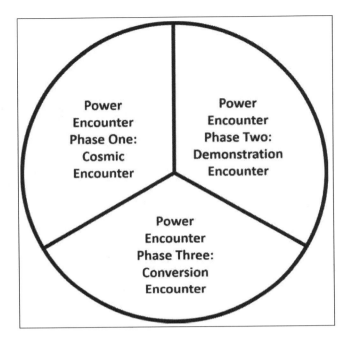

Figure 3. Hovey's Model of Tippett's Three Phases of Power Encounter.

As noted above, the term "phase" does not indicate hierarchy. For example, in practice, many converts from an animistic background have begun their journey to Christian faith by asking Christians to pray for them in the context of some challenge they are facing. At that point in their experience, they have no concept that God is supreme, or that Jesus is Lord. However, they have seen God's power demonstrated in miracles, or have heard about it from the Christian who has offered to pray for them. From a conceptual point of view, their request for prayer is similar to them approaching a shaman in time of need. For that reason, it is not uncommon for those people to offer to pay for the services rendered after the prayer, thus demonstrating that to them it was like a request to a "shaman." This highlights that their understanding of God is very limited at that point. When the Christians involved are sensitive to these animistic issues, in the context of their prayer they can take the opportunity to explain "who" they have prayed to, and "who" healed the person, should God answer that prayer in that way. By adding this explanation, they can point the enquirer to God. By this process, the prayer opportunity is reinterpreted for the person to be a phase two demonstration encounter of God's reality, presence, power, and love. When this is done well, the door is open for that person to understand the other phases of power encounter, namely, God is supreme and Jesus is Lord. Experiences like this have often been the beginning of such a person subsequently coming to a realization of God's phase one cosmic encounter, and also, to come to Christ via allegiance change, demonstrated in a phrase three conversion encounter. Having made a commitment to Christ as described above, in the ongoing maturation of such a person in their faith, no doubt there will be testing times as God leads them into deeper encounters with himself. At such a time, any one of these phases could be important all over again, although in a different way than occurred in the initial experience.

I believe that all three of Tippett's usages of the term power encounter need to be recognized conceptually and experientially when strategizing ministry for people of animistic backgrounds to come to vibrant Christian faith. When that is done, then the usefulness of Tippett's important concept of power encounter is maximized. I now turn to discuss in further detail what I perceive as the different phases of Tippett's concept of power encounter.

Power Encounter Phase One: Cosmic Encounter

Tippett highlights the point that the Christian message is itself a message of power encounter,[90] that is, God demonstrating ultimate authority over Satan and Satan's forces. My conceptual phase one refers to this "cosmic encounter" of Tippett's understanding and practice of power encounter. In *The Jesus Documents,* Tippett makes this point clearly in his chapter on the Gospel of Mark when he says, "The figure of Jesus comes through as the *Lord of Power* . . . There is so much in the story of Jesus, as Mark records it, that speaks to the encounters that the converted animist . . . knew . . . and will . . . know . . ."[91]

This cosmic encounter and victory will eventually be demonstrated throughout all eternity.[92] In the meantime, it is demonstrated in a series of encounters in the lives of people who receive the salvation God has provided. So, by extension, a power encounter occurs when a person comes to Christ, and every time such people make decisions that advance them in

90. Tippett, "Liminal Years," 11, 16, 18.

91. Tippett, *Jesus Documents,* 30–31.

92. Tippett, *Verdict Theology in Missionary Theory,* 89–91.

their life of committed discipleship to God. In *Before All Else Fails*, I used this sense of the term power encounter, to describe Abraham's primary allegiance challenges.[93] This process then is the "perfecting" dimension at work that was examined earlier. So the concept of power encounter is crucial in Tippett's understanding of God's intervention in human history, both through time, and also in the lives of individuals, and as outworked in societies.[94] To illustrate Jesus at work as phase one cosmic encounters, Tippett's analysis of Mark's Gospel shows this well,

> Jesus Christ is Lord; with power; and his kingdom brings a power encounter. He comes to the sinner, the sick, and the demon-possessed; and he helps the victim through his distress with an amazing demonstration of power in a salvation experience . . . passage of a victim from a state of sin, suffering or possession into an experience of peace of mind.[95]

The story of my own experience on the Sepik River in Papua New Guinea shows another way of seeing this. This relates to one very traditional village that, although it was in an area where a mainline church had been present for many decades, the people continued to pride themselves in their prowess with their traditional supernatural powers, including their primary god, who was seen to be enshrined in a ceremonial chair. That prowess included supernaturally providing for their own needs of provision and protection, as well as causing harm to their enemies. A number of people from that village, especially women, became born again Christians as they responded to the gospel while attending a Pentecostal church for some time in a coastal town. When they returned home they started having Pentecostal prayer meetings that could sometimes get quite emotional. As a result, they were strongly opposed by the village elders. As I observed this over a number of months of contact with the new Christians, I realized that the elders were afraid of what was happening, because they recognized that real supernatural power was involved, demonstrated in healings and even dreams that they had when they persecuted the Christians. From their point of view, supernatural power that they could not control by their own rituals was dangerous, because the *mana (pawa)* could break out at any time and cause illness, calamity or even death. Knowing that was not the case, I tried to arrange a meeting in which this could be explained to them in animistic

93. Hovey, *Before All Else Fails*, 71n4.

94. Tippett, *Introduction to Missiology*, 82–83.

95. Tippett, *Jesus Documents*, 31.

terms that they would understand. However, overnight the village elders prepared for the meeting next morning by using warfare preparation rituals, with the goal that supernatural harm would come upon the group of Christian as we entered the village in the morning. No harm came to us, so the meeting began. Although I was with a group of local Christians, because I was a white missionary who had been conducting weekly Bible studies with the new Christians for some months, attention was directed towards me as the "leader" of the group and as the representative of God. It was in that frame of reference that the priest of the primary god in the village shouted at me, using words something like, "Have you come to get rid of our village god (by name)? Our god (by name) is the most powerful god. Therefore, your plans to get rid of our god can never come to reality." In recounting this story, I am using the local concept of this statue being a god in the telling of the story. When they referred to this god, they were either referring to the statue of this god or the spirit being behind it. The two metre high statue comprised a large carved stool with a human figure being the backrest of the stool. The human figure had an elaborately decorated headdress. There was a personal spirit associated with that statue who was thought to be very powerful in *mana (pawa)* terms. Also, due to the way this village and the nearby villages had descended from a single community in a common location, the local belief was that this god held sway over more than just this one village. This was represented in the statement, "This is the most powerful god."

While I was concerned for his sake with the terms of reference he was establishing, I was at least pleased that the priest was using their formal debating technique. That would afford me the right to reply. However, when I tried to use that right, I was shouted down, there was threatened violence against our whole group and we were asked to leave, while being spat on by the women as we left and returned to the Christian hamlet. At 6 am the next day, a messenger from another village warned us that an armed group was coming to confront us. All we could do was pray. By the time they arrived, they had cooled down, which we saw as an answer to prayer. As a result, we were able to have some discussion—while they showed us the bicycle chains, etc. that they had brought to use as weapons. In that discussion though, none of the statements relating to the supernatural challenge from the day before were withdrawn. Then I was respectfully asked to leave the whole area. I requested permission to conduct a farewell Bible study with the Christians before leaving, which was agreed to.

Leaving out interesting sub-themes to the story, three weeks later, on Easter Friday, the statue of their god that the priest was referring to was discovered on its face early in the morning without its decorative headdress. By mid-morning, that headdress was found 160 kilometers away, lying on the road outside the church where I was preaching for the Easter Friday morning service[96] with no natural explanation as to how it could have travelled there. The combined river and road travel time was too long, even if someone had travelled from the village to the town on the coast that day, and even if someone had been brave enough to carry the god's headdress. On analysis, it can be seen that this encounter and its terms of reference were established by the village people themselves, as they said that their god was the most powerful god and no other god could get rid of it. Because of those unique factors, in their case it was a phase one cosmic level encounter. In the mind of the village elders, on later reflection it would have also been evident as a phase two demonstration encounter, but that would have been after processing the significance of the phase one encounter.

This analysis has identified this phase one cosmic power encounter as an important phase of power encounter in Tippett's thinking. At the same time, the analysis has also shown phase one cosmic encounter as an important phase for a person coming from an animistic background to be able to engage with God with confidence as they encounter other supernatural factors that have been a part of their lives until then. This point is made well when Tippett points new converts to the Gospel of Mark. As he says in *The Jesus Documents*,

> it is a straightforward narrative of what our Lord did, a gospel of power, . . . The literary climax of the narrative of the day of the cross is that the sarcasm of the priests about his kingship (15:32) rebounds on them seven verses later with the confession of the Roman soldier, a Gentile. (15:39).[97]

It is essential that appropriate teaching for people of animistic background may start with information about Jesus as healer. However it must continue on to show the full implications of that experience. Jesus is not just powerful cosmic ancestor who will heal anyone on earth, as animism could easily label him. Jesus is Lord.

96. Davies, *Invading Paradise*, 15.
97. Tippett, *Jesus Documents*, 32.

Power Encounter Phase Two: Demonstration Encounter

My conceptual phase two of Tippett's understanding and practice of power encounter or "demonstration encounter" refers to the times that God's power is demonstrated through miraculous intervention in human affairs. Lest this description of phase two demonstration encounter appear to be similar to the story above, and therefore seem confusing, it should be remembered that that story above was set in the phase one terms of reference that the priest had announced. I also observed above that subsequently they would have also come to see this experience as what I am referring to as a phase two encounter. But that realization would have come with later reflection, not in the immediate terms of reference. This is an important distinction, because, as Tippett points out, "The animists have come from a world of power encounter and presumably they, therefore, need a God who speaks and demonstrates with power."[98] As demonstrations of God's power occur, it captures the interest of people of animistic background and the door is potentially opened for them to take the attendant message of salvation seriously as indicated by Tippett[99] and Rynkiewich.[100] As the message and the power demonstrations converge, they point to a person—Jesus himself. As opportunity and need arose, Tippett developed special liturgies to minister in this way in specific situations.[101] He thought of these as the normative dimensions from the life of Jesus.[102] As an expression of this, Tippett questioned the Methodist and Anglican missions regarding their medical work in the Solomon Islands: "If the Church was committed to a healing ministry by our Lord, then these (medical) visits should be accompanied by prayers, as He showed himself in the days of His flesh."[103]

For the sake of endorsing type two power encounter at the cost of his own popularity, it is worth observing the way Tippett used the term "pentecostal" in his descriptions of the early movements in Fiji. At the time that he wrote those manuscripts, that term was not accepted positively outside Pentecostal churches themselves, so his use of it is surprising,[104] and

98. Tippett, "Evangelization of Animists"; Tippett, *Introduction to Missiology*, 331.

99. Tippett, *Integrating Gospel and the Christian*, 246–49.

100. Rynkiewich, *Soul, Self, and Society*, 144–45.

101. Tippett et al., *No Continuing City*, 218–21.

102. Tippett, "Holy Spirit and Responsive Populations," 86–87; Tippett, *Integrating Gospel and The Christian*, 180.

103. Tippett, *Solomon Islands Christianity*, 121.

104. Tippett, "Road to Bau," 163; Tippett, "Dynamics of Church-Planting," 33, 40, 48,

again highlights his willingness to describe things as accurately as he could from his own observations. The fact that Tippett highlighted this point was significant, because this was prior to the renewed emphasis of supernatural miracles amongst many non-Pentecostal churches that has subsequently become a reality through the influence of the Charismatic movement and or the Third Wave movement.[105] Tippett's research took him beyond the cessation theories of many of his Reformed contemporaries, which is the belief that signs and wonders and miracles ended with the close of the New Testament era. Jon Ruthven's *On the Cessation of the Charismata: The Protestant Polemic on Postbiblical Miracles*[106] places this argument in historical context, including showing why a perspective like Tippett's fits better with contemporary thought. Furthermore, Tippett was particularly concerned about those who felt that the records of Jesus' own ministry were to be interpreted mythologically, considering how damaging that view was to the growing faith of converts from animism. Dundon observes,

> Tippett's argument with western theologians on this matter, notably Bultmann, was to receive some vindication later in the century. Rudolf Bultmann had based his program for the demythologisation of Christianity on a scientific worldview in which good and evil spirits could not coexist with advanced science and technology. Hans Frei later challenged this view in his seminal work, *The Eclipse of Biblical Narrative*, Yale University Press, New Haven, 1974.[107]

Opal Reddin in *Power Encounter: A Pentecostal Perspective (Revised ed.)*[108] says that a power encounter was a demonstration of power to get the attention of a person of animistic background.[109] Subsequently, summarizing material from a number of sources,[110] still writing about what I am calling a phase two demonstration encounter, Reddin makes the statement, "This

50, 60, 62, 64, 70, 71, 72, 104, 114, 121.

105. Knight, "God's Faithfulness and God's Freedom"; Brown, *Global Pentecostal and Charismatic Healing*; Wagner, "Missiology and Spiritual Power," 92.

106. Ruthven, *On the Cessation*.

107. Dundon, "Raicakacaka," 136n215.

108. Reddin, *Power Encounter*.

109. Reddin, *Power Encounter*, 3.

110. Wimber and Springer, *Power Evangelism*, 4; Wagner et al., *Church Growth*.

definition is in line with Tippett's usage of the term,"[111] to which I would add, "at least his phase two usage."

Charles Kraft's article "Three Encounters in Christian Witness" interacts with Tippett's concept of power encounter. This article was first published in *Evangelical Missions Quarterly* in 1991 as "What Sort of Encounters Do We Need in Our Christian Witness" and has since been published in several places, the most recent being in *Perspectives on the World Christian Movement (Fourth Edition).*[112]

While acknowledging what I am calling phase three conversion encounter, Kraft's article focuses on what I am calling phase two of Tippett's demonstration encounter. Kraft says that the article rounds out an area he sees as lacking in Tippett's concept of power encounter. In order to make that point, he moves away from what I am referring to as Tippett's phase three conversion usage of power encounter, to replace the term "power encounter" in the article with the term "power demonstration"[113] as if they were equal. There are two problems when Tippett's term is only used in this demonstration sense. First, it does not represent Tippett well, when compared to all that he wrote about the three phases of power encounter. Additionally, the important role of phase three conversion use of Tippett's term power encounter, "classic power encounter" as Kraft later described it,[114] is left unfulfilled. So, while talking about this new concept of "power demonstration," as if it was the total Tippett concept of power encounter, Kraft correctly points out that demonstrations of power without a change in allegiance in fact do not change anything. His point is, power demonstration miracles alone for an animist is a truncated process, which, if not followed up in order to see that person progress to conversion and allegiance change shown in a phase three power encounter, the result is likely to be fragile or split level Christianity, to use Bulatao's term that will be described later. At the same time, it is important to acknowledge that Kraft's emphasis on truth and allegiance is valid, but simply not in such stark contrast when Tippett's conversion power encounter is kept in focus. A similar phenomenon can be seen in Kraft's 2014 "Power Encounter" article.[115]

---

111. Reddin, *Power Encounter*, 4.

112. Kraft, "Three Encounters in Christian Witness," 445–50.

113. Kraft, "Three Encounters in Christian Witness," 446.

114. Kraft, "Power Encounter," 44.

115. Kraft, "Power Encounter."

While Reddin and Kraft have focused on the need for phase two demonstration power encounters, not all scholars were equally positive about actively seeking demonstrations of God's power through the life and ministry of people in ministry. This tension is demonstrated by the fact that two volumes of the Evangelical Missiological Society Series entitled *Spiritual Power and Missions: Raising the Issues*[116] and *The Holy Spirit and Mission Dynamics*[117] were dedicated to various authors perspectives on these different points of view.

On the other hand, in Paul Hiebert, Dan Shaw and Tite Tiénou's *Understanding Folk Religion: A Christian Response to Popular Beliefs and Practices*,[118] there is no significant engagement with Tippett's missiological concepts including those of animism or power encounter. The index reference for "power encounter" directs the reader to a section that refers to miracles "to show the world God's superiority by means of power encounters,"[119] a phase two demonstration encounter use of the term, with no reference to Tippett. The index reference to "Tippett" yields two obscure entries, namely his taxonomy of spirit possession[120] and an analysis of Tippett's types for glossolalia,[121] using tables from Tippett's unpublished manuscript "Glossolalia as Spirit Possession: A Taxonomy for Cross-cultural Observation and Description."[122] Interestingly enough, this work is not referenced in the text or in the bibliography. Similarly, the description of *mana*,[123] while drawing on and acknowledging Codringron[124] as a primary source, also draws on Tippett's concepts, for example the concept of "*mana* = electricity, taboo = insulation" from "The Integrating Gospel"[125] with no acknowledgment of Tippett. In their bibliography, *Solomon Islands Christianity*[126] is the only reference to Tippett. In contrast, they incorrectly

116. Rommen, *Spiritual Power and Missions*.

117. McConnell, *Holy Spirit and Mission Dynamics*.

118. Hiebert et al., *Understanding Folk Religion*.

119. Hiebert et al., *Understanding Folk Religion*, 374.

120. Hiebert et al., *Understanding Folk Religion*, 180.

121. Hiebert et al., *Understanding Folk Religion*, 182.

122. Tippett, "Glossolalia as Spirit Possession."

123. Hiebert et al., *Understanding Folk Religion*, 68.

124. Codrington, *Melanesians*.

125. Tippett, "Integrating Gospel," 169.

126. Tippett, *Solomon Islands Christianity*.

attribute the term "spiritual warfare" to Tippett.[127] Using their term "spiritual warfare," they describe a concept much closer to the information, faith, and allegiance tension that is the precursor to my analytical phase three of Tippett's conversion power encounter. However, this is not consummated conceptually or in the hypothetical case study.

The goal of the book is to address the issue of what they refer to as "split level Christianity."[128] At this point, they acknowledge that they are using a term that Jaime Bulatao wrote about in a similar way in 1966 as he described Christianity in the Philippines.[129] Bulatao says, "Split-level Christianity may be described as the coexistence within the same person of two or more thought-and-behavior systems which are inconsistent with each other."[130] Some background to Bulatao's writing is worth noting in the context of Tippett's writing. Although Bulatao was a Catholic missionary working in the Philippines, writing this article in 1966 means that he was a contemporary of Tippett. Bulatao was describing similar challenges to those that Tippett was describing in material like "Probing Missionary Inadequacies at the Popular Level,"[131] *Solomon Islands Christianity*,[132] and *Peoples of Southwest Ethiopia*.[133] However, looking through Tippett's seemingly endless bibliographies, including his published Bibliography for Cross-cultural Workers,[134] there are no references to Bulatao.

Hiebert, Shaw and Tiénou, after extensive philosophical, cultural and historical analysis, have a shorter section about their goal summarized as,

> Finally, churches must deal with the challenges raised by folk religions. If they do not, their public witness will be compromised by the private practice of their members. Only when all areas of life are brought under the Lordship of Christ will churches have a vibrant life and winsome witness in the world.[135]

127. Hiebert et al., *Understanding Folk Religion*, 269n4.

128. Hiebert et al., *Understanding Folk Religion*, 15.

129. Now republished in the anthology, Bulatao, *Phenomena and Their Interpretation*, 22–31.

130. Bulatao, *Phenomena and Their Interpretation*, 22.

131. Tippett, "Probing Missionary Inadequacies."

132. Tippett, *Solomon Islands Christianity*.

133. Tippett, *Peoples of Southwest Ethiopia*.

134. Tippett, *Bibliography for Cross-cultural Workers*.

135. Hiebert et al., *Understanding Folk Religion*, 391.

Their stated means to achieve this goal was the use of Hiebert's "critical contextualization" approach.[136] While their goal aligns with the goal that Tippett's concept of power encounter is aiming to achieve, in the context of their description of the pervasiveness and virulence of the problem, one wonders if the suggested solutions focused around Hiebert's concept of "critical contextualization"[137] are sufficient for the task without actively utilizing the three phases of Tippett's power encounter that have been identified.

Tippett's unpublished volume, "Cross-Cultural Conversion in Oceania"[138] is replete with many phase two demonstration encounter stories, as the gospel moved from island community to island community across the Pacific. Some of these are also reported in his *Solomon Islands Christianity*.[139] In that era, there were not so many stories of healings, or similar demonstrations. Rather, it was the case that non-Christians observed God at work in the lives of the Christians, or at times, actually setting traps for them to confirm which god was strongest. On the island of Ulawa the sacred grove was desecrated by the Christians who had been brought to faith by Clement Marau. "The astonished [non-Christian] spectators were too afraid to interfere and adopted a 'wait and see' attitude." When the Christians were not harmed, many of the non-Christians became Christians.[140]

Power Encounter Phase Three:
Conversion Related Power Encounter

My conceptual phase three of Tippett's understanding and practice of power encounter or "phase three conversion encounter," is the phase that Tippett more commonly referred to as "power encounter." This relates to the ocular demonstration of allegiance change, creating a break from power sources of the past that is so necessary for effective Christian growth of people of animistic backgrounds. In that more restricted context, Tippett uses the term power encounter to describe the act by which converts from an animistic background turned from the powers they previously feared, served or from whom they have received supernatural assistance. The converts

---

136. Hiebert et al., *Understanding Folk Religion*, 22, 369–70, 386–87.

137. Hiebert et al., *Understanding Folk Religion*, 22, 369–70, 386–87.

138. Tippett, "Cross-Cultural Conversion in Oceania."

139. Tippett, *Solomon Islands Christianity*.

140. Tippett, *Solomon Islands Christianity*, 105; Tippett, "Cross-Cultural Conversion in Oceania," 27–28.

from animism themselves then focused and demonstrated their new allegiance to God, utilizing culturally appropriate actions such as destroying their symbols and repositories of power, breaking a taboo or desecrating a sacred site. In that act of power encounter they were declaring that they could potentially die unless God protected them. This is significant because if those people had engaged in such actions even accidentally while they were followers of that power it would have been harmful, if not deadly to them. This danger applied to their family and associates as well. Several examples of this can be seen in the descriptions of individual power encounter experiences that occurred in the village of Mowi, Sepik River, Papua New Guinea during 1977 where specific details on the implications for family members are documented.[141] But now that this person has become a Christian, it is done intentionally to demonstrate their new allegiance, trusting God to protect them in the encounter. In *The Evangelization of Animists*, Tippett addresses the same phenomenon from the perspective of the New Testament record, "Was it not the same in the days of New Testament Ephesus?"[142] He is referring to the burning of magical books in the city of Ephesus (Acts 19:17–19). He then answers his question generally by saying, "The biblical evidence of this demand for commitment to Christ in some form of dramatic encounter shows the converts demonstrating that the old way no longer has power over them."[143]

As those actions are taken and the people experience God's protection, that power encounter, which Tippett often referred to as an "ocular demonstration,"[144] sets the stage for their ongoing walk with the Lord as they are provided with appropriate assistance in their discipleship.[145] The point is, the exclusivity of the message of Christ means that the path of radical choice is the only path by which to come into relationship with God. When the person becoming a Christian does so on these biblical terms, this will be via a demonstration of their complete change of allegiance.

In the case studies that Tippett presents in a number of his writings, he shows that this happened at various points in the process of conversion.

141. Hovey, "Power Encounter at Mowi."

142. Tippett, *Introduction to Missiology*, 328.

143. Tippett, *Introduction to Missiology*, 329.

144. Tippett, *Solomon Islands Christianity*, 108; Tippett, *People Movements in Southern Polynesia*, 82; Yamamori and Taber, *Christopaganism or Indigenous Christianity?*, 99; Tippett, "Let the Church Be," 22; Tippett et al., *No Continuing City*, 218.

145. Tippett, *Introduction to Missiology*, 82–85; Tippett, *Integrating Gospel and the Christian*, 181.

For some, it was an initial demonstration of their change of allegiance. Tippett tells of a Tongan chief, who, before anyone else knew of his change of allegiance, and as his first public demonstration of his new faith, clubbed the priestess with a banana stalk while she was possessed by a god.[146] For others, it was something that they moved purposefully towards in their journey of faith. By engaging in the phase three power encounter as they progressed in their faith, they cut off the animistic tendency to simply add more power sources to the previous power sources that they have feared, worshipped, served, manipulated, and from which they have drawn power and assistance. This second approach is evident in my "Power Encounter at Mowi" article, as seen in just one of the similar stories in that article,

> two weeks before everybody else got around to destroying their fetishes etc., Naramauk had been thinking about how the Lord had helped him with his sickness, and how he had been continually sick as long as he practiced magic . . . So he decided that he'd finish his association with this `pawa' (supernatural enabler) [*mana*]. Consequently, he . . . ate the food which he had tabooed to control this 'pawa,' namely certain berries, vines, and bamboo shoots.[147]

This has been the more normal time sequence of phase three power encounter that I have observed in ministry on the Sepik River in Papua New Guinea. That is, a conversion experience without a phase three power encounter first of all, followed by a time of fellowship and teaching that builds their faith in God as supreme. This sets the stage for them to engage in the phase three encounter. This is in contrast with many of Tippett's historical stories from the Pacific, where the phase three encounter was the first encounter, according the records available to Tippett.

Through all of these insights, Tippett provides the animistic theology of power encounter and why, what this study is calling "phase three power encounter" made so much sense culturally to an animist.[148] Speaking of the Tongan movement into Christianity he says that from an indigenous religious point of view,

> Here are a people in a mana-oriented society, for whom there can be no possible change of faith without a change of mana. There must be a demonstration, physical or symbolic, but at least ocular—a power-encounter . . . This is how the islanders saw

146. Tippett, *People Movements in Southern Polynesia*, 81.

147. Hovey, "Power Encounter at Mowi," 15.

148. Tippett, *Integrating Gospel and the Christian*, 245.

themselves situated. If we see these demonstrations within the cultural matrix and philosophy of life of the island people, we must admit their behavior was quite meaningful.[149]

Gailyn Van Rheenen's *Communicating Christ in Animistic Contexts*[150] agrees with Tippett's concept and usage of what this study is calling phase three conversion power encounter,[151] however he does not talk about proactive phase two demonstration encounters as a normal part of life and ministry and as a precursor to phase three power encounter experiences. Nevertheless, Tippett reminds the missionary engaging in ministry in an animistic context for the first time that his or her credibility and effectiveness depends on their own acceptance of the people's worldview on the reality of "sorcery, spiritism, or other similar phenomena."[152] That acceptance will also require the missionary, through an act of faith, to see those powers overcome by the greater power of the one "who said 'All power is given unto me' (Mt. 28:18)" and who promised to give His disciples 'power (*eksousia*) . . . over all the power (*dunamis*) of the enemy' (Lk. 10:19)."[153] By thus taking the Bible "at its face value and act[ing] on it, they may discover the Bible a completely new book to them,"[154] a Tippett phase one cosmic power encounter statement. This is because the Bible, according to Tippett "can be better understood when we view it from a worldview more approaching that in which it was originally written,"[155] that is, a worldview that recognizes the spirit world as being real and active, which means acknowledging the need to take animistic practices seriously.[156]

Wonsuk and Julie Ma's book, *Mission in the Spirit: Towards a Pentecostal/Charismatic Missiology*[157] is unique in that it uses Tippett's term "power encounter" in two of the ways that Tippett uses it, sometimes describing phase two demonstration encounters while at other times similar to the phase three conversion usage of Tippett's power encounter. On one occasion they refer to "Tippett's example of eating a sacred turtle" as a

149. Tippett, *People Movements in Southern Polynesia*, 82.
150. Van Rheenen, *Communicating Christ in Animistic Contexts*.
151. Van Rheenen, *Communicating Christ in Animistic Contexts*, 89.
152. Tippett, *Introduction to Missiology*, 84.
153. Tippett, *Introduction to Missiology*, 84.
154. Tippett, *Introduction to Missiology*, 85.
155. Tippett, *Introduction to Missiology*, 85.
156. Van Rheenen, *Communicating Christ in Animistic Contexts*, 62–65, 86–89.
157. Ma and Ma, *Mission in the Spirit*.

"non-compliance to taboos."[158] Although the way they utilize these several meanings can be confusing because the difference is not clearly distinguished, it is worth noting that this volume includes previously published materials, so possibly follows the theme of each of those publications without adjusting it when editing it into this one volume. At the same time, their multifaceted usage is consistent with Tippett. As they range between these meanings in their case study from Northern Luzon, Philippines, they document how both phase two demonstrations of power in miracles and specific phase three conversion encounter experiences were critical in the planting, growth, and healthy contextualization of Christianity in the communities that they studied. Because these societies were oriented to supernatural power, this type of "power contextualization" to use their term, was crucial. They compared this approach to the "Context-Priority" and "Text-Priority"[159] approaches other Christian mission organizations used in the area, and concluded that the "power contextualization" approach was much more appropriate.[160] As a result, there were multiple virile churches and people movements, even though not overcoming all difficulties.

Ma and Ma[161] bring their case studies from the Philippines to bear on the question of how to have long term viable and virile Christianity. Their view is that Hiebert's goal of "critical contextualization"[162] as a way to achieve the goal of viable and virile Christianity, is, using standard mainline and evangelical ministry approaches, only achievable with unnecessary difficulty in the context of people of animistic backgrounds. The problem is that the key issues that have to be transformed for the goal of critical contextualization to be achieved relate to core practices and core beliefs within the worldview of the people, going all the way to their allegiances. These issues are too close to the core of culture and identity for the people themselves to allow cultural experimentation initiated by outsiders. Gospel messengers from the outside endeavouring to bring form and meaning changes in relation to core activities and core beliefs by words alone is not a viable option. This is especially the case when those core activities and beliefs are supernaturally related.

---

158. Ma and Ma, *Mission in the Spirit*, 65.

159. Ma and Ma, *Mission in the Spirit*, 62–65.

160. Ma and Ma, *Mission in the Spirit*, 65.

161. Ma and Ma, *Mission in the Spirit*, 65–71.

162. Hiebert, "Critical Contextualization," 290.

Furthermore, using both of their ways of referring to power encounter, phase two power demonstration in miracles and then phase three conversion power encounter, they agree with Tippett that "The power encounter for the new convert is both a symbolic act and a step of faith. However, this is not the end of the road, but rather the beginning. A growth in knowledge and grace has to follow."[163] According to Ma and Ma's case studies, ministries that used prayer for healing and other miracles as part of their approach were able to overcome a major problem in ministering to the tribes of Northern Luzon. In their traditional culture, miracles were the exclusive domain of their traditional spirit world beings through the practices carried out by their designated practitioners. So, when miracles occurred with God as the source, this opened their traditional worldview to change. With that as a starting point, then continuing for as long as was necessary, with patient evangelistic preaching and discipleship teaching, but always accompanied by prayer for miracles, over time that openness to worldview change increased. This then prepared the way for individual commitments to Christ,[164] and then for family and community wide people movements,[165] which however they describe using the old and subsequently rejected term "mass" conversion.[166] As this is allowed to happen over time, with the correct input at each step of the way, it leads to allegiance change, as people come to a robust faith in Christ. As an expression of that allegiance change, phase three conversion power encounters took place at an individual and group level. This confirmed the allegiance change, because a "change of faith had to be power demonstrated."[167] This also establishes a non-negotiable base for future Christian growth, as the gods of former allegiances had their power challenged. Ma and Ma's research shows this as the preferred model over "Context-Priority" and "Text-Priority" approaches in laying the best foundation for long term healthy growth.[168]

As specific examples of phase three conversion encounter, in our ministry on the Sepik River, Papua New Guinea, we were either present

163. Tippett, *Introduction to Missiology*, 321–22; Ma and Ma, *Mission in the Spirit*, 70; Ma and Ma give the correct page number for their reference to Tippett here, but the wrong book. Their reference to Tippett, *People Movements in Southern Polynesia*, 70, should be a reference to Tippett, *Introduction to Missiology*, 70.

164. Ma and Ma, *Mission in the Spirit*, 69; see also, 252.

165. Ma and Ma, *Mission in the Spirit*, 53, 121.

166. Ma and Ma, *Mission in the Spirit*, 53, 121.

167. Tippett, *People Movements in Southern Polynesia*, 81.

168. Ma and Ma, *Mission in the Spirit*, 71.

for, or heard detailed stories of at least five villages across three language groups where the people had included village wide phase three conversion encounter experiences as part of the way they demonstrated their new primary allegiance. Being with them during their decision-making process, and being present when they implemented their individual and group decisions was an experience I will never forget. It would have been good to record for history the full detail of what happened in those years, months, weeks, and days leading up to those encounters. But the fact that these were life and death experiences of people who were very important to me meant that they were too important to devalue their experiences by having a foreigner record their stories. My private records of one such village did get published in two places that are referenced here.[169]

There had been a village wide people movement in that village led by one of the local men. Following that, over a six month period, there were many healings, which, as phase two demonstration encounters, built the faith of the new believers. Then progressively there were individual phase three conversion power encounters, followed by an all-village bonfire arranged to follow a Sunday morning service. In that ceremony, one of the imported gods alone had been bought for the equivalent of three years wages. Six months later there was another major phase three encounter precipitated through a dream that led to the priest challenging the primary god of the village. Following this, now that the spirit house was no longer needed as the repository for the village god, its use was changed to be the village church. This was convenient seeing the congregation could no longer fit into their old church building as a result of the people movement.

One of Tippett's very important observations regarding phase three conversion power encounter is encapsulated in the question of what happens when it is not part of the process of conversion for people of an animistic background. In that case, with former allegiances left unchallenged, the door is left open for reversion if and when God subsequently does not answer their prayers according to their anthropocentric expectations. For Tippett this situation was so critical that it even raised the question of whether the "conversion" included the necessary allegiance change in the first place, or if it was potentially "another form of animism" as he describes the results in such cases.[170] The reason is that they have not engaged in the heart/worldview level third phase power encounter experi-

169. Hovey, "Power Encounter at Mowi," 15–18; Forbes, *Church on Fire*, 176–79.
170. Tippett, *Introduction to Missiology*, 329.

ence. In doing so, they have maintained the potential for access to their former power sources just in case they were needed if Christianity did not seem to work for them.[171] The effectiveness of Christianity in such cases is of course judged by their own animistic, need oriented, anthropocentric point of view that has continued unchallenged. The result has been unrecognized forms of syncretism and polytheism that appear under the guise of Christianity. Tippett gives two examples of this. One was a young man who had walked away from his Christian experience saying, "But now it is all empty and worth nothing."[172] The second was the story of a pastor who was particularly close to the missionary, who, after many years asked the missionary for the secrets Jesus had given him, thus demonstrating a cargoism mentality.[173] As explained in my book *Before All Else Fails*,[174] the better known term is "cargo cult," however John Strelan's *Search for Salvation: Studies in the History and Theology of Cargo Cults*[175] shows that cargo cults need to be distinguished from the endemic cargoism (philosophy of cargo) that underlies the whole phenomenon. In these cases, and in a broader sense, Darrell Whiteman's term, "dynamic religion,"[176] referring to Melanesian religions, would be an example of the potential of this issue at work, as external religious behaviour is able to adjust to the current situation without a concomitant change of worldview and allegiance. In those cases, the traditional Melanesian religion adjusts to embrace some new rituals while remaining essentially unchanged at core level.

Tippett does not assume that a third phase conversion power encounter experience, even if followed through resolutely up to this point, will take care of all issues forever. As with all Christians, there was the ongoing need for discipleship and maturation in order to see people well-grounded in the faith and subsequent leadership development to enable strong indigenous churches to be planted in those formerly animistic environments.

CONCLUSION

In relation to Tippett's fourth life theme on the importance of strategic missiology and strategic missionary practice, in this chapter I have analyzed

171. Tippett, *Introduction to Missiology*, 320.

172. Tippett, *Introduction to Missiology*, 330.

173. Tippett, *Introduction to Missiology*, 330.

174. Hovey, *Before All Else Fails*, 150–51.

175. Strelan, *Search for Salvation*, 110.

176. Whiteman, "Melanesian Religions," 94–96.

the challenges of and opportunities for ministry in animistic contexts, and have demonstrated Tippett's significant contributions in relation to this area of ministry. This is because cross-cultural witnesses discover animism in the tropical forest and in the urban jungle, as demonstrated by identifying the large part of the world's population who see and interpret life from an animistic worldview. As highlighted by Tippett, many of these people are open to the gospel when it is presented to them in the categories of their own worldview.

I demonstrated how Tippett's insights were able to contribute to his guidelines for practical application, starting with his biblical basis for ministry to animists which was enhanced by his emic, insider understanding of that animist worldview. The practical usefulness was articulated using his "pay attention" pointers for effective ministry in animistic contexts.

One of the most significant contributions Tippett made to the field was his concept of power encounter. The term was coined by him, but used by many others in different ways. Through extensive interaction with this material I have concluded that Tippett wrote about three essential phases of power encounter. All three are important, however Tippett especially believed that phase three power encounter experiences are essential as animists break with their supernatural past using ocular demonstrations of their new allegiance to God. When these are part of the process of conversion, it sets the stage for virile ongoing discipleship.

The following chapter, which flows nicely with this chapter on animism, will examine Tippett's contribution to an understanding of how indigenizing Christianity can and should fit into the cultures where it is planted as part of Tippett's strategic missiology and practice.

9

Alan Tippett's Strategic Missiology 3
Cultural Fit

"missionary shortcomings have been more cultural than theological. This may well account for the fact that missionary techniques have been severely criticized from outside the Church and sadly neglected from within."[1]

"The function of missiology in our day and generation, then, is to show that Christianity can be universal by being particular."[2]

THIS CHAPTER CONTINUES THE analysis of Alan Tippett's fourth life theme regarding the importance of strategic missiology and strategic missionary practice. Tippett's statements above regarding missionaries' cultural failings and missiology's purpose articulate his argument that Christianity can and should fit culturally into any society where and as it is planted and as it develops. In this chapter I will argue that Tippett viewed the concept of cultural fit as vital for the dynamic process of conversion and in establishing a Christian identity. He viewed cultural fit as imperative in creating a genuinely indigenous church, with appropriate worship and structures that reveal the "true selfhood" of that Christian community. Finally, Tippett maintained that functional substitutes were essential in providing alterna-

---

1. Tippett, *Verdict Theology in Missionary Theory*, 143.
2. Tippett, "Retrospect and Prospect," 2.

tive options to meeting felt needs while distinguishing faith in Christ from the forms used to communicate, understand, and practice that faith.[3]

As such, through Tippett's insights, refined by the perspectives of other scholars, the significance of Tippett's argument regarding the cultural fit of Christianity anywhere on earth will be demonstrated. His view that cultural shortcomings can be avoided and or overcome as they are brought to the fore and addressed will also be supported.

THE IMPORTANCE OF CULTURAL FIT
IN THE CONVERSION PROCESS

From an early stage in his ministry-focused life, Tippett demonstrated his belief that the opportunity for and invitation to conversion needed to be in the frame of reference of those to whom he ministered. The stumbling block of the cross needed to be the only barrier holding those people back from accepting the gospel message. Since his own conversion in Melbourne, Australia, in 1929, the conversion of others was something that Tippett gave his life for, both in his personal witness and ministry as well as in his research and writing. John Gration's statement engages both of these points, when he says, "So although there is only one way to God, and that through Christ (see Acts 4:12; John 14:6), there are a thousand ways to Christ, and the variety of religious experience as seen in conversion bears witness to this fact."[4] The following sections will look at conversion from a range of perspectives while focusing on cultural fit from Tippett's point of view. I will demonstrate that the gospel can integrate into any culture while showing the process that converts need to go through in their progress towards Christian maturity.

The Integration of the Gospel through Cultural Fit

In Tippett's in-depth analysis of the gospel's entry and impact in Fiji in "The Integrating Gospel," he uses a hypothetical scenario to help his readers realize the importance of the package in which the gospel is delivered in relation to the likely acceptance or rejection of that message. His question to his Western background readers is, how different would their attitude to Christianity be if Paul had stayed on in Arabia, shaped his ministry to that culture rather than shaping it in Asia Minor and Europe, and, as a result,

3. Tippett, *Verdict Theology in Missionary Theory*, 120.
4. Gration, "Conversion in Cultural Context," 157.

if the gospel had come to Westerners in Arabian cultural garb? He reflects, "Some of us would feel perhaps that Christianity was a bit of an imposition, and I'm quite sure we would have many nativistic movements to resist it."[5]

Tippett's understanding of the church is also crucial to understanding his concept of conversion. To him, while repentance, the aspect of turning *away* from something, was important in his understanding of conversion, this was balanced by a strong emphasis on understanding that conversion also meant the person turning *towards* something. Evangelism that did not have the goal of connecting the person with the body of Christ in their community was a truncated process. That is why the cultural shape of the church was important along with the cultural shape of the presentation of the gospel.

Conversion as a Dynamic Process in Christian Mission

Tippett's article, "Conversion as a Dynamic Process in Christian Mission"[6] diagrammatically represents the process of conversion using a series of diachronic periods culminating in synchronic points. The underlying thinking is that if the conversion process is understood well, so that, as much as humanly possible, the individual is assisted through this process, more people will go through the process and become mature Christians. Tippett's diagram outlining his 1977 model (see figure 4) begins with a diachronic period of awareness that may represent a short or long period of time, as the person, and even the society becomes aware of the Christian message. This is then focused or consummated by a synchronic point of realization (R) as the developing awareness is crystallized in the person's understanding.

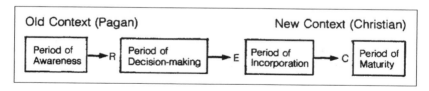

Figure 4. "Conversion as a Dynamic Process," from Tippett, Alan R. "Conversion as a Dynamic Process in Christian Mission."[7]

5. Tippett, *Integrating Gospel and the Christian*, 136.
6. Tippett, "Conversion as a Dynamic Process."
7. Tippett, "Conversion as a Dynamic Process," 219.

This is followed by a diachronic period of decision-making crystallized by a synchronic point of encounter (E). That is when the decision is implemented, and when applied to a person coming to Christian faith from animism, would include, what was discussed in the previous chapter as a phase three power encounter experience. Or, as Tippett describes it, "The act itself must be an ocular demonstration with a manifest meaning to Christian and pagan alike. It must leave no room for doubt that the old context may still have some of their allegiance."[8] It is informative to read of several locations in Oceania, where, according to Tippett, local people themselves did not consider converts to have completed formalizing their conversion unless they had engaged in this encounter.[9]

As Tippett continued to use his model as a tool to filter his research of situations where people had turned to Christ, he came to realize that simply coming to a point of decision and encounter was insufficient. There needed to be a period of incorporation during which the person/people were embodied into the Christian family, followed by a point of consummation (C) through which the person formalizes their long term commitment to the Lord and to their involvement in the church body. This would lead into an enduring period of maturity. While more could be said about preevangelism, evangelism, conversion, discipleship and Christian maturity, crystallized by the (R), (E), and (C) experiences, it is an illuminating model.

Richard Hibbert: Negotiating Identity and Cultural Fit

Richard Hibbert's article, "Negotiating Identity: Extending and Applying Alan Tippett's Model of Conversion," published in *Missiology*,[10] highlights first of all the general usefulness of Tippett's model. Having established that base, Hibbert draws on his own ministry engagement and on the experiences of others to interact with Tippett. He does this while reflecting specifically on ministry in Muslim and Hindu contexts. In doing so, his article highlights another diachronic period that is needed following the point of encounter yet preceding the period of incorporation. Hibbert refers to this as the "Period of Identity Negotiation"[11] (See figure 5).

8. Tippett, "Cross-Cultural Conversion in Oceania," 14.
9. Tippett, "Cross-Cultural Conversion in Oceania," 30.
10. Hibbert, "Negotiating Identity."
11. Hibbert, "Negotiating Identity," 69.

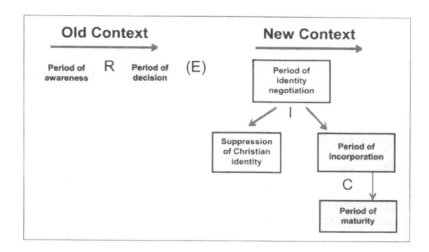

Figure 5. "Socioreligious Identity," from Hibbert, Richard. "Negotiating Identity: Extending and Applying Alan Tippett's Model of Conversion"[12]

Due to the socioreligious issues in Muslim and Hindu societies, the person who has come to faith in Jesus has to decide on their socioreligious identity after conversion as they are integrating their conversion decisions. As will be seen below, there are positive and negative consequences arising from each of the alternatives they face.

One approach is that the convert could maintain their identity with their Muslim or Hindu family and community.[13] In doing so, they would thus maintain their sense of cultural wholeness while leaving the door open over time for them to be able to witness to their family and community because they are still linked with that community. This phenomenon is increasingly common in such contexts, with the 679-page tome entitled *Understanding Insider Movements: Disciples of Jesus Within Diverse Religious Communities* edited by Harley Talman and John Jay Travis[14] providing the most significant documentation to date.

In relation to people coming to faith in Jesus from Muslim backgrounds, similar concepts have been pursued, with John Travis' article,

12. Hibbert, "Negotiating Identity," 63.

13. Hibbert, "Negotiating Identity," 64.

14. Talman and Travis, *Understanding Insider Movements*.

"Must all Muslims Leave Islam to Follow Jesus?"[15] providing a rallying point for much recent reflection and practical application in approaches to Muslims. Work by others, including Joshua Massey,[16] Travis's ongoing work,[17] Dudley Woodberry,[18] the May 2011 edition of "Mission Frontiers" themed "Jesus Movements" and Daniel Roberts,[19] along with two recent doctoral dissertations, Wolfe[20] who refers to Tippett quite a bit as he develops his case and Pruett,[21] etc. show that this is currently a very important topic. As part of the interaction on this topic, Timothy C. Tennent[22] is one scholar who is quite opposed to the phenomenon of Insider Movement.

When the insider approach is used as a ministry approach, it does however leave the challenge of how the insider followers of Jesus will participate in discipleship, fellowship, worship, Christian teaching, and service, essential components in the perfecting process. Furthermore, existing believers near them may not have ready access to them to provide assistance and resources to aid in that perfecting process. A positive point is that, as the phenomenon of insider movements is developing, useful models of *ecclesia* are emerging. Additionally, as the numbers involved in these insider movements increase in individual locations, there are growing opportunities for those communities of believers to develop. This opens the opportunity, in the case of Muslims, for this to be done within their community of Muslim Followers of Jesus or *jamats*. Consequently, they don't have to "deny" their birth identity as Muslims in order to "affirm" their second birth identity as followers of Jesus.

The second approach referred to by Hibbert is for the convert to identify with the Christian community,[23] thus meeting their discipleship, fellowship, worship, Christian teaching, and service needs. However, this usually results in at least isolation from their family and community, if not outright persecution. A consequence of this approach is that it significantly limits opportunities to witness to their family and community.

15. Travis, "Must all Muslims Leave Islam?"

16. Massey, "God's Amazing Diversity."

17. Travis, "Appropriate Approaches in Muslim Contexts."

18. Woodberry, *From Seed to Fruit.*

19. Roberts et al., *Family I Never Knew.*

20. Wolfe, "Insider Movements."

21. Pruett, "Barriers and Bridges."

22. Tennent, "Followers of Jesus."

23. Hibbert, "Negotiating Identity," 63.

Therefore, analyzing the overall perspective of Hibbert's article, this is an endorsement of Tippett's model, while making a genuine attempt to extend and reapply Tippett's model. When reading this article alongside much of what Tippett wrote, Tippett would never advocate someone being cut off from their family and community as being a goal. However, in the process of people coming to faith in contexts where they feel they are left with limited choices, Hibbert's article helps to see the decision-making process that such a person faces.

Another aspect worth noting is Tippett's point when talking about converts who have come to Christian faith from an animistic background via a power encounter experience. In that context, Tippett was concerned that some Christian organizations delay baptism for that person until they are more acquainted with the new belief system. Having made such a monumental decision to engage in the power encounter, there is an immediate need for encouragement and a sense of belonging. Therefore Tippett suggests that, "there should be an intermediate state somewhere into which the convert from paganism is incorporated."[24] Something like this may be needed as an extension and reapplication of Hibbert's model using Tippett's insights.

Maintaining Identity in Multi-Individual Groups for Cultural Fit

Observing Tippett and Hibbert's article and models, one is left with the question of how both of these models would relate to the parts of the world where multi-individual groups are turning to Christ from Muslim and Hindu backgrounds. Furthermore, it raises the question linked to Tippett's insights about people movements, that is, what more could be done in Muslim and Hindu context to re-develop ministry strategies that aim for new multi-individual mutually interdependent decisions for Christ in those contexts. The point is, when people movements occur, in contrast to individual conversions, they assist with the identity negotiation factor. That is because identity is maintained within the group during the process in which the group is making a multi-individual decision to become followers of Jesus. Similarly, the individual within that group would be able to establish a new identity as a Jesus follower, along with the other members of their group who are doing the same thing. This could be similar to the situation addressed in Hoefer's *Churchless Christianity*, where 200,000 people

---

24. Tippett, *Verdict Theology in Missionary Theory*, 129.

of both Hindu and Muslim backgrounds in Tamil Nadu State, India, have come to believe in Jesus as their saviour, but have not been baptized, or joined the structures of existing churches.[25]

Although Hibbert applies Tippett's model to individuals, Tippett's article is primarily addressing issues related to multi-individual decisions. The tension between assumptions regarding individual decisions and the assumptions regarding multi-individual decisions is brought to the fore in relation to Melanesia when Michael Rynkiewich[26] reflects on "personhood." He compares a Westerner's individualistic concept of personhood, which he believes has influenced most mission strategies, with that of a Papua New Guinean in-group concept of personhood, which he argues should influence ministry approaches in Melanesia. As seen earlier, Bruce Malina's description of the societies of the New Testament era[27] are not dissimilar to the Melanesian "individual" described above, who is an individual by virtue of the group. This "group-embedded, collectivistic personality is one who simply needs another continually in order to know who he or she really is,"[28] rather than being an individual within the group. So Malina's findings would lend their weight to the significance of Tippett's model of conversion when ministering in similar societies. Together, the concepts of Tippett, Hibbert, Rynkiewich, and Malina demonstrate the cultural fit needed in the conversion process. Meanwhile, Tippett's simple but comprehensive model was shown to be applicable in guiding questions of cultural fit in the range of situations that were examined.

DYNAMIC INDIGENEITY: CHRISTIANITY WITH CULTURAL FIT

Cultural fit was vital to Tippett because he held that for the church to truly be the church, it needed to be an indigenous church. The theological issues of this were explored in chapter 5, while in this chapter, the strategic aspects of this are examined. Tippett's perspective about the necessity of the church being indigenous needs to be nuanced for two reasons: first, because his use of the word "indigenous" in this context does not imply "traditional," second, because other terminology is often used in the contemporary world instead of the word "indigenous." For example, the terminology used to

25. Hoefer, *Churchless Christianity*.
26. Rynkiewich, "Person in Mission," 156.
27. Malina, *New Testament World*, 62.
28. Malina, *New Testament World*, 62.

describe the application of indigenous church concepts today has changed significantly, as documented by Kraft in this sequential list: indigenization; contextualization; dynamic equivalence; critical contextualization; inculturation, and culturally appropriate.[29] Bevans[30] categorizes the various approaches to indigenization/contextualization in his five models: Translation; Anthropological; Praxis; Synthetic; and Transcendental. Nevertheless, this part of the study will continue to use Tippett's term "indigenous church," while acknowledging that these more recent terms are the terms in current usage. This is done because Tippett's own insights can initially be seen more clearly by using his terminology. The subheadings to be handled will cover such areas as: cultural fit: Christianity being universal by being particular; cultural fit and the church's "true selfhood"; cultural fit and indigenization: other scholars' perspectives and implementing dynamic indigeneity for cultural fit. Once again, Tippett's insights and fundamental argument that Christianity can and should fit culturally into any society will be clearly seen.

Cultural Fit: Christianity Being Universal by Being Particular

The mechanisms and strategies by which cultural fit is achieved can be seen in the convergence of a number of practical perspectives, in particular in the context of dynamic indigeneity. Tippett emphasized the responsibility that missionaries have to understand the language and culture of the people they go to, and the importance of having church worship and structures that are appropriate to the cultural communities in which the gospel is being proclaimed and in which churches are being planted. As Kraft[31] points out, this could be either in a traditional context or an urbanized Western context, depending on the cultural fit of the congregation. Or, as Tippett's states, "The function of missiology in our day and generation, then, is to show that Christianity can be universal by being particular."[32] Tippett's stated goal has sometimes been appreciated and implemented intentionally, while at other times this goal was achieved more intuitively. An example of using these approaches intuitively can be seen in the unique linkage between "contextualization" and Pentecostal approaches in mission. This is explained by

29. Kraft and Gilliland, *Appropriate Christianity*, 3–4, 15–34; Kraft, *Issues in Contextualization*.

30. Bevans, *Models of Contextual Theology*, 32.

31. Kraft and Gilliland, *Appropriate Christianity*, 74.

32. Tippett, "Retrospect and Prospect," 2.

Allan Anderson as, "Pentecostalism has contextualized Christianity, mostly unconscious of the various theories . . . and mostly unnoticed by outsiders. The experience of the fullness of the Spirit is the central plank . . . and it is in this focus on experience that contextualization occurs,"[33] thus adding an aspect of praxis to the theoretical reflections, an emphasis that was close to Tippett's approach. However it occurred frequently and the compounding end result on biblical Christianity globally today is summarized cogently by Dana Robert's article, "Shifting Southward: Global Christianity Since 1945," when she says,

> What at first glance appears to be the largest world religion is in fact the ultimate local religion. Indigenous words for God and ancient forms of spirituality have all become part of Christianity. Flexibility at the local level, combined with being part of an international network, is a major factor in Christianity's self-understanding and success today. The strength of world Christianity lies in its creative interweaving of the warp of a world religion with the woof of its local contexts.[34]

Thinking anthropologically, while utilizing Malinowski's "new autonomous entity"[35] concept, Tippett points out that at any time and place, there are no such entities as the "old way" and the "new way."[36] There is only "the total entity of the living situation in which we are immersed, in which the traditional and the civilized interpenetrate."[37] All of the traditional and modern roles are "inextricably involved."[38] The missionary is one of the elements in that complex, who is best advised to "identify" so that "he may influence change significantly in the right direction" rather than to "become an irritant."[39] As can be seen, the term "indigenous" for Tippett is a dynamic term. It is of the people—right now, for the people—right now. "Indigenous" does not somehow require people to do things that may have

33. Anderson, "Contextualization in Pentecostalism," 34.
34. Robert, "Shifting Southward," 56.
35. Malinowski, "Anthropology of Changing African Cultures," xix.
36. Tippett, *Verdict Theology in Missionary Theory*, 135.
37. Tippett, *Verdict Theology in Missionary Theory*, 135.
38. Tippett, *Verdict Theology in Missionary Theory*, 136.
39. Tippett, *Verdict Theology in Missionary Theory*, 135–36.

been more appropriate for their grandparents.[40] This is seen in Tippett's analysis of a published case study from Lagos, Nigeria:[41]

> In a brief period of 50 years the mission (or indigenous Church) has to face three entirely different situations—the old *traditional* one, the *transitional* one and the new *emergent* one. Its forms and techniques will reflect the change. If they do not, then the mission will become irrelevant. The danger is that as the forms change the old biblical faith may go. This is why *faith and form* must always be clearly differentiated.[42]

Tippett's article "Conceptual Dyads in the Ethnotheology of Mission Today" in his compilation, *Evangelical Response to Bangkok*[43] and his chapter entitled "Cultural Compulsives" in *God, Man and Church Growth*[44] illustrate well his emphasis on designing strategies, ministry, and church planting approaches appropriate to each dynamically changing situation, people group, and era. As biblical Christianity is able to fit culturally into any culture or language group, the message of the gospel truly becomes a message for the whole world, a universal gospel.

Cultural Fit and the Church's "True Selfhood"

For Tippett, rather than emphasizing the three-self model of the indigenous church that was well known in his day, it was more important to release the "true selfhood" of the church. He was concerned about the shallowness of the popular self-governing, self-supporting, and self-propagating three-self model of the indigenous church that protestant, and especially evangelical churches had inherited from the writing of Henry Venn in the 1860s, documented by Max Warren.[45] In *Introduction to Missiology*[46] Tippett traces the origins of the term as proposed by Venn, the secretary of the Church Missionary Society from 1841–1872.[47] In order to deal with the issues of certain mission fields under his jurisdiction, Venn wanted to see

---

40. Tippett, *Verdict Theology in Missionary Theory*, 118–21.

41. Marris, *Family and Social Change.*

42. Tippett, *Verdict Theology in Missionary Theory*, 120.

43. Tippett, "Conceptual Dyads in the Ethnotheology," 244.

44. Tippett, "Cultural Compulsives," 174.

45. Warren, *To Apply the Gospel.*

46. Tippett, *Introduction to Missiology*, 85.

47. Warren, *To Apply the Gospel*, 13.

missionary-led field-mission structures transition to become indigenously led national church structures. Venn's action word was "'euthanasia,' the notion that the mission had to die that the church might be born."[48]

As the slogans of Venn's concepts have been promulgated, it has been assumed that the now morphed missionary structure could come to the point where it was taken over by indigenous leaders and the national structure is able to "become self-governing, self-supporting, and self-extending."[49] This three-self model was further popularized by Melvyn Hodges' books, namely, *The Indigenous Church*[50] and *The Indigenous Church and the Missionary.*[51] These books dealt with issues of Hodges' era and were written from his Latin American experience, especially as related to main stream Pentecostal churches. These were a stimulus in the direction Venn intended. Having described Venn's theory and its history, Tippett points out that it was seldom put into practice. The reasons he gave are telling; "Missionary paternalism and their lack of faith in the ability of their converts to take control prevented their letting go."[52] It is telling that Roland Allen's book, *The Ministry of the Spirit*, originally published in 1932, was addressing this very issue by highlighting the role of the Holy Spirit in equipping, guiding, and empowering national Christians to be the leaders of their own churches and movements.[53]

Tippett added his anthropological insights to the Venn model to provide guidelines aimed to produce churches that would function as appropriate local expressions of church "selfhood." The goal was that those churches would utilize the impetus of the biblical message while being developed to suit their own cultural, social, and national context. In particular, his insights were focused on the formation level of those churches, realizing that being formed in an appropriate way would position those churches for a great future. He then describes the foundations of his approach by which he comes to a very different conclusion than Venn, when he says,

> The concept of indigeneity has nothing whatsoever to do with the three selfs. Its true selfhood requires anthropological relevance and theological awareness, and effective pastoral ministry—nothing

48. Warren, *To Apply the Gospel*, 28.

49. Warren, *To Apply the Gospel*, 26.

50. Hodges, *Indigenous Church*.

51. Hodges, *Indigenous Church and the Missionary*.

52. Tippett, *Introduction to Missiology*, 85.

53. Allen, *Ministry of the Spirit*.

more and nothing less. It may draw from outside resources and personnel as long as they do not infringe on these requirements.[54]

While Tippett's concepts of appropriate indigeneity of the church permeated so much of what he wrote, his most crystallized writings on this topic can be found in *Verdict Theology in Missionary Theory*,[55] parts of which were repeated in *Introduction to Missiology*.[56] This included his extended list of the six marks of an indigenous church.[57] Expanded using quotes from Tippett, the list becomes:

> *The first mark of an indigenous Church is its self-image.* Does it see itself as the Church of Jesus Christ in its own local situation, mediating the work, the mind, the word, and the ministry of Christ in its own environment? . . .
>
> *The second mark of an indigenous Church is that it is self-functioning* . . . Only by effective internal growth in grace within a developing organic structure, where members interact and cooperate, and fulfill their natural functions can the Body be healthy and perform its appointed role in the world . . .
>
> *The third mark of an indigenous Church relates to its self-determining capacity.* Is the group an autonomous body, facing its own affairs as they relate both to the group and the group's outside relations? . . . Does its structure fit the decision-making patterns of the social structure or is it foreign? . . . that is, it should be something they can feel is their own. The greatest threat to an indigenous Church is the denominational character of Christian mission. We tend to plant denominational structures . . .
>
> *The fourth mark of an indigenous Church is its self-supporting nature.* This is the mark of stewardship. It has two aspects which may be covered by the questions: 1. Does the Church carry its own financial burdens? 2. Does it adequately finance its own service projects? . . . A truly indigenous Church regards the social problems of its environment as its own concern and should be doing more than distributing foreign aid. I do not mean to the exclusion of foreign aid, but the initiative should come from the young Church itself . . .

---

54. Tippett, *Introduction to Missiology*, 87.

55. Tippett, *Verdict Theology in Missionary Theory*, 148–63.

56. Tippett, *Introduction to Missiology*, 371–91.

57. Tippett, *Verdict Theology in Missionary Theory*, 154; Tippett, *Introduction to Missiology*, 378–81.

The fifth mark of the truly indigenous Church is its self-propagating fervor. Does the young Church see itself as being directly addressed by the words of the Great Commission? Is the matter of quantitative church growth from the pagan regions beyond of real concern to the young Church? . . .

The sixth mark of the indigenous Church is its devotion to self-giving. This is the mark of service. Does a young Church have its own service program? Does it exercise itself with facing and alleviating the social needs and problems of the local world in which it lives?[58]

Stephen Pavey reaffirms Tippett's "devotion to self-giving" criterion, when he states that "the measure of an indigenous church . . . can be determined by the degree to which it meets the needs of the poor and is perceived by the poor as relevant to their lived realities."[59]

Cultural Fit and Indigenization: Other Scholars' Perspectives

Tippett provides a description of how an indigenous church functioned contextually in an enclosed village society in the early days of the church in Fiji in *Oral Tradition and Ethnohistory: The Transmission of Information and Social Values in Early Christian Fiji, 1835–1905,*[60] when he says,

An indigenous church, defined anthropologically, must be the relevant integrator (Malinowski, Bronislaw, (1961) *The Dynamics of Culture Change.* New Haven: Yale University Press page 48) or governor (Wallace, Anthony F. C. (1966). *Religion: An Anthropological View.* New York: Random House page 4) of the integral system or institutions (Malinowski, Bronislaw (1960) *A Scientific Theory of Culture.* New York: Oxford University Press pages 38–39) which, combined, make up the whole society. Certainly this is so for a communal society like that of Fiji which provides the case study for this paper. An indigenous church, defined theologically, must have the self-awareness that enables it to see itself as the Body of Christ communicating the word, the mind, and the love of Christ to the society that it holds together: and to do this in a culturally accepted manner . . . When we speak of an indigenous church we are dealing with a self-activating organism, a dynamic phenomenon—not a static system. An indigenous church must also have

58. Tippett, *Verdict Theology in Missionary Theory,* 155–58.

59. Pavey, *Theologies of Power and Crisis,* 103.

60. Tippett, *Oral Tradition and Ethnohistory.*

a contextualized gospel or it cannot relate to the world that is its field of ministry. Internally and externally we must have dynamic relationships.[61]

Responding to that, Walter Hollenweger,[62] having identified Tippett as a "well-informed and independent thinker,"[63] highlights that "the process of adaptation/transformation/rejection of pagan traditions and rites"[64] that Tippett describes in relation to Fiji is an ongoing challenge as that biblical message goes into other societies as well. Other parts of his analysis, not so pertinent to this study, included his assumption that, further processing would result in "a more ecumenical, intercultural theology."[65] This however would require a new level of positive interaction between biblical studies and anthropology, which Hollenweger was not optimistic about. He also sees a role of the World Council of Churches and State Christianity as meaningful structures assisting the fulfillment of some of Tippett's goals.

Glenn Schwartz, a former colleague of Tippett's at Fuller SWM, built his ministry in Africa utilizing Tippett's indigenous church concepts.[66] His emphasis on overcoming unhealthy dependency means that he is more narrowly focused than Tippett, yet he uses Tippett's six points referred to above from *Verdict Theology*.[67] Schwartz then adds three items to Tippett's list, "1) an indigenous theology; 2) an indigenous form of worship; and 3) an indigenous church structure."[68] Schwartz attributes these additional points to Glasser in an unreferenced footnote[69] yet he uses Tippett's examples of structure.[70]

One point that Schwartz does clarify well is that the term "indigenous" can be used in many ways, and can even be used as a means of self-expression by a movement or a church. However these aspects of self-expression would always need to be evaluated against a grid of this foundational

61. Tippett, *Oral Tradition and Ethnohistory*, 1–2.
62. Hollenweger, "Oral Tradition and Ethnohistory," 517–21.
63. Hollenweger, "Oral Tradition and Ethnohistory," 519.
64. Hollenweger, "Oral Tradition and Ethnohistory," 520.
65. Hollenweger, "Oral Tradition and Ethnohistory," 520.
66. Schwartz, *When Charity Destroys Dignity*.
67. Tippett, *Verdict Theology in Missionary Theory*, 171–72.
68. Schwartz, *When Charity Destroys Dignity*, 172.
69. Schwartz, *When Charity Destroys Dignity*, 172.
70. Tippett, *Verdict Theology in Missionary Theory*, 172.

understanding[71] of an indigenous church. He uses the African Independent Churches phenomenon[72] (these days, African Initiated Churches) and the Three Self Movement in China as examples of churches that would benefit from this sort of evaluation.

Other scholars on the other hand, while not ruling out Tippett's culturally focused approach to indigeneity, have stayed closer to Venn's model. For example, Charles Van Engen[73] listed his "Seven Stages of Emerging within Missionary Congregations."

1. Pioneer evangelism leads to the conversion of a number of people.

2. Initial church gatherings are led by elders and deacons, along with preachers from outside the infant body.

3. Leadership training programs [select], train, and commission indigenous pastors, supervisors, and other ministry leaders.

4. Regional organizations of Christian groups develop structures, committees, youth programs, women's societies, and regional assemblies.

5. National organization, supervision of regions, and relationships with other national churches begin to form.

6. Specialized ministries grow inside and outside the church, with boards, budgets, plans, finances, buildings, and programs.

7. Indigenous missionaries are sent by the daughter church for local, national, and international mission in the world, beginning the pattern all over again.

Van Engen's list can be seen as an expansion on Venn's three-self model, adding the benefit of 100 years of mission insight. As such, it does not rule in or rule out indigeneity as advocated by Tippett, although realistically achieving each of these points would be difficult without cultural sensitivity on the part of the missionary. A brief case study from Fiji illustrates this point: When the culturally sensitive "anthropological" approach was used for the first forty years of the Methodist church, it was moving strongly towards a "coactive" situation, to use John Carter's term.[74] However, later in the nineteenth century, mono-cultural colonial attitudes took over

71. Tippett, *Verdict Theology in Missionary Theory*, 164–66.
72. Tippett, *Verdict Theology in Missionary Theory*, 166–68.
73. Van Engen, *God's Missionary People*, 43–44.
74. Carter, "Indigenous Principle Revisited," 73–82.

and delayed the process for sixty-five years. That was reactivated in the 1940s as Tippett was on the field, followed by a twenty year lead up to the independence of the national Fiji Methodist movement in 1964.[75] However, even that was in jeopardy when culturally insensitive missionaries subsequently became part of the team. After independence, missionaries, ostensibly serving under national leadership, rationalized national Fijian needs for literature production out of existence through budgetary mechanisms controlled by those missionaries.[76] This heightens Tippett's emphasis on missionaries being trained in anthropology and then using culturally appropriate approaches in the initial formation of an indigenous church movement.

On the topic of dynamic indigeneity, *Appropriate Christianity*, edited by Charles Kraft[77] brings the perspective of a range of authors to bear on the topic of "contextualization" using many of its more recent formulations. In that book, Tippett is acknowledged as a forerunner on the topic, while commending some of his insights. However even in this compilation of 519 pages in twenty-eight chapters by eighteen authors, it is surprising that there are still only fourteen references to Tippett. Other contributors to this volume only engage marginally with Tippett's insights. For example, DeNeui appropriately questions Tippett's prediction that animism would disappear in ten to twenty years, which I have also referred to in this study as being a Tippett over-statement. However he seems to misunderstand Tippett when he suggests that Tippett's prediction was an example of, "Religious-oriented evolutionary thought [that] gave rise to the notion that animism would eventually die out to the higher religions, preferably Christianity."[78] In a broader reading of Tippett, DeNeui would have found an ally for his observation that attempts to eradicate animism without understanding it "merely drove it underground,"[79] his point being a point that Tippett also emphasized strongly. Nevertheless, *Appropriate Christianity*[80] with so many contributors representing so many years of field experience and research, comprising so many pages of significant insight, is a major contribution to

---

75. Dundon, "Raicakacaka," 60.

76. Tippett et al., *No Continuing City*, 256–57.

77. Kraft and Gilliland, *Appropriate Christianity*.

78. DeNeui, "Typology of Approaches," 418.

79. DeNeui, "Typology of Approaches," 418.

80. Kraft and Gilliland, *Appropriate Christianity*.

this whole area of dynamic indigeneity/appropriate Christianity that was so important to Tippett.

Implementing Dynamic Indigeneity for Cultural Fit

One key aspect of cultural fit relates to the advocate for Christianity effectively communicating the Christian message cross-culturally. In his chapter "The Meaning of Meaning" in *Christopaganism or Indigenous Christianity*,[81] Tippett uses Linton's[82] concepts of form, use, function, and meaning, then adds his concept of "values" as well. From there he progresses through his concepts of approximate equivalence of meaning, narrative reconstruction in assisting people of another culture to understand a message couched in a culture different from their own, and eventually progresses to the concept of dynamic equivalence. It is interesting to note that Tippett only uses this term after Kraft's article, "Dynamic Equivalence Churches: An Ethnotheological Approach to Indigeneity"[83] was published in *Missiology* and when he does use it, Tippett does not refer to the source of the term. In using dynamic equivalence, as much as possible, the communication conceptually transports the audience from their own world into the world of the original message, thus making it possible for them to understand the message within that world. From that point they are empowered to interpret the message accurately within their own world.[84] This then is the process by which dynamic indigeneity is achieved.[85]

In *Verdict Theology*, Tippett accumulates some of his anthropologically informed insights focused towards the missionary's role in church planting, aiming for cultural fit.[86] Using his headings as a set of six guidelines, he says:

1. Those who plant churches across cultures should do so in terms of those cultures.

2. Those who engage in cross-cultural church-planting should preserve as many of the indigenous forms as possible.

---

81. Tippett, "Meaning of Meaning."
82. Linton, *Study of Man*.
83. Kraft, "Dynamic Equivalence Churches."
84. Tippett, "Formal Transformation and Faith Distortion," 175–89.
85. Kraft and Gilliland, *Appropriate Christianity*, 19–22.
86. Tippett, *Verdict Theology in Missionary Theory*, 168–74.

3. Those engaged in church planting cross-culturally should explore the need of functional substitutes.

4. Those planting cross-cultural churches need to safeguard the faith against the incorporation of pagan beliefs.

5. Church-planters should expect that indigenous churches themselves will produce a multiplicity of structures and leadership patterns.

6. There must be a power encounter of some kind for an indigenous church to emerge from the early stages.

He then explains what it will look and feel like for the missionary who is taking up the challenge of ministering in the context of these guidelines,

> If these six points are considered together it will be apparent that the church-planter, while maintaining a fixed faith in Christ as Saviour and Lord, and the Bible as norm for faith and practice, will need to be the most flexible with respect to the forms in which or through which the faith is practiced and transmitted. To be indigenous a Church has to belong to a culture, to be in it and to speak to it. It has to be the body of Christ ministering to that world which is its very own and we as missionaries must be prepared to let the church be itself.[87]

Although this is not a complete "manual for church planting," the seven pages of Tippett's writing that these headings have been extracted from give some very important guidelines that come from Tippett's areas of strength. Even if working with an existing church movement, the list could form an appropriate set of questions by which to evaluate the strengths and weaknesses of that movement in its existential situation.

FUNCTIONAL SUBSTITUTES: ADVANCED CULTURAL FIT

Tippett's aim, through the introduction of functional substitutes, was to prioritize the cultural fit with biblical Christianity, while at the same time, encouraging local people to find culturally satisfying ways of replacing aspects of their own culture that were not compatible with biblical Christianity.

---

87. Tippett, *Verdict Theology in Missionary Theory*, 175.

Functional Substitutes as Key Facilitators of Cultural Fit

Two extreme examples of Christianity not fitting well set the parameters of what this study of functional substitutes aims to achieve. First, Tippett uses the case study of *Juan* in "Christopaganism or Indigenous Christianity,"[88] in which Juan, calling himself a Christian, is still involved in a blend of pre-Christian and non-Christian religious practices. In that example, the "fit with biblical Christianity" was compromised by allowing the new belief system to be overruled by the old belief system, resulting in Christopaganism. At the other extreme, the approach of the Judaizers, leading up to the Council of Jerusalem in Acts 15, required gentiles to receive the gospel in the Jewish cultural frame of reference of the Jewish evangelists. As a result, the "fit with culture unless incompatible with biblical Christianity" was compromised to allow the evangelists to feel comfortable with the "fit" with their culture. However, looking back, the Judaizers believed that they were enforcing the requirements of biblical Christianity. Therefore, the Jerusalem Council in fact came to understand and to implement a broader understanding of biblical Christianity. Converts could come to Christ within their culture, without conforming to the Jewish culture. Andrew Walls makes a useful contribution in the context of embedding the church in any society in his article, "The Gospel as the Prisoner and Liberator of Culture." In that he identifies the "indigenizing principle" by which the church is able to "feel at home" in any culture. At the same time he highlights the concomitant "pilgrim principle," by which the gospel is in initial tension with any culture as it permeates and influences it.[89] Because the concept of functional substitutes was so important in Tippett's missiological theory for the sake of effective mission practice, this study will explore functional substitutes in a number of ways, while recognizing that Tippett considered his work in the field of functional substitutes to be one of his most important contributions to missiology.

In his research and writing on the concept of "functional substitutes," Tippett argued that functional substitutes were an essential component in establishing and stabilizing the cultural fit of Christianity as it was planted anywhere in the world. This is because, in his view, Christianity needs to be indigenous to truly be the church. In order for this to be implemented effectively, the Christian conversion experience itself needs to be recognized as a major cultural change experience. As the new faith is embedded in

88. Tippett, "Christopaganism or Indigenous Christianity," 19–27.
89. Walls, "Gospel as the Prisoner," 98–99.

that culture, it is normally the case that within the culture there will be elements that are demonstrably incompatible with their new faith. Therefore, so that Christianity is able to maintain a locally satisfying feel, those elements will need to be replaced with locally satisfying alternative activities and practices. Tippett uses the term functional substitute to describe the new replacement elements that the local people apply in order to meet their felt needs and maintain a sense of cultural cohesion and integration during this experience. Gailyn Van Rheenen[90] uses the term "cultural substitutes" for a similar concept.

When this process of implementing functional substitutes is carried out well, in an appropriate timeframe for each element, then there will be a strong sense that Christianity is truly their own. In this process, it is ideal, but by no means a requirement, that functional substitutes draw on local cultural elements, although Tippett warns that local cultural elements could have the tendency to bring syncretistic aspects with them, so the local people would need to be spiritually alert in this process.

The goal of functional substitutes in facilitating the cultural fit of Christianity in a society could be illustrated using an analogy from the concept of "transculturation" that has come into missiology from Bible translation. Daniel R. Shaw's book, *Transculturation: The Cultural Factor in Translation and Other Communication Tasks*[91] spells out this concept and its implications in a range of ways, especially as it relates to translation. As part of that, he opens up the concept of "idiomatic translations" then moves to "transculturation." As allies in his quest for transculturation, he draws on the work of Beekman and Callow, who say, "The goal of a translation is that it is to be 'so smooth in vocabulary, so idiomatic in phrase, so correct in construction, so smooth in flow of thought, so clear in meaning, and so elegant in style, it does not appear to be a translation at all, and yet, at the same time, faithfully transmits the message of the original.'"[92] The turn of phrase used here to describe language translation is inspiring, if not a little challenging. Functional substitutes, when understood well and applied effectively by local people, as they innovate the culture change brought about in their lives by the gospel, provide the means to enable Christianity to fit into their culture in the same spiritually, emotionally, and psychologically satisfying way, and to do this without theological compromise. For this

90. Van Rheenen, *Communicating Christ in Animistic Contexts*, 38.
91. Shaw, *Transculturation*.
92. Beekman and Callow, *Translating the Word of God*, 32.

to occur effectively, it needs to be a local initiative, not forced by outside evangelists/missionaries.

In the ongoing examination of functional substitutes, the following themes will be explored: the theory of functional substitutes for cultural fit will be examined, the significance of functional substitutes and church growth as the fruit of cultural fit will be investigated. Other scholar's perspectives on functional substitutes will provide balance while the effectiveness of functional substitutes will be examined theoretically and illustrated in case studies.

Theory of Functional Substitutes for Cultural Fit

While reflecting on conversion, Tippett frequently referred to a "need for change being felt." In that context, Tippett often refers to Sapir's[93] study of the way clusters of sounds in a language hold together and remain unchanged until all change at the same time.[94] This was also researched at a broader cultural level by other anthropologists, Kroeber[95] for example. Tippett then applies this idea into the culture change aspects of conversion to show that often essential significant change in morals and behaviour can occur at the time of conversion, without causing significant disruption to the foundations of the culture. His extended description of the changes that came in the first twenty years of the gospel entering Fiji in *The Road to Bau and the Autobiography of Joeli Bulu*[96] illustrates this powerfully. Things that had previously seemed so central to the society—warfare, human sacrifice, cannibalism, temples, priests, prostitution, polygamy,[97] widow strangling, euthanasia, etc., were all able to change while leaving the society intact. That was because it was a situation propitious for change, and also because the missionaries were sensitive to cultural issues, and cultural approaches when addressing matters that needed to be reflected on in the light of their new faith.[98]

93. Sapir, *Language*, 182.

94. Tippett, *Introduction to Missiology*, xv, 286, 397, 409–10.

95. Kroeber, *Anthropology*, 403.

96. Tippett, *Road to Bau*.

97. Tippett, "Polygamy as a Missionary Problem"; Tippett, *Verdict Theology in Missionary Theory*, 146.

98. Tippett, *Road to Bau*, 88–92; Tippett, "Formal Transformation and Faith Distortion," 181.

A touchstone to guide in the development of Christian functional substitutes is maintaining a clear differentiation between faith and form.[99] That way, the goal of maintaining Christian faith and meaning can remain in focus, while the form can be flexible to meet the needs of the people. To give one of many examples that could be cited, Tippett's description from the island of Bau in Fiji, when Chief Cakobau made the killing stone into a baptismal font illustrates this well. The stone used so often for death that it symbolized death, now commemorates the movement from death to life in the ritual of baptism.[100] That example makes another point very well; the criterion for determining the effectiveness of a functional substitute is by observing the acceptance of and meaningfulness to the local people, regardless of how an outsider feels, realizing that this stone now used in this way could seem extreme to an outsider.

In my own thirty-one years of ministry experience in Papua New Guinea, I had the opportunity for contact with hundreds of churches in my roles of field missionary, consultant to the National Executive Council of the Assemblies of God of Papua New Guinea (AOG PNG) and Ministry Training Department Director for AOG PNG. From the opportunities that those roles afforded me I was able to observe the integration of Christian faith in a large number of communities in many parts of PNG. The most common functional substitutes that I became aware of fitted two categories. The first was the replacement of magic ceremonies with prayer events. This applied to areas of healing, plus agricultural and hunting cycles. The other was the way multi-village, multi-day Christian conventions became celebration events to replace the traditional festivals (*singsing*). The degree of the impact at that level can be illustrated by diachronically observing the transport system used for those traditional and Christian events. When I first arrived in Papua New Guinea as a young auto-engineer, I was often asked to drive the truck to provide the free transport for Christians as a way of encouraging them to come to the Christian conventions. As we drove along the road, we would see crowds of people walking to the more popular traditional festivals. The contrast was pronounced, when, twenty-five years later, I saw hand written posters advertising traditional festivals, which

---

99. Tippett, *Verdict Theology in Missionary Theory*, 120.

100. Tippett, *Christian (Fiji 1835–67)*, 3. The photograph of this stone was not included in the reprint edition of this book (Tippett, *Integrating Gospel and the Christian*), so the reference to the original book is maintained.

included the statement "free transport provided." By that time, it was the Christians who would walk for days to get to the Christian conventions.

Building on concepts from Malinowski's *integral institutions,*[101] Tippett showed how complicated and interrelated multi-individual groups are. To address this issue, Tippett developed his concept of the "functional substitute in church planting and the incorporation of converts into the fellowship of believers."[102] The concept of functional substitutes, without that name, were stimulated in his thinking by researching what happened as Christianity came into Fiji in the 100 years prior to his arrival. Consequently, his understanding of it came initially from archival research while seeing the fruit of that impact 100 years later as he carried out his ministry. Although certain anthropologist's concepts helped him in articulating his own thoughts, however he developed the view that missiology was its own field of study, so could borrow from other fields of study without accepting their underlying philosophies. A key foundational concept of importance to the missionary is that any change to a social institution will have a ripple effect to other institutions in that society. The significance of functional substitutes to field strategies can be seen in so many of the topics already examined: people movements, ministry in the context of animism, power encounter, and the indigenous church. Additionally, functional substitutes provide a dynamic link between each of those other concepts with, "Indigenous Christianity achieved by means of functional substitutes"[103] being Tippett's description.

Functional Substitute and Church Growth: Fruit of Cultural Fit

Tippett was more prolific on the topic of functional substitutes than other authors, with few others writing on the topic. Coming into missiology from his field experience,[104] informed by informal historical and anthropological research prior to his formal studies in those areas, he was uniquely positioned to see the importance of this tool to facilitate the cultural fit of Christianity. He expanded his statement about the significance of the concept in a footnote in "Parallaxis in Missiology—To Use or Abuse" by saying, "The notion of the functional substitute is basic to church growth

---

101. Malinowski and Kaberry, *Dynamics of Culture Change.*
102. Tippett and Priest, *Fullness of Time,* 344.
103. Tippett, *Introduction to Missiology,* 188.
104. Shaw et al., "Contextualization, Conceptualization, and Communication," 97.

anthropology."[105] He then adds a list of his writings to illustrate that point.[106] Because of his research into facilitating people coming to Christ in people movements, Tippett was aware of the way that multi-individual experience uniquely facilitated deeper cultural issues to be addressed as part of the conversion experience. This then opened the door for functional substitutes to be utilized rather than running the risk of cultural voids resulting from the conversion experience.

When significant and satisfying functional substitutes are not implemented, the resultant cultural voids, to use Tippett's term, open the door for a range of problems to occur: (1) enclosed Christianity cut off from its community as it becomes a Christian enclave; (2) unstable Christianity as people continue to look to the old way in order to meet their needs in times of crisis; (3) the people's sense of cultural and societal identity is threatened, thus damaging the society's sense of well-being; (4) syncretism is possible when incompatible elements of the old system are permanently accepted into the new, or (5) nativistic movements may occur when an attempt is made to re-create the old institutions, which, however, include borrowed elements of the new.[107] Of great concern to Tippett was the fact that all of these responses, possibly attributable to the lack of cultural fit due to the absence of key functional substitutes, would have a negative effect on church growth.

Functional Substitutes and Cultural Fit— Other Scholars' Perspectives

While investigating functional substitutes, becoming aware of some of the academic debate that Tippett's view generated can be helpful in understanding his concept, and the place where his concept interfaced with other scholars and with Great-Commission-focused missiology. For example, Eugene Nida was a pioneer of missionary anthropology who worked with the American Bible Society but generally moved in different philosophical

105. Tippett, "Parallaxis in Missiology," 140.

106. Those writings were Tippett, *Solomon Islands Christianity*, 401; Tippett, *People Movements in Southern Polynesia*, 202, 250; Tippett, *Fijian Material Culture*, 10, 17, 167–72; Tippett, *Peoples of Southwest Ethiopia*, 295; Tippett, *Deep-Sea Canoe*, 100, 106–11; Tippett, *Verdict Theology in Missionary Theory*, 128, 167, 171; Tippett, "Parallaxis in Missiology," 140.

107. Tippett, *Introduction to Missiology*, 47; Tippett, *Oral Tradition and Ethnohistory*, 54.

circles to Tippett,[108] although some of Tippett's articles were published in *Practical Anthropology*, a journal that was strongly influenced by Nida for a number of years. Tippett reports that Nida did not agree with him about the importance, applicability or usefulness of functional substitutes. In his interaction, Tippett summarizes Nida's[109] argument by saying that,

> functional substitutes attempted by missionaries have been 'almost wholly unsuccessful' because of the 'highly integrated character' of the non-Christian rites to be modified, because the changes have been imposed from outside, and because they have not aimed at solving the basic psychological needs.[110]

Tippett responds by saying. "Certainly, any of these reasons may defeat the purposes of the advocate of change, but it is quite wrong to say . . . 'almost wholly unsuccessful.'"[111] He then explained, timing in implementing functional substitutes is crucial, as the openness of the situation for the initial culture change of conversion is probably also open for these other adaptions and adjustments at approximately the same time. Furthermore, if this is done well during the time of conversion, the stage will be set for the development and implementation of subsequent functional substitutes, as other cultural voids become apparent. It must be remembered that functional substitutes are a phenomenon within the local culture, in response to cultural voids in that culture. Functional substitutes are not a mechanism whereby a missionary is able to try to change a part of the culture they don't like or that they in isolation from the local people see as incompatible with Christianity. Functional substitutes may be suggested from a range of sources, however it is the people themselves who determine what is truly satisfying to them, even though an outsider like a missionary can be a resource person for them in this process.

Some anthropologists and missiologists argued that Tippett borrowed concepts from the "functionalists" who, they allege, viewed culture as a closed system, with everything tightly integrated. As such, that closed system view of culture was seen to be too neat to be representative of real life and/or too inflexible to represent Christian theology, leaving no room for the convicting and converting work of the Holy Spirit.[112] This was not

---

108. Tippett et al., *No Continuing City*, 281–82.

109. Nida, "Initiation Rites and Cultural Themes."

110. Tippett, *Introduction to Missiology*, 185.

111. Tippett, *Introduction to Missiology*, 185.

112. Wan, "Critique of Functional Missionary Anthropology," 19.

Tippett's view, but as scholars formed their own negative opinion about "the functionalists," Tippett's use of the term "functional substitute" meant that the concept was already found wanting in their minds. This is well articulated in Buswell's article, "Conn on Functionalism and Presupposition in Missionary Anthropology,"[113] in which he delineates the negative summary of functionalism as used by its critics, saying,

> We may begin by observing that functionalism is characterized by its critics in terms of at least seven principles:
>
> 1. A society or a culture is seen as static.
>
> 2. A society or a culture is ideally in a state of equilibrium.
>
> 3. A society or a culture is to be investigated and described synchronically rather than diachronically, i.e. in terms of existing structural relationships without reference to time or history.
>
> 4. The society or culture is seen as an autonomous organism functioning independently of other organisms.
>
> 5. The functionalist puts a positive moral evaluation upon stability, continuity, and the maintenance or restoration of equilibrium.
>
> 6. The functionalist puts a negative moral evaluation upon social or cultural change.
>
> 7. The functionalist, therefore, is a conservative and a traditionalist, usually interested in maintaining the *status quo*.[114]

Later, speaking about Harvie Conn's perspective, Buswell says,

> I cite these extreme examples simply to indicate . . . the extent of the problem. Happily, Harvie Conn is by no means as extreme in his view of functionalism . . . "Functionalism" has central and basic meanings based upon the fundamental recognition of cultural integration. To recognize that societies and their cultures are internally integrated systems of interacting, functioning parts is not a matter of dispute. Nor is it necessary, thereby, to imply that these parts are always totally functional, stable, unchanging, or that the whole system is static. Quite obviously sociocultural phenomena are always changing no matter what abstract model or ideal type

113. Buswell, "Conn on Functionalism and Presupposition."
114. Buswell, "Conn on Functionalism and Presupposition," 72–73.

one might describe for the analysis of the character and constituent elements of society.[115]

It is worth highlighting again at this point that Tippett came into the formal study of anthropology and history after significant field experience. As such, he was protected from the extremes of theoretical positions by his field experience. For Tippett, his involvement with functionalism was as a tool for ministry, not as an anthropological theory to which he was narrowly committed. In contrast to the allegations of functionalism's closed system, Tippett saw it as a method to understand and facilitate culture change. For those who did not understand Tippett in this way, it is understandable that they criticized him and functional substitutes, albeit unnecessarily.

Taber uses an approach similar to the critics of functionalism referred to above to generally critique missiological anthropology, and then, starting with Tippett and focusing on Kraft, to critique functional substitutes. From that point, he directs his attention to the applications of functional equivalent approaches, as if they were almost equivalent to functional substitutes themselves.[116] Rynkiewich[117] later critiques functionalism in missiological anthropology, but subsequently provides a case study where functional substitutes would have made Christianity more satisfying in later generations[118] if they had been utilized. So, it can be seen that Tippett's teachings on the application of functional substitutes has been debated at a theoretical level, but at the practical level of having Christianity fit culturally, it was endorsed even in the third and fourth generation, as the great-grandchildren of the original converts were reflecting on their experience in Rynkiewich's article.[119]

Cultural Fit through Effective Functional Substitutes

Tippett saw the importance of implementing functional substitutes in meaningful ways in order to maintain uncompromising biblical Christianity, while ensuring a positive sense of cultural fit. From his research of functional substitutes, he was aware that there were factors that increased the likelihood of functional substitutes being successful. With a goal of

---

115. Buswell, "Conn on Functionalism and Presupposition," 74.

116. Taber, *World Is Too Much*, 145–48.

117. Rynkiewich, "World in my Parish," 316.

118. Rynkiewich, "Do Not Remember," 315.

119. Rynkiewich, "Do Not Remember," 315.

being helpful to practitioners, he summarized and explained those factors, particularly in *Introduction to Missiology*[120] as:

1. Missionaries may intentionally be agents of change, but it is the local people who become the cultural innovators, when, as converts, they adopt or adapt the suggested changes. Unless this is the case, then the suggested changes will only be temporary. In another context, using Barnett's concepts, Tippett points out that a functional substitute is not actually a functional substitute until the people themselves have not only accepted the proposed substitute but have attributed a meaning to the new institution that meets their need and fulfils the original purpose purposed for the replacement.[121] The issues addressed here, as previously referred to from Beekman and Callow,[122] are examined with the goal of the complete integration of the Christian message in the lives of the people in a full orbed way. I use the expression "full orbed way" due to the truism that the Christian message comforts the disturbed and disturbs the comfortable. In missiological circles today, cognitive studies using concepts such as schema theory and relevance theory aim to explore these areas further. Scholars pursuing these approaches include Shaw, Burrows and Rynkiewich.

2. Cultural voids occur when conversion or any other major social change is accepted but no adequate substitute is found to replace those things that are rejected in this process. These voids are due to "the felt but unmet needs"[123] and the resultant tensions often "burst forth in some form of nativism."[124]

3. Particular difficulties arise when people convert individually. This is because the functional substitutes that would be needed to avoid cultural voids are social mechanisms that require acceptance of the social group. By contrast, "When social groups become Christian . . . by means of their own communal decision-making patterns

---

120. Tippett, *Introduction to Missiology*, 185–86.
121. Tippett, *Introduction to Missiology*, 184.
122. Beekman and Callow, *Translating the Word of God*, 32.
123. Tippett, *Introduction to Missiology*, 185.
124. Tippett, *Introduction to Missiology*, 185.

within the social structure, functional substitutes are frequent and effective."[125]

4. "Indigenous forms, rites, festivals, and so forth, which can be given a new Christian value content, have greater likelihood of finding permanent acceptance than foreign forms and rituals."[126]

5. Functional substitutes can comprise many different things. As Tippett says, "A functional substitute may be a form, a ritual, a symbol, a role, an idea, a craft, an occupation, an artifact, an economic pattern, or it may even be the Christian religion itself under certain ideal circumstances."[127]

6. Many of the unsuccessful attempts at implementing functional substitutes have "only been tried years after the eradication of the original institution."[128] By contrast, when appropriately designed functional substitutes have been implemented "at the time of the primary religious change"[129] effectiveness has been more typical.

7. "People movements to Christianity . . . occur when . . . *a need for change* is felt. A time propitious for the change of religious belief is also a time propitious for the creation and implementation of functional substitutes."[130] This is why functional substitutes have to be established as soon as possible and by local people, not by outsiders. When this does not occur, there will not only be the difficulty in seeing functional substitutes becoming permanent when they are implemented later on, but the "battle for an indigenous church (i.e. belonging to the people and to the culture) can be lost or won at this point."[131]

Or to use his statement from *Cultural Compulsives*,

> Frequently, especially in people movements, religious change is rapid. This is why church growth places so much stress on the consummation of such spontaneous expansion, on the preservation of

125. Tippett, *Introduction to Missiology*, 185.
126. Tippett, *Introduction to Missiology*, 185.
127. Tippett, *Introduction to Missiology*, 186.
128. Tippett, *Introduction to Missiology*, 185.
129. Tippett, *Introduction to Missiology*, 185.
130. Tippett, *Introduction to Missiology*, 185.
131. Tippett, *Introduction to Missiology*, 186.

indigenous forms in indigenous churches, the planting of groups with the same structural and leadership patterns as the culture pattern, and the use of the vernacular. To maintain this moving equilibrium missiological anthropology advocates such procedures as the use of functional substitutes. This has been more developed in church growth writing than in any secular anthropology.[132]

Observing Functional Substitutes in Action for Cultural Fit: Case Studies

To further clarify the role of functional substitutes in facilitating the cultural fit of Christianity, case studies of functional substitutes in action in several contexts will illustrate the points being made.

First, Darrell Whiteman's PhD research, published as *Melanesians and Missionaries: An Ethnohistorical Study of Social and Religious Change in the Southwest Pacific*[133] is significant because Tippett suggested that Whiteman carry out this research in the Solomon Islands. This research would follow up on Tippett's *Solomon Islands Christianity*.[134] One of the major goals was to research the functional substitutes and cultural voids that had had an impact on the acceptance of the gospel in the Solomon Islands, and the resultant shape of the church coming from that adaption.[135] Whiteman's study provides a diachronic view of big picture culture change and functional substitutes as seen in the Anglican Melanesian Mission areas of the Solomon Islands, from which much can be learned.

One of the key findings in his study is that, through intense culture change taking place as a result of culture contact, functional substitutes will occur, whether strategized for or not. Furthermore, when functional substitutes do not address all the issues in the society, cultural voids will occur, leaving the likelihood of functional substitutes being implemented later without reflection on the imported elements of culture, in this case, the church. The result over a protracted period of time is fascinating, and comes back to Tippett's emphasis on the need for missionaries to understand culture and to be proactively involved with the church as it decides on its own functional substitutes. Some examples show this clearly:

132. Tippett, "Cultural Compulsives," 183.
133. Whiteman, *Melanesians and Missionaries*.
134. Tippett, *Solomon Islands Christianity*.
135. Whiteman, *Melanesians and Missionaries*, 18–20.

Indigenous building construction: The Anglicans used indigenous construction and decoration in their church buildings, which was the beginning of a functional substitute.[136] However it seems that they did not notice that those skills were well developed because of the inter-clan, inter-village competitive aspects that were a traditional part of the ceremonial building program. Over time however, building elaborate (and expensive) church buildings became a functional substitute for that competitive feature of traditional culture that had been a cultural void since they no longer built their shrines and men's club houses for the traditional purposes.[137]

Worship style: While the church buildings were indigenous, the worship style conducted in those buildings was foreign.[138] Subsequently this opened the door for other denominations to make impact in the communities where the Anglican Church was already functioning, by bringing more satisfying worship styles—a functional substitute to counter a cultural void that the people were sensing. However, the multi-denominational options became a functional substitute for traditional inter-village cleavages,[139] obviously an unintended consequence as far as all of the missionaries and Christian workers were concerned.

Leadership structures: The very formal structures of Anglican Church leadership became a functional substitute for the diminishing role and influence of traditional big men.[140] Whether the end result of this was the best model of Christian leadership is another question.

Mana related practices: While the church was opposed to magic and other *mana* based supernatural activities, the fact that the church instituted ceremonies for the "blessing" of canoes, houses, etc. became a functional substitute for the old system. This in fact reinforced that system as people did not understand the difference between *mana* activities and a Christian blessing ceremony.[141]

A second example in the 1970s and 1980s, is from the time when I was involved in church planting and leadership development in the villages of the Sepik River in Papua New Guinea. I eventually became aware of the concept of functional substitutes and related concepts from reading

136. Whiteman, *Melanesians and Missionaries*, 18–20.

137. Whiteman, *Melanesians and Missionaries*, 377.

138. Whiteman, *Melanesians and Missionaries*, 18–20.

139. Whiteman, *Melanesians and Missionaries*, 174.

140. Whiteman, *Melanesians and Missionaries*, 224.

141. Whiteman, *Melanesians and Missionaries*, 355.

Tippett while on the field. In implementing the insights that I learned, the process was to prioritize making the Christian message as understandable as possible in the local contexts, taking language, thought forms, and communication style into account. Then it was up to the local people to make their own decisions in how this would work out in their lives. Prayer events instead of magic ceremonies as part of the agricultural cycle were implemented in a number of communities. Also, all night Christian celebrations using new songs that the Christians had created became a feature. These became functional substitutes for the all night non-Christian dances that the young people across large parts of Papua New Guinea had developed. These non-Christian dances were already a functional substitute to meet the deep seated cultural need for "celebration" that in the past had been tied in with their traditional festivals (*singsing*). Furthermore, the fact of overnight involvement in their culture was a strong symbol of actively demonstrated commitment. As a result, the short term significance of those functional substitutes was positive. The longer term fruit of this has two aspects to it. One is the fact of the strength of the existing churches while the other is the new churches being planted on the Sepik River as those churches continued in outreach.

This story of functional substitutes on the Sepik River is also expanded and localized in a story told to me several years ago by a Bible translator friend that I had worked near in Papua New Guinea. From USA, trained as an anthropologist, for a number of years he informally was my cultural mentor and was of great help to me. He had lived in a village and translated portions of the Bible. At the same time, he and his family personally invested their lives into people in that community in such a way as to make the Gospel very real for them. Twenty-five years later, he returned to that village for some further language work. While there, one of the local Christian leaders told him excitedly that during my friend's planned stay the village, they would host a major multi-village (and multi-language) Christian event. They were excited about the visitors, especially Christians, who were coming from other villages. Prior to the transformation that the gospel had brought, the thought of visitors from many of those other villages could only have brought fear. But now, not only were they coming, but those villages were bringing their music bands along with their portable generators and electronic instruments. My translator friend was shocked at what seemed to be such an intrusion from the outside world—and must have let it show. The leader was most concerned, and, because it was a private meeting, decided to challenge my friend. His summary was, "When you were here, you told us that you wanted us to make Christianity our own. As part of that, you wanted us to express our Christian faith in any way we wanted to, in order to make it attractive and meaningful to our people. This is the twenty-first century. This is how we want it. This is attractive to our people." My friend, when telling me the story, said that it was one of the most meaningful experiences of his life. The fact is, this style of celebration had become the functional substitute for the traditional multi-village festivals that were part of their lives before the gospel came. They had made Christianity their own, including borrowing features from outside their traditional culture, because that suited their contemporary situation better than traditional options would have done.

CONCLUSION

This chapter has examined the importance of strategic missiology and strategic missionary practice as Tippett's fourth life theme, this time applied to cultural fit. In three sequential sections I have shown that Tippett believed that Christianity can and should fit culturally into any society. Tippett was passionate to see people converted to Christian faith in culturally appropriate ways. He was also passionate to see the opportunity for the implementation of conversion carried out in such a way that it became the people's own experience, carried out in their own way. I have also argued in this chapter that Tippett's desire and use of research skills was to see Christianity dynamically fit into the life and lifestyle of the people using approaches of dynamic indigeneity. Where there was incompatibility between the local culture and biblical Christianity, Tippett advocated the use of functional substitutes as a way of bridging to a positive cultural fit, that can be described as dynamic indigeneity. I have identified Tippett's key insights and demonstrated why these insights were important for the fulfillment of the Great Commission in his day.

10

Concluding Observations

"God the Father Almighty laid his hand upon Alan Tippett and made him one of the apostles of effective evangelism throughout the entire world."[1]

This was McGavran's evaluation having worked closely with Tippett for 15 years, and having known him well for 26 years. Darrell Whiteman, who was profoundly influenced by Tippett, says much the same thing but in different words:

"Alan Tippett was a remarkable and complex man . . . He was that rare breed who combined the careful, meticulous eye of the scholar with the passion of a fiery evangelist."[2]

IN THIS STUDY I have analyzed the voluminous and conceptually broad writings of Alan Tippett, Australian Methodist missionary to the Fiji islands and world renowned missiologist, in order to identify the contributions he made to Great-Commission-focused missiology and mission practice in his era. I have argued that his contributions were vital in the development of Great-Commission-focused missiology, disseminated through his writing, lecturing, mentoring, conference presentations, and other avenues. Key areas were: the theological basis for his missiology; research methodol-

---

1. McGavran, "Missiologist Alan R. Tippett," 267.
2. Whiteman, "Legacy of Alan R. Tippett," 166.

ogies that provided accurate data for reflection; and cultural insights which guided his readers towards practical outcomes. This applied in key areas such as: the implications of societies that are propitious for innovation; societies that had the potential for people movements; the opportunities, challenges and appropriate ministry approaches in animistic contexts; and approaches that lead to indigenous Christianity. This study has revealed that, in each of these areas, his insights were relevant in his era, while laying a missiological foundation for generations to come. To achieve the goals of this study, a construct of five life themes was chosen as a meaningful way to distil the motive force behind Tippett's writings, enabling the volume and breadth of his writings to be encapsulated meaningfully.

A limited number of scholars have written summaries of Tippett's life and insights,[3] while one unpublished historical PhD dissertation on Tippett has been written.[4] However, there is a lacuna in relation to an in-depth work on his missiology. At another level, while the number of missiologists has grown significantly since Tippett came to see himself as a missiologist in 1964, many of them have not engaged with Tippett in the areas of his strength, even when writing about related concepts.[5] That identifies another gap in the scholarly interaction. It is also valid to highlight a range of literature that refers to Tippett in a fleeting way, but which does not engage with his key concepts,[6] again leaving a void.

At the same time, this study drew together the interaction of a number of scholars who have acknowledged and even extended Tippett's insights, highlighting those areas of convergence.[7] While filling these gaps in the scholarly literature, this study also builds on a strong foundation of work already conducted by many scholars regarding the relationship between Christian mission as elucidated in the Bible and the cultures of the world in which that mission is implemented. Identifying the unique Tippett insights

3. Kraft and Priest, "Who was this Man?"; McGavran, "Missiologist Alan R. Tippett"; Whiteman, "Legacy of Alan R. Tippett."

4. Dundon, "Raicakacaka."

5. Hesselgrave and Rommen, *Contextualization*; Hiebert et al., *Understanding Folk Religion*; Bosch, *Transforming Mission*.

6. DeLoach, "Knowing God in Melanesia"; Roxborogh, "Missiology after 'Mission?'"; Forman, "Study of Pacific Island Christianity."

7. Kraft, *Christianity in Culture*; Kraft and Gilliland, *Appropriate Christianity*; Kraft, "Power Encounter"; Van Rheenen, *Communicating Christ in Animistic Contexts*; McGavran and Wagner, *Understanding Church Growth*; Hibbert, "Negotiating Identity."

into this domain is one of the areas where this volume makes a major contribution.

Section 1 highlighted the historical and experiential factors that converged to contribute to, and or detract from, the development and influence of Tippett's mission insights as we know of him through his writings. Tippett's life story in chapter 2 provided an essential background to examine the development of Tippett's theory of mission as observed through his life themes. In a positive way, Tippett's upbringing influenced his focus on a relationship with God and the centrality of the church. Through his upbringing, ministry, and missionary experience he was able to lay the foundation for his developing research methodologies. Combining this with his studies, he developed his theories of mission that he came to refer to as post-colonial missiology.

Chapter 3 examined his increasing influence, in order to demonstrate his developing missiology and the global impact it was having. It begins as Tippett, somewhat unexpectedly, returned to Australia from Fiji in 1961. After twenty years of field service, he encountered a sense of isolation and frustration on returning to Australia. Remarkably, within five years of that time he had a PhD and was a senior faculty and founding member of Fuller Theological Seminary School of World Mission in the USA. From that role, he continued to influence mission around the world for the following twelve years until he retired in 1977. Tippett's written observations, although based on meticulous research, were prolific, as well as covering a wide range of missiological insights. The sudden and unexpected decline in Tippett's influence after his retirement is analyzed in depth in chapter 4 demonstrating that there were many factors at work. Some related to Tippett and decisions he made, such as locating to Canberra rather than the mission agency and ministry training hubs of Melbourne or Sydney. Many were external factors related to the church and mission world. His own denomination in Australia, for example, was not open to his influence, while even at Fuller SWM, many new programs were being developed which took the focus away from Tippett's areas of expertise. Nevertheless, through this analysis, his concepts, whether field based or in the academy, are not drawn into question to any marked degree.

Section 2 provided an understanding of three key areas of Tippett's missiology: relationship with God; centrality of the church; and appropriate research methods. Chapter 5 focused on theological dimensions, while chapter 6 focused on research methodologies. The insights identified in these two chapters lay a foundation for the articulation and practical out-working of his concepts later in the study.

Chapter 5 examines his first two life themes, namely, relationship with God and centrality of the church, thus establishing the foundations of Tippett's Bible based theology of mission. That theological analysis can be summarized as: an emphasis on the person of Jesus; his role as the risen Lord in instructing his followers to take the gospel message to others; their responsibility to form discipling communities called churches; the need for these discipling communities to be contextually appropriate to the culture of the new disciples; and churches to grow quantitatively, qualitatively and structurally-organically. Another unique aspect of Tippett's understanding of the church was to see it as the body of Christ, contributing heart, head, and hands to serve their community with service and social justice. However, this is initiated through a strong priority on evangelism and church planting, as a way of impacting more and more communities.

Another way in which Tippett provided the informational foundation for effective mission was in implementing appropriate research methods. This was his third life theme and is examined in chapter 6. His life of re-search was focused missiologically on history, anthropology, and ethnohis-tory. He saw research as seminal to provide verifiable data as the basis of missiology and to guide effective mission. He saw anthropological research having particular value for missionaries. Tippett found the ethnohistori-cal research method to be very fertile. The insights gained from it richly rewarded researchers for their painstaking efforts. While researching the use of ethnohistory, it was noted that it has seldom been used in missiologi-cal anthropology since Tippett's era. Tippett's research methodologies are a rich resource because they were designed on the basis of his field mission-ary experience. As a result, many of them are able to be used by missionar-ies while still involved in their ministry roles.

In Section 3, Tippett's key insights for strategic mission practice are identified, described, and analyzed by tracing his fourth life theme re-garding the importance of strategic missiology and strategic missionary practice. Tippett's research methodologies provided the ability to monitor, measure, and therefore project significant strategies for mission. Using the insights so generated as this life theme was examined, a trilogy of chap-ters, each engaging key strategic areas were analyzed using the overarching headings of societal decision-making, ministry in animistic contexts, and the cultural fit of the Christianity. These reveal that his paramount focus is clearly on field effectiveness.

Chapter 7, while focused on societal decision-making, examined people movements, societal receptivity, and the partnered ministry phases of discipling and perfecting. It identified that people movements facilitate large numbers of decisions for Christ and have a high likelihood of producing strong indigenous churches while reducing the foreign feel of Christianity. The mood-attitude of societal receptivity to the gospel has a major impact of the gospel's acceptance. The outworking of this in a society is a changing rather than a fixed phenomenon. Furthermore, changes in a given community's attitudes can occur quickly. Therefore mission leaders are encouraged to keep this in mind while making decisions regarding the deployment of personnel and resources in order to maximize mission impact. Yet no matter what ministry approaches are utilized, long term Christian maturity has to be prioritized.

As demonstrated in chapter 8, Tippett developed significant ministry-focused concepts in relation to ministry in animistic contexts. It was his early writing regarding animism that brought him to the attention of McGavran and thus to the world stage. Ministry approaches relating to animism were identified as applying to ministry in the "tropical forest" and in the "urban jungle." Furthermore, Tippett's sense of urgency for tribal animists was examined. He realized that the major cultural changes being thrust upon such societies often meant that they were open to other changes as well, such as being open to the gospel more than had been the case previously. Having established Tippett's understanding of the term animism, his biblical basis for ministry in animistic context is outlined. It was revealed that he combined this with his own emic, insider view of animism to provide the basis for his "pay attention" pointers to guide in ministry to animists. Based on Tippett discoveries, I formulated three phases of power encounter from his writings that engage animists with the Christian gospel: 1) God is supreme, 2) God is powerful, and 3) Jesus is Lord.

The paramount importance Tippett placed on the cultural fit of Christianity was the substance of chapter 9. Tippett's view was that for the church to truly be the church it needed to be indigenous. This chapter examined Tippett's model of the process of people being converted, observing how this works in the life of an individual or in a society coming to Christ in a people movement. The unique situation of people coming to faith in the context of the major world religions was also examined, adding the perspective of identity negotiation to Tippett's model. Dynamic indigeneity was examined from Tippett's view of the importance of ensuring the cultural fit of Christianity. At the same time, while indigeneity was an important goal for Tippett, he saw the goal of having biblically compatible Christianity as more important, hence the probability of some incompatibility between Biblical Christianity and the local culture. When that was the case, in order to avoid cultural voids, which can subsequently undermine Christianity, Tippett advocated the use of functional substitutes, that is, replacing an incompatible cultural element with a new element or elements that are compatible with biblical Christianity, yet meaningful and satisfying to the people in the culture.

While this study analyzed some of the major contributions Tippett made to the formation of twentieth-century missiology, it also uncovered some unexpected results. I was well aware of Tippett's emphasis on church growth before I began this project. However, as I went deeper into the research, I discovered that the concept of the church was the basis for and the expression of his missiology. It developed in his Australian pastorates and went to Fiji with him and was enhanced by living in a communal society, his biblical studies, his anthropology, and in his writing on the topic. Almost right up till his death he was working on a book about the church for local church studies.

The power of the tool of ethnohistory was another surprise. My initial engagement with ethnohistory was quite intimidating, as I heard Tippett lecture on ethnohistory as part of the course I took with him. The detail that Tippett went to in order to ensure that his findings were as accurate as possible was commendable. However, there was a sense that it was his "calling," and therefore somehow did not need to be taken that seriously by others in mission research in later eras. Yet in this study, it became obvious that approaching any situation with an ethnohistorical perspective, new and informative data can be found, new perspectives can be gained, and new solutions discovered. While Tippett's detailed approach to ethnohistorical research remains valid, an ethnohistorical perspective can be of benefit to mission leaders and field missionaries.

Over many years, my understanding of Tippett's concept of power encounter fitted well with my experience of ministry in animistic contexts. However, occasionally I noticed that he was emphasizing something different than the conversion-related power encounter experiences from his Pacific research. The further I went in my research of Tippett's concept of power encounter, the more I came to see that I was misreading Tippett. He never had to differentiate between the different aspects of power encounter in focus at that moment, because to him they were interrelated. Also, because he was clear in his own mind about which aspect of power encounter was in his focus at that time, delineating them was unnecessary. Recognizing these three phases in his writing helped in understanding the emphasis of other scholars, who were noticing the other phases of Tippett's concept as being primary.

The focus of this study was on the essential Alan Tippett. The nature of this study, especially considering the volume of Tippett's material to engage with, limited the ability to compare every one of his concepts with every missiologist since his day, including the present day. Therefore the emphasis of the study was focused on his era.

This study has opened up opportunities for further research, such as an analysis of mission in the twenty-first century, using an application of Tippett's insights. I suggest that there would be missiological significance in compiling a parallel analysis of the colonialism Tippett faced, and the neo-colonialism that characterizes so much of twenty-first-century mission, be it short term or long term mission. From that analysis and that comparison, the goal would be to see which, if any of Tippett's insights could provide positive guidance for the twenty-first century. Another fruitful area would be to compare missionary training in Australia, USA, and the UK in the period when Tippett was influential through Fuller Theological Seminary School of World Mission, especially identifying the factors related to Tippett that contributed to the differences.

In this study I examined the voluminous and conceptually broad writings of Alan Tippett, in order to identify the contribution he made to Great-Commission-focused missiology and mission practice in the twentieth century. This study primarily focused on the thirty-four-year time frame between 1954 and 1988, a crucial period for mission globally with the late 1960s being a watershed. Little research has focused on Tippett's outstanding life and work of, especially his later and influential role as a missiologist. At the same time, I identified some aspects of his writing that hampered his long term impact: he left no one volume that summarized his key insights in a unified way; many of his best insights were couched in local case studies; his insights were so broad and so detailed, they were difficult to access across the books and articles that were published in his lifetime; quite an amount of his crucial material has only been published posthumously with other key documents still unpublished. Despite those factors, I have been able to argue clearly that his contribution was vital in the development and dissemination of twentieth-century, Great-Commission-focused missiology and strategic missionary practice. Tippett held that the task of mission was founded on a biblical motivation. For that reason, he invested his lifetime to develop missiological insights to help in the fulfillment of that mission task. Key insight areas were: the clear theological basis for his missiology; research methodologies that provided accurate data for missiological and strategic reflection suited to a wide range of ministry contexts; his cultural insights were especially geared for effective mission in non-Western environments; his understanding of societies that are propitious for innovation; societies that had the potential for people movements; the opportunities, challenges, and appropriate ministry approaches in animistic contexts; and approaches that lead to indigenous, culturally appropriate Christianity at the local congregational level, and at the level of national church movements. I have demonstrated that in each of these areas, he served his generation well, and, in doing so, laid a mission and missiological foundation for generations to come.

Bibliography

Adams, Glenn. "Decolonizing Methods: African Studies and Qualitative Research." *Journal of Social & Personal Relationships* 31.4 (2014) 467–74.

Allen, Roland. *The Ministry of the Spirit.* London: World Dominion, 1960.

———. *Missionary Methods: St. Paul's or Ours?* London: Lutterworth, 1968.

———. *The Spontaneous Expansion of the Church and the Causes Which Hinder It.* London: World Dominion, 1927.

Anderson, Allan Heaton. "Contextualization in Pentecostalism: A Multicultural Perspective." *International Bulletin of Mission Research* 41.1 (2017) 29–40.

Anderson, William K. *Christian World Mission.* Nashville: Commission on Ministerial Training, Methodist Church USA, 1946.

Andrews, Lesie A. "Spiritual, Family, and Ministry Satisfaction Among Missionaries." *Journal of Psychology and Theology* 27.2 (1999) 107–17.

Arnold, Clinton E. *Ephesians, Power and Magic: The Concept of Power in Ephesians in Light of its Historical Setting.* Society for New Testament Studies Monograph Series. Cambridge: Cambridge University Press, 1989.

———. *Powers of Darkness: Principalities and Powers in Paul's Letters.* Downers Grove, IL: InterVarsity, 1992.

Asamoah-Gyadu, J. Kwabena. "Your Body Is a Temple: Conversion Narratives in African-Led Eastern European Pentecostalism." *Pastoral Psychology* 58.1 (2009) 1–14.

Bailey, Kenneth E. *Poet & Peasant* and *Through Peasant Eyes: A Literary-cultural Approach to the Parables in Luke.* Combined ed. Grand Rapids: Eerdmans, 1983.

Barnett, H. G. *Innovation: The Basis of Cultural Change.* 1st ed. New York: McGraw-Hill, 1953.

Barnett, Mike, and Michael Pocock. *The Centrality of Christ in Contemporary Missions.* Evangelical Missiological Society Series. Pasadena, CA: William Carey Library, 2005.

Beekman, John, and John Callow. *Translating the Word of God, with Scripture and Topical Indexes.* Grand Rapids: Zondervan. 1974.

Beidelman, T. O. *The Culture of Colonialism: The Cultural Subjection of Ukaguru.* African Systems of Thought. Bloomington, IN: Indiana University Press, 2012.

Bevans, Stephen B. *Models of Contextual Theology.* Faith and Cultures Series. Rev. and exp. ed. Maryknoll, NY: Orbis, 2002.

Birtwhistle, N. Allen. *In His Armour: The Life of John Hunt of Fiji.* London: Cargate, 1954.

Bosch, David J. "Church Growh Missiology." *Missionalia* 16.1 (1988) 11–24.

———. *Transforming Mission: Paradigm Shifts in Theology of Mission.* American Society of Missiology Series. Maryknoll, NY: Orbis, 1991.

Bowman, John Wick. *The Intention of Jesus*. Philadelphia: Westminster, 1943.

Boyd, David. *You Don't Have to Cross the Ocean to Reach the World: The Power of Local Cross-Cultural Ministry*. Grand Rapids: Chosen, 2008.

Brislin, Richard W. "Comparative Research Methodology: Cross-cultural Studies." *International Journal of Psychology* 11.3 (1976) 215–29.

Brown, Candy G., ed. *Global Pentecostal and Charismatic Healing*. Oxford: Oxford University Press, 2011.

Brown, George. *George Brown, D.D. Pioneer-missionary and Explorer, an Autobiography*. London: Hodder and Stoughton, 1908.

Brysk, Alison. *From Tribal Village to Global Village: Indian Rights and International Relations in Latin America*. Stanford, CA: Stanford University Press, 2000.

Bulatao, Jaime C. *Phenomena and Their Interpretation: Landmark Essays, 1957–1989*. Manila: Ateneo de Manila University Press, 1992.

———. "Split Level Christianity." In *Phenomena and Their Interpretation: Landmark Essays, 1957–1989*, 22–31. Manila: Ateneo de Manila University Press, 1992.

Burden, J. J. "Magic & Divination in the Old Testament." *Missionalia* 1.3 (1973) 103–12.

Burnett, David. *World of the Spirits: A Christian Perspective on Traditional and Folk Religions*. Oxford: Monarch, 2005.

Buswell, James Oliver. "Conn on Functionalism and Presupposition in Missionary Anthropology." *Trinity Journal* 7.2 (1986) 69–95.

Calverton, Victor Francis. *The Making of Man: An Outline of Anthropology*. The Modern Library of the World's Best . New York: The Modern Library, 1931.

Campbell, Jonathan. "Mission in Postmodern Contexts." In *Teaching Them Obedience in all Things*, edited by E. J. Elliston, 185–210. Pasadena, CA: William Carey Library, 1999.

Carmack, Robert M. "Ethnohistory: A Review of Its Development, Definitions, Methods, and Aims." *Annual Review of Anthropology* 1 (1972) 227–46.

Carter, John F. "The Indigenous Principle Revisited: Towards a Coactive Model of Missionary Ministry." *Asian Journal of Pentecostal Studies* 1.1 (1998) 73–82.

Carver, Tracey L., and Tina Cockburn. "Online Skill Development for Generation Y Students: A Case Study of an Online Negotiation Model for External Law Students." *The International Journal of Learning* 13.12 (2007) 81–89.

Casiño, Tereso C., et al. *Reaching the City: Reflections on Urban Mission for the Twenty-first Century*. Pasadena, CA: William Carey Library, 2012.

Cate, Patrick. "The Uniqueness of Christ and Missions." In *The Centrality of Christ in Contemporary Missions*, edited by Mike Barnett and Michael Pocock, 37–68. Pasadena, CA: William Carey Library, 2005.

Cavalcanti, H. B. "Human Agency in Mission Work: Missionary Styles and Their Political Consequences." *Sociology of Religion* 66.4 (2005) 381–98.

Chaves, Kelly K. "Ethnohistory: From Inception to Postmodernism and Beyond." *Historian* 70.3 (2008) 486–513.

Childs, Jay. "Church Growth vs Church Seasons." *Leadership*, 31.1 (Fall 2010) 38–41.

Christopher, A. J. *Colonial Africa*. Croom Helm Historical Geography Series. London: Croom Helm, 1984.

Clark, Sidney J. W. *The Indigenous Church: Evangelistic and Church Planting Work at the Big End*. Indigenous Church Series. 2nd ed. London: World Dominion, 1928.

Codrington, Robert H. *The Melanesians; Studies in Their Anthropology and Folk-lore*. Oxford: Clarendon, 1891.

Bibliography

Copeland, E. Luther. "Church Growth in Acts." *Missiology* 4.1 (1976) 13–26.

Daniélou, Jean "Preface: The Other Covenant." In *The Other Covenant: A Theology of Paganism*, xi–xiii. Glen Rock, NJ: Newman, 1968.

Dark, Philip. "Methods of Synthesis in Ethnohistory." *Ethnohistory* 4 (1957) 231–78.

Davies, Alun. *Invading Paradise: Inspiring Stories of AOG Missionaries in Papua New Guinea*. Melbourne: AOG World Missions, 1991.

Dayton, Edward R., and David Allen Fraser. *Planning Strategies for World Evangelization.* Rev. ed. Monrovia, CA: MARC, 1990.

Delavignette, Robert Louis. *Christianity and Colonialism*. Twentieth Century Encyclopedia of Catholicism. 1st American ed. New York: Hawthorn, 1964.

DeLoach, Daniel A. "Knowing God in Melanesia: Schemas Relevant to Vernacular Scripture Engagement." PhD diss., Fuller School of International Studies, 2016.

DeNeui, Paul H. "A Typology of Approaches to Thai Folk Buddhists." In *Appropriate Christianity*, edited by Charles H. Kraft and Dean S. Gilliland, 415–36. Pasadena, CA: William Carey Library, 2005.

Douglas, James D. *Let the Earth Hear His Voice: Lausanne Congress on World Evangelization. Official Reference Volume, Papers and Responses*. Minneapolis: World Wide , 1975.

Dundon, Colin. "Raicakacaka: 'Walking the Road' from Colonial to Post-colonial Mission: The Life, Work and Thought of the Reverend Dr. Alan Richard Tippett, Methodist Missionary in Fiji, Anthropologist and Missiologist, 1911–1988." PhD diss., Australian Defence Force Academy, School of History, 2000.

————. "The Tippett Library: Named after Rev Dr A R Tippett L Th MA PhD FLS." *Australian Journal of Mission Studies* 8.2 (2014) 11–16.

Duriau, Vincent J., et al. "A Content Analysis of the Content Analysis Literature in Organization Studies: Research Themes, Data Sources, and Methodological Refinements." *Organizational Research Methods* 10.1 (2007) 5–34.

Elliston, Edgar J. *Teaching Them Obedience in all Things: Equipping for the 21st Century.* Evangelical Missiological Society Series. Pasadena, CA: William Carey Library, 1999.

Fenton, William N. "Ethnohistory and its Problems." *Ethnohistory* 9 (1962) 1–23.

Forbes, George. *A Church on Fire: The Story of the Assemblies of God of Papua New Guinea.* Mitcham, VIC: Mission Mobilisers International, 2001.

Forman, Charles W. "The Study of Pacific Island Christianity: Achievements, Resources, Needs." *International Bulletin of Missionary Research* 18.3 (1994) 103–12.

Garrett, John. *To Live Among the Stars: Christian Origins in Oceania.* Suva, Fiji: Institute of Pacific Studies, University of the South Pacific, 1982.

Gibbs, Eddie. "How Appropriate Is the Church Growth Paradigm in Today's Mission Contexts?" In *Appropriate Christianity*, edited by Charles H. Kraft, 293–308. Pasadena, CA: William Carey Library, 2005.

Glasser, Arthur F. "Kingdom and Mission." Unpublished manuscript. Pasadena, CA: Fuller Theological Seminary, 1989.

Gottschalk, Louis Reichenthal, et al. *The Use of Personal Documents in History, Anthropology, and Sociology.* Bulletin. New York: Social Science Research Council, 1945.

Gration, John A. "Conversion in Cultural Context." *International Bulletin of Missionary Research* 7.4 (1983) 157–62.

Grim, Brian J., et al. "Yearbook of International Religious Demography." Leiden: Koninklijke Brill, 2016.

Grimes, Joseph E. "Ethnographic Questions for Christian Missionaries." *Practical Anthropology* 6.6 (1959) 275–76.

Hayward, Douglas J. "The Evangelization of Animists: Power, Trust or Love Encounter?" *International Journal of Frontier Missions* 14.4 (1997) 155–59.

Hayward, Victor E. W. "Call to Witness: But What Kind of Witness?" *International Review of Mission* 53.210 (1964) 201–8.

———. *Christians and China*. Belfast: Christian Journals, 1974.

———, ed. *African Independent Church Movements*. C.W.M.E. Research Pamphlets. Vol. 11, London: Edinburgh House, 1963.

Heitink, Gerben. *Practical Theology: History, Theory, Action Domains: Manual for Practical Theology*. Studies in Practical Theology. Grand Rapids: Eerdmans, 1999.

Henderson, G. C. *Fiji and the Fijians, 1835–1856*. Sydney: Angus & Robertson, 1931.

Hesselgrave, David J. "People Movements." In *Evangelical Dictionary of World Missions*, edited by A. Scott Moreau, 743–44. Grand Rapids: Baker, 2000.

———. *Planting Churches Cross-Culturally*. Grand Rapids: Baker, 1980.

Hesselgrave, David J., and Edward Rommen. *Contextualization: Meanings, Methods, and Models*. Pasadena, CA: William Carey Library, 2000.

Hibbert, Richard. "Negotiating Identity: Extending and Applying Alan Tippett's Model of Conversion." *Missiology* 43.1 (2015) 59–72.

Hibbert, Richard, and Evelyn Hibbert. "Expanding and Applying Tippett's Model of Conversion to Groups of Converts from other Major Religions." *Australian Journal of Mission Studies* 8.2 (2014) 34–41.

Hiebert, Paul G. "Critical Contextualization." *Missiology* 12.3 (1984) 287–96.

———. *Cultural Anthropology*. 2nd ed. Grand Rapids: Baker, 1983.

———. "The Flaw of the Excluded Middle." *Missiology* 10.1 (1982) 35–47.

———. *Transforming Worldviews: An Anthropological Understanding of How People Change*. Grand Rapids: Baker Academic, 2008.

Hiebert, Paul G., et al. *Understanding Folk Religion: A Christian Response to Popular Beliefs and Practices*. Grand Rapids: Baker, 1999.

Hitchen, John M. "Relations Between Missiology and Anthropology Then and Now—Insights from the Contributions to Ethnography and Anthropology by Nineteenth-century Missionaries in the South Pacific." *Missiology* 30.4 (2002) 455–78.

Hodges, Melvin L. *The Indigenous Church*. Springfield, MO: Gospel, 1953.

———. *The Indigenous Church and the Missionary: A Sequel to The Indigenous Church*. South Pasadena, CA: William Carey Library, 1978.

Hoefer, Herbert E. *Churchless Christianity*. Pasadena, CA: William Carey Library, 2001.

Hoekendijk, Johannes Christiaan. *The Church Inside Out*. Adventures in Faith. Philadelphia: Westminster, 1966.

Hogan, Philip. "Multi-Individual Conversion." *Church Growth Bulletin Second Consolidated Volume* 10.5 (1974) 415.

Hollenweger, Walter J. "Oral Tradition and Ethnohistory: The Transmission of Information and Social Values in Early Christian Fiji." *International Review of Mission* 71.284 (1982) 517–21.

Hook, Sidney. "Modern Quarterly, a Chapter in American Radical History: V. F. Calverton and His Periodicals." *Labor History* 10.2 (1969) 241–49.

Hovey, Kevin G. "Alan Tippett: Australian Missiologist." *Australian Journal of Mission Studies* 8.2 (2014) 30–33.

———. *Before All Else Fails, Read the Instructions: A Manual for Cross Cultural Christians*. 2nd ed. Brisbane: Harvest, 1995.

Bibliography

———. "Guest Editorial: Reflect, Reengage, Reinvigorate." *Australian Journal of Mission Studies* 8.2 (2014) 1–2.

———. "Guiding Light: Contributions of Alan R. Tippett Toward the Development and Dissemination of Twentieth Century Missiology." PhD diss., Alphacrucis College, 2017.

———. "Power Encounter at Mowi." *Australian Evangel* 35.3 (1978) 15–18.

Humble, Graeme. "Tippett for Today and Tomorrow: Functional Substitutes, Contextualization and Missiology." *Australian Journal of Mission Studies* 8.2 (2014) 49–55.

Hunt, Robert A. "The History of the Lausanne Movement, 1974–2010." *International Bulletin of Missionary Research* 35.2 (2011) 81–85.

Hunter, George G. "Multi-individual Conversion." *Church Growth Bulletin Third Consolidated Volume* 13.4 (1977) 111–17.

Jick, Todd D. "Mixing Qualitative and Quantitative Methods: Triangulation in Action." *Administrative Science Quarterly* 24.4 (1979) 602–11.

Johnson, Todd M., et al. "Christianity 2017: Five Hundred Years of Protestant Christianity." *International Bulletin of Mission Research* 41.1 (2017) 41–52.

Kärkkäinen, Veli-Matti. "Are Pentecostals Oblivious to Social Justice?: Theological and Ecumenical Perspectives." *Missiology* 29.4 (2001) 417–31.

Knapman, Claudia. *White Women in Fiji 1835–1930: The Ruin of Empire?* Sydney: Allen & Unwin, 1986.

Knight, Henry. "God's Faithfulness and God's Freedom: A Comparison of Contemporary Theologies of Healing." *Journal of Pentecostal Theology* 1.2 (1993) 65–89.

Knitter, Paul F. *No Other Name?: A Critical Survey of Christian Attitudes Toward the World Religions.* American Society of Missiology Series. Maryknoll, NY: Orbis, 1985.

Koranyi, Andras. "Mission as Call to Metanoia and Witness to Hope: A Historical Survey." *International Review of Mission* 88.350 (1999) 267–78.

Kraemer, Hendrick. *The Christian Message in a Non-Christian World.* London: International Missionary Council, 1938.

Kraft, Charles H. *Anthropology for Christian Witness.* Maryknoll, NY: Orbis, 1996.

———. *Communication Theory for Christian Witness.* Nashville: Abingdon, 1983.

———. *Christianity in Culture: A Study in Dynamic Biblical Theologizing in Cross-cultural Perspective.* Revised 25th anniversary ed. Maryknoll, NY: Orbis, 2005.

———. *Culture, Communication, and Christianity: A Selection of Writings.* Pasadena, CA: William Carey Library, 2001.

———. "Dynamic Equivalence Churches: An Ethnotheological Approach to Indigeneity." *Missiology* 1.1 (1973) 39–57.

———. *Issues in Contextualization.* Pasadena, CA: William Carey Library, 2016.

———. "Power Encounter." *Australian Journal of Mission Studies* 8.2 (2014) 42–48.

———. *SWM/SIS at Forty: A Participant/Observer's View of Our History.* Pasadena, CA: William Carey Library, 2005.

———. "Three Encounters in Christian Witness." In *Perspectives on the World Christian Movement*, edited by Ralph D. Winter and Steven C. Hawthorne, 445–50. Pasadena, CA: William Carey Library, 2009.

———. *Worldview for Christian Witness.* Pasadena, CA: William Carey Library, 2007.

Kraft, Charles H., and Dean S. Gilliland. *Appropriate Christianity.* Pasadena, CA: William Carey Library, 2005.

Kraft, Charles H., and Douglas D. Priest. "Who was this Man? A Tribute to Alan R. Tippett." *Missiology* 17.3 (1989) 269–81.

Kraft, Charles H., and Tom N. Wisley. *Readings in Dynamic Indigeneity.* Pasadena, CA: William Carey Library, 1979.

Kroeber, Alfred L. *Anthropology: Race, Language, Culture, Psychology, Prehistory.* New York: Harcourt, 1948.

Langridge, Albert K., and Frank H. L. Paton. *John G. Paton, Later Years and Farewell.* London: Hodder and Stoughton, 1910.

Latourette, Kenneth Scott. *A History of the Expansion of Christianity.* Contemporary Evangelical Perspectives. 7 vols. Grand Rapids: Zondervan 1970.

————. *Missions Tomorrow.* New York: Harper & Brothers, 1936.

————. *The Thousand Years of Uncertainty: A.D. 500–A.D. 1500. A History of the Expansion of Christianity.* 7 vols. Grand Rapids: Zondervan 1970.

Lausanne Committee for World Evangelization. *The Pasadena Consulation: Homogeneous Units Principle.* Lausanne Occasional Papers. 2 vols. Wheaton, IL: Lausanne Committee for World Evangelization, 1978.

————. *The Willowbank Report: Gospel and Culture.* Lausanne occasional papers. 2 vols. Wheaton, IL: Lausanne Committee for World Evangelization, 1978.

Linnenbrink, Günter. "Witness and Service in the Mission of the Church." *International Review of Missions* 54 (1965) 428–36.

Linton, Ralph. *The Study of Man.* New York: Appleton-Century-Crofts, 1936.

Liubinskas, Susann. "The Body of Christ in Mission: Paul's Ecclesiology and the Role of the Church in Mission." *Missiology* 41.4 (2013) 402–15.

Luzbetak, Louis J. *The Church and Cultures: An Applied Anthropology for the Religious Worker.* Techny, IL: Divine Word, 1963.

————. *The Church and Cultures: An Applied Anthropology for the Religious Worker.* 2nd ed. Techny, IL: Divine Word, 1970.

————. *The Church and Cultures: New Perspectives in Missiological Anthropology.* American Society of Missiology Series. Maryknoll, NY: Orbis, 1988.

Ma, Wonsuk, and Julie C. Ma. *Mission in the Spirit: Towards a Pentecostal/Charismatic Missiology.* Regnum Studies in Mission. Oxford: Regnum, 2010.

Malina, Bruce J. *The New Testament World: Insights from Cultural Anthropology.* 3rd ed. Louisville: Westminster John Knox, 2001.

Malinowski, Bronislaw. "The Anthropology of Changing African Cultures." In *Methods of Study of Culture Contact in Africa.* London: International African Institute, Oxford University Press, 1938.

Malinowski, Bronislaw, and Phyllis Mary Kaberry. *The Dynamics of Culture Change: An Inquiry into Race Relations in Africa.* London: Oxford University, 1945.

Markarian, Krikor. "Today's Iranian Revolution: How the Mullahs Are Leading the Nation to Jesus." *Mission Frontiers* 30.5 (Sep-Oct 2008) 6–13.

Marris, Peter. *Family and Social Change in an African City: A Study of Rehousing in Lagos.* Evanston, IL: Northwestern University Press, 1938.

Massey, Joshua. "God's Amazing Diversity in Drawing Muslims to Christ." *International Journal of Frontier Missions* 17.1 (2000) 5–14.

Matthey, Jacques. "From 1910 to 2010: A Post Edinburgh 2010 Reflection." *International Review of Mission* 99.2 (2010) 258–75.

Maurier, Henri. *The Other Covenant: A Theology of Paganism.* Glen Rock, NJ: Newman, 1968.

McCaughey, J. Davis. "Church Union in Australia." *The Ecumenical Review* 17.1 (1965) 38–53.

Bibliography

McConnell, C. Douglas. *The Holy Spirit and Mission Dynamics*. Evangelical Missiological Society Series. Pasadena, CA: William Carey Library, 1997.

McGavran, Donald Anderson. *The Bridges of God: A Study in the Strategy of Missions*. London: World Dominion, 1955.

————. *Church Growth and Christian Mission*. 1st ed. New York: Harper & Row, 1965.

————. *Church Growth in Mexico*. Grand Rapids: Eerdmans, 1963.

————. "Church Growth Strategy Continued." *International Review of Mission* 57.227 (1968) 335–43.

————. *Crucial Issues in Missions Tomorrow*. Chicago: Moody, 1972.

————. *Ethnic Realities and the Church: Lessons from India*. South Pasadena, CA: William Carey Library, 1979.

————. *How Churches Grow: The New Frontiers of Mission*. London: World Dominion, 1959.

————. "The Institute of Church Growth." *International Review of Mission* 50.200 (1961) 430–34.

————. "Missiologist Alan R. Tippett, 1911–1988." *Missiology* 17.3 (1989) 261–67.

————. "Principles and Policies Bearing on Church Growth." *Church Growth Bulletin Consolidated Volume I – V* 2.5 (1966) 149–54.

————. *Understanding Church Growth*. Grand Rapids: Eerdmans, 1970.

————. "Wrong Strategy: The Real Crisis in Missions." *International Review of Mission* 54.216 (1965) 451–61.

McGavran, Donald Anderson, and C. Peter Wagner. *Understanding Church Growth*. 3rd ed. Grand Rapids: Eerdmans, 1990.

McGavran, Donald Anderson, and Norman Riddle. *Zaire: Midday in Missions*. Valley Forge, PA: Judson, 1979.

McGee, Gary B. "Assemblies of God Mission Theology: A Historical Perspective." *International Bulletin of Missionary Research* 10.4 (1986) 166–69.

McGlynn, Angela Provitera. "Teaching Millennials, Our Newest Cultural Cohort." *The Hispanic Outlook in Higher Education* 16.1 (2005) 12–16.

McIntosh, Gary L. *Donald A. McGavran: Meet the Man Who Sparked the Entire Modern Church Growth Movement*. Los Angeles: Church Leader Insights, 2015.

McPhee, Arthur G. *The Road to Delhi: J. Waskom Pickett and Missions in the Twilight of the Raj and Dawn of Nationhood*. Rev. and exp. ed. Lexington, KY: Emeth, 2012.

McVeigh, Malcolm. "The Fate of Those Who Have Not Heard? It Depends." *Evangelical Missions Quarterly* 21.4 (1985) 370–80.

Michener, James A. *Hawaii*. New York: Random House, 1959.

Miller, Kevin, and Dave Goetz. "Finding the Eye of the Storm: An Interview with M. Craig Barnes." *Leadership Journal* 19.1 (1998) 20–27.

Moreau, A. Scott, et al. *Evangelical Dictionary of World Missions*. Baker Reference Library. Grand Rapids: Baker, 2000.

Mudimbe, Victor Y. *The Invention of Africa: Gnosis, Philosophy, and the Order of Knowledge*. African Systems of Thought Series. Bloomington, IN: Indiana University Press, 1988.

Nehrbass, Kenneth. *Christianity and Animism in Melanesia: Four Approaches to Gospel and Culture*. Pasadena, CA: William Carey Library, 2012.

Neill, Stephen. *Christian Faith and Other Faiths: The Christian Dialogue with Other Religions*. Oxford paperbacks. 2nd ed. London: Oxford University Press, 1970.

Neill, Stephen, and Owen Chadwick. *A History of Christian Missions*. The Pelican History of the Church series. Rev. for the 2nd ed. Harmondsworth, UK: Penguin, 1986.

Nettleton, Joseph. *John Hunt: Pioneer Missionary and Saint*. Methodist Missionary Library. London: C. H. Kelly, 1902.

Nevius, John L. *Methods of Mission Work*. Shanghai: American Presbyterian Mission, 1886.

Newbigin, Lesslie. *One Body, One Gospel, One World: The Christian Mission Today*. New York: Friendship, 1966.

———. *The Open Secret: An Introduction to the Theory of Mission*. Rev. ed. Grand Rapids: Eerdmans, 1995.

———. *The Open Secret: Sketches for a Missionary Theology*. Grand Rapids: Eerdmans, 1978.

Nida, Eugene A. *Customs and Cultures; Anthropology for Christian Missions*. 1st ed. New York: Harper, 1954.

———. "Initiation Rites and Cultural Themes." *Practical Anthropology* 9.4 (1962) 145–50.

Nida, Eugene A., and Charles R. Taber. *The Theory and Practice of Translation*. Boston: Brill, 2003.

Padilla, C. René. *Mission between the Times: Essays on the Kingdom*. Grand Rapids: Eerdmans, 1985.

———. "The Unity of the Church and the Homogeneous Unit Principle." *International Bulletin of Missionary Research* 6.1 (1982) 23–30.

Parshall, Phil. *Bridges to Islam: A Christian Perspective on Folk Islam*. Grand Rapids: Baker, 1983.

Parsons, Greg H. "Celebrating the Work of God Through the Life of an Innovator: Ralph D Winter (1924–2009)." *Mission Frontiers* 31.3–4 (Aug 2009) 6–11.

Paton, John Gibson, and James Paton. *John G. Paton: Missionary to the New Hebrides; an Autobiography Edited by his Brother, James Paton*. London: Banner of Truth, 1965.

Pavey, Stephen. *Theologies of Power and Crisis: Envisioning/Embodying Christianity in Hong Kong*. American Society of Missiology Monograph Series. Eugene, OR: Pickwick, 2011.

Pelto, Pertti J., and Gretel H. Pelto. *Anthropological Research: The Structure of Inquiry*. 2nd ed. Cambridge: Cambridge University Press, 1978.

Phillips, Susan. "Tippett Missiological and Anthropological Collection." *Australian Journal of Mission Studies* 8.2 (2014) 17–20.

Pickett, J. Waskom. *Christian Mass Movements in India: A Study with Recommendations*. 2nd Indian ed. Lucknow, India: Lucknow, 1933.

———. *Church Growth and Group Conversion*. 3rd ed. Lucknow, India: Lucknow, 1956.

Pinnock, Clark H. *A Wideness in God's Mercy: The Finality of Jesus Christ in a World of Religions*. Grand Rapids: Zondervan, 1992.

Pinola, Sakari. *Church Growth: Principles and Praxis of Donald A. McGavran's Missiology*. Åbo, Finland: Åbo Akademis Forlag, Åbo Akademi University Press, 1995.

Priest, Doug. "The Genesis of the Missiology of Alan R Tippett Series." *Australian Journal of Mission Studies* 8.2 (2014) 26–29.

———. "Vintage and Vantage: Alan R Tippett Now and Then." *Australian Journal of Mission Studies* 8.2 (2014) 3–10.

———, ed. *Fullness of Time: Ethnohistory Selections from the Writings of Alan R. Tippett*. Edited by Doug Priest, The Missiology of Alan R Tippett Series. Pasadena CA: William Carey Library, 2014.

———, ed. *Missiology of Alan R. Tippett Series*. Pasadena CA: William Carey Library, 2012–2015.

Pruett, Greg. "Barriers and Bridges for the Gospel among Yalunka Folk Muslims in West Africa." PhD diss., Fuller Theological Seminary School of Intercultural Studies, 2014.

———. Review of *Fullness of Time, Ethnohistory Selections from the Writings of Alan Tippett. Australian Journal of Mission Studies* 8.2 (2014) 58.

Ramseyer, Robert L. "Anthropological Perspectives on Church Growth Theory." In *The Challenge of Church Growth*, edited by Wilbert R. Shenk, 65–77. Institute of Mennonite Studies. Missionary Studies, 14. Elkhart, IN: Institute of Mennonite Studies, 1973.

Read, William Richard, et al. *Latin American Church Growth*. Church Growth Series. Grand Rapids: Eerdmans, 1969.

Reddin, Opal, ed. *Power Encounter: A Pentecostal Perspective*. Rev. ed. Springfield, MO: Central Bible College, 1999.

Reeson, Margaret. *Pacific Missionary George Brown 1835–1917: The Wesleyan Methodist Church*. Canberra: Australian National University Press, 2012.

———. "Wednesdays with Alan Tippett: A Gift of Wisdom." *Australian Journal of Mission Studies* 8.2 (2014) 21–25.

Richards, E. Randolph, and Brandon J. O'Brien. *Misreading Scripture with Western Eyes: Removing Cultural Blinders to Better Understand the Bible*. Downers Grove, IL: IVP, 2012.

Richardson, Don. "Redemptive Analogies." In *Evangelical Dictionary of World Missions*, edited by A. Scott Moreau, 812–13. Grand Rapids: Baker, 2000.

Robert, Dana L. "Shifting Southward: Global Christianity Since 1945." *International Bulletin of Missionary Research* 24.2 (2000) 50–58.

Roberts, Daniel, et al. *The Family I Never Knew*. Freemantle, WA: Vivid, 2012.

Rogers, Everett M. *Diffusion of Innovations*. 5th ed. New York: Free Press, 2003.

Rommen, Edward. *Spiritual Power and Missions: Raising the Issues*. Evangelical Missiological Society Series. Pasadena, CA: William Carey Library, 1995.

Rowe, George Stringer. *The Life of John Hunt: Missionary to the Cannibals of Fiji*. London: Hamilton, Adams, 1871.

Roxborogh, John. "Missiology after 'Mission?'" *International Bulletin of Missionary Research* 38.3 (2014) 120–24.

Royal Anthropological Institute of Great Britain and Ireland, and British Association for the Advancement of Science. *Notes and Queries on Anthropology*. 6th ed. London: Routledge and K. Paul, 1951.

Ruthven, Jon. *On the Cessation of the Charismata: The Protestant Polemic on Postbiblical Miracles*. 2nd ed. Tulsa, OK: Word and Spirit, 2011.

Rynkiewich, Michael A. "Do Not Remember the Former Things." *International Bulletin of Mission Research* 40.4 (2016) 308–17.

———. "Person in Mission: Social Theory and Sociality in Melanesia." *Missiology* 31.2 (2003) 155–68.

———. *Soul, Self, and Society: A Postmodern Anthropology for Mission in a Postcolonial World*. Eugene, OR: Cascade, 2011.

———. "The World in My Parish: Rethinking the Standard Missiological Model." *Missiology* 30.3 (2002) 301–21.

Salinas, Daniel. *Latin American Evangelical Theology in the 1970's: The Golden Decade*. Religion in the Americas Series. Leiden: Brill, 2009.

Samson, Jane. "An Historical Pilgrimage among 'The Last Heathen.'" *Material Religion* 2.1 (2006) 97–107.

Sapir, Edward. *Language*. New York: Harcourt Brace, 1949.

Schwartz, Glenn. *When Charity Destroys Dignity: Overcoming Unhealthy Dependency in the Christian Movement: A Compendium*. Lancaster, PA: World Mission Associates, 2007.

Seamands, John T. "The Legacy of J Waskom Pickett." *International Bulletin of Missionary Research* 13.3 (1989) 122–26.

Shaw, R. Daniel. "Beyond Contextualization: Toward a Twenty-first Century Model for Enabling Mission." *International Bulletin of Missionary Research* 34.4 (2010) 208–15.

———. "Every Person a Shaman: The Use of Supernatural Power among the Samo of Papua New Guinea." *Missiology* 9.3 (1981) 359–65.

———. *Kandila: Samo Ceremonialism and Interpersonal Relationships*. Ann Arbor, MI: University of Michigan Press, 1990.

———. *Transculturation: The Cultural Factor in Translation and Other Communication Tasks*. Pasadena, CA: William Carey Library, 1988.

Shaw, R. Daniel, and William R. Burrows. *Traditional Ritual as Christian Worship: Dangerous Syncretism or Necessary Hybridity?* Maryknoll, NY: Orbis, 2018.

Shaw, R. Daniel, et al. "Contextualization, Conceptualization, and Communication: The Development of Contextualization at Fuller's Graduate School of World Mission/Intercultural Studies." *Missiology* 44.1 (2015) 95–111.

Shenk, Wilbert R. *The Challenge of Church Growth: A Symposium*. Missionary Studies Series. Elkhart, IN: Institute of Mennonite Studies, 1973.

Smalley, William A. "Cultural Implications of an Indigenous Church." *Practical Anthropology* 5.2 (1958) 51–64.

Smalley, William Allen. *Readings in Missionary Anthropology*. South Pasadena, CA: William Carey Library, 1974.

———. *Readings in Missionary Anthropology II*. The William Carey Library Series on Applied Cultural Anthropology. Enlarged edition. South Pasadena, CA: William Carey Library, 1978.

Smart, Josephine. *The Political Economy of Street Hawkers in Hong Kong*. Centre of Asian Studies Occasional Papers and Monographs. Hong Kong: Centre of Asian Studies, University of Hong Kong, 1989.

Smith, Linda Tuhiwai. *Decolonizing Methodologies: Research and Indigenous Peoples*. 2nd ed. New York: Zed, 2012.

Søgaard, Viggo. *Everything You Need to Know for a Cassette Ministry: Cassettes in the Context of a Total Christian Communication Program*. Minneapolis: Bethany Fellowship, 1975.

———. *Media in Church and Mission: Communicating the Gospel*. Pasadena, CA: William Carey Library, 1993.

———. *Research in Church and Mission*. Pasadena, CA: William Carey Library, 1996.

St. Mark's National Theological Centre, Canberra. "A Guide to the Tippett Collection." https://stmarks.edu.au/wp-content/uploads/2017/08/TIPPETT-FINDING-AID-2015.pdf.

Stark, Rodney. *The Rise Of Christianity: How the Obscure, Marginal Jesus Movement Became the Dominant Religious Force in the Western World in a Few Centuries*. San Francisco: HarperCollins, 1997.

Stark, Rodney, et al. "Counting China's Christians: There are as Many Christians in China as there are Members of the Communist Party." *First Things* 213 (2011) 14–16.

Bibliography

Stark, Rodney, and Xiuhua Wang. *A Star in the East: The Rise of Christianity in China.* West Conshohocken, PA: Templeton, 2015.

Stephenson, Niamh. "Living History, Undoing Linearity: Memory-work as a Research Method in the Social Sciences." *International Journal of Social Research Methodology* 8.1 (2005) 33–45.

Strelan, John G. *Search for Salvation: Studies in the History and Theology of Cargo Cults.* Adelaide: Lutheran, 1977.

Taber, Charles R. *To Understand the World, to Save the World: The Interface between Missiology and the Social Sciences.* Christian Mission and Modern Culture. Harrisburg, PA: Trinity, 2000.

———. *The World Is Too Much With Us: "Culture" in Modern Protestant Missions (Modern Mission Era, 1792–1992).* Macon, GA: Mercer University Press, 1991.

Taiwo, Olufemi. *How Colonialism Preempted Modernity In Africa.* Bloomington, IN: Indiana University Press, 2010.

Talman, Harley, and John Jay Travis, eds. *Understanding Insider Movements: Disciples of Jesus Within Diverse Religious Communities.* Pasadena, CA: William Carey Library, 2015.

Taylor, William. *Pauline Methods of Missionary Work.* Philadelphia: National Publishing Association for the Promotion of Holiness, 1879.

Tennent, Timothy C. "Followers of Jesus (Isa) in Islamic Mosques: A Closer Examination of C-5 "High Spectrum" Contextualization." *International Journal of Frontier Missions* 23.3 (2006) 101–15.

Terry, J. Mark. "Indigenous Church." In *Evangelical Dictionary of World Missions,* edited by A. Scott Moreau, 483–85. Grand Rapids: Baker, 2000.

Thornley, Andrew. *The Inheritance of Hope: John Hunt, Apostle of Fiji.* Translated by Tauga Vulaono. Suva, Fiji: Institute of Pacific Studies, 2000.

Tiénou, Tite. "The Invention of the 'Primitive' and Stereotypes in Mission." *Missiology* 19.3 (1991) 295–303.

———. "Reflections on Michael A. Rynkiewich's 'Do Not Remember the Former Things.'" *International Bulletin of Missionary Research* 40.4 (2016) 318–23.

Tippett, Alan R. "Adventures in Missiology: Picture of a Growing Discipline." Unpublished manuscript. Pasadena, CA: Fuller School of World Mission, 1972.

———. "The Anthropological and Ethnohistorical Pilgrimage of a Missiologist." Unpublished manuscript. Pasadena, CA: Fuller School of World Mission, 1974.

———. "Anthropology: Luxury or Necessity for Missions?" *Evangelical Missions Quarterly* 5.1 (1968) 7–19.

———. *Aspects of Pacific Ethnohistory.* South Pasadena, CA: William Carey Library, 1973.

———. "Australia's Missionary Outreach in Our Time." Unpublished manuscript. Eugene, OR: Institute of Church Growth, 1962.

———. *Bibliography for Cross-cultural Workers.* South Pasadena, CA: William Carey Library, 1971.

———. "Bibliography 1934–1988." Unpublished manuscript. Canberra: St. Mark's Library, 1988.

———. *The Christian (Fiji 1835–67).* Auckland: The Institute Printing and Publishing Society, 1954.

———. "Christopaganism or Indigenous Christianity." In *Christopaganism or Indigenous Christianity?,* edited by Tetsunao Yamamori and Charles R. Taber, 13–34. South Pasadena, CA: William Carey Library, 1975.

————. *Church Growth and the Word of God: The Biblical Basis of the Church Growth Viewpoint*. Grand Rapids: Eerdmans, 1970.

————. "Church Planting in New Guinea and Papua." Unpublished manuscript. Eugene, OR: Institute of Church Growth, 1962.

————. "Conceptual Dyads in the Ethnotheology of 'Salvation Today.'" In *Evangelical Response to Bangkok*, edited by R. D. Winter, 42–57. Pasadena, CA: William Carey Library, 1973.

————. "The Contour of Ethnohistory." *Missiology* 4.3 (1976) 405–6.

————. "Conversion as a Dynamic Process in Christian Mission." *Missiology* 5.2 (1977) 203–21.

————. "Cross-Cultural Conversion in Oceania." Unpublished manuscript. Pasadena, CA: Fuller School of World Mission, 1976.

————. "Cultural Compulsives." In *God, Man and Church Growth*, edited by Alan R. Tippett, 167–85. Grand Rapids: Eerdmans, 1973.

————. "The Cultural Dynamics of Fijian Cannibalism." Unpublished manuscript. Pasadena, CA: Fuller School of World Mission, 1974.

————. *The Deep-Sea Canoe: The Story of Third World Missionaries in the South Pacific*. South Pasadena, CA: William Carey Library, 1977.

————. "The Distribution and Use of Documents in Oceania." Unpublished manuscript. Pasadena, CA: Fuller School of World Mission, 1972.

————. "The Dynamics of Church-Planting in Fiji (Ono, Viwa, Bau, Kadavu, Vanua Levu and the Hill Tribes of Viti Levu)." Unpublished manuscript. Eugene, OR: Institute of Church Growth, 1962.

————. "Ethnolinguistics and Bible Translation. A Diachronic Case Study: Fiji." In *1986 SIL Anthropology Seminar*, 67–78. Dallas: SIL, 1986.

————. "The Evangelization of Animists." In *Let the Earth Hear His Voice*, edited by J. D. Douglas, 844–55. Minneapolis: World Wide, 1975.

————. "Experiment in Data Collecting, Mexico." Unpublished manuscript. Pasadena CA: Fuller School of World Mission, 1965.

————. *Fijian Material Culture: A Study of Cultural Context, Function, and Change*. Honolulu: Bishop Museum, 1968.

————. "Florescence of the Fellowship." *Missiology* 3.2 (1975) 131–41.

————. "Formal Transformation and Faith Distortion." In *Christopaganism or Indigenous Christianity?*, edited by Tetsunao Yamamori and Charles R. Taber, 97–118. South Pasadena, CA: William Carey Library, 1975.

————. "Frontiers of Evangelism." Unpublished manuscript. Canberra: St. Mark's Library, 1986.

————. "Glossolalia as Spirit Possession: A Taxonomy for Cross-Cultural Observation and Description." Unpublished manuscript. Pasadena CA: Fuller School of World Mission, 1972.

————. "His Mission and Ours." Unpublished manuscript. Fiji: Davuilevu, 1960.

————. "The Holy Spirit and Responsive Populations." In *Crucial Issues in Missions Tomorrow*, edited by Donald Anderson McGavran, 77–101. Chicago: Moody, 1972.

————. "The Integrating Gospel." Unpublished manuscript. Fiji: Davuilevu, 1958.

————. *The Integrating Gospel and The Christian, Fiji 1835–67*. The Missiology of Alan R Tippett Series. Pasadena, CA: William Carey Library, 2015.

————. *Introduction to Missiology*. Pasadena, CA: William Carey Library, 1987.

————. "The Jesus Documents." Unpublished manuscript. Pasadena, CA: Fuller School of World Mission, 1975.

Bibliography

————. *The Jesus Documents*. The Missiology of Alan R. Tippett Series. Edited by Douglas D. Priest. Pasadena, CA: William Carey Library, 2012.

————. "Let the Church Be the Church." Unpublished manuscript. Canberra: St. Mark's Library, 1988.

————. "The Liminal Years: Selected Essays 1943–1976." Unpublished manuscript. Pasadena, CA: Fuller School of World Mission, 1976.

————. "The Meaning of Meaning." In *Christopaganism or Indigenous Christianity?*, edited by Tetsunao Yamamori and Charles R. Taber, 169–96. South Pasadena, CA: William Carey Library, 1975.

————. "The Nineteenth-Century Labour Trade in the South West Pacific: A Study of Slavery and Indenture as the Origin of Present-day Racial Problems." Washington, DC: The American University, 1956.

————. "No Continuing City." Unpublished manuscript. Canberra: St. Mark's Library, 1988.

————. "Not-so-secular City." *Christianity Today* 17 (1973) 8–9.

————. "Objectives of World Mission." Unpublished manuscript. Canberra: St. Mark's Library, 1986.

————. *Oral Tradition and Ethnohistory: The Transmission of Information and Social Values in Early Christian Fiji, 1835–1905*. Canberra: St. Mark's Library, 1980.

————. "The Other Covenant: A Theology of Paganism." *Reformed Journal* 21.9 (1971) 30–31.

————. "Parallaxis in Missiology: To Use or Abuse." *Missionaries, Anthropologists, and Cultural Change Vol* 25–26 (1983) 92–131.

————. *People Movements in Southern Polynesia: Studies in the Dynamics of Church-planting and Growth in Tahiti, New Zealand, Tonga, and Samoa*. Chicago: Moody, 1971.

————. *Peoples of Southwest Ethiopia*. South Pasadena, CA: William Carey Library, 1970.

————. "Polygamy as a Missionary Problem: The Anthropological Issues." *Practical Anthropology* 17.2 (1970) 75–79.

————. "Possessing the Philosophy of Animism for Christ." In *Crucial Issues in Missions Tomorrow*, edited by Donald Anderson McGavran, 125–43. Chicago: Moody, 1972.

————. "Probing Missionary Inadequacies at the Popular Level." *International Review of Missions* 49 (1960) 411–19.

————. "Report on the Curriculum Committee on Training Missionaries." *Milligan Missiogram* 1.3 (1974) 1–3.

————. "Report on the San Juan Episcopal Mission to the Navaho, Farmington, NM." Unpublished manuscript. Pasadena, CA: Fuller School of World Mission, 1967.

————. "Retrospect and Prospect." Unpublished manuscript. Canberra: St. Mark's Library, 1986.

————. "Road to Bau: The Life and Work of John Hunt of Viwa, Fiji." Unpublished manuscript. Bau, Fiji: Delanikoro, 1955.

————. *The Road to Bau and the Autobiography of Joeli Bulu*. The Missiology of Alan R Tippett Series. Edited by Doug Priest. Pasadena, CA: William Carey Library, 2013.

————. "Slippery Paths in the Darkness." Unpublished manuscript. Canberra: St. Mark's Library, 1988.

————. *Slippery Paths in the Darkness: Papers on Syncretism: 1965–1988*. The Missiology of Alan R Tippett Series. Edited by Doug Priest. Pasadena, CA: William Carey Library, 2014.

———. *Solomon Islands Christianity: A Study of Growth and Obstruction.* World Studies of Churches in Mission. London: Lutterworth, 1967.

———. "Spirit Possession as it Relates to Culture and Religion: A Survey of Anthropological Literature." In *Demon Possession*, edited by John Warwick Montgomery, 143–74. Minneapolis: Bethany Fellowship, 1976.

———. "Suggested Moratorium on Missionary Funds and Personnel." *Missiology* 1.3 (1973) 275–79.

———. "Taking a Hard Look at the Barbados Declaration." *International Review of Mission* 62.247 (1973) 287–94.

———. "Task and Method: How Anthropology and Theology Need to Integrate in Post Colonial Missiology." Unpublished manuscript. Canberra: St. Mark's Library, 1987.

———. "Theological Encounters: 1968–1972." Unpublished manuscript. Pasadena, CA: Fuller School of World Mission, 1972.

———. *Verdict Theology in Missionary Theory.* 2nd ed. South Pasadena, CA: William Carey Library, 1973.

———. *The Ways of the People: A Reader in Missionary Anthropology.* The Missiology of Alan R Tippett Series. Edited by Doug Priest. Pasadena, CA: William Carey Library, 2013.

———. "The Ways of the People: Reader in Anthropology." Unpublished manuscript. Pasadena, CA: Fuller School of World Mission, 1977.

———, ed. *God, Man and Church Growth: A Festschrift in Honour of Donald Anderson McGavran.* Grand Rapids: Eerdmans, 1973.

Tippett, Alan R., and Doug Priest. *Fullness of Time: Ethnohistory Selections from the Writings of Alan R. Tippett.* The Missiology of Alan R Tippett Series. Edited by Doug Priest. Pasadena, CA: William Carey Library, 2014.

Tippett, Alan R., et al. *No Continuing City: The Story of a Missiologist from Colonial to Postcolonial Times.* The Missiology of Alan R Tippett Series. Edited by Doug Priest. Pasadena, CA: William Carey Library, 2013.

Tomlinson, Matt, and Ty P. Kāwika Tengan. *New Mana: Transformations of a Classic Concept in Pacific Languages and Cultures.* Monographs in Anthropology Series. Canberra: ANU Press, 2016.

Travis, John. "Appropriate Approaches in Muslim Contexts." In *Appropriate Christianity*, edited by Charles H. Kraft and Dean S. Gilliland, 397–414. Pasadena, CA: William Carey Library, 2005.

———. "Must All Muslims Leave Islam to Follow Jesus?" *Evangelical Missions Quarterly* 34.4 (1998) 411–15.

Treloar, Geoffrey R. "Towards a Master Narrative: Theological Learning and Teaching in Australia since 1901." *St. Mark's Review* 210 (2009) 31–52.

Trompf, Gary W. *Melanesian Religion.* Cambridge: Cambridge University Press, 1991.

Tucker, Ruth. *From Jerusalem to Irian Jaya: A Biographical History of Christian Missions.* 2nd ed. Grand Rapids: Zondervan, 2004.

Turner, Harold W. "Further Dimension for Missions: New Religious Movements in the Primal Societies." *International Review of Mission* 62.247 (1973) 321–37.

Twiss, Richard. *Rescuing the Gospel from the Cowboys: A Native American Expression of the Jesus Way.* Downers Grove, IL: InterVarsity, 2015.

Tylor, Edward B. *Anthropology: An Introduction to the Study of Man and Civilization.* New York: D. Appleton, 1901.

van de Vijver, Fons, and Kwok Leung. *Methods and Data Analysis for Cross-cultural Research.* Cross-cultural Psychology Series. Thousand Oaks, CA: Sage, 1997.

Bibliography

Van Engen, Charles Edward. *God's Missionary People: Rethinking the Purpose of the Local Church*. Grand Rapids: Baker, 1991.

Van Engen, Charles Edward, et al. *Paradigm Shifts in Christian Witness: Insights from Anthropology, Communication, and Spiritual Power: Essays in Honor of Charles H. Kraft*. Maryknoll, NY: Orbis, 2008.

Van Gennep, Arnold. *The Rites of Passage*. London: Routledge & Paul, 1960.

Van Rheenen, Gailyn. *Communicating Christ in Animistic Contexts*. Grand Rapids: Baker, 1991.

Verkuyl, Johannes. *Contemporary Missiology: An Introduction*. Grand Rapids: Eerdmans, 1978.

Verstraelen, Frans J. ed. *Missiology: An Ecumenical Introduction*. Grand Rapids: Eerdmans, 1995.

Vogt, Evon Z. Review of *Innovation: The Basis of Cultural Change* by H. G. Barnett. *American Anthropologist* 55.5 (1953) 721–22.

Wagner, C. Peter. "Missiology and Spiritual Power." In *Paradigm Shifts in Christian Witness: Insights from Anthropology, Communication, and Spiritual Power: Essays in Honor of Charles H. Kraft*, edited by Charles Edward van Engen et al., 91–97. Maryknoll, NY: Orbis, 2008.

Wagner, C. Peter, et al. *Church Growth: State of the Art*. Wheaton, IL: Tyndale House, 1986.

Wallace, Anthony F. C. *Culture and Personality*. Studies in Anthropology Series. 2nd ed. New York: Random House, 1970.

Walls, Andrew F. "The Gospel as the Prisoner and Liberator of Culture." *Missionalia* 10.3 (1982) 93–105.

———. *The Missionary Movement in Christian History: Studies in the Transmission of Faith*. Edinburgh: T. & T. Clark, 1996.

Wan, Enoch. "Critique of Functional Missionary Anthropology." *His Dominion* 8 (1982) 18–22.

Warren, Max. *To Apply the Gospel: Selections from the Writings of Henry Venn*. Grand Rapids: Eerdmans, 1971.

WCC Department of Mission Studies. "The Growth of the Church." *Ecumenical Review* 16.2 (1964) 195–99.

———. "Growth of the Church: A Statement." *International Review of Missions* 57.227 (1968) 330–34.

Weir, Christine. "Fiji and the Fijians: Two Modes of Missionary Discourse." *The Journal of Religious History* 22.2 (1998) 152–67.

White, Carmen M. "Historicizing Educational Disparity: Colonial Policy and Fijian Educational Attainment." *History of Education* 32.4 (2003) 345–65.

Whiteman, Darrell L. "Anthropology and Mission: The Incarnatonal Connection." In *Catholic Theological Union Louis J. Luzbetak, SVD Lecture on Mission and Culture*, edited by Stephen B. Bevans, 2–43. Chicago: CCGM, 2003.

———. "Contextualization: The Theory, the Gap, the Challenge." *International Bulletin of Missionary Research* 21.1 (1997) 2–7.

———. "Contextualization, Model of." In *Encyclopedia of Mission and Missionaries*, edited by Jon Bonk, 90–96. Routledge Encyclopedias of Religion and Society. New York: Routledge, 2007.

———. "The Legacy of Alan R. Tippett." *International Bulletin of Missionary Research* 16.4 (1992) 163–66.

Bibliography

————. "Melanesian Religions: An Overview." *Point Series* 6 (1984) 87–121.

————. *Melanesians and Missionaries: An Ethnohistorical Study of Social and Religious Change in the Southwest Pacific*. Pasadena, CA: William Carey Library, 1983.

————. Review of *The Ways of the People*, by Alan Tippett. *Australian Journal of Mission Studies* 8.2 (2014) 56–57.

————, ed. *Missionaries, Anthropologists and Cultural Change*. 2 vols. Studies in Third World Societies. Williamsburg, VA: College of William and Mary, 1983.

Whiteman, Darrell L., and Gerald H. Anderson. *World Mission in the Wesleyan Spirit*. Vol. 44. American Society of Missiology Series. Franklin, TN: Providence House, 2009.

Williams, John, and Richard M. Moyle. *The Samoan Journals of John Williams, 1830 and 1832*. Pacific History Series. Canberra: Australian National University Press, 1984.

Williams, John, and Cook Islands Library and Museum Society. *A Narrative of Missionary Enterprises in the South Sea Islands: With Remarks upon the Natural History of the Islands, Origin, Languages, Traditions and Usages of the Inhabitants*. Facsim. ed. Rarotonga: Cook Islands Library & Museum Society, 1998.

Williams, Thomas, and G. C. Henderson. *The Journal of Thomas Williams, Missionary in Fiji, 1840–1853*. 2 vols. Sydney: Angus & Robertson, 1931.

Williams, Thomas, et al. *Fiji and the Fijians*. New York: D. Appleton, 1860.

Wimber, John, and Kevin Springer. *Power Evangelism*. 2nd ed. Ventura, CA: Regal, 2009.

Winter, Ralph D., and Steven C. Hawthorne. *Perspectives on the World Christian Movement: A Reader*. Pasadena, CA: William Carey Library, 1981.

Winter, Ralph D., et al. *Perspectives on the World Christian Movement: Fourth Edition*. Pasadena, CA: William Carey Library, 2009.

Wolfe, J. Henry. "Insider Movements: An Assessment of the Viability of Retaining Socio-Religious Insider Identity in High-Religious Contexts." PhD diss., Southern Baptist Theological Seminary, 2011.

Wood, A. Harold. *Overseas Missions of the Australian Methodist Church*. Vol. II (Fiji). Melbourne: Aldersgate, 1978.

Woodberry, John Dudley. *From Seed to Fruit: Global Trends, Fruitful Practices, and Emerging Issues among Muslims*. 2nd ed. Pasadena, CA: William Carey Library, 2010.

Yamamori, Tetsunao, and Charles R. Taber. *Christopaganism or Indigenous Christianity?* South Pasadena, CA: William Carey Library, 1975.

Yoder Neufeld, Thomas R. "Koinōnia: The Gift we Hold Together." *The Mennonite Quarterly Review* 86.3 (2012) 339–52.

Yu, Jie. "China's Christian Future." *First Things* 265 (2016) 49–54.

Index

Adams, Glenn, 24–25
"Adventures in Missiology: Picture of a
    Growing Discipline" (Tippett),
    82, 85
African Independent Church Movements
    (Hayward), 64
African Independent Churches (these
    days, African Initiated Churches),
    250
Ai Tukutuku Vakalotu, 35
"Alan Tippett, Australian Missiologist"
    (Hovey), 136
"Alan Tippett Symposium on Mission
    and Cross-Cultural Ministry,"
    16–17
Allen, Roland, 11, 246
American Society of Missiology,
    founding of, 69
Anderson, Allan, 244
Anderson, Gerald H., 13
Anderson, Norman, 103
Anderson, William, 108
Andrews, Leslie, 31
Anglican Diocese of Canberra and
    Goulburn, 51, 91
animism
    in context of ministry, 14–15, 192–95
    current understandings of, 198–200
    defined, 19
    definitions and application of,
        195–200
    "The Evangelization of Animists"
        (Tippett), 77, 186–87, 195, 206,
        226

gaining an insider view of, 200–204
numerical definitions of, 197–98
phenomenological definitions of,
    196–97
Tippett's contribution to mission in
    animistic contexts, 200–206
Tippett's structured points of
    application of, 206–13
use of term, 199
animist religion, use of term, 200
Annual Review of Anthropology, 148–49
anthropological field research, as
    providing information base,
    137–40
anthropological missiological research,
    65
anthropological research, as applied to
    mission, 140–48
*Anthropological Research: The Structure of
    Inquiry* (Pelto and Pelto), 139
Anthropological Writings 1962–1971
    (Tippett), 145
Anthropological Writings Fiji 1944–1963
    (Tippett), 144–45
anthropology
    applied anthropology, 68, 140, 148
    boundaries of appropriate use of,
        146–48
    Christian anthropologists, 10, 140–41
    contribution of Pacific missionaries
        to, 9
    as differentiated from Christian
        mission, 145

Lagos, Nigeria, 245
observing functional substitutes in
action for cultural fit, 265–68
Casiño, Tereso, 16
Cate, Patrick, 101–2
centrality of church, as Tippett's life
theme #2, 21, 22, 33–36, 99,
111–29
centrality of relationship with God, as
Tippett's life theme #1, 21, 22,
31–33, 98, 99–106
*The Centrality of Christ in Contemporary
Missions* (Barnett and Pocock),
102
CGRILA (Church Growth Research in
Latin America), 67, 133, 139–40,
144
Chadwick, Owen, 134
change, openness to, 182, 183, 184–85,
197, 231, 260
Charismatics, 8
Chaves, Kelly, 148, 149
Chief Cakobau, 5, 257. *See also* Ratu
Cakobau
Childs, Jay, 117–18
China
Christians in, 118, 185
Three Self-Movement in, 250
Christian anthropologists, 10, 140–41
"Christian Fellowship Church" (Tippett),
90
*Christian Mass Movements in India: A
Study with Recommendations*
(Pickett), 60, 169
*The Christian Message in a Non-Christian
World* (Kraemer), 12
Christian World Mission (Anderson), 108
Christianity
appropriate Christianity, 3, 15, 251,
276
with cultural fit, 242–53
fragile Christianity, 223
indigenous Christianity, 15, 26, 258,
270
split level Christianity, 223, 225
Tippett on initial impact of
Christianity on Fiji, 168

Tongan movement into, 228–29
*Christianity and Animism in Melanesia:
Four Approaches to Gospel and
Culture* (Nehrbass), 188
Christians and China (Hayward), 64
The Christian (Fiji 1835–67) (Tippett), 5,
37, 46, 50, 152, 169
*Christopaganism or Indigenous
Christianity* (Tippett), 198, 252,
254
"Christopaganism or Indigenous
Christianity" (William S. Carter
Symposium, Milligan College,
1974), 76
*Christopaganism or Indigenous
Christianity?* (Yamamori and
Taber), 76
Christopher, A. J., 41
Chrysostom, John, 108
church
growth as expression of nature of,
115–19
nature and essence of, 111–15
"true selfhood" of, 245–48
world church, 2
*The Church and Cultures: New
Perspectives in Missiological
Anthropology* (Luzbetak), 9, 141
church growth. *See also* Church Growth
theory
case studies about, 117–19
quantitative and qualitative
dimensions of, 119, 120, 129, 149,
165, 177, 180, 190, 248, 272
tridimensionl nature of, 119–21
use of term, 115–16
*Church Growth and the Word of God:
The Biblical Basis of the Church
Growth Viewpoint* (Tippett), 68,
104, 128–29, 169, 190
Church Growth Bulletin, 124, 126, 189
"Church Growth in Acts" (Copeland),
120
"Church Growth Missiology" (Bosch),
113

Index

"The Gospel as the Prisoner and Liberator of Culture" (Walls), 123, 254

Graham, Billy, 67, 76

Gration, John, 236

Great Commission
    defined, 18
    development of Great-Commission-focused missiology, 11–12
    practical Great-Commission-focused missiology, 13–16
    Tippett as advocate for priority of fulfillment of, 98, 106–11
    use of term, 2, 12

Great-Commission-Focus missiology, defined, 18–19

Greek New Testament, Tippett's use of, 7, 105, 107

Gribble, Mr., 64, 88–89, 174

Grime, Joseph, 139

"The Growth of the Church" (WCC), 11

guidelines for mission boards and field missionaries, as Tippett's life theme #5, 21, 22

"Halting Due to Redemption and Life" (McGavran), 170

Halverson, Richard, 21

Hawthorne, Steven C., 195

Hayward, Douglas, 14

Hayward, Victor, 64, 65, 109, 110

Henderson, G. C., 5, 151

Henry, Carl F. H., 102

Hesselgrave, David J., 14, 166, 177, 180

Hibbert, Richard, 17, 238–41, 242

Hiebert, Paul, 4, 14, 141, 198, 199, 211, 224, 225, 226, 231

"The Highest Priority: Cross-Cultural Evangelism" (Winter), 110

Hindus, 176, 194, 198, 238, 239, 241–42

"His Mission and Ours" (Tippett), 5–6, 12, 50, 104, 107

Historian, 148

historical context (of Tippett's work), 8–12

historical research, 9, 37, 133–36, 163

The History of Christian Missions (Neill and Chadwick), 134

The History of the Expansion of Christianity (Latourette), 134, 160

Hitchen, John, 9

Hodges, Melvyn, 246

Hoefer, Herbert, 15, 241

Hoekendijk, Johannes, 12, 76

Hogan, Philip, 174, 189

Hollenweger, Walter, 25, 249

Holy Spirit, 8

The Holy Spirit and Mission Dynamics, 224

"The Holy Spirit and Receptive Populations" (Tippett), 166–67, 185

homogeneous unit principle, 78, 186–87

Hovey, Kevin G., 177

"How Appropriate is the Church Growth Paradigm in Today's Mission Contexts?" (Gibbs), 118

How Colonialism Preempted Modernity in Africa (Taiwo), 41

Hubbard, David, 66–67, 84–86

Human Agency in Mission Work: Missionary Styles and Their Political Consequences (Calvacanti), 13

Hunt, John, 8, 45, 46, 50, 159

Hunt family, 181

Hunter, George, 124

Iberville, Canada, WCC consultation at (1963), 61–63, 64

ICG (Institute of Church Growth). *See* Institute of Church Growth (ICG)

identity negotiation, 238–41, 274

idiomatic translations, 255

importance of appropriate research methodologies, as Tippett's life theme #3, 21, 22, 36–47, 131–63

importance of strategic missiology and strategic missionary practice, as Tippett's life theme #4, 21, 22, 47, 164–268

In His Armour: The Life of John Hunt of Fiji (Birtwhistle), 38

perfecting, 164, 166, 189, 190, 218, 240, 273

persecution, persistent proclamation in contexts of, 188–89

personal interviews
Tippett's use of, 139–40, 144
use of term, 190

personal journals, use of, 153–55

personal relationships, triangle of, 153–55

personhood, use of term, 242

Perspectives on the World Christian Movement: Fourth Edition (Winter et al.), 13, 223

Perspectives on the World Christian Movement (Winter and Hawthorne), 69, 195

Phenomena and Their Interpretation: Landmark Essays, 1957–1989 (Bulatao), 141

Pickett, J. Waskom, 11, 13, 48, 61, 169, 170, 173, 181

"Piety Curve of a Weak Congregation," 138

pilgrim principle, 254

Pinnock, Clark H. A., 102

Piper, John, 102

PNG (Papua New Guinea), missionaries in. *See* Papua New Guinea (PNG), missionaries in

Poet & Peasant; and Through Peasant Eyes: A Literary-cultural Approach to the Parables in Luke (Bailey), 159

"Possessing the Philosophy of Animism for Christ" (Tippett), 101, 200, 202

post-colonial missiology, defined, 19

power contextualization, 230

power encounter, 6, 81, 192, 193, 200, 202, 206, 207, 210, 213, 214–33, 234, 241, 253, 258, 270–71, 274–75

Power Encounter: A Pentecostal Perspective (Revised ed.) (Reddin), 222–23

"Power Encounter at Mowi" (Hovey), 228

"Power Encounter" (Kraft), 223

"power interview techniques," 143–44

Practical Anthropology, 10, 75, 139, 141, 260

"Pre-Christian Religion" (Tippett), 195

pre-evangelism, 188, 189

Priest, Doug, 81, 162

primal religions, 199

"Principles and Policies Bearing on Church Growth" (McGavran), 126

"Probing Missionary Inadequacies at the Popular Level" (Tippett), 47, 48, 50, 57, 194, 225

problem of cultural voids, in Tippett's "pay attention" statements, 2–6, 212

problem of incorporation, in Tippett's "pay attention" statements, 2–6, 212

problem of meaning, in Tippett's "pay attention" statements, 206, 209–10

problem of motivation, in Tippett's "pay attention" statements, 206, 208–9

problem of power encounter, in Tippett's "pay attention" statements, 206, 213

problem of proclamation-only gospel, in Tippett's "pay attention" statements, 206, 207–8

problem of social structure, in Tippett's "pay attention" statements, 206, 210–11

"Problems of Encounter" (Tippett), 195

"The Process from Animist to Christian Forms" (Tippett), 195

proclamation-only gospel, problem of, in Tippett's "pay attention" statements, 206, 207–8

"The Prophetic Attitude to Idolatry (Isaiah 44)" (Tippett), 204

Pruett, Greg, 240

Queens College (Melbourne), 34

Ramseyer, Robert L., 184–85